D0917104

THE FIRST CODE TALKERS

THE FIRST CODE TALKERS

Native American Communicators
in World War I

WILLIAM C. MEADOWS

University of Oklahoma Press : Norman

Publication of this book is made possible through the generosity of Missouri State University, Springfield.

Library of Congress Cataloging-in-Publication Data

Names: Meadows, William C., 1966– author.
Title: The first code talkers : Native American communicators in World War I / William C. Meadows.
Description: First. | Norman : University of Oklahoma Press, 2021. | Series: The civilization of the American Indian series ; volume 281 | Includes bibliographical references and index. | Summary: "An ethnohistory of known Native American Code Talkers of World War I, exploring the origins of code talking, misconceptions and popular myths, recognition of military service, and the impact on code talkers during World War II" —Provided by publisher.
Identifiers: LCCN 2020020849 | ISBN 978-0-8061-6841-8 (hardcover)
Subjects: LCSH: Indian code talkers. | World War, 1914–1918—Cryptography. | World War, 1914–1918—Participation, Indian.
Classification: LCC D570.8.I6 M43 2021 | DDC 940.4/8673—dc23
LC record available at https://lccn.loc.gov/2020020849

The paper in this book meets the guidelines for permanence and durability of the Committee on Production Guidelines for Book Longevity of the Council on Library Resources, Inc. ⊗

For Saori K. and Keito V. Meadows

I am bringing a distant nation against you—
An ancient and enduring nation,
A people whose language you do not know,
Whose speech you do not understand.

Jeremiah 5:15

CONTENTS

List of Tables   xi

Acknowledgments   xiii

Introduction   1

1 The Origins of Native American Code Talking   7

2 The Eastern Band of Cherokee Indians   33

3 The Oklahoma Choctaw   43

4 The Oklahoma Choctaw after the War   122

5 The Oklahoma Cherokee, Comanche, Osage, Sioux,
  and Ho-Chunk   176

6 Recognition   197

7 The Legacy of Native American Code Talkers
  in World War I   222

Conclusion   250

Appendices:
A US Army Campaigns in World War I   253
B World War I Code Talker Biographies   254
C World War I Messages Sent in Choctaw   273
D Code Talker Timeline, 1918–2020   275

Notes   281

Sources Cited   313

Index   351

TABLES

1 Sources Identifying Choctaw Code Talkers by Name   90
2 Choctaw Code Terms   105
3 Bridges in Oklahoma Named for Choctaw Code Talkers   219
4 Native American Code Talkers in World War I   224

ACKNOWLEDGMENTS

The research for this work involves Native American soldiers from several tribes and armed forces units and data encountered in small, scattered increments over nearly thirty years. This work allowed me to meet many individuals across the country. First I offer my sincere gratitude to individuals who provided interviews, documents, photographs, and contacts in their respective tribal communities:

Cherokee Nation of Oklahoma: Richard Allen

Choctaw: Chief Gregory Pyle; Chief Gary Batton; Judy Allen, historic projects officer and former editor of *Bishinik,* now *Biskinik*; Nuchi Nashoba, president, Choctaw Code Talkers Association; Regina Green, Choctaw Nation Museum; James Parrish and Teresa Billy, School of Choctaw Language, Choctaw Nation of Oklahoma; the Choctaw Code Talkers Association; Evangeline Wilson, Margaret Wilson McWilliams, Kathryn Hooker, Lila Douglas Swink, and Sarah Elizabeth Sawyer

Comanche: Albert Nahquaddy Jr., Lanny Asepermy, Robert Atchavit, Comanche Indian Veterans Association

Eastern Band of Cherokee: American Legion Post 143 (Stephen Youngdeer), Cherokee, NC

Osage: John Henry Mashunkashey

Hochunk: Ona Garvin

I extend my deepest appreciation to Judy Allen (Choctaw), who has shared documents with me since the mid-1990s, served as my host during research in Choctaw Country, was seminal in helping the Choctaw code talkers gain federal recognition, and who read and commented on a draft of this work; and to Nuchi Nashoba (Choctaw) for sharing information on the Choctaw code talkers, reading a draft of this work, and welcoming my participation in the Choctaw Code Talkers Association. Both have done so much to preserve knowledge of the Choctaw code talkers. I also extend my sincere gratitude to Sgt. Maj. Lanny Asepermy (Ret.) (Comanche), who for many years has been a valuable friend and consultant. Lanny shared many resources on Comanche veterans and long welcomed my interaction with the Comanche Indian Veteran's Association, which in 2015 honored me for my work with Comanche code talkers at one of their monthly meetings; I am forever grateful for their kindness and friendship.

I also extend my thanks to Erin Fehr (Yupiq) of the Sequoyah National Research Institute in Little Rock, Arkansas, and to Sarah Elizabeth Sawyer (Choctaw). I came to know Erin after contacting the Sequoyah Institute in 2017 regarding their code talker exhibit and was later asked to write the text for a permanent website on WW I code talkers for the institute (Meadows 2018). Erin shared sources on code talkers as she encountered them. I met and began to network with Sarah during the research for her historically based novel on the Choctaw code talkers (Sawyer 2018), and we began sharing archival sources.

In September 2018, Erin located and visited with Mrs. Kathryn Horner Widder, daughter of Lieutenant Colonel Elijah W. Horner. During their visit, Mrs. Widder provided Erin and Sarah with news clippings and military documents of her father. On October 27, 2018, the one hundredth anniversary of the date that the Choctaw first used their language against the Germans at Forest Ferme, I had the pleasure of interviewing Mrs. Widder and her son John Widder and examining these documents. Mrs. Widder showed me the framed picture, displayed in their family home, that her father had kept since World War I of him and five of the Choctaw code talkers. These documents clarified several key issues not addressed in other archival sources about the Choctaws. The Widders' generosity greatly strengthened the manuscript.

Since the early 1990s, I have visited many archives for this work. I offer my sincere thanks to Keevin Lewis (Navajo) and Ellen Alers of the National Museum of the American Indian; Towana Spivey (Chickasaw), Fort Sill Museum Archives; Matt Reed (Pawnee) and Michael W. Bell, Oklahoma History Center; Angela Ragan, archivist of American Legion Post 143 (Stephen Youngdeer); Lisa Sharik, Texas Military Forces Museum; Russell Horton, Wisconsin Veterans Museum; Matt Despain, Rose State College; and the staffs of the Oklahoma History Center and the National Archives in College Park, Maryland, St. Louis, Missouri, and Washington, DC, for facilitating my visits. Ellen Siebert, curator of collections at the Indiana University Museum of Archaeology and Anthropology, provided copies of Joseph K. Dixon's materials on the Choctaw Telephone Squad in World War I. I have benefitted greatly from my former student First Sergeant Dan McMurray (US Army Retired) who continues to teach me about searching military records and assisted me in finding several records. Dr. Harald Prins, Kansas State University, has graciously shared archival sources, information, and insights from his research on Native American veterans.

My thanks also to Missouri State University for 2015, 2016, and 2019 faculty research grants that allowed me to visit archives, and to the College of Humanities and Public Affairs for providing subvention funds. Deborah Williams and Shannon Conlon, Missouri State University Meyer Library Interlibrary Loan, greatly aided me by fulfilling my many requests for old, obscure documents. My thanks to Dustin Thompson, Center for Archaeological Research, who drew excellent maps for this work. Finally, my sincere thanks to Alessandra Jacobi Tamulevich, senior acquisitions editor at the University of Oklahoma Press, for her wonderful help and encouragement with this project and to copyeditor Richard Feit for his editorial insights and contributions.

INTRODUCTION

Of the many accounts originating from the First World War, those of Native American telephone communicators and their undecipherable transmissions became one of the most intriguing genres of battlefield legends (Stallings 1963:281, 288; Tate 1986:432; White 1979:17–18). The Native languages of these US military personnel allowed messages to be sent faster and with greater security than existing communications and coding technology allowed, giving the US military a valuable advantage in combat communications where they were used. These groups of Native communicators were not intentionally recruited and trained to devise codes in their languages, but were formed late in the war to send messages in their vernacular languages, which, being essentially unknown outside tribal contexts, were as effective as formal encrypted codes. At least one group created specially encoded vocabulary specifically for military items.

Although the term "code talkers" did not develop until near the end of World War II, the participating individuals in both wars have collectively become known by that title. Many Americans know of the Navajo code talkers of World War II, but few know that code talking had its origins in World War I and that over thirty tribal groups were eventually involved in World Wars I and II. While the Navajo code was declassified in 1968 and the Navajo Code Talker Association was formed in 1971, many non-Navajo code talkers went unrecognized for decades.

This work focuses on Native Americans in the American Expeditionary Forces who used their Native languages to send messages during World War I. Many paths merged to create this account. The Choctaw (Chata Yakni) first formally recognized their code talkers in 1986. In 1989, the French government and the state of Oklahoma jointly recognized the Choctaw code talkers of both world wars and the Comanche (Nʉmʉnʉʉ) code talkers of World War II. While living and conducting ethnographic fieldwork in Anadarko, Oklahoma, in 1997 and 1998, local business owner Liz Pollard visited with me about her interest in seeking federal recognition for the Comanche code talkers of World War II. Beginning with a hand-signed petition seeking federal recognition for the Comanche code talkers, Pollard went on to create an online petition in 2001 and a mock congressional resolution urging Congress to honor all Native American code talkers. "It's been frustrating because there seems to be a lot of public support," Pollard told the *Arizona Republic* in 2001. "But I can't get anyone in Congress interested, including the only Native American senator, Ben Nighthorse Campbell."[1] Increased awareness and recognition efforts began coalescing, resulting in Senator Campbell heading a Senate committee to investigate honoring all Native American code talkers (Meadows 2011, 2016).

In the Indian communities I work in the names Indian, Native American, Native, and non-Indian and non-Native are all still commonly used by Native Peoples, as well as Indigenous. While Native names for their respective populations are introduced for the groups discussed in this work, such as Chata Yakni for Choctaw and Nʉmʉnʉʉ for Comanche, popular glosses are also still widely used. Reflecting community use, these terms will be used interchangeably.

During the 1990s, I conducted research with the surviving Comanche code talkers and members of the Choctaw Nation. When I published the *Comanche Code Talkers of World War II* (Meadows 2002), which included a section on the Choctaw in World War I and brief accounts of other groups in both world wars, I had no idea of the road it would lead me down. In September of 2002, Liz Pollard passed my contact information to Tim Jones, who was then conducting research on code talkers for the Smithsonian's National Museum of the American Indian. Mr. Jones contacted me, and I became a consultant for the museum's traveling *Native Words, Native Warriors* exhibit. I soon received more and more requests to speak on the subject.

In August of 2004, the office of Senator Tom Daschle called, asking me to testify and submit written documents at a Senate committee hearing in Washington, DC, on all the information I had on Native American code talkers. Representatives from the Choctaw, Comanche, Meskwaki, and Lakota Nations joined me in presenting information on September 23, 2004, the day the National Museum of the Native American opened on the Washington Mall. With the new documentary evidence we were able to bring before Congress, this event furthered efforts to introduce federal legislation to recognize all non-Navajo code talkers. I soon began receiving phone calls, emails, and other communications and data relating to code talking among other tribes, as well as requests to help identify other code talkers. Several tribes continued lobbying congressional representatives to pass proposed legislation. Four years later, the Code Talker Recognition Act of 2008 was signed into law, awarding congressional recognition to each tribe having code talkers and presenting a Congressional Gold Medal to each tribe and a Congressional Silver Medal to each surviving code talker or his family (Meadows 2011, 2016).

This work led me to collaborate with members of several tribes (Acoma, Assiniboine, Cherokee, Choctaw, Comanche, Ho-Chunk, Hopi, Laguna, Lakota, Meskwaki, Muscogee, Navajo, Oneida, Osage, Pawnee, and Pima) in documenting code talkers in both world wars. As the *Native Words, Native Warriors* exhibit traveled the country, I was asked to speak at several openings, and since the mid-1990s to speak on Native American code talkers at army, navy, and marine bases, universities, museums, tribal gatherings, and civic and historical institutions across the country. These events allowed me to meet many wonderful people and have been some of the most enjoyable work of my career.

As difficult as it is to research the service of any lower-ranking serviceman in World War I and II, tracking code talkers is even harder. Native American service members were fewer in number, kept fewer journals, and published fewer written accounts of military service than non–Native American veterans. While some works on Native American military service have appeared, Native American veterans have only recently begun to publish or coauthor similar accounts (Holiday and McPherson 2013; Holm 1996; Medicine Crow and Viola 2006; Mihesuah 2002; Nez and Avila 2011; Stabler 2005; Viola 2008).

Other differences regarding the numbers of servicemen (Native versus non-Native) in both world wars—including cultural background (familiarity and rapport in Native communities), residence (rural, sometimes remote, reservations), and economic differences (ease of contact via telephone and internet)—also favor non-Native participation in military unit reunions and histories. The focus of divisional and regimental unit histories, written by non-Natives, favored larger, predominantly non-Native units over smaller ethnic groups and individuals, and offer little about Native Americans in military service. Even in the accounts of units with large numbers of Native Americans (Arthur 1987; Braun 2005; Kidston 2004; McCartney 1948; Nelson 1970; Whitlock 1998), Native Americans are often mentioned only in passing in the territorial settlement, and nothing is included of their later military service (Cooper and Smith 2005). Other sources are brief favorable anecdotal accounts (usually martial or physical stereotypes attributed to Native Americans) or unique meritorious service and awards (Fisher 1947) such as Medal of Honor winners (Whitlock 1998:101–103, 243–245, 289–291).

Research is further complicated by the fact that code talking in World War I was a relatively brief and impromptu phenomena developed during combat and had no existing basis or formal classification. With no standardized presence or military occupational specialty (MOS) code for so-called Indian communicators (who eventually became known as code talkers), this type of service does not appear in military records, such as division signal battalion files. In World War II, code talking was indicated only in the military discharge forms (DD-214) of the marine corps' Navajo code talkers (MOS 642 Code Talker) and in descriptions on some discharge documents of Hopi in the army's 81st Division, and some Army Air Corps units. Native language use is also usually absent in the personnel files of WW I and II servicemen. Most sources come from accounts of military officers, newspapers, and tribal communities.

Though the internet has increased access to data, internet-sourced data must be used critically. Many sources contain unsupported claims or errors, lack citations and contextual data, or simply repeat earlier accounts taken at face value.[2] How these issues affect what is known about code talkers is addressed throughout this book. Newly discovered primary sources allow a more critically examined, revised, and much expanded account of the Choctaw, as well as more complete narratives about other groups. Many primary sources are presented to allow the reader to examine the basis of my arguments.

Until all military records are digitized and available for comprehensive searches, archival work in scattered repositories remains a daunting task. Some information may never be found. The National Personnel Records fire of July 12, 1973, in Overland, Missouri, resulted in an 80 percent loss of US Army personnel discharge records from November 1, 1912, through January 1, 1960, and 75 percent of US Air Force personnel discharged September 25, 1947, to January 1, 1964, for names alphabetically after James E. Hubbard.[3] While some have been reconstructed from records at other locations, many files are now incomplete or lost. Most files comprise only general military service information and contain nothing relating to communications services.

The subject of WW I code talkers involves decades of public knowledge based primarily on several frequently reprinted news articles that are accurate in some aspects and inaccurate in others. This trend has produced an oral and documentary history that has largely been taken at face value by scholars, Native tribes, and the general public. This body of knowledge has never been critically examined or questioned through analysis, source examination, or comparison with primary sources, including military records, officers' firsthand accounts, and censuses. As such, *The First Code Talkers* is a classic exercise in ethnohistorical methodology and source criticism, especially in its sifting through a large body of fragmentary and frequently repeated news sources.

As William Stein (1986) discusses, newspapers are produced primarily for consumption and profit. With a powerful underlying motivation to boost sales, varied forms of bias are possible. Stein's analysis of the newspaper coverage of an 1885 Andean peasant movement demonstrates a heavy bias favoring the ruling elite attempting to maintain their socioeconomic and political dominance. Blanton and Cook (2002:145–162) show how news accounts of female American Civil War veterans often sacrificed detail and accuracy—even when possessing the facts—to fit Victorian social standards and romantic notions of ideal behavior. The historical accounting of Native American code talkers has been similarly bent by prevailing cultural dispositions; as this work demonstrates, while some popular beliefs about Native American code talkers are accurate, others are not.

This work is a mix of archival and newspaper documents, oral history, ethnographic fieldwork, military unit histories, and individual soldiers' experiences set in the larger backdrop of World War I. Data on most WW I code talkers are sparse, with more documentation and inquiry on the Choctaw than other groups. Consequently, chapters vary greatly in length and detail due to available data. Chapter 6 combines the stories of several groups with WW I code talkers about whom little is known.

Since most WW I veterans were deceased by the 1970s and 1980s, this work required an ethnohistorical approach comprising much oral history that was closely compared with archival data. I have taken on several difficult questions that have yet to be fully examined but that continue to be taken at face value, are cited uncritically, and remain problematic. What factors led to the formation of Native-language military communicators in World War I? From what tribe did the first code talkers in World War I come? Was code talking actually classified as secret after the war? Were code talkers ordered or sworn to secrecy regarding their service? When did declassification occur, and did any leaks occur? Who originated the idea to use the Choctaw, and how many Choctaw were used in WW I? What were the actual military accomplishments of Joseph Oklahombi, the Choctaw infantryman long reputed to be the most decorated Oklahoma soldier of World War I? These and other issues are addressed in their respective chapters.

This work expands on my earlier publications on code talkers (Meadows 2002, 2006, 2009, 2011, 2016, 2018), with much new data on Eastern Band and Oklahoma Cherokee, Choctaw, Comanche, Ho-Chunk, Osage, Lakota and other Sioux. This work presents data indicating that members of the Ho-Chunk and Eastern Band of Cherokee were used prior to the Choctaw, long considered the first code talkers in WW I. Neither have been recognized under the Code Talkers Recognition Act of 2008 (Meadows 2011, 2016).

At present, research on Native American code talkers of World War I is scant, comprising just a few pages scattered among a handful of sources. This book seeks to provide a more comprehensive account of the development, use, experiences, postwar influences, and recognition of these soldiers. I do not claim to have identified every group or individual who served as a code talker; we will likely never know every instance of this service. The impact of WW I code talkers on World War II, however, is better known and discussed.

The book consists of eight chapters. Chapter 1 reviews Native American service in World War I and addresses the origins of Native American code talking. Chapter 2 focuses on Eastern Band Cherokee (The Eastern Band of Cherokee Indians, EBCI, Tsalagiyi Detsadanilvgi) in the 30th Division. Chapter 3 explores the Oklahoma Choctaw (Chahta Yakni) in the 36th Division in World War I. Chapter 4 follows the Choctaw code talkers after the war. Chapter 5 features other tribes with WW I code talkers, including Oklahoma Cherokee (Tsalagihi Ayeli), Comanche (Nʉmʉnʉʉ), Ho-Chunk (Winnebago), Osage (Wazhazhe), and unspecified Sioux. Chapter 6 focuses on efforts to recognize code talkers. Chapter 7 describes the legacy of Native American code talkers in World War I and examines the impacts of Native language use in the war, the reasons that Native languages worked as codes, and the impact of code talking on US military signals intelligence, tribal language maintenance, code talking in World War II, and ethnic identity. Chapter 8 offers conclusions regarding WW I code talkers.

I hope this work will serve as a foundation for further inquiry into the unique service of Native American code talkers in World War I and II and that it will be a source of documentation and pride for their tribes and their descendants.

1

THE ORIGINS OF NATIVE AMERICAN CODE TALKING

Military intelligence is a complex endeavor.[1] In military operations, secure communications are as important as weapons and troops. To coordinate actions in combat, there must be constant communications between units. This is especially vital where combat units operating over a wide area require radio communications. To ensure success, those in charge of military strategy and tactics require up-to-the-minute reports from the front lines. Any transmissions falling into enemy hands aid the enemy in countering planned actions. Military forces soon understood that the side that could send faster, more secure messages held an enormous advantage, one that could make the difference between winning and losing a battle or a war.

Of all forms of communications, the human voice has long been considered the most difficult to encrypt. In World War I, American forces were plagued by the Germans' ability to intercept and break coded communication transmissions based on English until a handful of unique and secure codes using unknown Native American languages were developed shortly before the war's end. Early in World War II, American intelligence units broke Japan's foremost diplomatic code, which used an electromechanical machine that the United States called "Purple." The Purple machine enciphered messages on the sending end and deciphered them at the receiving end. The intelligence resulting from breaking the Purple machine was code named MAGIC. Although of little aid in the Pacific Theater, it proved beneficial in the European Theater. Because Japanese ambassador to Berlin Baron Oshima Hiroshi sent back nearly 1,500 messages regarding German military affairs in Europe—some as long as thirty single-spaced typed pages—the United States learned much about the so-called Atlantic Wall from his messages. Despite problems in translating double veils of sophisticated ciphers and the complexity of numerous Japanese homonyms, the United States continued reading this code until V-J Day (Maslowski 1995:69–70).

Based on US Navy code breakers' partially solving the Japanese navy's primary code, JN25b, just before the Battle of the Coral Sea, ULTRA intelligence (the code name for intelligence gained from breaking Japan's army and navy military codes) in the Pacific, and later in Europe, sometimes provided timely information (Maslowski 1995:70–81). Despite immense mathematical complexity and frequent changing of codes and coding machines, Japan also enjoyed the same advantage through their own code-breaking efforts.

Cryptography, from the Greek *kryptos* (secret) and *graphos* (writing), is the science of forming, sending, and rendering secure signals and extracting information (Bruce 1973:13). Codes can be sent in any human-generated form, including speech, writing, or transmitted signals such as Morse code or semaphore signaling. The history of secret communications and its associated disciplines—cryptography, cryptology (the science and study of cryptography), and crypt analysis—has a long history (Bruce 1973; Kahn 1967, 1983; Maslowski 1995:52; Van Der Rhoer 1978). Throughout the history of warfare, military leaders have sought the perfect code—one no enemy could break regardless of the ability of their intelligence staff. For centuries, political and military personnel have developed codes to disguise their messages. The two most common forms of sending secret messages are codes and ciphers. Codes are systems of symbols used to represent an understood meaning among those familiar with the code formation. They are systems of secret message transmission. Codes use symbols to represent a message's true meaning and are understood only by those familiar with the code and the agreed-upon associated meanings. Coded messages reveal little to an enemy if intercepted, unless the enemy is able to break the code system and figure out the true meaning conveyed by the symbols. Ciphers are substitution systems using a standardized list of equivalents to transform regular symbols, such as letters, to represent another symbol. In a cipher system, the letter A, for example, might represent the letter F, B might represent G, and so on (Bruce 1973; Kahn 1967; Van Der Rhoer 1978). Making and breaking codes and ciphers has long challenged human ingenuity and analytical skills, providing much of the drama surrounding cryptography and cryptology (Bruce 1973:14).

Written codes have been used for various political, military, and religious purposes. The earliest known use of cryptograms, or coded messages, began nearly four thousand years ago among Egyptian political leaders. In ancient Babylonia and Assyria, a rare and unusual type of cuneiform was used in signing and dating clay tablets. The ancient historian Herodotus mentions the use of secret messages among the Greeks. Hebrew literature used at least three forms of letter substitutions. Mesopotamia, India, Persia, Scandinavia, Anglo-Saxon Britain, and parts of

Arabia also used cryptic scripts for various political purposes. The Yezidis of northern Iraq employed a cryptic script in their holy books for fear of religious persecution, and Tibetans have used cryptic scripts since the 1300s (Kahn 1967:71–105).

Cryptography has contributed to the political and military demise of some of the world's greatest armies, empires, and historical figures, including the Persian and Roman Empires, Elizabethan England, Mary Queen of Scots, Alexander II of Russia, Admiral Yamamoto of Japan, and the defeated powers in both world wars (Bruce 1973). In 405 BCE, the Spartan general Lysander used the first known system of military cryptography against the Persians through a device known as a skytale. This device consisted of a strip of papyrus, parchment, or leather wrapped tightly around a wooden staff. A secret message was written on the parchment down the length of the staff, and the parchment was unwrapped and then sent. Once unwrapped, the disconnected letters made no sense until the material was rewrapped around another pole of equal diameter, restoring the original positioning of the words to reveal their coherent messages. Julius Caesar used cryptographic messages in the Gallic Wars (Bruce 1973:15; Kahn 1967:1–105). In western Europe, political cryptology emerged during the Middle Ages (Kahn 1967:106), increasing in complexity with the development of voice radio, telephone, computer, and internet communications.

Between the American Civil War and World War II, military intelligence, like warfare itself, shifted from being human centered, personalized, and qualitative to being increasingly machine centered, bureaucratized, quantitative, and technological. During the Civil War, most operational military intelligence was human intelligence (humint), consisting of human-centered activities including spying, reconnaissance, observation, conversation, interrogation, and captured enemy documents. The need to communicate rapidly over long distances by sending signals led to the development of signals intelligence (sigint), or intelligence gathered by the interception of signals, including forms such as flags, flares, and telegraph. The telegraph led to enemy wiretapping and the development of encryption or coded messages. Although all humint sources (including modifications such as aerial and photo reconnaissance) in the Civil War were also present in both world wars, they had declined in overall importance.

In contrast, sigint, which was relatively unimportant in the Civil War, evolved so dramatically that it comprised the majority of military communications and constituted an intelligence revolution. Centering on radio, sigint became essential for efficient military operations at both tactical and strategic levels, and with radio waves free for the taking, complex enciphering of messages became necessary (Maslowski 1995:52–69). The level of communications systems in large, complex wars like World War I and II were staggering. Sophisticated mathematics, coding and decoding systems, frequent code changing, code-machine formation, and restructuring to statistically increase code complexity are but a few of the many aspects involved in these enormously complex communications systems. Sometimes thousands of individuals worked to break a single critical enemy code (Maslowski 1995).

Prior to 1917, US communications intelligence (comint) was both sporadic and poorly documented. Comint is intelligence produced through the study of foreign communications, including the breaking, reading, and evaluating of enciphered communications. Cryptology is a synthetic term applied to the combined activity of cipher construction and breaking or encoding and decoding messages; the terms "cryptography" and "cryptanalysis" are applied to these activities, respectively. The history of American cryptanalysis begins largely with entry into World War I with the first formally organized cryptanalytic office established by the US War Department in June 1917. Even the most sensitive codes and ciphers were simplistic and naïve by current standards. At this time, American codes were hand-coded and hand-applied cipher systems that usually overlaid double-entry codebooks. Breaking these systems required skill and patience, but not the elaborate electronic and tabulating devices of later periods. During World War I, American code breakers comprised a relatively small group of lexicographers, mathematicians, and individuals with a background in the hobby of cipher construction (Spector 1998:3).

Kahn (1983) and Singh (1999, 2002) present much of the crypt analytic development of the twentieth century, including the achievements of the various crypt analytic agencies in World War II. Yet despite changes in warfare, technology, and communications transmission, the basic purpose of military intelligence has remained unchanged. Sending and breaking intelligence, of course, is another matter.

Most codes are based on the codist's native language. If widely used, that language will also likely be known by one's enemy, and regardless of the code's structure, the enemy will eventually begin to break it through clues provided by limited numbers of phonemes, vowels and consonants, and the grammatical patterns of the language. However, the use of "hidden" languages—those that are little known outside their cultural group and have little or no written form—can be very effective for transmitting communications. The use of obscure languages in warfare predates World War I, as the British used Latin to confuse their adversaries in the Second Boer War of 1899–1902. In the US, many largely unwritten Indigenous languages existed, and as hidden languages, they made a unique contribution to American military communications during both world wars.

Native American Military Literature and Code Talking

One counter to Axis efforts to break American military communications in both world wars involved voice transmissions in languages that had either never been heard or had been little studied by German or Japanese military forces. One such genre of languages, for which neither Germany nor Japan was prepared or able to counter, was Native American. Despite a voluminous literature on World War I, military scholars have long dismissed Native American contributions as too peripheral or insignificant to merit wide recognition. Extensive accounts of Native American participation in World War I are few and fairly recent (Barsh 1991, 2001; Britten 1997; Dempsey 1983, 1988, 1999, 2006; Grillot 2018; Krouse 2007; White 1979, 1982, 1984; White 1990; Winegard 2012). More extensive works have been written on Native American participation in World War II (Collier 1942; Bernstein 1991; Franco 1986, 1990a, 1990b, 1999; Parman 1994:59–70; Townsend 2000), the collective role and experiences of Native veterans (Hale 1982, 1992; Haynie 1984; Meadows 2017; Tate 1986; White 1979), Korea (van de Logt 2006), Vietnam (Holm 1985, 1992, 1996), and the role of veterans in tribal ceremonial culture (Meadows 1991, 1995, 1999, 2010; Viola 2008).[2] Some works focus on individual Native communities and their veterans (Dempsey 1988; Hale 1992; Johnson 1977; van de Logt 2006, 2010).

Little scholarly work has been published on Native American code talkers. Of the major sources on military codes and code breaking, only Kahn (1967:549–550) and Singh (1999:193–202) briefly mention code talkers. Other works only briefly mention Native American—primarily Choctaw—telephone operators in World War I (Brager 2002:74–75; Gilbert 2012:189–190, 202n22–23; Hale 1982; Raines 1996:283n56; Stallings 1963:288; White 1976:22). The largest non-fiction publication on the Choctaw code talkers is in Meadows's larger work on the Comanche (2002:14–27).

Most works on code talkers focus solely on the Navajo in World War II. Numerous newspaper accounts, non-academic journal articles, and over sixty other sources (fifteen books, including six children's books, twenty-five articles, seven archival locales, oven ten documentary films, and the MGM motion picture *Windtalkers*) discuss or focus on the Navajo code talkers.[3] Two recent works provide the first collaborative accounts with Navajo code talkers Chester Nez (Nez and Avila 2011) and Tom Holiday (Holiday and McPherson 2013). Other recent works include Mack (2008), McClain (1994, 2012), Gorman (2015), and Tohe (2012).

A few US armed forces publications briefly mention the Navajo in World War II (Morison 1953:376; Newhouse 1948:39; Thompson and Harris 1966:218). Walker (1980, 1983) briefly describes the use of Navajo and Muskogee Creek in World War II and code talking in both world wars from limited press releases. Some works focusing on the Navajo briefly mention the Comanche in World War II, often with incorrect data and uncritically cited sources (Bernstein 1991:46; Bixler 1992:42; Daily 1995:50–52; Hale 1992:416; Paul 1973:7; Townsend 2000:144, 150; White 1979:18). Based on published sources, Holm (2007:69–84, 109–120) published a young reader's book on Navajo and other World War II code talkers, and Robinson (2011) provides brief accounts from interviews with World War II code talkers.[4]

Prior to Meadows's (2002) work, only three sources mention the Comanche: two brief works written by a Comanche code talker (Red Elk 1991:113–114, 1992:1–9) and a work by Gawne (1998:264). Meadows (2006, 2009, 2011, 2016, 2018) later published four articles and a webpage on Native American code talkers in both world wars and their federal recognition. Recently, Andrea Page (2017), a Hunkpapa Lakota, wrote about seven WW II Lakota code talkers in the 1st Cavalry Division.

As the anniversary of World War I (1914–18) approached, many new historical works on the "Great War" appeared. Yet few mention code talking in World War I or its expansion in World War II (the notable exception is Yockelson 2016:291–292). Thus, the Navajo have long been believed to have been the first and only Native American code talkers (Paul 1973:7). Although they were the largest and best-known group of code talkers, the Navajo were not the first in either world war. While military intelligence has long used cryptography and codes to ensure secure communications and gain advantages in warfare, Native American military service as code talkers has a more recent history.

World War I and Native Americans

The first major battle of World War I was fought on the Eastern Front at Tannenberg in August 1914. Here, the Germans monitored radio communications of the Russian forces, who at that time had few radio operators and limited encryption systems. As most Russian messages were sent in the clear (without encryption), Germans simply listened to and translated them. Redeploying several divisions countering the Russian battle plan, a massive German victory ensued, with seventy-six thousand Russians killed or wounded and ninety-two thousand taken prisoner. A second victory in September virtually wiped out the Russian Second Army, a loss that set the Russians back six months (Downing 2014:103–104). These battles demonstrated the importance of infiltrating enemy radio communication and developing new forms of secure voice transmission.

Although World War I began in 1914, the United States remained neutral for two and a half years, delaying its entry until 1917. Before the US entry into the war, many Native Americans from northwestern states had crossed the border to enlist in Canadian units; others had enlisted in the US Army, Navy, and Marines (US Congress 1920:2211). Determined to keep America neutral, President Woodrow Wilson used the slogan "He kept Us out of War" in his 1916 reelection campaign. Americans disapproved of Germany's violation and subsequent invasion of neutral Belgium. German foreign secretary Alfred Zimmerman proposed a German-Mexican alliance against the United States, promising Mexico the return of much of the lands lost in the US-Mexican War. When British intercepted the proposal and informed the United States of it, it fueled existing desires to declare war against Germany.

Germany's announcement in January 1917 of resumption of unrestricted submarine warfare prompted a US ultimatum. Germany's reply that it would allow one US ship per week to sail through the war zone, but only if painted in red and white stripes, was viewed as an insult (Lawson 1963:19). Resuming unrestricted submarine warfare on February 1, 1917, the United States severed diplomatic relations with Germany on February 3. On March 27, German U-boats sank four American ships, leading President Wilson to call for a special session of Congress seeking a declaration of war, which followed on April 6, 1917.

During World War I, US Army divisions were organized in a form known as a square organization. The average American infantry division contained two infantry brigades, each with two infantry regiments, three machine gun battalions, one field artillery brigade with three artillery regiments, and a divisional trench mortar battery. Each infantry regiment contained three battalions of four rifle companies and a machine gun company. Companies contained four platoons, six officers, and 250 men. At full strength, a regiment held 112 officers and 3,720 men. A full division contained 17,666 riflemen, 260 machine guns, and 72 guns (forty-eight 75 mm and twenty-four 155 mm). Headquarter, engineering, communications, and supply units brought the division's membership to roughly twenty-eight thousand men (Hallas 2000:52; Otte 2018:235–236).

On May 18, 1917, Congress passed a selective service act. On June 5, the federal government enacted the first call to register for the draft, requiring all citizen and non-citizen males between the ages of twenty-one and thirty to register with local draft boards. Drawings began on July 20 in Washington, DC. Native American males holding US citizenship (slightly less than two-thirds of all Native Americans in 1917) in this age range were also required to register and were subject to the draft. Despite their legal status, most Native Americans without US citizenship waived their exemption for military service and voluntarily enlisted; others were drafted (Finger 1986:288; Britten 1997:57–58).

In 1917, the Native American population was approximately 350,000 (Wood 1981:249); by April 1918, over six thousand were serving in the US armed forces.[5] By the end of September 1918, over seventeen thousand Native American men had registered for the draft (Britten 1997:51–52). Estimates of the number of Natives who served in the American Expeditionary Forces (AEF) during World War I range as high as 10,000 by the Bureau of Indian Affairs (BIA) to 17,300 by the US adjutant general (US Congress 1920:2163, 2175–2176). The later figures are likely the number registered for the draft; because of inconsistent racial categories on draft and enlistment forms and self-identification, the precise number will never be known. Britten (1997:83–84) and Franco (1999:60) report that eventually, some 12,000 to 12,500 served, with nearly 1,000 in the navy. This represents over 25 percent of the adult male Native American population eligible for military service (the number inducted after the September call is unknown). Compared to their total population at the time, Native Americans volunteered and were inducted at a rate nearly twice that of the rest of the American population. Holm (1996:99) reports that nearly two-thirds of all Native American veterans were volunteers, while Britten (1997:73, 199n28) reports around 6,000 enlistments to 6,500 draftees. Nevertheless, the ratio of volunteers was high (Britten 1997:59, 73, 84).[6]

It is often stated that Native Americans in the twentieth century have served in US armed forces conflicts in higher numbers in relation to their total population than any other ethnic group in America. While widely uncited, this claim may originate from Commissioner of Indian Affairs Cato Sells's 1918 report *The Indian's War Activities*. Sells wrote, "Considering the large number of old and infirm Indians and others not acceptable under the draft, leaving about 33,000 of military eligibility, I regard their representation of 9,000 in camp and actual warfare as furnishing a ration to population unsurpassed, if equaled, by any other race or nation. I am very proud of their part in this war."[7] The *Stars and Stripes* reported that approximately thirty-three thousand Native Americans were eligible for service in World War I and that members of sixty tribes served in twenty American divisions, from one in the 29th Division to "several thousand" in the 36th. The number of tribes involved may have been even higher.[8]

Nineteen months of combat and additional occupation duties greatly affected Native American citizenship, economics, cultural retention, and political changes. Before the war, national debates occurred in America and Canada concerning whether to integrate Native Americans into the US and Canadian militaries, whether to form separate all–Native American military units, and whether to attempt to determine their loyalty and reliability (Dempsey 1983; Hale 1982; Parman 1994:60–61; Tate 1986;

White 1990:78–79). When the Indian Cavalry Program was ended in 1897, official military policy ceased forming all-Native units, henceforth integrating them into white units (Britten 1997:25). Some evidence suggests that Native Americans encountered fewer problems adjusting to military life in largely Native American units, which occurred in western states with high Native American populations (White 1990:79–80).

However, efforts to form all–Native American units in the US Army continued. During the Spanish-American War in 1898, some Indian agents and military officers suggested forming such units. In April of 1898, W. A. Mercer, Indian agent at the Omaha and Winnebago Agency in Nebraska, wrote to the adjutant general of the US Army and to Assistant Secretary of War George D. Meiklejohn, proposing the formation of a regiment of Native Americans from his region and a transfer from the Indian Service back to military duty. Intending to lead the all-Native unit, and after "We have licked the Spaniards," he planned to return as Indian agent.[9] In 1900, Major John J. Pershing also proposed forming a Native militia.[10]

Before the war, Joseph K. Dixon, of the Eastman Kodak Company and the Educational Bureau at the John Wanamaker Store in Philadelphia, emerged as a champion of Native American rights and citizenship.[11] Financed by Rodman Wanamaker, Dixon participated in three photographic expeditions documenting Native Americans (Barsh 1993:97–100; Krouse 2007:8–10). Although describing himself in 1913 as "Dr. Joseph K. Dixon, leader of the expeditions to the North American Indian to perpetuate the life story of these first Americans," his efforts moved beyond photography and documentation to advocacy for Indigenous rights. Aimed at promoting Native American citizenship, Dixon and his party visited eighty-nine reservations over six months where American flags, flag raisings, and the signing of a declaration of allegiance were presented to 169 tribes. Dixon's goal of securing citizenship for all Native Americans shifted to campaigning for greater Native participation in the US military (Barsh 1993: 100–111; Krouse 2007:10–11).

Dixon urged members of Congress to recruit Native Americans as guards for patrolling the US-Mexican border during and after the Mexican Revolution. Many Native American soldiers were already participating in this campaign. In 1917, Representative Julius Kahn (California) and Senator Boies Penrose (Pennsylvania) introduced legislation calling for the formation of all–Native American cavalry units. That year, Dixon testified on behalf of Kahn's Indian Cavalry Bill (HR 3970), calling for the formation of ten or more regiments of mounted Native Americans in the US Army. Although the bill died in committee as a result of the War Department's and Indian Commissioner Sells's strong opposition to its segregational basis, Dixon continued championing all–Native American military units and citizenship (Britten 1997:38–50; Krouse 2007:11–12; Tate 1986:425–426; US Congress 1920:2163; White 1976:20–21).[12]

During World War I, several governmental and military officials, including secretary of the interior Franklin K. Lane and some Native tribal leaders, proposed raising all-Native units for military service as high as the division level.[13] Other Natives and non-Natives supported forming all-Native units. In January 1918, Pine Ridge Indian agent Henry M. Tidwell wrote Sells desiring to form an all-Native unit (Lynn-Sherow and Bruce 2001:86). The following month, nearly thirty Cheyenne and Arapaho in Native dress, led by Chiefs Yellow Hawk, Magpie, and Little Wolf, addressed Governor Robert Lee Williams at the Oklahoma State Capitol, requesting to be allowed to fight in defense of their country and proposing the formation of ten regiments of Native American cavalry. Little Wolf explained that "the Indian wants to fight for his country and will go where he is sent but they would like best to fight on horseback so he can get up and go fast after the enemy." White Horse reportedly stated, "I want to fight for my country and if Uncle Sam will give me a good horse I will make a good soldier and scalp the kaiser."[14]

While serving with the 4th Division in the Meuse-Argonne campaign in 1918, Lieutenant John R. Eddy, formerly superintendent of the Crow Indian Reservation, "recommended the organization and training of Indians as rangers and their assignment in small groups throughout the Army for special service as scouts." Eddy "was seconded by Lieut. Red Cloud who, while attending a school at Langres urged that they be formed into special Signal Corps units" (Wise 1931:533), which suggests that they were either already aware of Native American languages being used for military communications or were considering it. Other supporters included several members of the Society of American Indians (SAI), a Native-led reform organization dominated by well-educated "red progressives," including Edward Ayer, a member of the Board of Indian Commissioners; Frances LaFlesche of the Bureau of American Ethnology; Joseph K. Dixon; and Carlos Montezuma, among others (Hertzberg 1971:170).

These efforts were opposed by Secretary of War Newton D. Baker, Major General Hugh Lennox Scott, US Army chief of staff Peyton C. March, Commissioner of Indian Affairs Cato Sells, and some Indian agents and members of the SAI, including its president, anthropologist Arthur C. Parker (a member of the Seneca nation) (Britten 1997:42–45; Hertzberg 1971:170; Krause 2007:11; US Congress 1920:2164, 2172–2173). March and Baker opposed separate units, stressing the purported failure of Native American cavalry units of the 1890s. Baker was also concerned with continuing segregation policies in relation to problems encountered with black troops and communities during the war, while March did not believe enough Native Americans could be recruited to fill several cavalry units, let alone maintain replacements for potentially high casualty rates (Britten 2007:42–43).[15] The editor of *American Indian Magazine* also opposed separate Native American army units on the grounds that it represented a form of segregation interfering with Native American freedom of choice (Hertzberg 1971:170). The magazine described its chief arguments against such formations, referencing stereotypes associated with a form of cultural stereotyping known as the "Indian Scout Syndrome" (Holm 1996:88–89).

The idea of forming separate Native American units arose from several sources, and the arguments to support the idea were many—that Native Americans were superior in some ways, that they occupied a lower social station, and that they belonged to a separate and peculiar race whose nobility and fighting skills could best be maintained on the battlefield by regiments of the race—all such arguments being used to support the need to segregate Native Americans from white European Americans. Much of the clamor for a spectacular Indian regiment or battalion arose from the showman's brand of "Indian" as seen in the circus (Hertzberg 1971:171n8).

Scott, who initially supported the Kahn Bill and had the most successful all–Indian Scout unit in the 1890s, later reversed his position, perhaps in response to Secretary of War Baker's opposition to it (Britten 19197:40–41). Both rejected Lane's proposal on the grounds that replacements for a Native American division at the front would be difficult to provide and thus maintain separate units (Britten 1997:42–44; Scott 1928:562–563; Tate 1986:426). With US divisions during World War I as large as twenty-eight thousand men, this would have been impractical. Scott also saw no reason why Native Americans could not serve harmoniously in Caucasian organizations, acknowledging that "the separate Negro organizations we cannot avoid" (Scott 1928:563).[16]

The decision not to form all–Native American units in World War I resulted more from disagreement within the military's higher echelon concerning logistics of numbers and replacements, social issues of segregation, and widespread government goals to assimilate Native Americans into mainstream American society—all of which would be necessary for the larger goal of enhancing the development of a larger, more mechanized, more complex modern army—than from any issue having to do with the performance of Native American soldiers. Along with concerns for language and culture shock, additional resources, training, and ability, implementing all–Native American units within larger units did not match the army's priority of efficiency (Britten 1997:40–45; Dunlay 1982:196; Scott 1928:169–170; Sells 1918:874; White 1990:78–79).

Scott was supported by Commissioner of Indian Affairs Cato Sells who actively promoted Native American assimilation. Federal officials and pro-assimilation reformers believed Native American participation in the war would accelerate assimilation and entrance into American society. Sells felt that integrated units would also increase Native education levels while "moving him away from tribal relations and towards civilization" (Sells 1918:874). When Sells visited the 36th Division at Camp Bowie in late 1917, he noted that Native American troops had invested heavily in liberty bonds, were receiving the "best of treatment," and espoused a "wonderful spirit of patriotism," but he noted:

> I am much opposed to having the Indians in independent units, large or small. I am firm in my opinion that they should be . . . mixed indiscriminately among the whites, elbow to elbow, so that they will absorb the English, habits and civilization of their white brothers. In this way only can they advance. I want no discrimination either for or against them, but believe they should be advanced on their merit, and always advanced when they do deserve it.[17]

Secretary of War Baker also rejected the idea of forming separate Native American units largely on historical and social grounds, a position he maintained throughout the war (Britten 1997:43; Wise 1931:529–532; White 1979:13–14). Arthur C. Parker, SAI president, supported the war effort, assimilation, and even intermarriage with whites, noting, "Segregation had done more than bullets to conquer the red man." Parker was highly supportive of assimilation for both Native Americans and immigrants (Britten 1997:44; Hertzberg 1971:156–170). Gabe Parker (Choctaw), superintendent of the Five Civilized Tribes in Oklahoma (1918:22), also strongly opposed all–Native American military units while supporting assimilation, stating, "This is an all-American war and we are not running our population through a blood grader to separate the English from the Italian. All we ask of an American is that he is an American and not Hun-American. Those last we grade out."

Many viewed military service as a major step in moving American Indigenous Peoples away from tribal cultures and toward "civilization" by assimilating them into mainstream American culture. Ironically, while the US government, the BIA, missionaries, and assimilationists embraced military participation as a means to integrate and assimilate Native Americans into American society and divorce them from their Native traditions, the military expected Natives to retain their "warrior" characteristics, which they believed would benefit them, even if based on stereotypes. As Lynn-Sherow and Bruce (2001:86–87) explain, "Ironically, the perceived special talents (bellicosity, stealth, marksmanship, devotion to unit) of the Indian soldier as valued by the military were precisely those traits that the BIA hoped would be erased through his service in the armed forces."

Native Americans often embraced the "Wild West" and "Indian scout" stereotypes associated with the profiling of their inherently natural "warrior" skills, as it brought reputation, respect, and status in the eyes of both their home communities and non–Native Americans (Bernstein 1991:41; Britten 1997:99–115; Holm 1986:83–90; Krouse 2007:66–79, 118–132; Winegard 2012:29–31).

Nearly all US policy regulating Native American participation in World War I prioritized assimilation. Lynn-Sherow and Bruce (2001:86–87) point out that "in general, Indian service in the military strengthened and supported the three major goals of assimilation policy: the decline of Indian culture, customs, and language; the instillation of pride in American citizenship; and the elimination of all 'special privileges' historically associated with Indian peoples such as their legal status as tribal members and commonly held reservation land."

Despite integration into regular regiments, the army inadvertently established a few units, mostly on the company level, in which most or all members were Native. The 2nd, 5th, 36th, 40th, 41st, 42nd, and 90th Divisions contained sizable contingents of Native American soldiers. Between six hundred and a thousand Natives from fourteen tribes were stationed in the 36th Division at Camp Bowie, Texas. At Camp Travis, Texas, nearly a thousand tribal members from Oklahoma, mainly from the Choctaw, Chickasaw, and Creek tribes, were in the 90th Division, a National Army draft division, with the 358th Infantry Regiment composed mostly of Native Americans. At one point, the 358th Infantry Regiment from Texas and Oklahoma was reported to be "a complete Indian regiment," and from a total of 1,440 men, only 260 returned. One newspaper estimated that there were some 1,500 Native American soldiers stationed in four Texas camps. Lieutenant Ben Cloud, 164th Infantry Regiment, 41st Division, reported fifty to seventy-five Native Americans in Company B. Many Natives in the Arizona National Guard were eventually transferred to a predominantly all-Indian company in the 158th Infantry Regiment, 40th Division. Significant numbers of Native American replacements were sent to other divisions. Following heavy losses at Château-Thierry, the 2nd and 3rd Battalions of the 165th Infantry, 42nd ("Rainbow") Division, each received fifty Native American replacements, most from the 36th Division. The Canadian army also had between three thousand and four thousand Native troops in its forces (Britten 1997:74–75, 116; Hale 1982:40; US Congress 1920:2168, 2185–2186).[18] Although a few companies were primarily Native American in membership, a result of demographic factors, the US military had no "officially recognized" Native American units in either of the two world wars (White 1979:11–12), unlike segregated American black units. Yet these concentrations of Natives are what allowed code talking to develop.

Citizenship

While many still believe Native Americans were not US citizens during World War I, this is only partially true. Over one-half to two-thirds of Native Americans possessed US citizenship by this time. Existing legislation determining US citizenship for Natives included provisions in some earlier treaties, allotment through the Dawes Act of 1887, forced patenting, and instances of women marrying a Native or non-Native citizen. A March 3, 1901, act gave citizenship to the Five Civilized Tribes in Indian Territory (later Oklahoma) (Britten 1997:176).[19]

Generally, Native Americans were considered citizens if they lived in the old Indian Territory as of March 3, 1901. Non-citizens included those not allotted or allotted after May 8, 1906, and still under federal trust status. Because nearly one-third or more of all Native Americans had not been granted US citizenship, many were not legally subject to the draft or qualified for voluntary enlistment. Anyone allotted before the 1906 Burke Act or residing apart from his or her tribe and living "like a white man" was eligible for conscription, as were children of citizens, children with one or more parent allotted after May 8, 1906, in accordance with the government allotment program prior to their child's birth or adulthood, and anyone declared a citizen by legislation (Parman 1994:60; White 1979:9).

The Selective Service Act caused great confusion for Natives. Because citizenship came through varied means and legislation varied among Native groups, much confusion regarding who were US citizens and who were not ensued. Many non-citizens believed draft registration meant instant conscription. When the United States entered the war in 1917, thousands of Native Americans entered the armed forces regardless of their existing legal status. Others were conscripted. Refusing to take advantage of their draft exemptions, some took the military oath to defend the US Constitution without possessing citizenship or any rights under it. Despite widespread media presenting a positive pan-Native response to registration and the draft, tribal and individual reactions varied. Some largely non-citizen, less-acculturated, and more isolated Southwest and Great Basin groups took little interest in the war, were suspicious of American motivations, and resisted draft registration. Greater participation and support came from Plains, Southeast, and Great Lakes communities that had longer contact and greater assimilation with Americans. Some four thousand servicemen from the southeastern Five Civilized Tribes reflected a high enlistment rate, with some six hundred serving in the 36th Division, an activated Oklahoma National Guard unit. While some individuals questioned and contested the legality of being drafted, because of uncertainty of citizenship and agreements made in earlier treaties, most complied and no violence resulted

(Britten 1997:51–71, Weingard 2012). In reality, there was no typical Native American serviceman; diversity existed through factors of tribal culture, lifestyle, acculturation, education, US citizenship or ward status, and enlistment motivations (Parman 1994:63).

Native Motivations for Military Service

In light of past treatment from non-Native Americans, many contemporary non-Natives question why large numbers of Native Americans voluntarily enlisted in the US armed forces. Most scholars of Native Americans in World War I and II offer two explanations. Journalists and popular writers often attribute high rates of Native military service to an innate or biologically and culturally determined love of warfare. These positions are typically not supported with any data, and cultural anthropology has long demonstrated that culture is socially and environmentally—and not biologically—determined. More academic scholars tend to stress Native attempts to legitimize themselves as American citizens (Bernstein 1991:22–42; Parman 1994:107–111; Rawls 1996:5). These authors attribute increased military service to Native Americans' becoming subject to the draft, their attempts to share in American democracy, increased prewar employment and urban migration, increased military and war industry, and ensured employment, status, income, and a taste of the white world.

As early as 1931, Jennings C. Wise (1931:319–323) recognized defense of homeland as a significant factor in Native participation in World War I. However, these influences were experienced in different combinations and to different degrees by every soldier, Native and non-Native alike. Although a correlation exists between Native American populations possessing strong warrior traditions and acting on incentives to form economic and military alliances through enlistments in American military forces during periods of economic hardship (Britten 1997:20), these multi-factorial developments are simply too complex to designate a single cause.

Indigenous responses to World War I were highly diverse, and no single Native American response accurately represents the motivations and decisions of all Native American veterans (Britten 1997:51–72; 130). The same applies to later wars. Most prior works give little attention to Native American cultural motivations for enlisting, related cultural practices, and their return home. While increased interactions with non–Native Americans fostered acculturation to some degree, it simultaneously intensified ethnic identity by revitalizing Native traditions such as prewar protection and postwar honoring ceremonies, dances, songs, giveaways, naming ceremonies, and the creation of Native American Legion Posts (Britten 1997:84, 149–151; Grillot 2018; Meadows 1995:407–409; Parman 1994:60, 63). The process of Native American militarization is far more complex than most scholars and general readers realize, and the topic has been largely overlooked by authors relying on archival documents over interviews with Native American veterans (Holm 1996:100–102, 117–128; Meadows 1995, 2002; 2017).

As Holm (1996:100–101) explains, many authors attribute Native American participation in the US military to dependency theory, whereby joining the military is an act of self-legitimization as an American ally and then as an American citizen. This assumes that Native Americans have internalized colonization, lost their autonomy, been deprived of political experience, and seek entrance into the larger American polity. Holm (1996:100–101) notes that "from the viewpoint of dependency analysis, American political and military elites have accepted Indians as being politically reliable because they have supposedly adopted the same basic value system as whites in order to gain greater benefits from the state—either in terms of limited economic opportunity or a degree of social, cultural, and/ or political autonomy. The militarization of Native Americans can be seen as the result of a continual process."

While American military and governmental leaders promoted integrated military service to increase acculturation, dependency theory is too simplistic, correlating with neither Native American nor non–Native American data. Native American participation was clearly not solely draft oriented, as 50 percent or more of all Natives in World War I voluntarily enlisted.[20] Enlistment was also not strictly from dependency or a desire to assimilate into mainstream American society. If dependency and assimilation were desired, the widespread postwar ceremonialism that rekindled past tribal traditions, and continues to the present, should not have occurred (Britten 1997:84, 149–151; Meadows 1995:407–409; Parman 1994:60–63). The BIA and the Board of Indian Commissioners initially attempted to prohibit such celebrations as acts of disloyalty and attempts to subvert the will of the government. However, Commissioner Cato Sells later acquiesced amid the nationwide cultural revivals held for returning Native servicemen (ARCIA 1919:12; Britten 1997:149, 186–187; Holm 1978:208).

Native Americans did not join the armed forces in World War I solely from a sense of national patriotism or to legitimize themselves as American citizens. Nearly one-third of all enlistees were already allotted, and despite existing inequalities, many already knew that they were both members of their respective tribes and American citizens. Most Native American World War I veterans joined the armed forces for a complex combination of reasons, including traditional cultural motivations (warrior-based themes), acculturative influences (military-style boarding school, National Guard service), contemporary economic factors (employment), and patriotic ideology for the defense of their own land and people, as well as of the United

States, all of which they were a part of. Veterans' accounts demonstrate that while several dominant reasons are found, there was no one single Native American response to the war and that a combination of many factors existed. Economic opportunity, travel, adventure, escape from reservation conditions, support of dependents, citizenship status, patriotism, a desire to defend their homeland, devotion to tribal and American ideals of freedom and democracy, improving civil rights, and raising Native and American social status were all significant factors. Other factors included geography, demographics, education levels, boarding-school and paramilitary-training experiences, vocational skills, levels of acculturation, individual and tribal relationships with the federal government and the BIA, Indigenous-reform influences, and conscription (Britten 1997:60–67; Franco 1999:62–67; Holm 1992:101–102; Krouse 2007:17–18; LaBarre n.d.; Parman 1994:64–76; SIFCJ 1984:68; White 1990).

Traditional Cultural Motivations

Traditional Native American motives for engaging in warfare include factors of alliance, treaties, geography, protection of homeland, economics, politics, traditional definitions of martial and social status, patriotism, and other factors. While the largest sample of firsthand data on Native motivations for enlisting in World War I comes from Dixon's surveys (Krouse 2007), larger cultural patterns and data suggest continuing traditional Native cultural and martial values.

For some tribes, the content of treaties was taken seriously. Several tribal treaties with the United States contained obligatory clauses requiring Native Americans to "lay down their arms forever," or "war no more against the white man except in self defense." The Onondaga and some other tribal governments declared war on Germany independently, viewing military service as part of their own treaty obligations to the United States (Holm 1992:346).

Reservation-era service as scouts, cavalry, and US marshals provided younger men lacking war records access to a semblance of martial service, material culture, and status in a period when traditional martial roles were severely curtailed (Meadows 1999:378–381). Scouting service also provided an outlet for the restlessness of young men in reservation contexts (Dunlay 1982:48, 200; Feaver 1975; Price 1977) who blended elements of two diverse military systems during a period of immense sociocultural and economic change. Comanche and Kiowa had proven themselves in pre–reservation-era warfare (Mooney 1898; Richardson 1933) and had established their later military worth and allegiance in the all-Native cavalry of Troop L at Fort Sill, Indian Territory, from 1891–97 (Meadows 2015:57–66; Nye 1937).

Native Americans have served in every major English, French, Spanish, and American conflict in the New World (Britten 1997:10–17; Holm 1996). As early as 1778, General George Washington (Bucholtz et al. 1996:1) observed, "I think they [Native Americans] can be made of excellent use, as scouts and light troops." Natives have fought alongside European and American powers in King Philip's War (1675–1676), the French and Indian War (1754–1763), the Revolutionary War (1776–1783), the War of 1812, and on both sides in the American Civil War. Recognizing Native American skills in scouting, the US Army established the Indian Scouts in 1866, with members of various Plains and Southwest tribes (Crow, Pawnee, Cheyenne, Tonkawa, Apache) serving as scouts and auxiliaries in Plains and Southwest campaigns, Theodore Roosevelt's Rough Riders in the Spanish American War in Cuba in 1898, the Philippine Insurrection of 1899–1902, the Boxer Rebellion of 1899–1900, and in General John Pershing's expedition into Mexico against Pancho Villa in 1916–17. Although officially active from 1891–97, the Indian Scouts were technically deactivated with the last member's retirement at Ft. Huachuca, Arizona, in 1947 (Bucholz et al. 1996:1; Dunlay 1982; Feaver 1975; Price 1977; Tate 1986:418–421).

For younger males, World War I was the first opportunity to fulfill traditional tribal roles as warriors through military service, while simultaneously achieving other statuses. As Bruce White (1990:76) notes, "For Indians, military service facilitated self-defense and revenge on enemies, the acquisition of plunder, the attaining of status, and prestige through military exploit, escape from the boredom of reservation life and farming activities, accommodation to white power, and improving relationships with dominant whites."

In this context, some Natives approached military service not solely in terms of patriotism to America, but as an opportunity to fulfill personal and cultural goals that raised their tribal sociopolitical position. While the BIA and the armed forces saw military service as a means to assimilate Native Americans, many approached service based on Native values, finding ways to syncretize and indigenize their service, especially upon returning to their tribal communities (Holm 1996:69, 101, 117, 191).

Many Indigenous veterans believed military service would gain them respect from both Native Americans and white European Americans and that it would enable them to protect their land and people according to traditional value systems and link them to traditional family and tribal male cultural roles and heritage as warriors. Service in the US military became a modern—and in some ways, the only viable—means of regaining traditional prestige as a warrior through warfare. Native Americans combined military service with their own tribal customs and value systems and were enlisting because of factors related to their own social and cultural backgrounds, not solely from the preconceptions and stereotypes of American society (Holm 1996; Meadows 1995). Many Native veterans saw military service as traditionally protecting their land and their people, as well as the United States, which equated to exactly what their forbearers did and were honored for. Natives emphasized their desire to join in the common defense of tribal lands and America, were clearly fighting for "their" country, and saw any enemy attack on the United States as an assault on them as well. This is nothing short of patriotism for their respective tribes, traditional homelands, and the United States.

Some Natives preferred to remain with other Natives in combat (Britten 1997:60–63; LaBarre n.d.; Parman 1994:64), thus maintaining traditional concepts associated with pre-reservation ideologies involving kinship, war party, warrior sodality, and group cohesiveness (Meadows 1995, 2010). The motivations of Native WW I veterans clearly contained culturally based factors as reflected in the maintenance of a strong warrior ethos and by maintaining and reviving many cultural practices still technically prohibited by Indian Agency efforts to suppress them. Military service provided not only a contemporary link to past warrior roles and prominent social status, but also a link to the maintenance and subsequent postwar revival of other tribal cultural forms, including dances, songs, economic redistribution through giveaways, religious practices such as protective prayers, medicine and post-service purification, naming ceremonies, induction into men's societies, Native titles of status, and women honoring male veterans (Holm 1996; Meadows 1995, 1999, 2010, 2017; Parman 1994). Thus, a syncretic blend of two previously distinct military traditions developed into a new form allowing for the continuation of traditional martial values and culture in a manner more conducive to modern US military service.

Acculturation and Economic Factors

The acculturation-oriented structure of the boarding-school experience preconditioned many Native Americans to military-style regimented daily activities. Army life posed few problems for Native American boarding-school students, who were intimately familiar with regimented military-style discipline, uniforms, drills, and time schedules. Training correlated with traditional martial themes and values that fostered Native soldiers regaining their warrior status as veterans in the modern US military. Several cases are recorded of boarding schools preconditioning Native Americans for military service and serving as recruiting centers (Barsh 1991:278–279; Britten 1997:60–65; Hale 1982; Holm 1992; 1996:99; Lynn-Sherow and Bruce 2001; Meadows 2002:80–84; Parker 1918:22; Parman 1994:63, 64;

Tate 1986). School reports list numbers of active and former students who served in World War I, such as 415 students from Haskell.[21]

Boarding schools for Native Americans also preconditioned some individuals for communications duties through training in related fields. As John Eddy described in 1919, "The Indian [is] competitively prepared by his technical training in special government and public schools to render advanced battalion and regimental intelligence services. He has received military training at Carlisle, Haskell, Riverside, Chilocco, Phoenix, and Chemawa and he has qualified since graduating from such schools as telegrapher, telephone operator and draughtsman."[22]

Boarding schools often fostered a military-school environment. Many army officers, serving in detached positions, held key positions in the Indigenous school system, and it was widely assumed that Native American students were inherently discipline problems (Newland and Delaney 1996:2–4). From its beginning in 1884, Haskell organized students in a military battalion with military-style uniforms, regimented formations, marching to classes and meals, and squad drills. Small-arms drilling was added in 1913. Boarding schools in turn likely preconditioned men for service in National Guard units, in which many served as a source of monthly income prior to both world wars.

Commissioner Sells turned all BIA programs toward ensuring victory in the war cause, fervently urging Native Americans to enter military service to capitalize on the opportunity to assimilate. The reasons for such high rates of Native military service becomes obvious as Native Americans were heavily recruited, consciously and rigidly conscripted, and demonstrated a high rate of volunteerism for several generations (Holm 1992:345–346). Government control over reservations and the availability of annual tribal censuses accelerated promoting Native enlistment and registration, and Secretary of War Baker allowed Indian agencies to act as recruiting and induction centers. While the drafting of Native Americans was handled by local draft boards, agency and school officials supported the recruitment of volunteers, and Indian Service employees were required to serve as registrars and members of registration boards (Hale 1982:39–40, Holm 1996:99). Native recruits were often older than non-Natives. In 1917, the Choctaw code talkers ranged in age from nineteen to thirty-five, while the recruits at Camp Funston were twenty-four to twenty-seven (Lynn-Sherow and Bruce 2001:93).

Native Americans in World War I

After the US entrance into World War I on April 6, 1917, Native Americans were among the first American troops to reach France, arriving in the last week of June 1917 and fighting in every major engagement (see appendix A) from Château-Thierry in May 1918 to the Meuse-Argonne offensive in September-November of 1918 (Britten 1997:75). Dozens of Native servicemen were awarded decorations of valor, including the French Croix de Guerre (Cross of War), yet their contributions were largely negated in two ways. First, news coverage on Native Americans in the war was extremely limited; the *Stars and Stripes* ran only four articles on Native Americans in the war. Second, with the exception of accounts of General Pershing's use of Apache scouts, news coverage on Native Americans was overly stereotyped in racist terms and overtones. One *Stars and Stripes* article on the Choctaw was titled "Yank Indian was Big Help in Winning the War."[23] Walter Snow, decorated in every major campaign that the Americans fought during World War I, was described as "Redskin Hero of Verdun Can't Stalk Ivories as He Did Huns" (Hale 1982:39–41). As Russel Barsh (2001:375) aptly surmised, "By the time Americans entered the European war in 1917, they had become intoxicated with the Indian Warrior ideal, both as a representation of the worthy adversary and as their own *alter ego.*"

An April 1918 article on the 142nd Infantry Regiment at Camp Bowie, Texas, containing many Indigenous Oklahomans, both commended and disparaged their abilities:

> The Indian is the best light infantry soldier in the world. . . . Military experts at one time believed that the Indian would never make a well disciplined soldier. His ancestors had lived a free and easy life, it was in his blood, he fought his wars without regard to organization and the thousand and one things that make discipline.

Soldiers by Instinct

"It all came to him by instinct. For centuries, his ancestors were soldiers, even if undisciplined. They possessed military strategy and poise, two traits that have been inherited by the present Indians so the discipline came more easily with them than with many other American troops."[24]

Native reformers Gabe Parker (Choctaw) and Arthur C. Parker (Seneca) applauded the Native military service, and their promotions included stateside fundraising efforts, albeit often in promoting integration with non-Indigenous soldiers in preparation for citizenship.[25] The 1918 *New York Times* article "On the Warpath" emphasized the perceived natural abilities of Native Americans in warfare: "The Indians were always excellent fighters; scouting in the open warfare which prevails at present affords an opportunity for display of their peculiar talents, and excursions into No Man's Land would suit them even better."[26] Another article, noting that Native Americans from Manitoba in the Canadian forces "have done excellent work at scouting in No Man's Land," quoted a Canadian captain encouraging the American military to recruit Native Americans:

> These Indians with us have performed services that never could have been performed by a white man. The Indian of North America has it in his bones to be a good fighter and a crafty one. We have them in nearly every regiment. Again and again during the last two years, I have seen them go out at night between the trenches, without firing a shot, without making the slightest noise or creating the slightest disturbance, come back leading a half dozen or so Germans, from whom valuable information has been gained.[27]

Some tactics were frequently associated as being "Indian." Doughboys attacked machine-gun nests "by crawling forward Indian fashion" or "adopted Indian style tactics, crawling forward on their stomachs"(Lawson 1963:76, 109, 126). The Lufbery Circle, a defensive air maneuver in which planes were flown in a circular formation so that each pilot could protect the plane in front of him, "was based on the method American pioneers used in drawing their covered wagons into a circle in protection against the Indians." Pilot Frank Luke was described as "silent as an Indian and had few friends" (Lawson 1963:86, 93).

However, while the military had great confidence in the scouting and fighting abilities of Native Americans, they did not hold the same regard for their leadership abilities. During World War I, the army believed that Native Americans made good and even exceptional soldiers in scouting, reconnaissance, fighting at night, and sense of direction, but lacked initiative, were not "natural leader[s]," and could not contribute much in terms of leadership, command, or advancement. Indians were considered most effective under the guidance and direction of more experienced white officers.[28]

Most Americans idealized Native Americans as natural warriors with super-elevated scouting and fighting abilities. Native Americans were believed to possess elevated abilities of stealth, bellicosity, marksmanship, unit loyalty, perseverance, physical endurance, exceptional sense of direction, and a love of warfare. Stallings (1963:281) acknowledged their athletic ability, noting that the Native American and Mexican American members of the Oklahoma National Guard "probably had the finest legs in France." After taking Saint-Etienne, the 71st Brigade approached and helped take Machault, then continued a rapid nighttime advance. As Stallings (1963:287–288) colorfully described:

> The cowboys and the Indians, the Mexicans and the Okies from the wide-open spaces were not the kind to be fenced in. . . . They went

thirteen miles in a single day. They were committed to a night attack tough enough for veterans, and were successful in the black confusion of a ravine—the Indians among them said that nighttime was the only time for fighting. No one, not even their company officers, even understood how their swift units held together . . . more than any other Yank infantry they defied the maxims of warfare. . . . When they reached the canal that paralleled the Aisne River, [Major General] William R. Smith halted them so that he, not they, might draw a few deep breaths.

Even when stereotypes proved true, this only increased the likelihood of Indians being asked or assigned to dangerous tasks.[29]

Views of Indians as warriors, their willingness to undertake assigned tasks, low levels of complaining, and glorification by the press resulted in Native Americans regularly being given some of the most dangerous assignments as scouts, snipers, and messengers. Known as the Indian Scout Syndrome (Holm 1996:88–89), this trend led to high casualty rates among Native American servicemen. In World War I, around 5 percent of all Native Americans were killed, compared to 1 percent for the entire AEF (Barsh 1991:278, 298). This was partly a result of the majority serving as infantry versus communications and rear-echelon positions. For non–Native Americans, the very stereotypes they once considered uncivilized and contrary to progress were now seen as beneficial. As Barsh (1991:290) described, "The negative stereotypes of Indian savagery had become virtues." The accomplishments of World War I Native servicemen were widely heralded and covered in American newspapers but often took on mythic proportions, sometimes exaggerated and misleading, that only reinforced existing stereotypes of the "natural ability" of Native Americans as warriors turned soldiers.

News articles described Native Americans as "redskins," "warriors," and "chiefs" and made references to scalping. An October 11, 1918, *Stars and Stripes* article proclaimed the ongoing Argonne campaign as the most bitterly and desperately resisted, with one section describing the Germans as the "hundreds upon hundreds of those great man-killers of the war" that had to be rushed blindly, overwhelmed with tanks, or, more often, to be "stalked warily, cunningly, craftily as the redskins stalked their foe in primitive America." Even when expressed in admiration, such attributes only furthered limited perceptions of Indians and reinforced the Indian Scout Syndrome.[30]

Native American soldiers frequently distinguished themselves in action, only validating these images in the eyes of non-Natives. In June 1919, Joseph K. Dixon recorded the following account from Captain E. W. Harner [Horner] of Company E, 142nd Infantry Regiment:

The Indian was always the equal of the white man, sometimes his superior. One-half of my Company were Indians. There was not a straggler among them. As illustration, the officers all say that the Supply Station and Dressing Stations are always thronged with a group of stragglers, but they all said they never saw an Indian among them.

When wounded, they were stoical and would bear it unflinchingly. They never uttered a moan.

In censoring their mail, I got a glimpse of their inside life. They would write home, "George Good Eagle died." They would say, "He is no more. He died like a good American."

They were good scouts. A natural instinct in finding their way greatly aided them. The Indians in Company K he [they] would ask to go alone. "Why?" He was asked. "Because white boys get scared and give me away. If I go alone, I can get the information. They make noise."[31]

A 1919 *Stars and Strips* article applauded several attributes of Native servicemen, including being uncomplaining, having good runners, being good shots, being stoic under fire, using signals readily, being "fond of the excitement patrol work holds," and winning decorations for bravery. Especially noteworthy was their "uncanny sense of direction," in blindfolded tests with non–Native Americans, scouting and patrol work in combat, and in particular their ability at night.[32]

Dixon recorded how Coporal Alexander Chuculate (Cherokee), Company E, 142nd Infantry, captured prisoners at St. Etienne:

Chuculate was left with 37 prisoners in the trenches. He was there three hours. These [men had] captured 50 Boche. Two marines took the bunch back to the rear. The other man was blown to pieces by a shell. Chuculate said, "I was left alone. I knew by scouting that there were a bunch of Boche in the dugouts. I began a rapid fire, first at one end of the dugouts, then at the other end, then the middle, to give them the impression that there were a bunch of us. I finally stood up and ordered my men forward, to give the impression that there were a big bunch of us, and kept on firing.

"Twenty-five Boche came out of their holes and threw up their hands. I then ordered my men (imaginary men, of course,) to move forward, and I took the 25 prisoners back to headquarters."

This story is vouched for by Captain Horner.[33]

While Euro-American "rules of engagement" may not always have been understood, other actions reflect the Native commitment to fight and dedication to their cause. Of Richard Hinman (Ponca), Company E, 142nd

Infantry, Dixon recorded, "This man Hinman was mad because Capt. Horner made him quit killing the Boche. Made him take prisoners as they came out of the dugouts. Instead of taking them prisoners as they came out, he used his bayonet. He was fairly provoked, indignant all the way through. Said that he enlisted to kill the Germans, and now when he had the opportunity, they wouldn't allow him to do it."[34]

From February to June 1919, and again in September, Joseph Dixon undertook his last major project promoting Native Americans and citizenship by documenting their military service through photographs and personal testimony. During visits to several military bases, hospitals, ships, and debarkation camps in Massachusetts, New Jersey, New York, and Washington, DC, Dixon met with military officers and servicemen, photographing and recording notes on 186 Native servicemen that were compiled into eight notebooks. In late 1919, Dixon expanded his own survey sample by developing his own questionnaire. He increased this collection in 1920, eventually collecting data on 1,672 men with an additional 1,174 records from the US Army's Historical Section. Dixon planned to publish the material in a book to support American Indian citizenship titled *From Tepees to Trenches*, but the volume never reached fruition (Britten 1997:110–115; Krause 2007:12–14). Significant data on the Choctaw code talkers comes from his work.

Native Americans also contributed to the war effort in other ways. Reservation communities were widely praised for volunteer work in increasing food production, collecting scrap, forming home guard units, knitting clothing, packaging supplies, holding Liberty Bond drives, and engaging in civil defense activities, patriotic rallies, clubs and associations, Red Cross work, and other activities (Britten 1997:132–147; White 1990:82). By the end of January 1918, members of the Five Civilized Tribes of Oklahoma had purchased $82,000 of war savings stamps and were preparing to purchase another $100,000 the following day.[35] Native Americans also contributed by responding to President Wilson's April 10, 1917, call to increase agricultural production for use at home and overseas. Embraced as a means to further Native self-sufficiency, promote assimilation, and end the status of Native Americans as government wards, the BIA viewed the wartime emergency as a catalyst toward their goals. The BIA changed its leasing policies, opening up extensive reservation acreage for lease to non-Indian farmers. Despite mixed results, the total acreage farmed, numbers of Native Americans farming, land improvements, lease earnings, locally available food, and contributions to the war effort all increased significantly (Wood 1981).

World War I provided new and larger military and economic opportunities on the largest scale to date (Parman 1994:64–76). Economic

motivations provided additional incentives and increased urban reloca-
tions for jobs in wartime industries, setting the stage for the larger off-
reservation exodus that occurred during and after World War II. Blending
Native and non-Native US armed forces culture, these factors were syncre-
tized to create a uniquely duel form of Native military service and range of
Native American cultural experiences.

2

THE EASTERN BAND
OF CHEROKEE INDIANS
(TSALAGIYI DETSADANILVGI)

While Native American code talking began in World War I, determining who first served as code talkers is difficult. The Choctaw have long been believed to have been the first Native American group to use their language for coded communications in World War I, on October 26, 1918.[1] This chapter focuses on an archival source describing how the Eastern Band Cherokee from Qualla Boundary in North Carolina began using their native language in the same fashion before the Choctaw (Stanley 1931).

A document written by Captain John Stanley (1931:6) reports how Eastern Band of Cherokee began using their native language for military communications on October 8 or 9, 1918, eighteen to nineteen days prior to the Choctaw. However, for members of other tribes that performed the same service in the war, we currently lack documentation bearing the dates of their first use. Thus, two things become apparent: individuals in several American Expeditionary Forces units were having similar ideas regarding the employment of Native American languages to ensure secure military communications; and available documentation indicates that the chronological sequence of the earliest known Native American code talkers to date was Ho-Chunk, then the Eastern Band Cherokee, then the Choctaw. However, determining who was first is perhaps not as important as documenting the service of all code talkers in the war. With this context in mind, we will now examine what is known about the Eastern Band Cherokee in World War I.

The Eastern Band of Cherokee Indians, 30th Infantry Division

Following passage of the Selective Service Act of 1917 in May of that year, many Eastern Band Cherokee men began leaving school to enlist in the army or navy or to volunteer in other service-oriented tasks (Finger 1986:285). John Finger (1986:288) reports that sixty-eight Eastern Band

Cherokee served in World War I, but he does not mention any use of the Cherokee language for military purposes. More recently, Angela Ragan, post historian of American Legion Post 143 (Stephen Youngdeer Post) of Cherokee, North Carolina, has increased this list to seventy-nine (Ragan 2012).[2] Russel Barsh (1991:298n8) states that "most Eastern Cherokee servicemen (77 percent) went overseas, chiefly with the 30th Division."

During the Somme offensive, from September 29, 1918, until the end of the war, a group of Eastern Band Cherokee were used as military communicators in the 105th Field Artillery Battalion, 30th Infantry Division. The 30th Division was initially comprised of National Guard units from North Carolina, South Carolina, and Tennessee.[3] Much of the 30th had just returned from the campaign on the US-Mexican Border when it was called into federal service on July 25, 1917. Sent to Camp Sevier, South Carolina, the division began preparing for the war. The addition of draftees that October brought the division up to full strength, totaling around twenty-seven thousand men. In May of 1918, the 30th traveled to New York, arriving in England on May 24. After a short stay in England, the division continued to France, where it was attached to the British army. That June, the 30th underwent extensive combat training under British supervision and exchanged American for British equipment (Murphy and Thomas 1936:10–74, Marshall 1998:52–53).

In June 1918, the 27th and 30th Infantry Divisions were combined to form the American Second Corps, but at the insistence of Britain, the two divisions were detached from the American First Army to serve with the British. After nearly a month of training, both divisions were sent to the British Second Army, the 27th joining the British 19th Corps and the 30th Division joining the British Second Corps. On July 2, 1918, the 27th and 30th Divisions were sent into the trenches at Ypres, Belgium. On August 16, the 30th was sent to support two British divisions on the front-line trenches south of Ypres, where they held captured German positions with little action during a nearly month-long standoff. On August 19, the British initiated a campaign near Ypres that became known as the Ypres-Lys offensive. During this drive, the 30th was brought to the front and prepared to enter its first battle. On the night of August 18, the 60th Infantry Brigade (119th and 120th Infantry Regiments) was brought onto the front line, where it remained into early September (Marshall 1998:53–55; Murphy and Thomas 1936:63–85).

On September 3, the division was withdrawn from the front and transferred to the British Fourth Army. By September 25, the division was holding a position opposite the German Hindenburg Line near Bellicourt, France. On the night of September 27, the 119th and 120th Infantry Regiments moved into the front lines. Supported by British tanks, the

119th and 120th went "over the top" early on the morning of the 29th, breaking through the Hindenburg Line despite taking heavy casualties of nearly three thousand men. The 30th was credited as the first to break the Hindenburg Line, capturing significant arms, equipment, and nearly 1,500 Germans. That afternoon, Australian troops passed through the 30th to continue the attack. The 30th was pulled from the front the following day but returned on October 5, where it took part in severe fighting until October 19, when it received orders to withdraw from combat. The 30th was undergoing reorganization when the Armistice was declared on November 11, 1918. The division remained in France until April 1919, when it was sent home and discharged, but it was not a part of the occupation forces (Marshall 1998; Murphy and Thomas 1936:86–149).

Captain John W. Stanley

The primary source detailing the use of the Cherokee communicators comes from Captain John W. Stanley, who served as a first lieutenant in Company C, 1st Battalion, 2nd Infantry Regiment, 1st Infantry Brigade, North Carolina. Later he served in Company C, 1st Battalion, 119th Infantry Regiment, 60th Infantry Brigade, 30th Infantry Division while stateside, including six months service on the Mexican border (Murphy and Thomas 1936:156, 176, 188).

On October 17, 1917, while at Camp Sevier, South Carolina, then first lieutenant Stanley submitted a request to the commanding general of the 30th Division via the division signal officer, Colonel Frank B. Meeks, to be transferred from Company C, 119th Infantry, to the division signal corps. His prewar experiences and request to transfer would prove fortuitous later in the war. As Stanley's transfer request states:

1. It is requested that I be transferred from Company, "C" 119th, Infantry to the Division Signal Corps under Maj. Taylor.
2. This request is made for the reason that I have had about fifteen years' experience as Telegraph Operator, and, as I am very fond of the Signal Corps, feel that I would make a success in this branch of the service.

The request was forwarded noting, "approved for try out."[4]

On November 3, Major G. L. VanDeusen of the signal corps forwarded the request, noting, "1. Lieutenant Stanley's services with this battalion have been entirely satisfactory. He has special qualifications for Wire Company work. His transfer to this battalion is recommended." The following day, a major in the National Army, a division signal officer, recommended the transfer be completed and notified the commanding general of the

30th Division.[5] On November 6, headquarters, 30th Division, issued Special Order No. 61, transferring Stanley to the 105th Field Signal Battalion. In November 1917 he began serving as battalion exchange officer and signal officer.[6]

During World War I, Stanley served as a first lieutenant in Company B (Wire), 105th Field Signal Battalion, 30th Division, in France (Murphy and Thomas 1936:156, 176, 188). Based on Stanley's account, Eastern Band Cherokee men were culled from the 119th and 120th infantry regiments, 60th Brigade, and possibly from other units, in the 30th Infantry Division, during the Battle for Montbrehein from October 6–12, 1918 (Murphy and Thomas 1936:107–118, 335; Stanley 1931). In 1930–31, Captain Stanley was attending an "advanced course" in the Infantry School, Fourth Section, Committee H, at Fort Benning, Georgia. There he wrote an account recording the details of how the Cherokee were used in World War I (Stanley 1931). The account was part of a series of "personal experience monographs and student papers" written largely by officers and describing combat operations, actions, and campaigns fought during the war.[7]

Stanley (1931:1) stated that "this monograph is based almost entirely upon memory. Search as I may, I have been unable to locate any official records of the detailed operations of the 105th Field Signal Battalion during the Somme Offensive." After relieving the signal troops of the 75th British Division on September 25, 1918, in the area where the 30th Division was to attack, the 105th experienced considerable difficulty in keeping phone lines intact. By October 6 or 7, the 105th discovered that their messages in English were being intercepted by the Germans, who were taking immediate counteractions, including artillery, almost as soon as the messages had been sent. When a colonel at the division headquarters called another colonel who was a regimental commander to check on that unit, the latter responded that all was fine, and that "they are shelling us pretty heavy but their shells are striking about 100 yards in rear of my reserves." As their conversation continued for a few minutes the shelling suddenly shifted to the reserve line's location as well as directly on the regimental commander's dugout, which he was conveying to the division headquarters. As the regimental officer continued, "By Jove, they are planting them right on my reserve line. There! One landed right on top of my dugout." Only belatedly realizing that his communications were not secure, the regimental commander had not only given the Germans information on their position and corrected the range for their artillery, but also had acknowledged for them precisely when they were on target. According to Stanley, the Germans maintained "powerful interception sets" at this time, and to speak uninhibited from the brigade level forward at this time was dangerous. Despite the realization of the communications breach and their pleas, signal personnel were unable to convince some commanders of this danger (Stanley 1931:1–5).

The following day, October 7 or 8, the danger was beginning to be realized, and Captain Stanley of the 105th Signal Battalion was summoned by the division signal officer to a meeting of the signal officers to discuss ways to counteract this problem. At the meeting Stanley proposed a solution (1931:5–7):

> Pardon this personal reference, but at this meeting I pointed out to the Division Signal officer that the old 1st N.C. Regiment which was split up at Camp Sevier, S.C. in 1917 and its personnel assigned to the 119th and 120th Infantry Regiments contained quite a number of Cherokee Indians which were now somewhere in the division, and that in my opinion, if a number of the most intelligent of them were placed as each telephone, and that they transmit all messages in their native tongue, I felt sure that even a battalion commander could use them in transmitting commands in perfect safety. The matter was taken up with the division commander, and the next day found every command post from brigade forward, including some company command posts, [with] a telephone with a Cherokee Indian beside it. Needless to say, there were no further messages intercepted by the enemy that we heard of. About the second or third day after this system was put into effect, a colonel of the enemy intelligence staff was captured and sent back to Division Headquarters for questioning. He could speak English exceedingly well, and after the officers at Division Headquarters had about finished their examination of him, he asked permission to ask a question himself, which was granted. It ran something like this, "Gentlemen, we have officers in our army that can speak and translate the majority of the languages in the world, but none of them can understand the language you Americans are using over the telephone. Now please, gentlemen, won't you tell me what it is?" There was quite a bit of laughter but no one gave the secret away. From then on until October 12, 1918, at which date I was ordered back to the United States as an instructor, the Cherokees were kept on the job with continued success, and I understand were used until the end of the war.

While the history of the 30th Division (Murphy and Thomas 1936:113–118, 335) covers the division's activities during this period, it provides little insight into the use of the Cherokee. This is not surprising, as they represented only a small number of men in an entire army division. After experiencing heavy fighting that resulted in breaking through the Hindenburg Line at Bellicourt on September 29–30, the division was moved back to the

Herbecourt-Le Mesnil area on October 2. On October 4, the division was ordered to reenter the front line, and on the 5th and 6th they relieved the 2nd Australian Division in preparation for the assault on Montbrehein. Because the 60th Brigade had borne the brunt of the fighting at Bellicourt, they were placed in reserve of the 59th Brigade, who led the assault on October 7. Late on the afternoon of October 9, the 120th Regiment of the 60th Brigade passed through the 118th Regiment of the 59th Brigade to continue the attack. On the morning of the 10th, the 119th on the left and the 120th on the right carried the center of the advance. The assault continued until October 11, capturing sixteen square miles of enemy-held territory including the towns of Busigny, Becquigny, Vaux-Andigny, Escaufort, St. Souplet, St. Benin, La Haie Meneresse, other smaller towns, and many farms. While the 60th Brigade suffered heavy casualties, many German prisoners and much German materiel was captured, while over two thousand civilians were freed (CMHUSA 1988:167–168; Murphy and Thomas 1936:118).

On the night of October 11 and into the following morning, the 30th was relieved by the American 27th Division and, badly depleted, assembled in the Bohain-Premont-Busigny area as corps reserve until reentering the front line on October 15–16. The 105th Field Signal Battalion established its headquarters at Montbrehein from October 12 to 22. The 30th would fight again in the Battle of La Selle River from October 17–20, after which they were stationed in the Querrieu Area until the war ended (CMHUSA 1988:167–168; Murphy and Thomas 1936:118, 236, 335).

Stanley (1931:7) concluded with three recommendations derived from lessons learned from this campaign, the latter two of which applauded the Cherokee, while recommending the future use of their language in combat communications: "Second. The successful use of the Cherokee Indians in transmitting messages over the telephone in their native tongue. Third. If I ever have the honor to command troops in battle again, and any American Indians are available, I will in all probability insist upon their use over the telephone."

Assuming that Stanley's account is valid—and there is no reason to believe it is not—the next step is to try to determine who these men might have been. During World War I, the 30th Division contained the following units among other auxiliary units (Murphy and Thomas 1936:55–58):

59th Brigade, Infantry:
109th Infantry Regiment
110th Infantry Regiment
108th Machine Gun Battalion
60th Brigade, Infantry

119th Infantry Regiment
120th Infantry Regiment
115th Machine Gun Battalion
55th Brigade Field Artillery
113th Field Artillery Regiment
114th Field Artillery Regiment
115th Field Artillery Regiment
105th Trench Mortar Battery
Engineer Troops—105th Regiment
Signal Troops—105th Field Signal Battalion
Division Units—30th Headquarters Troop; 113th Machine Gun
  Battalion

Identifying the Cherokee

Attempting to determine how many Cherokee served in the 30th Division, their identities, and which individuals were used for Native voice communications service has been extremely difficult. Stanley (1931:6) noted that "every command post from brigade forward, including some company command posts, [had] a telephone with a Cherokee Indian beside it." However, it is difficult to determine the exact number of positions manned. In addition, Stanley (1931:Fig. 3) provides a figure of a laddered communications circuit used prior to the fight, and a "Plan of Wire Communication" (Stanley 1931:Fig. 2) that was presumably used during the battle. While this figure contains eighteen communication posts (including the division command post, a series of division message centers, brigade command posts, right and left regiments, forward battalions, and message centers), it contains no company designations.

Based on the organization of US Army divisions in World War I (Hallas 2000:52; Otte 2018:235–236), with a Cherokee at each command post from brigade through battalion, just the two infantry regiments of a single brigade would require at least nine code talkers, with twenty-four rifle companies and six machine gun companies contained within the six battalions. Unfortunately, we do not know how many positions were manned by Cherokee.

Identifying individuals who may have served as code talkers in the 119th and 120th has also been difficult. Stanley (1931) does not provide the exact number of Cherokee who were used as communicators, their names, or exactly how many locations they were used at. However, this is not unusual, as it represented simply an assignment given to a number of individuals who probably ranged in rank from private to no higher than corporal or sergeant. In addition, no mention of these events is found in the brief regimental histories of the 119th (Conway and Shuford 1919:48–52) or 120th Infantry Regiments (Walker et al. 1919:28–29).

There appear to have been many Cherokee in the 119th Infantry Regiment. In 1919, Roland Dixon recorded, "119th Regiment Inf. 30th Div. had 50 or more Indians. The Cherokees were originally from North Carolina."[8] While all of these men may not have been Cherokee, the statement that the Cherokee were from North Carolina suggests that many of the fifty men were of that tribe, as the Cherokee had a history of serving in the North Carolina National Guard that became part of the 30th Division.

To identify Cherokees in the 30th Division, I attempted to obtain rosters for all Cherokees who served in World War I, then all units of the 60th Battalion of the 30th. Two primary sources were found. First, a list of all Eastern Band Cherokee men registered for the draft as of November 2, 1917, was published in an edition of *The Indian Leader*.[9] While other men were subsequently drafted or enlisted, this list provides 115 Eastern Band men. Second, Angela Ragan (2012) has identified and compiled data on seventy-nine Eastern Band Cherokee from North Carolina who served in World War I.[10] Of these men, at least sixteen are listed as being in the 81st Infantry Division.

In reviewing the membership roster of the 119th Infantry Regiment (Conway 1919), only one name correlated with known WW I Eastern Band Cherokee veterans collected by Ragan (2012): Pfc. Ute Crow of Company H, 119th Infantry Regiment. Crow had served nine months as a private in the 1st North Carolina Infantry prior to registering for the draft on June 5, 1917.[11] Conway (1919:76) lists Pfc. Ute Crow, Company H, 119th infantry Regiment, as being wounded October 10, 1918, and returning to his unit October 27, 1918.

I have been able to identify fifteen other Cherokee who were in the 30th Division during World War I. Steven Youngdeer and Cain George served in Company D, 115th Machine Gun Battalion (Ragan 2012). Multiple sources (Finger 1986:301; Morrison and Graham Jr. 1961; Murphy and Thomas 1936:328) confirm Youngdeer and George as members of Company D of the 115th and are listed as private first class (Pfc.) in the unit roster, which sailed from Philadelphia on May 11, 1918. They are also both listed in the casualty list of Company D as privates, dated December 28, 1918. Cain George is listed as "Slightly" wounded, being "Gassed" on September 2–3, 1918. As Youngdeer (Serial number 1,305,666) was "Seriously wounded by Shrapnel" on September 1, 1918, and died of his wounds two weeks later on September 15, 1918 (Morrison and Graham Jr. 1961:13–14, 24; Murphy and Thomas 1936:328), he could not have participated in the use of the Cherokee language the following month. American Legion Post 143 at Cherokee, North Carolina, is named in his honor.

Other Cherokee in the 30th Division (Ragan 2012) include the following:

William Amos Bradley, 13th Battery, 9th [119th] Regiment
Curtis Cooper, Company A, Radio Dispatch, 105th Signal Battalion
Soggy (Saughee) Youngbird, Company E, 105th Ammunition Train

Records in the National Archives also contain several Eastern Band Cherokee who were in the 30th Division, many in the 118th Infantry:

Pfc. Charlie Bullard, Company G, 118th Infantry
Pvt. Alonzo Collins, Company G, 118th Infantry
Pfc. Ute Crow, Company H, 119th Infantry Regiment
Pvt. Willie Dial, Company G, 118th Infantry
Pvt. Stancil Jumper, Company E, 105th Ammunition Train
Pvt. Angus Locklear (Serial No. 1877919), Company G, 118th Infantry
Pvt. Charlie L. Oxendine Company G, 118th Infantry
Pvt. William Runway [Runaway], Company B, 118th Infantry
Pvt. Martin L. Sanderson, Company G, 118th Infantry
Pvt. Henry G. Tyler, Company F, 118th Infantry (no frontline service)[12]

While Dial, Locklear, Sanderson, Crow, and Oxendine saw action at Ypres and at Cambrei-St. Quentin, the list of their dates of frontline service indicate that only Dial, Locklear, and Oxendine in the 118th, and Crow in the 119th Infantry, saw action after October 6, when their language is reported to have been used.[13] However, because only a few individuals have their dates of service listed in these files, the files are likely incomplete and do not reflect all Cherokees who may have been present after October 6, 1918. The possibility of other Eastern Band Cherokee not yet identified is also likely, especially in light of Dixon's reference to fifty members in the 30th Division.

Unfortunately, extant records inhibit the positive identification of any individual Eastern Band Cherokee who served as military voice communicators (code talkers) in World War I. Because the 119th and 120th included many North Carolina National Guard members, other Eastern Band Cherokee likely served in the 30th but may not have been identified as Native Americans or included in tribal veterans' rosters and are often difficult to identify because of a high prevalence of non–Native American surnames.

There are likely more Eastern Band Cherokee who served in World War I than Ragan (2012) and I have been able to identify, especially in light of Barsh's (1991:228n8) and Dixon's 1919 figures and Foreman's account (1943:215) that "the Eastern Band of Cherokees, on the Qualla reservation in North Carolina, sent one hundred soldiers and a nurse with the American Expeditionary Force." Regrettably, Foreman's sources are not specified throughout her text.

Although the individual Eastern Band Cherokee involved are currently unknown, Stanley's (1931) account demonstrates that several used their native language for military communications in combat during World War I and prevented German forces from deciphering the content of their transmissions. Based on Stanley's account, these individuals provide one of the early documented cases of what would become known as code talking. Under the provisions of the Code Talkers Recognition Act of 2008, the Eastern Band of Cherokee merit congressional recognition as having had Native American code talkers who served in World War I.

3

THE OKLAHOMA CHOCTAW

The best-known Native American code-talking group of World War I is the Choctaw of southeast Oklahoma who served in the 36th Infantry Division. During much of the war, the 36th contained nearly six hundred Native Americans speaking twenty-six languages and dialects, only four or five of which had ever been written.[1] These men were mostly from southeastern tribes, the largest of which were collectively known at the time as the "Five Civilized Tribes," with smaller numbers from Plains and Prairie tribes in Oklahoma. Most were forcibly removed in the 1830s to reservations in Indian Territory, now Oklahoma. Before the war, over half had served in the Texas-Oklahoma National Guard in the 36th ("Panther") Division and trained at Camp Bowie at Fort Worth, Texas, under Major General Edwin St. John Greble (AIM 1917a; White 1978, 1979:8–9). Information on the Choctaw code talkers has increased markedly since the mid-1980s through Oklahoma newspaper articles in the Choctaw tribal newspaper *Bishinik* (Meadows 2002:14–27; and Morris 2006).[2]

During the Mexican border crisis of 1916, several Oklahoma and Texas National Guard regiments and smaller organizations were mobilized. After serving along the Rio Grande River in 1916 and early 1917, elements of the Oklahoma National Guard (1st Oklahoma Infantry Regiment, 1st and 2nd Cavalry Troops, Field Hospital, Ambulance Corps, Infirmary, Engineers) were sent home but were soon reactivated for service in World War I (Houston 1975; White 1979:9, 1984:4–5). Some Oklahoma Native Americans already had considerable military service; Walter Veach (Choctaw), for example, had served since 1910, and Sergeant W. J. McClure (Choctaw) of Durant, Oklahoma, had served in the 38th United States Volunteers in the Philippines, in border service with the Oklahoma Infantry, and as a captain of cavalry in the Oklahoma National Guard.[3]

Many Native American Oklahoma WW I veterans were in their twenties, married, and with children. Among the Choctaw, Joseph Oklahombi was married; Albert Billy, Mitchell Bobb, and Otis Leader were all married with at least one child; and Ben Carterby was married with four children. While many Native Americans declared no military service on their draft registration, Ben Carterby wrote "Indian School Training" on his draft registration card reflecting the military nature of these institutions. Carterby was a US Native American policeman in Bethel and Smithville, Oklahoma, when he registered for the draft on June 5, 1917.[4]

Seeking new recruits, US armed forces recruiters regularly visited Native American boarding schools such as Haskell, Chilocco, and Phoenix. A well-published photograph of fourteen Choctaw recruits in civilian clothing posed around an American flag with a uniformed non-Native army soldier was taken at Armstrong Academy northeast of Bokchito, Oklahoma. In the Choctaw community, it is reported that this group comprised most of the Armstrong Academy baseball team. When a number of students at the school expressed a desire to enlist, they sought and were granted permission by the school superintendent.[5]

This photo has also long been circulated and frequently labeled as the "Choctaw Nation Code Talkers from World War I" or the "Code Talker School," and many Choctaw assert that the fourteen individuals in the photo were code talkers. While several of the Choctaw code talkers did attend Armstrong Academy, several factors make this association impossible. First, the idea to use the Choctaw did not develop until October 1918, over a year after some who became code talkers enlisted for military service. Second, the ages of the code talkers varied greatly. With birth dates ranging from 1882 to 1899, they were nineteen to thirty-five years old in 1917. Their ages, children, occupations as noted on their draft registration cards, and limited schooling indicate most were not in the same grade. Most were not in school when the war begun. Third, the young men in the picture wear civilian clothing and haircuts; both would have been replaced after entering basic training or at any subsequent period of active service. While some of those depicted may have become Choctaw code talkers, they are not readily recognizeable and the photo is likely that of Choctaw students enlisting in response to the uniformed recruiter's visit.

The Choctaw Nation received the photo from the Oklahoma Historical Society, where it had been labeled "Choctaw Code Talkers." Who identified the photo is unknown. Assuming the label to be correct, it has been repeatedly published as such by the tribe and others for many years. Upon inquiring about the photo, tribal officers stated that members of the tribe recently realized that the photo was a recruiting photo and could not be the Choctaw code talkers, because the faces of the young men in the photo do not match those of known code talkers.[6]

Solomon Louis, who was underage for military service, also desired to enlist. Being as large and strong as the older boys and an orphan, no one knew his exact age or objected when he joined others to enlist.[7] One source states that Louis, born in 1899, joined with six other Choctaw at the same time. The other six and their birthdates include Ben Carterby (1891), Robert Taylor (1894), Calvin Wilson (1895), Pete Maytubby (1891), James Edwards (1898), and Jeff Wilson (Nelson).[8] The fact that not everyone started school at the same age or graduated at the age of eighteen, and the proximity of their birthdates, make their simultaneous attending of school and enlistment possible, although it is not supported by their military personnel files. If the individuals in the photo all enlisted together, they would have had the same enlistment date and been issued serial numbers that were close in numerical sequence. The enlistment dates of the Choctaws identified as code talkers (appendix B) span over a year and vary regarding enlistment location and serial numbers.

During the spring and summer of 1917, the 1st Oklahoma Infantry, which included most of the Oklahoma National Guard, was mobilized and brought close to full strength at Fort Sill, near Lawton, Oklahoma. Company H of the 1st Oklahoma Infantry from Durant, Oklahoma, was sent to Fort Sill at this time. Containing only ninety-six men upon arrival, it was far below full strength. When Company H arrived at Fort Sill, only three of the Choctaw who were later reported as code talkers were in the company: James Edwards, Tobias Frazier, and Walter Veach (Barnes 1920:205–206).

By early June, the number of new recruits placed in Companies H and L approached "probably 300" Native Americans, with Choctaw, including the Armstrong Academy baseball team, comprising the majority. One-third or more were estimated as full bloods, with the remainder mixed-bloods of varying degrees. After a few weeks of training at Fort Sill, they were sent to Camp Bowie at Fort Worth, Texas. On August 5, 1917, the Oklahoma and Texas National Guards were federalized (White 1979:9, 1984:5–10, 44).

Arriving at Camp Bowie in Fort Worth in late August 1917, the 1st Oklahoma Guardsmen learned that because the War Department planned to form large numbered regiments without state distinctions, they would not retain their separate state identity. During the next two months, the 1st Oklahoma and 7th Texas Infantry Regiment comprised a temporary brigade commanded by Roy Hoffman, former colonel of the Oklahoma regiment and now brigadier general. In mid-October, the 1st Oklahoma and 7th Texas were merged to form the 142nd Infantry Regiment, 36th Infantry Division. As the aggregate number of companies remained the same, many officers in the older National Guard regiments had to be transferred or discharged (White 1979:9, 1984:25–49).

Colonel Alfred W. Bloor commanded the 142nd Infantry. An attorney from Austin, Texas, Bloor served in military units at Texas A&M University; in the 1st Infantry Texas Volunteer, Company L; 1st Texas Volunteer Infantry in the Spanish-American War; as a first lieutenant in the Governor's Cadets of the Texas Volunteer Guard; and in the 1st Texas Infantry, National Guard. In 1902, he was promoted to major in the 1st Texas Infantry. He was later transferred to the 2nd Texas Infantry as a major and promoted to lieutenant colonel in 1914. In 1917, Bloor was promoted to colonel in command of the 7th Texas Infantry, which was later incorporated in the 142nd Infantry Regiment. From the formation of the 142nd until it was mustered out of service, Bloor served as commanding officer and was the only colonel in the 36th Division to remain in command of his regiment throughout the war (Maxfield 1975:16).

From its initial formation, the 1st Oklahoma Infantry was considered to be the most ethnically diverse National Guard unit. While some Natives were in other Oklahoma units, most belonged to the 1st Oklahoma Infantry. Most had been in Company H, organized at Durant under Captain Walter Veach, and Company L, organized at Antlers under Captain Ben Davis Locke, both reportedly half Choctaw. Both companies served on the Mexican border in 1916 (Houston 1975; White 1979:9). The division also contained individuals of Mexican, German, English, Irish, Italian, Polish, Chinese, Assyrian, Filipino, Turkish, Danish, Swedish, and other backgrounds.[9]

In November of 1917, Captain Walter Veach was placed in command of the formation of an all-Native company at Camp Bowie, Company E, 142nd Infantry Regiment. Upon leaving Durant, Oklahoma, Veach took with him the old Company H of the 1st Oklahoma comprised mainly of Choctaw. Company H was combined with Company L, 1st Oklahoma, also made up primarily of Native Americans from Oklahoma, to form Company E, 142nd Infantry. At this time, the company contained seventy-two Native Americans of various Oklahoma tribes. Other companies in the regiment contained Cherokee, Chickasaw, Osage, Pawnee, Kiowa, Comanche, and Creek. More than two hundred additional Native Americans were brought into the regiment through the draft in early November.[10] As reported from Camp Bowie, "All of these will be transferred to the company and the Caucasians who now constitute a part of the company will be transferred to the other companies in the command. Under the present organization there are 250 men to each infantry company in the United States Army; so there will be more than enough redmen to form the company. Only One of the Kind. As far as can be ascertained there is not another purely Indian company in the army, especially one commanded by an Indian."[11] As official US armed forces policy prohibited the formation of all-Native units, it is unclear why these actions were taken.

Captain Benjamin Davis Locke was relieved as commander of Company L, 142nd Infantry, and reassigned to the 61st Depot Brigade, while Captain Walter Veach was assigned to command Company E, 142nd, 71st Brigade. A long-time guardsman, Veach entered as a private in 1910 and worked his way up through the ranks as a commissioned officer "by sheer ability and common sense." He is reputed to have enjoyed the "unbounded confidence" of his Native American troops and was anxious to do them "proud." Serving under Veach were 1st Lt. Hylan Mitchell of Durant, 1st Lt. Ben H. Chastaine of Tulsa, 2nd Lt. Elijah W. Horner of Durant, 2nd Lt. Carl Edmonds of Antlers, and Veach's brother, 2nd Lt. Columbus Veach, who had previously served under his brother as a first sergeant (White 1979:11, 1984:44).[12] Horner will later figure prominently in the formation of the Choctaw code talkers and Chastaine regarding their postwar publicity. Of the officers surviving consolidation and reassignment at Camp Bowie, only Walter and Columbus Veach (Choctaws), Captain Charles H. Johnson of Pawnee, Oklahoma, and First Lieutenant Moses Bellmard (Kaw) are reported as Native American. Former commanding officer of Company E, 1st Oklahoma Infantry, Johnson was made commanding officer of Company C, 143rd, a largely white company, with Bellmard as one of his officers.[13]

Many Natives from Companies H and L, 1st Oklahoma Infantry, were later distributed throughout companies in the 142nd. Most of the Native American and about thirty white enlisted men were assigned to Company E, forming a largely Native American company. Nearly two hundred Oklahoma Native American draftees and volunteers arriving from Camp Travis in late October 1917 were placed in Company E and other units in the 142nd. These additions, almost exclusively Native Americans from Oklahoma, totaled 208 men from fourteen tribes in Company E, the majority Choctaw and Cherokee.[14]

While stationed at Camp Bowie, the membership roster for November 17, 1917, lists 89 Choctaws, 68 Cherokees, 15 Chickasaws, 7 Osages, 7 Creeks, 6 Seminoles, 5 Delawares, 2 Shawnees, 2 Quapaws, 2 Poncas, 2 Caddos, 1 Peoria, 1 Arapaho, and 1 Cheyenne.[15] Other members from Pawnee, Kaw, and Comanche tribes served in other units. The 143rd Infantry Regiment also contained many Natives. In May 1918, additional Native American draftees from Oklahoma arrived, bringing the total number in the 36th Division to around six hundred. Approximately 50 percent of the Indigenous soldiers were Oklahoma National Guardsmen while the rest were voluntary enlistments or draftees who entered the National Army. No other division in World War I is said to have contained more Native Americans and Mexicans than the 36th Division (White 1979:9,12; 1984:44–45, 50). W. D. Cope reports that the 36th, from which replacements for other divisions going overseas had been periodically drawn during their training, received around 6,200 draftees from Texas and Oklahoma in May 1918.[16]

Like most Native Americans in the 90th Division, those in the 36th had attended government-run boarding schools for Native Americans. These included local boarding schools such as Armstrong Academy and large off-reservation boarding schools such as Carlisle, Haskell, and Chilocco. Several Native Americans in the 142nd had played sports at these schools (White 1979:13, 1984:45). Education levels among the Indigenous troops in the 36th varied greatly. Some individuals spoke little or no English upon induction, which resulted in some being discharged for language deficiency; others improved "by observation alone" or at company night schools established to teach Native Americans to write their names and converse in English. A February 1918 news article reports a similar program and the ordering of texts at Camp Bowie to teach "a working knowledge of French to all officers and enlisted men, including all Indians, in the division."[17]

Others were academy and college graduates commended for their penmanship and typing abilities, and noted collegiate and professional athletes such as Harold C. Mahseet, who had played football for one year at Haskell Institute in Kansas and two years at the Oklahoma Agricultural College at Stillwater. A member of the 36th Divisional Team, Mahseet was declared the greatest tackle in the American Expeditionary Forces (AEF) by his comrades. Tex Richards had also played at Haskell.[18] With the formation of the 142nd, many surplus officers and men from the 1st Oklahoma and the 7th Texas were sent to other units. As many had belonged to units that had served together since the Spanish-American War, the transfers caused a marked decrease in morale and discipline and a problematic rise in the numbers of AWOL (absent without leave) troops. During the fall of 1917, athletics were being emphasized in the army as a means to restore morale and discipline. Bloor persuaded regimental chaplain Charles H. Barnes to direct the regiment's athletics. Having coached football for years, Barnes organized football teams in the regiment. The 142nd won game after game until losing the division championship to the 111th Engineers by a score of 3-0. The 142nd also formed a seven-man all–Native American basketball team from Company C, with one member from Company D. Winning twenty of their first twenty-one games, they soon became the regimental team (Maxfield 1975:16–17, 20).

Besides focusing on assimilation to Euro-American culture, many Native American schools maintained a military-oriented program emphasizing attendance, marching, uniforms, discipline, order, and schedules that preconditioned Indigenous students for military service. Although English fluency varied greatly within the student body, students were already familiar with specific words related to military procedure, such as "attention," and drilling calls. Consequently, many Native Americans were better at drilling than were English-speaking non-Natives.[19] Service in National Guard units only further familiarized Native Americans with military-style life and procedures. Captain Walter Veach (Choctaw) "obtained the foundation for his military career in the Indian schools and in his new company he has found several men who attended the same institution where he secured his early education."[20]

Education levels of the Choctaw who were reported to have served as code talkers varied greatly. National Archives service reports for some of these men list five years at Jones Academy and one year at Armstrong Academy for Ben Carterby, one year of public school for Robert Taylor, and "No Education" for Joseph Oklahombi.[21] Victor Brown attended Armstrong Academy, Tyler Commercial College, and graduated from Haskell Institute in Kansas. Later, he attended Southeastern State College in Durant, Oklahoma.[22] James Edwards attended Armstrong Academy in Oklahoma and the Folsom Methodist Training School in Smithville, Oklahoma.[23]

Many of the Choctaw had attended Armstrong Academy, a Native American boarding school located near Doaksville (later Bokchito) in Pushmataha District, Bryan County, Oklahoma. The school was managed by several entities and ran intermittently from 1841 until it burned, along with its records, in 1921. From 1893 to 1921, the school housed many orphaned boys. Fourteen of the Choctaw code talkers are reported to have attended Armstrong Academy prior to enlisting for military service, including Solomon Bond Louis and Victor Brown. This is likely, as the academy was located in Bryan County, and the majority of the Choctaw code talkers came from Bryan and McCurtain counties, Oklahoma. Containing a military structure, the academy taught Native Americans the initial rigors of the military.[24]

Of the additional three hundred Native American draftees arriving from Camp Travis in 1917–18, most were less educated and composed the majority with English deficiencies.[25] While most appear to have had a good command of English, some were so deficient that they had to be placed beside other bilingual members who could translate orders for them (White 1979:13, 1984:45). Some were determined to be so deficient in English that they were discharged. As a March 3, 1918, release from Camp Bowie reports:

> In the findings of an efficiency board the division is losing some of its most picturesque characters. These are the Indians from Oklahoma who were brought into the service through the draft. Most of these men speak English so poorly and are so deficient in other ways

that it has been found almost impossible to teach them the rudiments of [the] military. One or two are volunteer soldiers who have been in the service for years but who have been found deficient in this day of modern war where so many things that require intelligence are brought up daily.[26]

An April 11, 1918, article in the *Daily Oklahoman* reports that the 142nd contained 1,500 Oklahomans with "two companies of Indians from Oklahoma, more than 400 men."[27] Because many of the Native Americans in the 36th came from reservations that had been allotted, many were individual landowners, with some possessing considerable oil holdings. Although some members received sizable royalty checks while in service, the nature of the post-allotment era in Oklahoma makes it very likely that others were poor. Nevertheless, as Company E contained a significant number of well-educated and wealthy Native Americans, it became known as the "Millionaire Company."[28]

While knowledge of English was a problem for some Oklahoma Indians during World War I, many were well acculturated into American society in many other ways. As Kiowa photographer Horace Poolaw (Smith 2016) and historians Peter Iverson (1985), Alexandra Harmon (1999), and Russel Barsh (2001:376) have shown, by the 1910s, many young Native American men were quite "modern" in appearance. Despite studio photographs depicting the wearing of traditional dress, scores of everyday images from this era depict young Native Americans sporting up-to-date and often dapper American attire (men wearing suits, women wearing dresses, high heels, stockings, and handbags and showing finger waves and other period hair styles), wearing sun glasses, smoking cigarettes, attending baseball games, watching silent movies, going to church socials, and standing beside Model T's and Ford coupes. Many photos of this era remain in the homes of Oklahoma Native Americans today.

Unlike most US soldiers, many of the Native American members were married, having the financial means to support their families while in service. Regardless of economic background, the performance of the Native Americans as soldiers was praised in several news accounts that highlighted their physical endurance, rapid learning, and exuberance (exhibiting "so much spirit that the officers find difficulty holding them in check"); one went so far as to acclaim that "the Indian is the best light infantry soldier in the world."[29]

At Camp Bowie, training was broken up by visits from family members from Oklahoma, noted government officials, and sports. Prior to a highly anticipated November 25 football game between the 142nd and 143rd Infantry Regiments, "Chief" Harold Mahseet, playing tackle for the

142nd, was featured in the *Fort Worth Star Telegram*. Although probably not needed due to the high level of voluntary enlistment, Bureau of Indian Affairs commissioner Cato Sells visited Native American soldiers at camps Bowie, MacArthur, Logan, and Travis in November and December of 1917 to encourage them and to tell them why the war was justified.[30]

In early April 1918, Five Civilized Tribes superintendent Gabe Parker (Choctaw) visited the Native troops at Camp Bowie for two days. In addition to watching the units drill and praising their development, his visit was primarily to encourage Native Americans to sign up for soldiers' insurance, which most did for $5,000 and $10,000 benefits.[31] Being an orphan and realizing he had no beneficiary of his military insurance, Solomon Louis wrote to Mary Patterson, a Choctaw girl he had met at a Southeastern College football game in Durant, Oklahoma, while attending nearby Armstrong Academy, and whom he had been dating for approximately four years. Patterson was also an orphan, living with her aunt when she met Louis. Louis related that he wished to make her his beneficiary and that she should come meet him at the training camp at Fort Worth. He also asked her if, with her aunt's consent, they could be married, which they were on November 30, 1917.[32]

In the spring of 1918, the 36th was notified that it would embark for Europe. On April 11, the division paraded through the streets of Fort Worth as a farewell review prior to leaving Camp Bowie and in honor of the aging general Edwin St. John Greble, who had been found physically unfit for overseas duty. Described as the "greatest crowd in Texas History," the large gathering included the governors of Texas and Oklahoma. "Again it was the sight of Captain Walter Veach and his purely Oklahoma company of Indian boys that made the massive ranks of fathers and mothers and brothers and sweethearts tear their lungs out with cheering."[33]

In July and early August of 1918, the 36th traveled by rail to the East Coast. The 142nd Infantry was processed at Camp Mills, New York, and boarded ships at Hoboken, New Jersey. Embarking from Hoboken on July 18, 1918, several of the Choctaw who were later identified as code talkers were assigned to Company E of the 142nd Infantry. Among these were Captain Walter Veach, Mitchell Bobb, George and Joseph Davenport, Tobias Frazier, Noel Johnson, Solomon Lewis (Louis), Pete Maytubby, Robert Taylor, and Cabin (Calvin) Wilson. The company strength was then at 171 men.[34]

The 142nd arrived and disembarked in Brest, France. After a short rest at Pontanezen barracks, where part of the regiment was reviewed by French president Henri Poincaré, the 142nd proceeded by rail to the 13th Training Area (Bar-sur-Aube), 120 miles southeast of Paris. Here, the 71st and 72nd Infantry Brigades of the 36th, including the Choctaw in Company E of the

142nd and supporting units, participated in rigorous pre-combat training under the supervision of new divisional commander, Major General William R. Smith, who assumed command on July 13 (White 1979:14).

Although for security reasons, the exact location of soldiers could not be revealed, the Red Cross provided "Soldiers' Mail" notification cards for soldiers to inform their families of their safe arrival in Europe. The family of James Edwards still retains the Red Cross notification card he sent to his mother. The back of the card contains the statement, "THE SHIP ON WHICH I SAILED HAS ARRIVED SAFELY OVERSEAS." Below this are entries for name and organization followed by underlined blank spaces; the handwriting reads "Name Corp James Edwards organization Co. E 142nd Inf.," followed by "American Expeditionary Forces."[35]

While the 36th's training in the United States had focused on tactics for trench warfare, by the time they arrived in France, the prolonged deadlock on the Western Front had been broken. Training for more open and mobile fighting was needed, and at Bar-sur-Aube, numerous hikes, maneuvers, and field exercises were undertaken by the division to prepare them.[36] Lieutenant Ben H. Chastaine of the 142nd described how the Oklahoma Native Americans not only excelled during the training, but also contributed to developing improved tactics.

> A model platoon of Oklahomans was organized and developed a flanking form of attack that attracted attention at corps headquarters and brought a representative from General Headquarters of the American Forces. In these exercises and maneuvers the Oklahomans took advantage of every fold in the ground to surround the foe once he had uncovered his position. Old formations were deserted for something akin to individual movements and what was known as the "gang" formation was developed to a high degree. In this the men were spread far apart to an extent that they were never targets for machine gun and rifle fire and left the enemy artillery at a loss for a target worthy of the name. In this respect the Indians of the Oklahoma troops showed to remarkable advantage.[37]

Upon reaching the training area at Bar-sur-Aube, significant staff reorganization occurred as part of the change to the "G," or general staff, system. A group of outside instructors and observers closely studied the regiment's officers. Captain Walter Veach, whose capability had been questioned at Camp Bowie, was removed as Company E commander and replaced with Captain Carter C. Hanner of Stillwater, Oklahoma. Hanner was later killed in action during the 142nds' first combat at St. Etienne and replaced by Elijah W. Horner. Veach was among forty-five officers, including General Hutchings, who were sent to Blois for reclassification

or were discharged. Others were later transferred. Three 1919 news articles, two by fellow 142nd officer Captain Ben Chastaine, report of Veach's
discharge prior to entering combat. Two of the articles report that "Captain
Walter Veach, commanding company E, was discharged from the service
and returned to the United States" and "Veach . . . was discharged and
sent home before the 142 Infantry, to which he was assigned, got into the
fighting." Veach's military records state that he was discharged on October 14, 1918.[38] Walter Veach also does not appear in the 142nd regimental
roster at the time it went on the front line on October 5, 1918 (Barnes
1922:345). Although Veach was instrumental in helping recruit Natives
who ended up in the 142nd, these sources indicate that he could not have
participated in subsequent combat or in the use of the Choctaw language
in late October 1918. Some officers were reassigned within the division or
to other divisions, especially the 42nd ("Rainbow") Division. Around fifty
men from each company in the 142nd, which removed a significant number of Native Americans, were transferred as replacements to the 42nd
already on the front lines. Lieutenant Bellmard (Kaw) was reportedly sent
to a "1st Corps School."[39] Lieutenant Chastaine (1932:1) of Company A,
142nd, reports arriving in France "somewhat short" of their authorized
strength of 250 men, followed by similar transfers of men to other units,
resulting in 141 enlisted men and six officers by September 1918.

Of the 142nd's Native American officers, only Lieutenant Columbus E.
Veach, who was sent to Company G, and Captain Charles H. Johnson,
the commanding officer of Company C, remained. Although a 1919 *Daily
Oklahoman* article states, "Oklahoma Indian tribes sent three captains and
one major to France, Charles H. Johnson, Ben Davis, and Walter Veach,"
White (1979:14, 20n35) reports that only Johnson would go with the 36th
to the front, as Veach was removed at Bar-sur-Aube prior to the 142nd's
entering combat.[40] However, Bellmard appears on the 142nd's roster as a
first lieutenant in Company C when the regiment went on the line (Barnes
1922:345).

Other factors left the 36th ill prepared for combat. The division landed
in France some 1,500 men less than authorized by military tables of organization. On September 10, the 111th Engineers were transferred to the First
American Army, while two thousand trained infantrymen were dispatched
as replacements to other American divisions, many to the 42nd. Unfortunately, the artillery brigade was separated from the rest of the division at
Bar-sur-Aube, and as the division had no tanks, the men had to enter the
front lines with no experience in maneuvering with an artillery barrage
or tanks. The division was also short of many kinds of equipment. Also
complicating matters, the influenza epidemic had set upon the division at
Bar-sur-Aube, further reducing the division's strength. Nevertheless, with

their morale noted as "very high," their training was soon cut short as the regiment was needed on the front line.[41]

The Meuse-Argonne Offensive, September 26–November 11, 1918

In 1820, Choctaw chief Pushmataha is said to have predicted that some of his listeners would live to see the day "when the highly improved Choctaw shall hold office in the councils of that great nation of white people, and in their wars with nations of the earth, mixed up in the armies of the white man, the fierce war whoops of the Choctaw warrior shall strike terror and melt the hearts of the invading foes" (MCHS 1982:25). Choctaw tribal historian Charley Jones often told this story in his history classes reminding his students that the "Choctaw War Cry would be heard in many foreign lands."[42] This prediction became a reality in World War I and remains as Choctaw continue to serve in the US military in foreign lands (Milligan 2003:249).

In the closing days of World War I, Choctaw and other Native Americans in the US Army's 36th Division became instrumental in the success of the AEF's battles at St. Etienne and Forest Ferme. Until the late summer of 1918, American forces had fought largely under French army command. That August, the independent First United States Army was formed under General John J. Pershing. Their first action would be at St. Mihiel on September 11–12 and was a turning point in this sector of the front. On the first day, American forces took more than twelve thousand German prisoners. The battle triggered a steady retreat toward the Rhine River, and German forces began collapsing under the steady advance of the AEF.

Following the Allied success at St. Mihiel, the Germans knew they were in a precarious position. Over the next two weeks, the AEF frantically prepared for its next major offensive against Germany, the Meuse-Argonne campaign. This involved a large-scale, forty-seven-day Allied offensive along sixty miles of the Western Front. British, French, and Belgian forces advanced in the north, while the French-American forces advanced around the Argonne Forest. Named for the region between the Meuse River and the Argonne Forest, the campaign lasted from September 26 to November 11, 1918, and is credited for leading directly to the Armistice (CMHUSA 1988:225–229; Stallings 1963:223–226).

The Meuse-Argonne offensive centered on a well-defended front. The initial battlefield focused on a twelve-mile sector of the Meuse River Valley with heights on one side and the thick undergrowth of the Argonne Forest on the other. Four elevated areas in the valley offered natural strongholds: the heights of Mountfaucon, Romange, Bois de Barricourt, and Bois de

Bourgogne. The Germans also held four successive lines of defense, each containing defensive trenches, concrete emplacements, and barbed wire. American Expeditionary Forces intelligence predicted that Allied troops would face five enemy line divisions, four divisions of reinforcement within twenty-four hours, and two additional divisions on the second day. Within a week, the campaign would be further complicated by rain, cold, and outbreaks of influenza and pneumonia that swept through the ranks (Gilbert 2012:185, 187).

The American attack north and northwest of Verdun was aimed at the German's principle railroad supply line that ran between Carigan, Sedan, and Mezieres. The center point of Sedan lay fifty-three kilometers from the front line. Severing the line would prohibit the Germans from holding their positions to the west and northwest of Sedan. The 36th, assigned with the US 2nd Division under the French Fourth Army, was flanked by the French Fourth Army on their left and the American First Army on its right (Spence 1919:6, 82–83; Brager 2002:56).

Hoping to end the war quickly, the Americans concentrated on breaking through the German forces comprising the defensive Hindenburg Line concentrated along this section. Characterized by heavy growth and steep ravines, the terrain was strategically defensive and offensively problematic (Britten 1997:79). Thirty-five miles north of this area lay the vitally important, laterally running, rail hub at Sedan. Capturing this station would break the railroad net critical to supplying the German army in France and Flanders by dividing the German armies, forcing a collapse of the German positions along the Western Front. Because of the difficulty of crossing the Ardennes Mountains in winter, capturing Sedan would also prevent the Germans from retreating to the Rhine River and reorganizing for a last-ditch stand until a peace could be obtained. These movements sought to stop, then reverse, a strong German push that would help hasten the end of the war. Anticipating this push, the Germans had strategically constructed a series of barriers along a series of east-west ridges containing an almost continuous zone of trenches, barbed wire, and fortifications nearly ten miles in depth (Hallas 2000:239; Stallings 1963:223–226).

Severing the Lille-Metz railroad would cut the German's ability to move supplies and troops both east and west. The American Army would advance northward between the Meuse River and the Argonne Forest, while the French Fourth Army would attack on the west. At the same time, French, British (including Canada, Australia, and New Zealand), Belgian forces, and the US 27th and 30th Divisions under the British-led II Corps, would assault German positions along other sectors of the Western Front to the north. The Meuse-Argonne was the largest, most costly, and bloodiest battle of the AEF in World War I and in US military history, resulting in over 187,000 Allied casualties and losses, including 117,000 Americans (CMHUSA 1988:227–229; Stallings 1963:223–226).

With the offensive planned to begin in late September, General Pershing desperately needed all available divisions on the front lines. French soldiers remained on the front line to conceal the preparations. Conducted at night, nearly 220,000 Allied soldiers were moved out of the sector, as 600,000 Americans moved in. Three US corps would attack along the front; with I Corps (77th, 28th, 35th Divisions) on the left, V Corps (91st, 37th, 79th Divisions) in the center, and III Corps (4th, 80th, 33rd Divisions) on the right (Hallas 2000:239–240).

The 36th's training was shortened, and on October 3, it was assigned to the Army Reserve under the French Fourth Army, part of the French "Armies of the Center" that had met stiff resistance advancing on the Champagne Front. On October 4 and 5, they were taken northward by rail to the vicinity of Chalone-Epermay, north of Somme-Py and south of the Aisne River, to relieve part of the 2nd Division, which had captured Blanc Mont Ridge. The night of the 4th, the 71st Brigade and 111th Field Signal Battalion were taken by truck then marched to the front east of Reims, north of Somme-Py, and south of the Aisne River (Chastaine 1920:68–70).

The US 36th and 2nd Infantry Divisions would support Pershing's push into the Argonne Forest by attacking to the left in the Champagne, focusing on the German forces around St. Etienne and Forest Ferme (Chastaine 1920:57–73).[43] Two days later, the 36th began moving to their new assignment and on the following day were chosen to participate in an offensive in the Champagne area.

The American 36th and 2nd Divisions were charged with breaking the German's control of the most critical point in that section of the front. On October 5, the 71st Brigade (141st and 142nd Infantry Regiments and the 133rd Machine Gun Battalion) was ordered to relieve a part of the 2nd Division that had suffered severe casualties on the 3rd near St. Etienne in capturing Blanc Mont Ridge. As the offensive unfolded, the 36th would participate in two major actions in the offensive: St. Etienne and Forest Ferme (Chastaine 1920:57–73).[44]

Five officers in the 142nd wrote detailed accounts of the unit's actions in the war: regimental commander Colonel Alfred W. Bloor (1919, 1922); commander 2nd Battalion Major William J. Morrissey (1919); commanding officer, Company A, First Lieutenant Ben H. Chastaine (1920); regimental chaplain, First Lieutenant Charles H. Barnes (1922); and First Lieutenant and later commanding officer, Company E, Captain Elijah W. Horner.[45] These accounts and unit histories allow a reconstruction of these battles and the Choctaw's role in them.

St. Etienne

During the attack of October 6, 1918, the 2nd Division almost drove the Germans off of Blanc Monte Ridge near St. Etienne, but nearly 1,100 of the 2nd and 4th Brigades were killed, wounded, or captured. When the Germans held their position along the northern slopes of Blanc Monte, the 36th was called in to relieve the 2nd (CMHUSA 1988:225–227; White 1979:14–15; 1984:113–119). Chosen because it could reach the front faster than the 72nd Brigade, the 71st Brigade arrived late on the night of October 6 and continued digging in the next morning. Facing the brigade were three under-strength German divisions that had stalled the French corps. German resistance in this sector of the front was especially strong, and if lost would jeopardize the entire German line along the Meuse-Argonne sector (Coleman 2002:212). The 71st Brigade had barely prepared their positions when the 142nd and portions of the 2nd Division were ordered to go over the top to take the village of St. Etienne and resume pushing toward the Aisne River.[46]

This operation required the 142nd to advance down the northern slope of Blanc Mont toward and along the sunken road to Saint-Etienne-a-Arnes. Within the 1st Battalion of the 71st Brigade, Company D, 141st Regiment was placed in a forward position. In the upcoming assault, Joseph Oklahombi (Choctaw) and other men in Company D would perform a notable feat, described in detail in chapter 4. Despite inadequate maps, deficient briefings, and a lack of combat experience, the first action of the inexperienced 71st Brigade began at 5:55 A.M. on October 8 (Coleman 2002:212).

Because the Germans had the ability to monitor US communications, field telephones were not used to transmit orders prior to the attack and were hand delivered. This impediment had serious impacts, resulting in some units being notified too late to fully convey the orders and others not notified before the attack, in some instances from messengers being killed en route (Bloor 1919; Spence 1919:117).

Following a brief period of misdirected artillery, the advance proceeded under a cold drizzle and over difficult terrain through a wooded area dissected by ravines and guarded by a network of German barbed-wire entanglements. Members of the 1st Battalion, 141st Regiment, immediately encountered heavy rifle and machine gun fire and intense artillery shelling from the Germans. Despite the resistance, small groups advanced forward, engaging the enemy machine gun emplacements (Coleman 2002:212).

The Germans were slowly cleared out or pushed back from a wooded knoll to the right. Then the 3rd Battalion, minus Company K, assigned as reserves and advancing under machine gun fire from the cemetery, church, and a ditch running from the cemetery to the southwest corner of the village, enveloped and overran the cemetery, capturing around 208 Germans. By 10:30 A.M., the Americans established a line along the road to the north and running northeast out of St. Etienne. Soon encountering machine gun fire from the German trench positions in front of the town, the Americans were forced to dig in for defense. This position was held until a German counterattack was launched at 4:30 P.M., forcing the 141st back to its earlier position.[47]

For the 141st, the fighting on October 8 was costly, with seven officers and 182 enlisted men killed and eighteen officers and 348 enlisted personnel wounded. The regiment held its advanced position through the night of the 8th, despite intense enemy ground fire and expecting a German counterattack (Coleman 2002:213). Although the fighting continued for two days, including German ground and air attacks, it soon became apparent that the Germans could only periodically check the determined American advance. Late on the 9th, the Germans began withdrawing all along the front west of the Argonne Forest. The Americans gained nearly six hundred yards, capturing nearly six hundred Germans and seventy-five machine guns but suffering nearly 1,600 casualties in two days, with over 1,300 on the 8th.[48]

Chaplain Barnes (1922:30–31) described the ferocity of the fighting the 142nd faced at St. Etienne.

> They encountered a terrific artillery and machine gun fire from the enemy. The machine gun fire coming principally from a network of machine guns nests over which our artillery was firing. The air was full of whizzing, whistling, screaming, bursting instruments of death.
>
> Picture if you can that scene. Recall all the frightening descriptions you have read in newspapers and magazines. Call on all the power of your imagination and see those men as they move slowly, steadily, forward into barbwire entanglements, while gigantic cannon are booming, huge shells screaming through the air, high explosives bursting, shrapnel whizzing on all sides, snipers firing from hidden positions, machine guns click, click, click, doing their deadly work while the air is filled with gas. That was the reception given the 142nd Infantry that cold October morning. Their advance was slow and costly . . .
>
> For three days and nights the enemy kept up a continuous bombardment, serving everything at his command, including plenty of gas. Death lurked on all sides and the field was strewn with dead. That scene and experience drove some men mad while others looked like demons. Only a scant ration could be brought to the line and

that under cover of darkness. No water was available and the juice from canned tomatoes had to serve to quench the thirst. Words have never been coined that will express the terror and hell that reigned on the front line during those days.

Though the 142nd suffered severe losses—34 of 58 officers and 657 of 1,715 enlisted men killed or wounded—the regiment captured some 520 German prisoners and fifty machine guns and inflicted heavy casualties on the German troops (Franks 1984:30).

On October 10, troops of the 36th entered St. Etienne. The following morning, patrols confirmed that the Germans had withdrawn as the 72nd Brigade attacked through the 71st, pursuing the enemy. The actions of the Native Americans in Company E, 142nd Infantry Regiment, the "Millionaire Company," were lauded in the news article "13 Redskins Tribes in Single Company."[49]

As the 2nd Division withdrew from St. Etienne, its artillery brigade remained to provide temporary support to the 36th while the 72nd Brigade moved forward to the front line. The 71st and the 72nd brigades then continued to push the attack, forcing the German forces from the heights to the north of St. Etienne to gradually withdraw from Machault, Dricourt, Vaux-Champange, Chufilly, Givry, Attigny, and other villages on October 11, before halting and establishing a new front line along the Aisne River on the 13th. The Germans fought strong rearguard actions over these three days. The front line continued to change from October 13 to 23, as the 36th occupied a position extending from Fontenille Ferme to Givery. The withdrawal of the French 23rd Division forced the 36th's boundary lines to extend to the left and right to nearly four miles in width, although the left side was soon reestablished at its original position.[50]

The Germans were withdrawing but had made the 142nd pay a high price for the victory. The 142nd suffered considerable losses in taking St. Etienne. On the morning of October 7, the 142nd Infantry Regiment had fielded 91 officers and 2,333 men. By the 11th, only 53 officers and 1,690 men remained available for duty. During a lull in the fighting, the 71st Brigade was reorganized, but according to Chastaine (1920:163–176, 1932:30), the heavy loss of manpower had reduced the battalions "to the size of a full company while regiments were only slightly larger than full strength battalions."

Elijah W. Horner left a detailed handwritten account of the 142nd's actions during October and November 1918. In Company E of the 2nd Battalion, most of his account, dated November 10, 1918, focuses on the actions of October 8 at St. Etienne. It provides further detail regarding the presence and actions against the cemetery, a large dugout, the taking of

German prisoners, and the over-extension of a small portion of the Allied line during the assault.

OBSERVATIONS AND EXPERIENCES AT THE FRONT
By Capt. E.W. Horner, 142nd Inf.

On the morning of October 7th, 1918, the Second Battalion of the 142nd Infantry took its place alongside a battalion of Marines of the Second Division on the Champaign front. Three companies occupied frontline positions, and the remaining company was in support. The Marines told us that the German lines were only a hundred yards in front; but we were inclined to be skeptical, until bullets from snipers' guns began singing by our heads. Then we knew it must be so.

We remained in position until the morning of October 8th, at which time we received orders to go "over the top." Our battalion was in the assault—companies "G" and "H" in the assaulting wave and "E" and "F" in the supportive wave. I was in command of the First platoon of Company "E," commonly known as the Indian company.

No sooner had our barrage started than the Germans started firing at our positions. It was an accurate and deadly fire both from artillery and machine guns. I lost two of the best Indians I had—two corporals—right in the holes where they had kept watch before we jumped off.

Company "G" started and got to our position and was held up by the fire from dozens of machine guns directly in front. I attached my platoon to the left end of "G" company and we all went over together. My men advanced by short rushes until the first machine guns were reached. It seemed that there was not a square foot of air space through which bullets were not flying. In less than fifteen minutes from the time of starting, many machine guns were silenced and taken, and hundreds of Germany's elite—the Prussian Guards—were on their way to the rear of our lines.

There was a tendency to bunch up after the first positions had been taken. The men were soon made to realize that others remained intact ahead, and they scattered and started for them with the same dash and determination that they had evinced at the start. There were no shirkers. Every man was advancing. By this time many officers had been killed or wounded, and platoons and companies had become mixed. They fought on, however, regardless of whom they were fighting with. Soon other positions were taken, and the strip of woods between our starting point and the town of St. Etienne was ours. After the woods had been taken several small tanks came from the rear. They were too late and were of no service that I could see.

The town of St. Etienne was about a kilometer ahead. The space between was an open field traversed by barbed wire entanglements. The German artillery had direct observation of the whole field and were able to shoot point-blank at any part of it. To the right, in the sector where the 141st Infantry was attacking, was a timbered area infested with machine guns, arranged to sweep the open field. Our men saw the town and started for it. The artillery opened up on us. The 141st wasn't as far advanced as we were, and consequently the machine guns in the timber also fired at us. The town was reached, and a large number of prisoners who had assembled in a cemetery just to the right of town, were taken. Just before reaching the town a dugout in which perhaps fifty Germans were located was captured. They formed in a column of squads and started back through our lines. Their own artillery, upon seeing the close formation, fired into them. I saw several fall.

The number of men who had penetrated as far as the town was amazingly small. It was impassible to advance farther, because the artillery implacements [sic] were very near. Machine guns all the while were pouring their fire in our direction. There was nothing to do except dig in. The line thus formed was thin indeed and it was a projection not connected at either end with friendly troops. In fact, from all information we could get, both the right and left were a kilometer behind. This position was held from about noon on October 8th till about dusk. Knowing that a counterattack would surely come, and knowing also that the few disorganized men could not withstand such an attack, advantage was taken of a moment when the German artillery was firing on our own artillery to make our way back to the line of resistance. The artillery fire was again directed at us, but there were so few and we were in such an open formation that no hits were registered. Two men were hit by machine guns but were not killed. The new line had been established in edge of woods overlooking St. Etienne, and that position was held until; the 144th Infantry took the offensive.

On the night the Germans withdrew their men and artillery and started for the Aisne, they used some very clever tricks to keep it becoming known that they had started to retreat. The heavy artillery fire was kept up until perhaps 9 P.M. Then it was observed that gas shells were falling a little short of our line. A line of gas shells fell in front of and the entire length of our line. The wind was in our favor and none of the gas reached us. Machine guns during the greater part of the night, swept our lines at intervals. Next morning we knew that those things were only to make us think they were still there in force, and we knew that the gas barrage was to prevent our pursuing them.

After this first day of fighting I was the only officer left with the company, and I was alone with the company for the remainder of the front line tour.

The 71st Brigade followed in support of the 72nd Brigade, and upon reaching the Aisne, took over a sector to their right. Company "E" was sent to the line of observation for two days. This sector was not subject to as heavy fire as we had previously encountered. Several patrols were sent out from the company, but no casualties resulted . . .

E.W. Horner
Capt., 142nd Inf.
10th November, 1918.[51]
Forest Ferme

By October 13, the 36th Division had advanced along the south bank of the Aisne River, where they prepared for the next assault. These movements placed the 36th face to face with German troops strategically positioned in an elevated U-shaped peninsula or horseshoe on the south bank of the Aisne, three miles east of Antigny. Formed by the river making a ninety-degree turn around an elevated area before it continued westward, this loop provided a strategic salient for the Germans. This area would become known as Forest Ferme (Forest Farm), named after a nearby abandoned farmhouse near the base of the peninsula. The toe of the horseshoe extended to the north and was flanked by the German lines on the north side of the river. The hamlet of Rilly-aux-Oies lay at the top of the peninsula, which was approximately three kilometers in width across the base and two and a half kilometers in depth. Across the base of the horseshoe, the Germans had constructed a series of wire entanglements, a well-organized trench system, small caliber *Minenwerfer* (short-range mortars), and light artillery dominated by interlocking machine-gun positions with two especially strong points. Inside the pocket were the German 195th and 9th Regiment, 3rd Prussian Guard Division. The latter was considered to be "one of the best German divisions" and fronted the right of the 36th. The whole position was covered by German artillery on the hills along the north side of the Aisne. Because this elevated pocket afforded the Germans advantages in observation and in launching raids or counterattacking the Americans, and because it provided flanking fire for other German positions across the river to the north, it required elimination before the Americans could effectively cross the Aisne. The assault would not be easy, requiring a direct frontal assault across a wide area of unprotected terrain toward an elevated position.

As Brigadier General W. D. Cope explained:

The land within this loop was considerably higher than the ground immediately to the south, which was occupied by the 71st Brigade, and this position was of great tactical value to the enemy, since it could be used for observation posts, and in case of an attack on the Allied lines, would serve as a bridge-head and debouching point. For this reason, and because it would serve as a convenient salient from which to launch an attack on the German position north of the river, it was of utmost importance that this stronghold be wrested from the enemy.[52]

The Operations Report of the 36th Division states,

The Boche had fortified the mouth of the loop with a series of strong points, defended by approximately sixty machine guns, and in the 141st Infantry sector, consisting of 1400 meters frontage extending along the west half of the loop, six prepared machine gun emplacements of concrete were found, two consolidated trenches, one minenwerfer emplacement, and twenty dug-outs, showing indication of machine gun occupancy.[53]

After two failed attempts by the French 73rd Division on the evenings of October 16 and 17 followed by the defeat of a German counterattack, the 36th Division was assigned to assault the position. After repositioning, the 36th's regiments included, from east to west, the 143rd, 144th, 141st, and 142nd. The 143rd was relieved on October 26. Spanning the neck of the peninsula, the 141st and 142nd prepared to assault the position, with the 144th in reserve.[54]

For several days, German artillery increased in intensity and accuracy. Following every troop movement, General Smith suspected that the Germans were monitoring their communications through intact lines that they had left behind. Following the placement of the 36th, German gun, mortar, and artillery fire increased. On October 25, the Germans unleashed a bombardment of several hours' duration two miles south of Chufilly and southwest of Voncq. Their artillery hit two companies of the 2nd Battalion and part of the Headquarters Company of the 142nd, elements of the 113th Machine Gun Battalion, and several artillery batteries stationed in the vicinity with mustard gas. Although some two hundred men were exposed, only forty-five "became gas casualties" (Brager 2002:74; White 1984:163).

AEF Field Intelligence

During World War I, a variety of intelligence-gathering methods were used. Maps, based primarily on topographical surveys and aerial photographs, provided assessments of topography. Observation posts, balloons, and direction-finding sites were used to identify the location of enemy units. During actual combat, flash and sound-ranging devices helped to pinpoint enemy fire to return more effective counterfire. Similar methods were employed with air intercept that copied communications between spotting aircraft and enemy artillery batteries. Because much of World War I focused on prolonged entrenched positions along a stalemated front, combat was dominated by artillery for its accuracy and ability to reach behind enemy lines. In turn, a significant portion of intelligence focused on locating enemy guns and concealments (Gilbert 2012:119).

To ascertain and counter enemy forces, knowledge of their location, composition, and objectives was required. To gather such intelligence, varied forms of information gathering were used, including scouts, direction finding, train watchers, photo intelligence, radio intercept, interrogation of prisoners, and captured documents, often obtained through trench raids. Advance warning of enemy plans and movements was vital to prepare countermeasures, and it was in these situations that radio and telephone interception was especially vital.

When codes were not being routinely broken, commanders often relied on trench raids to confirm the identification and composition of opposing forces through captured uniform insignia, documents, and prisoners. Throughout the war, raids became increasingly dangerous as enemy forces regularly moved out of their forward trenches, requiring patrols to venture deeper into enemy-held territory. Similar to British forces, US battalions contained scout detachments of fifteen enlisted men from which local commanders typically assigned up to two members to accompany raiding parties. Although trained to use trench knives to silently kill opponents, a primary duty of scouts was to search dead bodies for official and personal intelligence through documents, cut off identifying uniform insignia, and survey dugouts and positions of interest. Scouts also participated in more common assignments of concealed observation for reconnaissance (Gilbert 2012:120). The use of Native Americans as scouts often placed them in such assignments.

In concealed elevated positions, eight-man crews manned observation posts, often transmitting information to the rear via Morse code by telegraph or lighted blinker. There, a draftsman recorded relevant information onto a situation map and prepared reports for division intelligence. Radio intelligence sections employed listening stations near the frontlines. For much of the war, both sides used telegraph and telephone lines to communicate, though because these lines ran throughout the front lines, they were subject to wiretapping (Gilbert 2012:121–122).

Eventually, a form of ground relay was adopted, such as the French TPS (French for *telegraphie par sol* or "telegraphy by ground," sometimes referred to as earth wires), in which signal personnel drove iron poles into the ground to transmit at low frequencies up to distances of four to five kilometers. Because TPS and ground telephone required no wires or antennas, they provided communications that were less vulnerable to enemy artillery, as ground lines were frequently severed by artillery. However, ground-relay low-level communications were still susceptible to electromagnetic interception, which was dependent in part on soil type and dampness (Cameron 1919; Gilbert 2012:122).[55] This method involved constructing wire loops that were placed parallel to the enemy's lines of communication. Tiny electric currents were then magnified by means of an amplifier, allowing messages to be intercepted. Another method employed copper-mesh mats or metallic rods buried as near to the enemy's wires as possible, with wires leading to an amplifier, which rendered the signals audible.[56] Other methods of interception were possible against a single wire that used a ground return and two-wire systems when the lines were separated by at least twelve inches. In wooded areas, loop antennas were used for interception, often secured to treetops near but out of sight of enemy forces (Gilbert 2012:122).

One of the most dangerous duties performed by radio intelligence was serving at a listening station, typically located within a kilometer of the front lines. To work, the point of intercept had to be within three to four kilometers of the base line in use. If the signal originated from wires, the distance decreased to two or three kilometers. When German communications went silent, radio personnel at listening stations were required to extend their intercept lines farther into no-man's-land. As the enemy increased the depth of no-man's-land, listening-station personnel were forced to extend their lines farther into enemy-patrolled areas to install a new antenna. Often this required individuals to remain concealed ahead of their own lines for extended periods to establish and repair lines and to continuously check their lines to ensure that Germans had not tapped into them to pick up stray TPS signals from other friendly stations (Cameron 1919; Gilbert 2012:122–123).

In addition, inferences from radio transmissions could often be made from changes in operator accents, tones, loudness, greetings, choice of vocabulary, requests for locations, and dates. The signal loudness often allowed listening stations to estimate the transmitter's distance with some degree of accuracy. By drawing lines between the communication links, the chain of command within a division could be recreated. The telephone remained Germany's primary means of communication from the infantry battalion to the rear, and according to one captured document, imprudent phone conversations remained perhaps the most serious source of harm to the German front (Gilbert 2012:124).

Divisional Intelligence

During World War I, a brigade's primary area was defined as one mile to the rear of the enemy's front lines. The brigade was not originally considered a link in the intelligence system. Eventually, the adjutant became responsible for appointing a brigade intelligence officer to collect and maintain information in their immediate area, which was accomplished through observation. Of paramount interest were locations and strengths of improved trenches, machine-gun and trench-mortar emplacements, dumps, trench railways, reserve dugouts, observation posts, command posts, and the collection and transfer to division of captured documents and prisoners. At the brigade level, intelligence personnel were charged with monitoring communication to a range of one mile behind the enemy's front lines. At the division level, intelligence was typically responsible for a collection zone extending two miles behind enemy lines (Gilbert 2012:125).

Although the AEF had planned to reach the Hindenburg Line by October 1, halfway to their final objective, and had made a great effort, they did not reach it until the 16th. Newly constructed defensive positions were observed in the area. As French marshal Ferdinand Foch (Gilbert 2012:188) described, "There is no denying the magnitude of the effort made by the American Army. After attacking at Saint-Mihiel on September 12, it attacked in the Argonne on the 26th. From September 26th to October 20th, losses were 54,158 men—in exchange for small gains on a narrow front, it is true, but over particularly difficult country and in the face of serious resistance by the enemy."

Despite efforts to improve communications and interception methods, American units failed to implement communications security on a widespread basis. Suspecting that German forces were monitoring their communications and quickly shelling pinpointed locales, some officers confirmed their suspicions by sending messages with false coordinates, which resulted in German artillery quickly shifting to those locations. The terrain and defenses in the Meuse-Argonne area were also extremely difficult, reported by some as more so than any other sector of the front, helping German resistance remain unusually strong (Bloor 1919; Gilbert 2012:188–189; Stanley 1931:1–5; White 1982:164).

Sending messages in the clear with little concern for communication security was not only dangerous, but also commonplace throughout the war. Gilbert (2012:189) provides an example of this problem and how it was confirmed. Colonel James Rhea, an infantry brigade commander in the 2nd Division, reported occupying a French farmhouse. Shortly after the site had been reported as the new brigade command post and the coordinates of the farmhouse had been sent out, it began to receive German artillery. Suspecting the Germans were monitoring their communications, Rhea soon transmitted a false message in the clear announcing that the first message was in error and that the command post was at a building located 450 yards away from the previously located location. Within five minutes, the shelling ceased and was shifted to the false location, confirming his suspicions. When Dennis Nolan, the first to serve as the United States Army G-2 in intelligence, learned of the incident, he lamented, "This was 18 months after we had declared war and we had not succeeded in getting in the minds of all our officers the danger involved in this type of communications" (Gilbert 2012:189; Johnson 1929:318–319). A more secure method of transmitting messages was badly needed. This was not an isolated incident as demonstrated in chapter 2 with the 30th Infantry Division.

With the mass armies of World War I, field telegraph and telephone and wireless telegraphy offered the greatest promise for managing and controlling large units by commanders and were the most common forms of communication for sending messages via overhead wires in the rear and deeply buried cables near the front. These methods were viewed as adjuncts to offensive actions involving rapid movements of large units (Johnson 1994:6–7). But the first three years of the war in Europe stagnated into prolonged trench warfare. Despite a relatively confined battlefield, both telephone and telegraph were prone to frequent breaks in the line from enemy artillery explosions, even with lines laid deep underground (Holm 2007:108). Whether on the surface or buried, lines had to be laid in combat, including extensions or new lines following an advance, exposing crews to enemy fire. With fluid and sometimes irregular troop movements, connecting lines to particular command posts was often difficult. These drawbacks led to an increased reliance on messengers and wireless communications. As combat became more mobile in the last months of the war, military observation structures designed for trench warfare decreased. When infantry lines advanced, artillery needed to be brought forward to support them, a mobilization that was complicated by a lack of good roads. With each mile advanced, the distance from vital railheads to ensure supply, artillery support, and communication lines became less effective, and there was little or no time to "catch up" (Johnson 1994:288).

Even by 1918, secure communications proved difficult to obtain, despite the use of several forms including telephone, radio, TPS, buzzer phones, field rocket signals, lights, flags, carrier pigeons, and messages transported by runners.[57] Radios of the period were fragile and somewhat unreliable and were little used in the trenches. Wireless telegraph required that messages be translated from dots and dashes to written word, requiring valuable time in coding and decoding. The most useful form of communication allowing two individuals to communicate directly was the telephone, but its drawback was critical: with telephone, each side could easily monitor the other's communications.

Major General A. W. Greely described American methods of monitoring German communications and the dangers associated with its use:

> Intercepting work was rarely possible at a greater distance than five miles, and the apparatus for this purpose had to be set up in No Man's Land, not infrequently within a few yards of the outposts of a vigilant enemy. These message collectors consisted either of wire loops installed parallel to the enemy's lines or of copper meshes to metallic rods buried near the German trenches. Wires extended back from these installations to our base station, where vacuum-tube amplifiers so strengthened the feeblest currents that the German messages were clearly audible. The setting up of such equipment, necessarily made at night, was a most hazardous adventure, which caused the death or maiming of scores of heroic volunteers of the Signal Corps, but volunteers for these incursions into No Man's Land were never lacking.[58]

Numerous accounts reference the dangers and high casualties associated with men attempting to lay and repair communications line under small arms and artillery fire. The Americans became aware that that Germans were tapping into their radio circuits and telephone lines near St. Mihiel and St. Etienne, intercepting intra-divisional transmissions, and had broken the Allies' codes.[59]

Another problem was the high casualty rate of runners carrying messages from one location to another. As Major General A. W. Greely described, "Beyond doubt, the enemy's listening-in experts acquired definite and important information as to our plans and movements. . . . When all other methods failed runners were used, generally under conditions of greatest hazard and in the midst of vigorous fighting."[60] One source reports, "They were also capturing about one "messenger" out of four who served as runners between the various companies on the battle line."[61]

Bloor (1922:74–75) notes that "runners were slow and casualties high" and that runners—and in one instance an entire signal platoon—sometimes became lost at night, using up valuable time. White (1984:138) reports that the 36th had "many casualties among the runners, who made excellent targets as they carried messages between the regimental PCs and the forward positions." Other divisions experienced similar losses. When infantry and artillery units in the US 26th Infantry ("Yankee") Division experienced communication problems in combat on July 18, they were forced to make heavy use of runners who "died in droves" (Grotelueschen 2007:35).

Major General Greely reports that the signal corps suffered 1,331 killed, wounded, and missing and cites a study of three month's fighting indicating that the signal corps, a non-combatant body, lost a greater percentage of men than any other unit of service—line or staff—except infantry. Greely described some of the dangers experienced by signal corps troops: "Some perished through flares of star-rockets, which brought on a shower of machinegun bullets or the deadly barrage, generally German but at times American. Others when wounded met a lingering death by thirst or starvation in the labyrinth of shell holes and other craters, while some were killed outright as they sought entrance through or exit from the gaps in the enemy's wire entanglement."[62] Reflecting the disregard of danger and gallantry in service, over fifty Distinguished Service Crosses were awarded to American Signal Corps troops.

As the war continued, several new forms of technology and tactics were developed. "The deadly accuracy of artillery and machinegun fire has caused changes in methods of obtaining military information. Scouting has yielded pace to electricity. The Signal Corps by listening in obtained its information from the planes in the sky, the telephones in dugouts, the telegrams of T.P.S. (earth wires) and the radios at German stations."[63]

The Germans also knew that the Allies monitored their transmissions. Posters in German reading "The Enemy Is listening In—Beware of the Telephone" were recovered from German dugouts. Since practically every troop movement by the 36th drew German fire, it became obvious that the Germans were monitoring their movements through voice transmissions, in particular telephone. The most secure method of transmission was the signal corps' development of the buzzer phone, whereby a low current was used to send a message in dots and dashes that was then read telegraphically. To prevent theft by induction, the use of a return wire was required.[64]

At this time, encoding messages over telephone and telegraph wire presented a better means of preventing the interception of signals between commanders and forward echelon units. However, while coding provided a degree of security, it also inhibited messages from being read quickly or in real time, a result of the time needed to encode and decode them (Holm 2007:109). As Colonel Bloor described, "There was reason to believe every message or word going over our wires also went to the enemy." Consequently, transmitters were forced to code all-important messages, which "took valuable time."[65] Although the encoding and decoding required by the buzzer phone was slow and consumed precious time, runners took even longer to relay messages. The need for a code that could be deciphered instantly led the Americans to search for a faster, more secure means of communications.

Concerned with the effectiveness of the German artillery, General William R. Smith sought a means to decrease it. Suspecting that the Germans were monitoring the 36th communication by listening in through lead wires left intact during their withdrawal, Smith devised a plan to test his suspicion. Giving "some false orders over the phone" that "a contingent of troops would be on a certain hill," Major George A. Robinson, commander of the 111th Field Signal Battalion, reported that the hill was soon almost obliterated by German artillery.[66]

As the Americans gained control of the Champagne area after taking St. Etienne, including houses and dugouts recently abandoned by the Germans, they discovered many abandoned German communications lines intact. Since the Germans were already adept at tapping into American telephone lines and breaking radio codes, the Americans were suspicious as to why the enemy would leave intact lines in such exposed areas. Bloor (1919) reasoned they had been left behind deliberately, hoping that the Americans would tap into the abandoned German lines for their own communications and allow the Germans to monitor the Americans' conversations.

With the Forest Ferme assault quickly approaching, Smith needed a foolproof and instant means of communications (White 1984:164). It would come from the Choctaw Indians in Company E, 142nd Infantry Regiment, just fifteen days before the end of the war. When Bloor and his staff in the 142nd experienced this problem, they reasoned that the answer might well be in the Native languages spoken by troops in their units. One step ahead of the Germans, Bloor willingly played into their trap by using the captured German telephone lines and continuing open-air telephone transmissions. However, having Choctaws transmit the messages in their own language allowed the Germans to monitor but not decipher the transmissions. The communication problems and mistakes at St. Etienne would be remedied through the use of the Choctaw language.

The Assault on Forest Ferme

Following the German gas attack of October 25, Colonel Bloor decided to test the use of Choctaw-language messages on the evening of the 26th by withdrawing two companies of the 2nd Battalion (Companies E, F,

G, H), 142nd Infantry Regiment, from Chufilly to the neighboring village of Chardeny. The tactic worked. There was no German reaction to the messages and movements, which Bloor described as occurring "without mishap."[67] The following day, Choctaw troops were stationed at telephone terminals to transmit and receive messages. Sources confirm that "Indians—mainly Choctaws" were used (Barnes 1922:39; Chastaine 1920: 223–225; White 1984:164).

Generals Whitworth and Smith planned to attack the German position south of Rilly-aux-Oies on October 27. The attack would be led by the 71st Brigade, with two infantry regiments abreast, the 141st on the left and the 142nd on the right, with the 3rd Battalion of the 142nd leading the assault. The 71st Brigade would advance at 4:30 P.M., just before dark, to deprive the enemy the benefit of their observation posts. Prior to the assault, a twenty-minute standing artillery barrage would occur followed by a rolling barrage of artillery fired at the rate of one hundred yards every three minutes to cover the infantry assault (Franks 1984:29).[68] Captain Steve Lillard was chosen to lead the attack for the 3rd Battalion, 142nd Infantry (Ball 2010:357–358).[69]

Although depleted through losses at St. Etienne and the recent influenza epidemic, the veteran troops were considered able to stand against even a violent opposition. Companies B and D, 132nd Machine Gun Battalion, and the 142nd Regimental Machine Gun Company provided covering fire. Light guns, machine guns, and trench mortars raked the German positions, forcing them to remain in their dugouts. Company D, 1st Battalion, 141st Infantry was attached to the 2nd Battalion, while the remainder of the 1st Battalion (Companies A, B, C) was assigned as support. The 2nd Battalion, 142nd Infantry (Companies E, F, G, H) would support the 3rd Battalion (Companies I, K, L, M) (Barnes 1922:343–344; Chastaine 1920:223–225; White 1984:164).

Support battalions were ordered to follow a thousand meters behind the assault battalions. During the evening of October 26, the 143rd was relieved by the French 51st Division, while the 141st and 142nd were moved into place without arousing German suspicion. Under cover of darkness, the advance troops had moved forward and secreted themselves for observation near the German barbed wire, remaining there most of the follow day prior to the attack. The 144th also remained nearby.[70]

Sunday, October 27, began clear and sunny but became misty, with low visibility that afternoon, favoring the assault troops. The advance troops were pulled back several hundred yards to the rear, creating an open zone to begin the walking barrage of artillery and mortars toward the German positions while protecting troops from any shelling that fell short, prior to advancing. Orders were issued in Choctaw at 11:40 A.M. (appendix C).

More coordinated than at St. Etienne, all officers and men understood their assignments, having received early issue of orders, sketches, maps, instructions for the attack, and time for concealment. Assault troops were not notified of the time of attack until almost time to begin. At 4:10 P.M., a shot from the 2nd Artillery signaled the start of a preliminary twenty-minute barrage on the German positions, while the Forest Ferme position was raked with shrapnel. So many high explosive shells were directed on the enemy positions near Voncq across the river that the German artillery was completely neutralized. Following the artillery and smoke shells for cover, the rolling barrage began three minutes before the American infantry advanced. A rolling barrage consists of artillery lining up in a series of rows, usually two or three, behind its advancing infantry, then concentrating its fire in alternating, overlapping salvos on a series of parallel formations. By the time the last row fires, the first row is ready to fire again, and so on, providing an overlapping barrage that spares little in its way as one's infantry advances behind it. At 4:30 P.M., officers along the line blew their whistles, signaling the infantry to "jump off," or go over the top. Heading for two strong points, one at Forest Ferme and the other in a small wooded grove to the east, the troops followed behind the barrage so closely they were described as "leaning against it." Having concentrated their fire on the wire entanglements, the 2nd Trench Mortar Battery had a detail of wire cutters from the 2nd Engineers cut paths through the wire, leaving guides to direct the approaching infantry (Chastaine 1920:225–229; White 1984:165–166).[71]

Other factors helped. The late afternoon start placed the setting sun behind the advancing Americans and in the German's eyes. The timing of the attack with the approaching darkness minimized the value of German observation posts. Unlike at St. Etienne, all officers and men were fully briefed prior to the start of the attack. At St. Etienne, the rolling barrage had been placed too far ahead of the US troops, allowing the German defenders to recover. The accidental shelling of some US troops was also corrected at Forest Ferme. The troops followed the barrage so closely that when the Germans returned fire, their full-scale barrages landed behind the approaching US troops.

Allied artillery began shelling enemy positions across the river east of Givry to make the Germans think that they were preparing to cross the Aisne. The German artillery responded by ineffectively firing in advance of and then consistently behind the line of departure. Virtually untouched, the assault troops advanced in two waves positioned two paces apart and following a little over a hundred yards behind the artillery barrage. The first wave consisted of automatic riflemen and hand grenadiers, while automatic riflemen, "ordinary" riflemen, bombers, and rifle grenadiers composed the second wave. With the exception of an artillery battery commencing firing two minutes late and briefly hitting a company of the 142nd, which briefly scattered for cover then reformed and continued advancing, the attack went without incident (Chastaine 1920:228–231; White 1984:166).

Aided by the artillery barrage, smoke screen, and the cutting of the German barbed wire entanglements, the infantrymen advanced rapidly with little resistance, pouring into the German trenches, dugouts, and strong points. Using grenades to clear out trenches and dugouts, American troops had German prisoners quickly escorted to the rear by guards. Most of the Prussians were still in their shelters to escape the artillery barrage, and before they realized what had occurred, they were surrounded by the advancing echelons of Americans brandishing rifles, grenades, and trench knives in hand. Although some Prussians resisted, the vast majority surrendered on the spot. Sixteen dugouts were found.

On the right, the 142nd Infantry reached their objective at 5:10 P.M. then organized its position. Less than an hour after beginning the assault, troops fired green star shells into the air at 5:17 P.M., signaling mission accomplished. To the left, the 141st Infantry had reached its objective and organized its position by 6:10 P.M. After establishing liaisons between the two regiments, combat patrols from both regiments advanced to clean out the loop beyond Rilly-aux-Oies, capturing remaining pockets of machine guns and snipers harassing the captured positions. The 142nd maintained contact with French forces to the right at a point approximately four hundred meters north of Fontenill Farm.[72]

The success of the attack was also due in large part to the 133rd Machine Gun Battalion, whose forward machine gunners accompanied the infantry while rear gunners laid down a machine-gun barrage to cover the infantry advance. Reaching their objective, forward gunners helped to consolidate the advance by taking up positions, enabling them to repel any counterattack the enemy might attempt. The machine-gun barrage that was simultaneously fired through the artillery barrage supported the latter by providing a thick hail of fire that kept the enemy in their dugouts until the US troops were upon them. The attack was seemingly a complete surprise to the enemy.[73] The assault troops occupied the captured positions until they were relieved late on the evening of October 28.

Another important factor in the successes during the Meuse-Argonne campaign was the debut of two models of .30-caliber machine gun: the Browning machine gun model 1917 and the Browning automatic rifle M1918 (or BAR), first issued to US and French troops in September of 1918. Browning automatic rifles arrived with the 79th Division, which had come to France in July of 1918, and were issued the Browning machine guns on September 13. Both models were first used in combat later that month by a detachment of the 79th Division at the start of the Meuse-Argonne campaign. The BARs received generally positive reviews as long as their firing mechanisms were kept clean, and they were described as making an impact disproportionate to their numbers. Brownings were soon issued to the 80th Division, which was already in France, and to all US divisions embarking for France after July 1, 1918, including the 6th, 7th, 8th, and 29th. The 36th carried both types of Browning (Ballou 2000:57–62; Chinn 1951:179–181). At the time the 36th received Brownings, front line troops were using the automatic French Lewis gun.[74]

The BAR is a shoulder-fired rifle that provides semiautomatic and fully automatic fire from a walking position. Although it can be fired slung over the shoulder or from the hip, it was most frequently fired from a bipod. In 1916, the French developed the tactic of "walking fire," whereby units of infantry advanced as they fired, to counter the problems caused by heavy German MG08 Maxim machine guns that provided lethal crossfire from entrenched positions. The French developed "machine gun killing teams" consisting of small mobile squads of riflemen and grenadiers grouped around a gunner armed with a "machine rifle." Whereas heavier machine guns could not be fired while being carried, these lighter, portable, rifle-caliber automatic guns with a fixed ammunition supply could provide brief but heavy concentrations of suppressive fire while the operator was walking, capable of forcing the enemy to keep their heads down long enough for grenades to be thrown into German machine gun positions and neutralized. The BAR was designed to provide suppressive fire for advancing infantry carrying heavier machine guns who could not keep up with other units during assaults. Originally based around the use of the French CSRG 1915 Chauchat machine gun and M1909 Benét-Mercié machine gun, the BAR proved even better suited to this tactic (Ballou 2000:16; Chinn 1951:179–181).

In Europe, the BAR was more enthusiastically received than the heavier water-cooled Browning machine gun, and all of the Allied governments immediately requested purchase of more BARs upon arriving. The French requested fifteen thousand to replace the inferior machine rifle currently used by French and American troops that were sometimes so unreliable that many were discarded during combat (Ballou 2000:57–59; Chinn 1951: 179–181).

Efforts were made to keep the new machine guns secret. On March 4, 1918, L. L. Bracken, secretary of the US Federal Trade Commission, issued a gag order to the Colt and Browning companies from disclosing details of, or further publicizing, the Browning machine gun or Browning machine rifle (Ballou 2000:49). Although seventeen thousand Browning machine rifles—enough to arm twenty US divisions—had been delivered to AEF depots by June, 1918, their introduction into combat was delayed under order of General Pershing. Two official reasons were given. First, as the German army was retreating when the Browning models became available, there was no time for frontline units to exchange their French and British machine guns for Brownings or to replace their Chauchat automatic rifles with light Brownings. Second, once Pershing realized that the Brownings were superior to other machine guns on both sides of the war, it was deemed wise to wait until many divisions could be equipped with them and a plentiful future supply of them could be assured. Therefore, to prevent the weapon from falling into the hands of the Germans and to maximize their advantage once introduced, the BAR received limited use. With fifty-two thousand BARs manufactured by November 1918, greater numbers would have been used had the war continued. The war ended so quickly after their introduction that twenty-seven American divisions were still equipped with French .30-cal or 8 mm Chauchat machine guns and two divisions with British .303 Lewis machine guns (Ballou 2000:57–59; Chinn 1951:179–181). Chastaine reports that all of the 36th's infantry were armed with BARs while training at Bar-sur-Aube and that they used the new rifle during their entire period of combat.[75]

At Forest Ferme, elements of the 71st Brigade had thoroughly overrun elements of the Ninth Regiment, Third Prussian Guard Division, reportedly one of the best units in the German army. Although Forest Farm was a minor operation in the larger campaign, it further enhanced the 36th's reputation as an excellent combat division and garnered considerable praise from both American and French armies (Chastaine 1920:229–235; White 1979:15, 1984:167).

While reports vary, the 36th losses were small. Barnes (1922:39) reports that approximately "190 [German] prisoners were captured and the best information obtainable confirmed the fact that practically every officer of the command was killed, including the commanding officer, and other casualties were very great. Considering the strong position of the enemy our casualties were very few." The Americans suffered eleven killed and thirty-six wounded, some from delayed friendly fire at the start of the assault.[76]

Captain Ben Chastaine colorfully detailed the preparation and attack on Forest Ferme and its impact on the Germans:

CLEARING THE RIVER LOOP

As if in anticipation of the attack for three days prior to the 26th the artillery of the German forces concentrated on the village opposite the loop in the river, registering many direct hits in the foxholes occupied by the waiting troops and sending something like forty gas victims from the 142nd to the hospitals. Most of these losses were on the second battalion, which already had suffered severely. But the river loop had to be cleared.

All the artillery available for a considerable distance on either flank was brought to bear on the loop. All troops were held in readiness for instant service and just as dusk began to gather a thousand infernos were concentrated into the loop from which no German was to be allowed to make his way back to his own lines in safety. The light artillery firing high explosive shells bore on the enemy's wire and known machine gun locations while the heavier pieces made all of the back areas of the loop including the village of Rilly untenable. Every yard of territory in the loop was searched by direct and indirect machine gun fire.

170 German Prisoners

Then the barrage began to roll and the doughboys began to advance at the stipulated hour. They were veterans now. Whereas all had been uncertainty and confusion before St. Etienne, all was orderly and precision now. Before the Hun could come out of his dugouts and man his machine guns the infantry were upon him a little more than anxious that there would be some show of resistance to tempt the bayonet. But there was none. Approximately 170 prisoners were captured including several officers and the toll of dead was large. Seven men of the attacking force were taken by the counter battery work of the German guns and were wounded.

Immediately [as] the ground was taken it was organized for defense and cleared of possible "booby traps." Officers and men went about their tasks with a calmness and certainty. At the conclusion of the engagement it was declared to be one of the "cleanest engagements" of the great final drive.

Serious Loss to Foe

To lose the river loop, to allow the placing of allied artillery that much nearer the river[,] meant also that the Hun must abandon extensive occupation of the towns all along the east bank of the Aisne as far down as the Argonne and that his defense of that formidable barrier must soon crumble. Lines of communication to the rear from Vouziers and Grandpre were under serious threats of being cut if the allied forces should cross the river and this threatened to materialize any day.

This was the last scrap of the thirty-sixth Division and the seventy-first brigade had earned a reputation that might well be envied by units that had been in the field longer and received more official mention . . .

With the conquering of the additional square mile of territory described in the loop of the Aisne east of Attigny the 142nd had added additional luster to its already bright history in the war and established an esprit de corps that was destined to gain for it the reputation of being the most efficient organization in the fighting forces of the division.[7]

E. W. Horner's handwritten account of the 142nd's actions of October 1918 concludes with a brief section on the assault on Forest Ferme:

When the Third Battalion of the 142nd Infantry attacked in the bend of the river near Roche on October 27th, "E" Company was the right assault company of the support battalion. From my position I could see the whole attack. It was well planned and worked out very successfully. It was during this fight that I realized fully how much aid to an attack a rolling barrage is. The Allied airplanes also did valuable work here, which I had not noticed in the previous encounter.

Taken as a whole I consider the work done by the 36th Division, the first time up, very creditable.

E.W. Horner

Capt., 142nd Inf.

10th November, 1918.[78]

Use of the Choctaw Language at Forest Ferme

Underlying the success in taking Forest Ferme was the use of Choctaw to send secure military communications before and during the assault. The use of the Choctaws proved successful, as the German forces were unable to break their transmissions. As Lieutenant Ben Chastaine (1920:231–232) described,

In the preparations of the 142nd Infantry for the attack a novel scheme of keeping the movements of the troops secret was worked out. The entire country was covered by a network of abandoned German wires which were suspected of having been left purposely in such a condition that the enemy across the river could connect up with them and "listen in" to the messages being transmitted to various parts of the American lines. More than once there had been evidence to indicate that such things were being accomplished. To overcome this condition Colonel Bloor selected some of the most intelligent Indians from Company E, composed almost entirely of redmen from Oklahoma, and stationed them at the telephones. These Indians were members of the Choctaw tribe and when the written messages were handed to them in English they transmitted them in their own tongue and it is reasonably assured that no word of this was picked up by the Huns.

Captain Byron S. Bruce, medical corps, 36th Division, documented other messages sent in Choctaw in a letter.

On the night of October 27, 1918, when I had sent Hospital Corps men with an ambulance to Chufilly unauthorized to evacuate from that post, casualties from the Advance Battalion at Mery—Roche. I was notified through the Message center that the town had been again gassed by shells. I sent a message written out, for the Indian who was transmitting, I think, a Choctaw, to another Indian, this message:

> "Hospital Corps men removed to Marqueny taking ambulance. Notify surgeon, Advance Battalion to evacuate by litter to that point."[79]

This account supports Bloor's (1919) statement that "Indians were used repeatedly on the 27th in preparation for the assault on Forest Farm" with the Choctaw sending messages into the evening.

After capturing Forest Ferme, the 142nd was withdrawn from the front line late on the night of October 28. The 144th Infantry was relieved by the French 61st Division and the reserve battalions of the 141st and 142nd were relieved by the French 22nd Division. Some assault battalions and elements of the 141st were not relieved until early on the morning of the 29th. After resting a day at Camp Montepelier, the division was assigned as a reserve in the 1st Corps, 1st American Army, and sent to a rest area twenty miles from Verdun. During the next few days, the 36th marched southeastward toward Paris to Triaucourt-Bar-le-Duc to undertake training in preparation for the upcoming offensive toward Metz (Chastaine 1920:236–237; White 1984:167–173). By the end of October, US troop had advanced ten miles and cleared the Argonne Forest of German forces. To their left, the French had advanced twenty miles through more open country to the Aisne River. On November 3 and 4, the 142nd arrived and rested at Bar-le-Duc, 120 miles east of Paris, with headquarters at Louppy-le-Petit. They began retraining on November 5 and were scheduled to move toward the front again on November 11 (Barnes 1922:39–42; Brager 2002:77; Chastaine 1920:232–249; Franks 1984:30).

During this brief training, seven days at most (November 5 to 11) as the 36th held special memorial services on the 10th and the Armistice was signed on November 11, Choctaw were detailed for training in transmitting future messages. While some English terms had Choctaw equivalents, others did not. As Bloor's report demonstrates, terms were quickly developed to convey military arms and organizational levels. Patrol became "many scouts," a grenade became "stone," regiment became "tribe," casualties became "scalps," and 2nd Battalion became "two grains of corn." During this period, the Choctaw created specialized coded vocabulary to be mixed into the Choctaw language, creating a code within an unknown language, essentially a form of double code.

However, Bloor's letter states that the Choctaws were unable to use the language again following their training and code formation at Louppy-le-Petit, as their last combat occurred at Forest Ferme on October 27.[80] Less than two weeks later, and before the 36th saw action again, the Armistice was signed on November 11, ending "the war to end all wars."

In twenty-three days of combat, the 36th Division suffered 23 officers and 1,450 men killed, 35 officers and 427 men gassed, and 80 men missing in action. The 71st Brigade, containing the Choctaw code talkers, had borne the brunt of the fighting and suffered the most casualties. The 36th was also credited with capturing three heavy pieces of artillery, six pieces of light artillery, four howitzers, seventeen trench mortars, 277 machine guns, large quantities of small arms, and 813 German prisoners of war (Franks 1984:30; Maxfield 1975:87). Some of these figures may have been higher in light of reports from St. Etienne.

Following the Armistice, the 36th Division was briefly stationed north of Bar-le-Duc. After being assigned to the US Seventh Army Corps for less than a week, they were transferred to the First Army Corps under Major General William M. Wright. Leaving Louppy-le-Petit on November 18, they began marching southeast to the 16th (Tonnerre) training area. Ten days later, the 71st and 72nd Brigades established regimental headquarters at Flogny, one hundred miles southeast of Paris. There the 36th remained part of the First United States Army and passed time awaiting new orders. The 1st, 2nd, and 3rd Battalions were headquartered at La Chapelle, Carisey, and Lignieres, respectively. The 36th Division adopted a new divisional insignia of a blue arrowhead with a khaki-colored "T" across it, imposed on a khaki background. The design represented the contributions of soldiers from both Oklahoma, represented by the arrowhead, and Texas, represented by the "T." *Arrow Head* was selected as the name of a new division newspaper in the Tonnerre area. The 36th ("Panther") Division also became known as the Arrow Head Division, and both "Arrow Heads" and "Panthers" became nicknames for individual members of the division (Chastaine 1920:17, 248–272; Franks 1984:30; White 1978:18, 1979:20n40, 1984:173–207).

During this time, training exercises, roadwork, routine duties, inspections, furloughs to European leave areas, musical and theatrical events, and sporting events helped pass the time. The 36th Division almost became football champions of the AEF, but they lost to the 89th Division.[81] According to Captain Chastaine, Company E, the 142nd "maintained its identity as an Indian company until the division was demobilized." However, it had lost many of its Indian members "by transfer"; indeed, a February 25, 1919, photo taken at Carisney, France, shows increased Caucasian personnel (Chastaine 1920:17, 248–272; White 1979:20n40; 1984:181–207). Lieutenant Horner reported to Dixon that "one-half of my Company were Indians" and in 1941 an interview with Horner reported, "Of the 250 men in Company E, under Horner's command, 225 were Indians from Oklahoma, who spoke more than 13 dialects."[82] Captain Lincoln Lavine (1921a) reports that around 150 Native Americans remained in Company E during their combat in 1918. After the Armistice, Captain Columbus Veach was transferred to the 42nd Division (Chastaine 1920:17, 248–272; White 1979:14, 20n35, 1984:181–207). In June of 1919, Joseph K. Dixon recorded from members of Company E that "Co. E. was originally composed of Indians. Were then transferred in sections to the 42nd Division. Observe that there is an entire company, Company E, composed of Indians."[83]

In April 1919, the 36th Division was ordered home. The 142nd Regiment was processed at Le Mans and boarded the USS *Pueblo* at Brest, France, setting out for the United States on May 5. Approximately 150 miles out, the ship met severe head seas. When a major swell swept over the forecastle head, nearly sixty soldiers were thrown against the ship; two were wounded and two killed when they were swept overboard. The regiment debarked at Hoboken and was processed at Camp Merritt, New Jersey. Traveling by rail via St. Louis and Oklahoma City to Camp Bowie, Texas, the 142nd was mustered out of service in mid- to late June 1919 and began returning home (Chastaine 1920:271–278; White 1979:15–19, 1984:207–217).[84]

The Idea to Use Choctaw

Determining who originated the idea to use Choctaw has long been problematic. Colonel Bloor (Chastaine 1920:231–32; White 1979:17–18), Captain Elijah W. Horner (Imon 1977:87; Kahn 1967:55; Lavine 1921b:327–328), Major William J. Morrissey, a certain Captain Lawrence (Bishinik 1986b), other officers in the 142nd such as Lieutenant Mose Bellmard (Kaw), and the code talkers themselves (Albert Billy, Solomon Lewis, James Edwards, Tobias Frazier) have all been given or claimed credit for conceiving the idea of using the Choctaw language for communications transmission.[85]

Captain Lavine (1921b:327) attributes the idea to then 1st Lt. E. W. Horner of Company E, 142nd Infantry, who was clearly involved in their use. There are several reasons to support his claim. First, many of the Choctaw who were reported to have served as code talkers (Mitchell Bobb,

James Edwards, Tobias Frazier, Noel Johnson, Soloman B. Louis, Pete May-tubby, Robert Taylor, Calvin Wilson, and George and Joseph Davenport) were all from Company E (Barnes 1922:363–365) and appeared in the company roster when it sailed from Hoboken, New Jersey, to France. Benjamin Hampton is listed in Company E, 142nd, when the 1st Oklahoma and 7th Texas were consolidated, but not at the time the regiment went on the line (Barnes 1922:293, 363–365). Second, Joseph K. Dixon took the well-published photo of Horner with five of the Choctaw Telephone Squad that included Solomon Louis, Mitchell Bobb, James Edwards, Calvin Wilson, and James Davenport, and Dixon interviewed Horner and several of these Choctaw at Camp Merritt in June 1919 and documented Horner's involvement with their use of Choctaw.[86] An interview with Solomon B. Louis reported that "Capt. E. W. Horner conceived the idea of asking certain Choctaw boys to talk over the telephone in Choctaw, so that the Germans could not understand the orders."[87] Third, lieutenants Horner and Chastaine, both in Company E since the formation of the 142nd, knew the men and Horner's involvement (Barnes 1922:245–246).

Dixon (US Congress 1920:2189) specifically credits Horner with the idea. During Congressional testimony on the reorganization of the US Army, Dixon explained, "I photographed in Camp Merritt the Choctaw telephone squad, together with Capt. Horner, who organized this telephone squad, and recently I have had an interview with Lieut. Col. William J. Morrissey, who was in command of the Second Battalion, One hundred and forty-second Infantry, Thirty-sixth Division." Dixon (US Congress 1920:2190) also testified, "It was then that Col. Morrissey and Capt. Horner conceived the idea of using the Indian in his own dialect, and . . . the messages were transmitted in the Choctaw dialect, which proved to be very effective during the short time that it was used."

In 1970, Solomon Louis described how Choctaw came to be used. Louis reports that it was following their fighting at St. Etienne in late October when his "company" was pinned down in their trenches by "crack Prussian and German Troops" and, having had all of their codes broken by the Germans, "were unable to get any messages out for help." When word passed that the Germans planned to go over the top at 7:00 A.M. the following morning, the Americans considered themselves doomed. While visiting with two other Choctaws in the trenches,

Cpl. Louis was suddenly interrupted in his conversation with two of the Choctaws. "Corporal, get out of that hole and come up here on the double" the stentorian voice of his company commander Capt. E. W. Horner bellowed out at him. "Yes Sir," Cpl. Louis said. As he was climbing out the captain asked, "How many of you Indians talk the same language?" Tossing a hasty salute at his commander, Louis quickly replied, "Eight of us sir." "We must get through to headquarters. So here's what I want you to do" Captain Horner told Louis. The captain then outlined the plan of using the Choctaw language to get the message through. "You do have a man back in headquarters don't you?" he asked. Assured that he did, the daring plan was outlined. "I sent Mitchell Bobb to man the field telephone," the 72 year-old Indian said as he recalled the historic event from his home in Bennington recently. "Acting on orders from Capt. Horner, told Louis, [the] field artillery [was directed] to send a barrage over at 5:55 A.M. It was just to last five minutes and then we were going over the top to surprise the Prussians ahead of their planned attack on us" Louis said.[88]

Louis reported that Mitchell Bobb, Ben Carterby, Robert Taylor, Pete May-tubby, James Edwards, Jeff Wilson [Nelson], and Calvin Nilson [Wilson] participated in the action, but he did not specify their arrangement.[89] (The writer misrecorded some of the surnames.)

This account raises factual, temporal, and logistical problems. The 36th attacked Forest Ferme late in the afternoon, not in the morning. They were not surrounded at St. Etienne, nor at Forest Ferme, where they had pushed the Germans back into a peninsula they were defending. Other German forces had already retreated across the Aisne. The reference to occurring in late October can only be Forest Ferme, as the 142nd was only in two major engagements, St. Etienne (October 8–12) and Forest Ferme (October 26–28).

Len Green reported in 1979 that Solomon Louis told him that the idea originated with a Captain Lawrence, a company commander who was walking through the company area one day when he happened to overhear Solomon Louis and Mitchell Bobb, both Company E, 142nd, conversing in their native Choctaw language. After listening to them for a few min-utes and realizing the possible communications advantage, he called Louis aside and asked, "Corporal, how many of you Choctaw boys do we have in this battalion?" After conferring with Bobb, Louis told Lawrence, "We have eight men who speak fluent Choctaw in the battalion, Sir." "Are any of them over in Headquarters Company?" Lawrence asked. "I think Carterby and Maytubby are over there," Louis replied. "You fellows wait right here," instructed the captain. Lawrence got onto a field telephone and discovered that Ben Carterby and Pete Maytubby were indeed attached to the Head-quarters Company. Lawrence told his commanding officer, Colonel Bloor, "Get them and have them stand by, I've got an idea that just might get these Heinies [Germans] off our backs." Calling Louis and Bobb together,

Lawrence told them, "Look I'm going to give you a message to call in to headquarters. I want you to give them a message in your language. There will be somebody there who can understand it." The message was given to Private First-Class Mitchell Bobb, who used the field telephone to deliver the first message in Choctaw to fellow Choctaw Ben Carterby, who then translated it back into English for the battalion commander, who would have been Major Morrissey. On field telephones at separate communication posts, the Choctaws quickly and accurately transmitted the messages. As Carterby was in Company D, 141st Infantry, the logistics of this connection are unclear.[90] No officer named Lawrence appears in the 142nd rosters when they entered combat (Barnes 1922:342–346, 363–365), suggesting Lawrence was confused with or misidentified as Horner.[91]

Determining Who the Choctaw Code Talkers Were

Determining the numbers and identities of the Choctaw who served as code talkers in World War I has also been extremely difficult. Several individuals have been reported and confirmed through archival sources including officers' correspondence, oral histories, photographs, and news reports. Some do not appear in such sources.

Early accounts from 36th Division officers, the *New York Sun*, Choctaw code talkers James Edwards and Solomon B. Louis, and other Choctaw state that six to eight Choctaw were used. Later sources include as many as nineteen individuals. Judy Allen of the Choctaw Nation stated that for a long time, the tribe had only the Bloor (1919) memo to go on and that other information came slowly over several years via news clippings, military records, and descendant oral testimony.[92]

Having interviewed some of the Choctaws and their commanding officer, Joseph Dixon testified (US Congress 1920:2190):

> And now let me refer to the telephone exploit of the Choctaws under Lieut. Col. Morrissey and Capt. Horner. There were six of them. It was on the 8th of October. They were in front of St. Etienne, the Champagne Front, working in conjunction with the French Fourth Army. They knew that the Germans had a superior listening-in system, and were finding out the entire movements of the American and French troops. Therefore the commander ordered over the telephone a movement of troops at a certain spot at 8 o'clock that night, which of course was a false command. At precisely 8 o'clock that night, the Germans put down a terrible barrage on the exact spot. It was then that Col. Morrissey and Capt. Horner conceived the idea of using the Indian in his own dialect, and therefore they placed six

Indians at the end of the telephone wire, three at headquarters and three on the firing line, and the messages were transmitted in the Choctaw dialect, which proved to be very effective during the short time that it was used. One can imagine that this barbed wire conversation was a barrage that nonplussed the puzzled Germans. There were, of course, difficulties in using Choctaw, as there were no words in the Choctaw tongue for many military technical expressions, so that it became necessary to make a table of substitutions.

For instance, we called regiment "the tribe," First battalion, "One grain corn," company, "Bow," platoon, "Thong," machine gun, "Little-gun-shoots-fast," artillery, "Big gun," ammunition, "Arrows," grenades, "Stones," rations, "Food," attack, "Fight," patrol, "Many scouts," casualties, "Scalps," gas, "Bad air" (just what it is).

Col. Morrissey states:

We found that the Germans knew absolutely nothing about our preparations, and were taken completely by surprise. This was the first time that we surprised the Germans during our stay in the lines, and I attribute it in many respects to the fact that the Choctaw language was used in making preparations for this attack.

And thus it comes about again that the Indian was needed to outwit the Hun.

Dixon's account contains errors, foremost of which was mixing the events of St. Etienne and Forest Ferme and the date of the use of the Choctaw language. Firsthand accounts from officers in the 36th clearly date the use of the Choctaw to October 26–27 (at Forest Ferme) instead of October 8 (at St. Etienne). Other details vary, including the number of men and the formation of code terms; these will be addressed later. However, Dixon's accounts provide useful insights into how the language was used and its effectiveness.

Lavine (1921a, 1921b:327) states that Horner assigned eight Choctaw to provide communications prior to the assault on Forest Ferme. Eventually, the Choctaw Nation reported nineteen WW I code talkers. In discussing this, one Choctaw Nation official stated that some of these individuals may not have actually served as code talkers.[93] As this section demonstrates, there are valid reasons for the different estimates.

For many years, I suspected that six to eight Choctaw were originally used at Forest Ferme, after which others were recruited for the week of code training at Louppy-le-Petit. This scenario is suggested by two sources but has never been examined by scholars. First, Lieutenant John Eddy's study on Native Americans in World War I states, "Captain E. W. Horner,

Co. E., 142nd Infantry . . . was called upon by Division G-2 to furnish if possible a number of Indians speaking the same language and capable of working telephones within the Division, the idea being to maintain secret transmissions of intelligence. Captain Horner detailed eight educated Choctaws for the work. They served efficiently in the experiment and it was a success. The use of Indian tongues certainly provides nearly absolutely safe code for important intelligence transmission."[94]

A second source is from Lieutenant Temple Black (Cheyenne), the 142nd regimental liaison officer. After the 142nd was relieved at Forest Ferme and moved to Louppy-le-Petit, Black was charged with solving the issue of the Choctaw language lacking equivalents for military terminology by developing "substitutive expressions for some of the military terms." As Black stated, "I was in charge of the work of training these Indians, so I selected three non-coms, and eighteen men to put through a course of instruction for code training."[95] Until a record of this detail is found, if it exists, we will likely never know who the twenty-one men were.

These sources suggest that no more than eight Choctaw were used at Forest Ferme and that the larger numbers of individuals reported as WW I Choctaw code talkers since the 1980s likely come from the larger body of men gathered for code training at Louppy-le-Petit, presumably including those used at Forest Ferme who were already familiar with the process. This also clarifies why so many accounts cite eight men as having been used at Forest Ferme. While many news and popular accounts focus on the assault, only Black's account details the training at Louppy-le-Petit.

Other sources, some from the Choctaw, also report numbers and names of code talkers. In April 1919, Jonas Durant, a Choctaw from Stigler, Oklahoma, also in Company E, 142nd, and just returning from France, named six Choctaw who were used.

German "kulture" as displayed by its efficiency was not able to cope with the telephone senders when the Indian boys were put on the wires by order of General Pershing. When the Germans left their own wire apparatus, thinking that the Americans would use them, and they would tap them and overhear the conversation. The Americans did use the German wires, but—General Pershing gave out an order that Choctaw Indian soldiers were to be used on the front line for communications duty. And the Choctaws were put to work, and they did work, and the Germans were fooled. The Indian soldiers spoke in their own language and the enemy did not understand the Choctaw lingo—at least they were indifferent enough to it so that the Americans didn't give a d-.

Jonas Durant of Stigler, a Choctaw Indian soldier, who has just returned from France and was on duty with these men, was visiting the Indian Agency the other day. Durant was in the 36th division and was under the command of Captain A. W. Harner [E. W. Horner]. With him were six other Choctaw men: Solomon Lewis [Louis] of Durant, James Edwards of Bokhoma, Noel Johnson of Smithville, George Davenport of Antlers, Calvin Wilson of Valliant and Joseph Davenport of Antlers.

Durant explained that the reason the Choctaw men were used was because they understood English and could read English. When an order was given them they would send it in the Choctaw language. The receiver of this message would then translate it back into English for the commander.[96]

The clause "with him" suggests that Durant participated in using Choctaw. An article in the *Arrowhead* (1919) reports that he received a Church War Cross for code talking.

Dixon's photos of the Choctaw Telephone Squad include Mitchell Bobb, James Davenport, James Edwards, Solomon Louis, and Calvin Wilson. A photo of Albert Billy and addresses for these men and for Pete Maytubby and a Choctaw listed as Pvt. Taylor [Robert Taylor] of Idabel, Oklahoma, are also included. The Dixon materials are listed as "Catalogue information and images for 8 images, including individual and group images of soldiers associated with the Choctaw Telephone Squad. Date: June 8, 1919."[97]

Captain Lavine (1921b:327) also states that eight Choctaw were used to send messages, but he provides no names. Five subsequent sources provide varied lists. A 1937 *Tulsa World* article, inferably based on information from "Soloman Lewis" (Louis), states that after Captain Horner thought of the idea to use the Choctaw,

Soloman Lewis [Louis] was called and asked to choose seven men who knew the language well. He selected Carterby, Wilson, Edwards, Maytubby, Nilson [Jeff Wilson or Nelson] and Taylor, who were placed on the front line, some distance apart. Joseph Oklahombi was also in the group. James Edwards was to be with the field artillery and Soloman Lewis at headquarters. It was not long until Lewis was in touch with Edwards, who told him that the Germans were making great preparations to go over the top. The others, all along the line, reported practically the same thing, but Ben Carterby's message came with more emphasis. He said, "Go quick and tell Colonel Brewer [Bloor] it is hell down here where I am. The Kaiser's crack troops are getting ready to go over the top tomorrow; they are the Prussian guards!"

In a short time, Colonel Brewer gave orders to be passed out in Choctaw to be ready to go over the top at 6 o'clock sharp the next morning ahead of the time set by the Germans. Also a message was sent to the field artillery to send a barrage over at 5:55 A.M.

When the division went over the top that day, over 500 German prisoners were captured in about thirty minutes. The ground was literally covered with dead German soldiers. About half of the company was killed and wounded.

This article also confuses the events at Forest Ferme with St. Etienne, including the time of the assault, as the Germans at Forest Ferme were south of the Aisne River, in a defensive position, few in number, had already repulsed two French assaults, and had made no offensive movement toward going over the top. The article also reports that Oklahombi distinguished himself by bringing two German prisoners toward the American lines, killing one before arriving.[98]

In 1938, the *New York Sun* reported that Solomon Lewis [Louis] chose himself, Ben Carterby, Robert Taylor, Calvin Nilson [Wilson], Pete Maytubby, James Edwards, Jeff Wilson [Nelson], and Joseph Oklahombi. In a 1941 article in the *Oklahoman*, James Edwards lists Mitchell Bobb, Calvin Wilson, Solomon Lewis [Louis], Joe Davenport, and Noel Johnson. A 1979 article states that Solomon Lewis reported himself, Bobb, Carterby, and Maytubby and later appeared in a 1986 edition of the Choctaw tribal newspaper *Bishinik*, although the article lists Lewis, Bobb, Carterby, Taylor, Nelson, Maytubby, Edwards, and Wilson. In August 1986, *Bishinik* listed eight men (Lewis, Bobb, Carterby, Taylor, Nelson, Maytubby, Edwards, Wilson) and asked anyone who was a descendant of or knew of a Choctaw code talker to write to the newspaper. Around 1990, *Bishinik* editor Judy Allen listed fourteen men (Billy, Bobb, Brown, Carterby, Edwards, Frazier, Hampton, Louis, Maytubby, Nelson, Oklahombi, Taylor, Walter Veach, and Wilson), based on family testimony and records. John Callaway and John Langelier also reported these names in publications. By 2000, the Choctaw Nation reported eighteen men whom Chief Gregory Pyle acknowledged in 2002 in a formal letter to the Six Nations of Virginia, adding George Davenport, Joseph Davenport, Noel Johnson, and Otis Leader.[99]

Benjamin Colbert Jr., mentioned as a possible code talker since at least the mid-1990s, was not on this list and was the only name not listed on the original monument at the Choctaw Capitol grounds. His inclusion is largely through information from Choctaw tribal historian Charley Jones. Colbert's assignment in Evacuation Hospital No. 19 and his late departure to Europe from New York on August 31, 1918, make his association with the 142nd Infantry and involvement with the code talkers logistically questionable.[100] Colbert, who was reported by descendants to have been a code talker, was removed from the list by the Choctaw Nation for lack of documentation, then reentered by the Department of Defense and recognized with a silver medal through the Code Talker Recognition Act of 2008.[101] While his name was not on the official 1986 gray granite memorial at the Choctaw Capitol in Tuskahoma, he was added to the black granite Choctaw code talker monument erected in 2018.[102]

Benjamin Hampton described using Choctaw during the war in a 1939 interview in the *Durant Daily Democrat,* while James Edwards named several of the other code talkers in describing his use of the language in a 1941 newspaper article.[103] Tobias Frazier described his participation in a 1966 news account.[104] George Davenport's 1950 obituary states that he was a code talker.[105] Otis Leader mentions using his language in a 1958 news article.[106] Some family members tell of postcards and letters sent home from France describing their use of Choctaw (Visionmaker 2010), but those that I have seen make no mention of language use.

In a 1942 letter, Captain E. W. named five men as having served in the original eight-man Choctaw telephone squad in World War I. They are listed with their rank, assignment, and birthplace in Indian Territory (I.T.), now Oklahoma.[107]

1. Pfc. Mitchell Bobb, Smithville, I.T., Co. E, 142nd Inf.
2. Pvt. James [Joseph] H. Davenport, Finley, I.T., 142nd Inf.
3. Cpl. James M. Edwards, Oak Hill, I.T., Co. E, 142nd Inf.
4. Cpl. Soleman Bond Lewis [Louis], Hochatown, I.T., Co. E, 142nd Inf.
5. Cpl. Calvin Wilson, Eagletown, I.T., Co. E, 142nd Inf.

Horner stated that three others were used, but he could not recall their names. As he reports, all were from Company E, 142nd Infantry, and they were most likely from the following;[108] Noel Johnson, the only member to die before returning home, is referenced by Edwards, and Jeff Nelson is pictured and named in the 1937 *Tulsa World* article:

6. Pvt. Noel Johnson, Smithville, Ok., Co. E, 142nd Inf.
7. Pvt. Jeff Nelson, Kullituklo, Ok., Co. E, 142nd Inf.

Others in Company E, 142nd include:

8. Pfc. George Davenport, Finley, Ok., Co. E, 142nd Inf.
9. Sgt. Tobias W. Frazier, Spencerville, Ok., Co. E, HQ, 142nd Inf.
10. Cpl. Pete Maytubby, Broken Bow, Ok., Co. E, 142nd Inf.
11. Pfc. Robert Taylor, Bokchito / Boswell, I.T., Co. E, 142nd Inf.
12. Pvt. Jonas Durant, Stigler, Ok., Co. E, 142nd Inf.

Other Choctaw in the 36th who were reported as code talkers by fellow code talkers, relatives, and printed sources include the following:[109]

13. Pfc. Albert Billy, Howe, Ok., HQ Co., 142nd Inf.

14. Cpl. Victor Brown, Good Water, Ok., HQ. Co. 143rd Inf.

15. Pfc. Ben Carterby (Bismark), Wright City, Ok., Co. D, 141st Inf.

16. Pvt. Benjamin W. Hampton, Bennington, Ok., 142nd Inf. Field Hospital.

17. Pfc. Joseph Oklahombi, Bokchito, Ok., Co. D, 141st Inf.

18. Pfc. Benjamin Colbert, Evacuation Hospital No. 19.

19. Sgt. Otis Leader, Scipio, Ok., Co. H, 16th Inf., 1st Div.

20. Capt. Walter Veach, Durant, Ok., Co. E, 142nd Inf.

Table 1 lists the names of the Choctaw who were reported as code talkers in World War I through sources from 1919 to 1990.

Lavine (1921a, 1921b:327) appears to have been the first to report that eight Choctaw were used, indicating that "Captain Horner simply detailed eight Indians in command of Chief George Baconrind, to transmit his orders in original Choctaw, pure and undefiled." The 1938 *New York Sun* article credits Solomon Louis with choosing the other seven. "They had been selected by Solomon Lewis [Louis] who was told to choose seven trustworthy men who wouldn't flinch. And he picked Ben Carterby, Robert Taylor, Calvin Nilson [Nelson], Pete Maytubby, James Edwards, Jeff Wilson, and Joseph Oklahombi was stationed with the field artillery and Solomon Lewis at headquarters."[110] Within hours, the location of the eight Choctaws had been shifted; as Bloor reported, eventually there was a Choctaw placed in "each P.C."[111]

The 142nd was fortunate enough to have two Native American officers who spoke several of the twenty-six native languages in the regiment.[112] Although only eight Choctaw are mentioned in the earliest sources, others have been added by tribal members based on family oral histories and by supporting records that demonstrate that they were in the 141st or 142nd Infantry Regiments during the same campaigns. The Choctaw Nation eventually identified nineteen and confirmed eighteen Choctaws who served as code talkers in World War I.[113] Beyond the five men named by Horner, it is difficult to determine through comparison of multiple overlapping sources with family oral history the identities of the other three used at Forest Ferme. Nelson and Maytubby are likely. Others presumably participated in the training at Louppy-le-Petit. If Brown, Carterby, Colbert, and Oklahombi were involved, it was likely during the training at Louppy-le-Petit as they were in other regiments, suggesting that a broader use of Choctaw was planned. Many accounts do not specify whether individuals used Choctaw at Forest Ferme or during their later training. Unless military records

TABLE 1   Sources Identifying Choctaw Code Talkers by Name

	Durant* (1919)	NYS (1938)	Edwards (1937)	(1941)	Horner (1942)	Lewis (DH 1970) (TO 1979)	Choctaw (1986)	Nation (1990)
Billy	—	—	—	—	—	—	—	x
Bobb**	—	—	—	x	x	x	x	x
Brown	—	—	—	—	—	—	—	x
Carterby	—	x	x	—	—	x	x	x
Colbert	—	—	—	—	—	—	—	—
G. Davenport	x	—	—	—	—	—	—	—
J. Davenport**	x	—	—	x	x	—	—	—
Edwards**	x	x	x	x	x	x	x	x
Frazier	—	—	—	—	—	—	—	x
Hampton	—	—	—	—	—	—	—	x
Johnson	x	—	—	x	—	—	—	—
Louis**	x	x	x	x	x	x	x	x
Maytubby	—	x	x	—	—	x	x	x
Nelson	—	x	x	—	—	x	x	x
Oklahombi	—	x	x	—	—	—	—	x
Taylor	—	x	x	—	—	x	x	x
Veach	—	—	—	—	—	—	—	x
Wilson**	x	x	x	x	x	x	x	x
Otis Leader	—	—	—	—	—	—	—	—
Jonas Durant	x	—	—	—	—	—	—	—

*Full source citations listed in Bibliography

**Code talkers confirmed by E. H. Horner (1942). Horner reported three others but could not recall their names.

clarifying both groups are ever found, it will be impossible to identify and confirm everyone involved.

How the Choctaw Were Used

News accounts provide several, often conflicting statements regarding where the Choctaw communicators were positioned during the Forest Ferme assault. The placement of the Choctaw are clarified in the accounts of the assault on Forest Ferme, in the location of the companies in the 141st and 142nd in division maps that are housed at the National Archives, and in White (1984:Map 6). The 141st Infantry regiment was positioned to

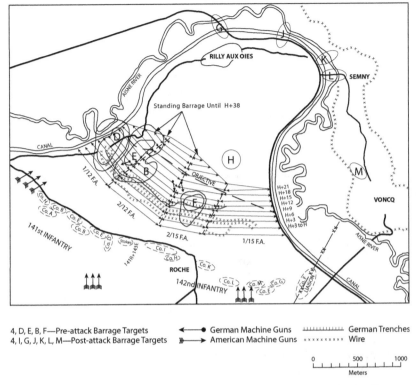

4, D, E, B, F—Pre-attack Barrage Targets   ◄———● German Machine Guns   ⊥⊥⊥⊥⊥⊥⊥⊥⊥ German Trenches
4, I, G, J, K, L, M—Post-attack Barrage Targets   ⫸———➤ American Machine Guns ××××××××× Wire

0   500   1000
Meters

Battle of Forest Ferme, France, October 26–28, 1918, Meuse-Argonne offensive. Adapted from White (1984:Map 6). Drawn by Dustin Thompson, Bernice S. Warren Center for Archaeological Research, Missouri State University, Springfield.

the left with Stokes mortars on its far right, while the 142nd Infantry was positioned to the right. Reserves from the 141st and the 143rd were placed between the 141st and 142nd. Six companies of the 142nd were on line at the start of the Forest Ferme assault (Companies I, K, L, M, G, and F), with Companies H and E in supporting positions.

Bloor (1919) reports that "Indians from the Choctaw tribe were chosen and one placed in each P.C. [command post]," while Lavine (1921a, 1921b:327) reports that eight Choctaw men were used. While it would be easy to assume that this referred to company command posts, in fact it referred to battalion and regimental command posts, as will be demonstrated. Since Bloor submitted his memo as the commanding officer of the 142nd Infantry regiment, it likely refers to the use of the Choctaw in the 142nd, which contained three battalions, and not to the entire 36th Division.

The 1918 *Stars and Stripes* article, reprinted in the *Fort Worth Star Telegram,* and the 1938 *New York Sun* article each contain inconsistencies and factual errors, namely confusing the 36th's participation at St. Etienne for St. Mihiel and mixing the events of the St. Etienne and Forest Ferme battles. However, the mention of the Choctaw using their language, the 36th facing "Prussian Guards," and the articles' context clearly refer to the battle at Forest Ferme on October 26–28, 1918.[114]

More importantly, the February 1938 *New York Sun* article was reprinted in the *Kansas City Star*. Another reprint ran the following month in the *Weiser Signal* in Idaho, where Horner then lived and was interviewed, followed by his comments and clarifications of the reprinted account.

> Captain Horner stated that due to the length of time since the occurrence there are several small discrepancies in the story. The Indians were used on the Champaign front instead of the St. Mihiel front while the 36th Division was part of the French army. The men belonged to Company E, 142nd infantry, instead of the unit mentioned in the story and captain Horner did not originate the idea. It came from regimental headquarters and he selected the Indians who were to carry it out. The Joseph Oklahombi mentioned in the article was not a member of Company E and had no part in the affair. Otherwise, Captain Horner said, the story is correct.[115]

The *New York Sun* article also maintains that after the Choctaw were placed at their assigned stations, the Germans listening in were soon confounded by the strange and unrecognizable sounds passing over the wires. After reporting positions and other matters of a routine nature, Edwards sent over a report to Solomon [Lewis] at headquarters that the Germans were making extensive preparations to attack. All along the line came messages in Choctaw to the same effect. Ben Cartaby [Carterby] had a little more to report.

> "Go quick and tell Col. Brewer [Bloor] it is hell down here where I am. The Kaiser's crack troops are getting ready to go over the top tomorrow. They are the Prussian Guards." Almost immediately, Col. Brewer gave orders to Lewis to be reported in Choctaw to go over the top at 6 o'clock the next morning in advance of the time set by the Germans. And at that same time, a message in Choctaw went to the artillery to send over a barrage at 5:55 A.M. The division went over the top as ordered. In a half hour the results had shown. The Germans had lost heavily and 500 prisoners were brought in.[116]

The 1938 *New York Sun* article, possibly drawing from the 1937 *Tulsa World* article, is problematic. Several firsthand accounts (Barnes 1922:37–39; Bloor 1919, 1922; Chastaine 1920:217–238; White 1984:160–169) indicate that the assault at Forest Ferme began at 4:30 P.M. on October 27, 1918. The

New York Sun account also mixes the St. Etienne and Forest Ferme assaults. The October 8 attack at St. Etienne began at 5:15 A.M. and resulted in the capture of "approximately 520" German prisoners, including some 208 from the cemetery (Bloor 1922:66–69). Since around 500 prisoners were captured at St. Etienne but only 190 were taken at Forest Ferme, and because the Forest Ferme attack occurred after that of St. Etienne, they clearly mistake the 142nd's two engagements and when Choctaw was actually used.[117]

In 1941, James Edwards reported that he had suggested the idea to use the Choctaw language.

> Edwards recalls that Americans officers were becoming alarmed at German wire-tapping. Every order phoned became known to the enemy. Surprises were impossible. "Maybe they can't talk Choctaw," Edwards told his commanding officer, Capt. E. W. Horner. The more the captain thought of the idea, the better he liked it, and Edwards was instructed to carry out his plan. He picked several others of his tribe—Mitchell Bobb, Calvin Wilson, Solomon Lewis [Louis], Joe Davenport, Noel Johnson, all fellow students at old Armstrong academy near Bokchito—and they formed a relay team.[118]

Four primary documents written by 142nd Infantry officers between 1919 and 1942 clarify many of the repeatedly published details. These documents clarify the date, context, organization, and method by which the Choctaw language was used to send coded messages during World War I.[119] The first is a report to the commanding general of the 36th Division, General Smith, dated January, 23, 1919, titled "Transmitting messages in Choctaw" and marked to the attention of Captain Alexander White Spence of Dallas, the official division historian. Written by Colonel Bloor (1919, 1922), this strategy was discussed in detail (White 1978:9, 1979:17–18).[120]

> Headquarters 142d Infantry, A. E. F.
> January 23, 1919. A. P. O. No. 796.
> From: C.O. 142d Infantry.
> To: The Commanding General 36th Division (Attention
>   Capt. Spence).
> Subject: Transmitting Messages in Choctaw
>
> 1 In compliance with Memorandum, Headquarters 36th Division, January 21, 1919, to C. O. 142d Infantry, the following account is submitted:
>   In the first action of the 142d Infantry at St. Etienne, it was recognized that of all the various methods of liaison the telephone presented the greatest possibilities. The field of rocket signals is restricted to a small number of agreed signals. The runner system

is slow and hazardous. T.P.S. is always an uncertain quantity. It may work beautifully and again, it may be entirely worthless. The available means, therefore, for the rapid and full transmission of information are the radio, buzzer, and telephone, and of these the telephone was by far the superior,—provided it could be used without let or hindrance,—provided straight to the point information could be given.

It was well understood however that the German was a past master in the art of "listening in." Moreover, from St. Etienne to the Aisne we had traveled through a country netted with German wire and cables. We established P.C.'s in dugouts and houses, but recently occupied by him. There was every reason to believe every decipherable message or word going over our wires also went to the enemy. A rumor was out that our Division had given false co-ordinates of our supply dump, and that in thirty minutes the enemy shells were falling on the point. We felt sure the enemy knew too much. It was therefore necessary to code every message of importance and coding and decoding took valuable time.

While comparatively inactive at Vaux-Champagne, it was remembered that the regiment possessed a company of Indians. They spoke twenty-six different languages or dialects, only four or five of which were ever written. There was hardly one chance in a million that Fritz would be able to translate these dialects, and the plan to have these Indians transmit telephone messages was adopted. The regiment was fortunate in having two Indian officers who spoke several of the dialects.[121] Indians from the Choctaw tribe were chosen and one placed in each P.C.[122]

The first use of the Indians was made in ordering a delicate withdrawal of two companies of the 2nd Bn. [Battalion] from Chufilly to Chardeny on the night of October 26th. This movement was completed without mishap, although it left the Third Battalion, greatly depleted in previous fighting, without support. The Indians were used repeatedly on the 27th in preparation for the assault on Forest Farm [Ferme]. The enemy's complete surprise is evidence that he could not decipher the messages.

After the withdrawal of the regiment to Louppy-le-Petit, a number of Indians were detailed for training in transmitting messages over the telephone. The instruction was carried on by Liaison Officer Lieutenant [Templeton] Black. It had been found that the Indian's vocabulary of military terms was insufficient. The Indian [term] for "Big Gun" was used to indicate artillery. "Little gun shoot fast," was substituted for machine gun, and the battalions were indicated by "one, two, and three grains of corn." It was found that the Indian tongues do not permit verbatim translation, but at the end of the short training period at Louppy-le-Petit, the results were very gratifying, and it is believed, had the regiment gone back into the line, fine results would have been obtained. We were confident that the possibilities of the telephone had been obtained without its hazards.

A.W. Bloor,
Colonel 142d Infantry
Commanding.[123]

This document demonstrates five important points. First, the idea to use the Choctaw occurred "while comparatively inactive at Vaux-Champagne," which is east of and after the 142nd action at St. Etienne. Second, the Choctaw were used only once on October 26–27 at Forest Ferme. Third, code terms were formed after this battle, while the division was at Louppy-le-Petit. Fourth, Bloor's letter mentions the following code terms:

"Big Gun"	artillery
"Little gun shoot fast"	machine gun
"one grain of corn"	1st Battalion
"two grains of corn"	2nd Battalion
"three grains of corn"	3rd Battalion

Fifth, as the 36th saw no more action before the war ended on November 11, 1918, the code terms devised at Louppy-le-Petit were never actually used in combat. This document is of great significance as the first official government document recording the use of Native American code talkers by the AEF in WW I files.[124]

The second source of military documentation is a letter titled "Terms used by Indians over telephone" and written by Lieutenant Colonel William J. Morrissey, commander, 2nd Battalion, 142nd Infantry Regiment, to Lieutenant Eddy of the Historical Section, on March 2, 1919. This letter lists fifteen Choctaw terms for military terminology that at the time had no Choctaw language equivalents.

2 March, 1919,
A.E.F., A.P.O. #796
From: William J. Morrissey, Lt.-Col., 142nd Infantry.
To: Lieut. John P. Eddy, Historical Section, G.S., G.H.Q
Subject: Terms used by Indians over telephone.

1. As per our conversation of recent date, I am sending you the following talle of substitutions. The column on the left indicates the terms that were found incapable of translation into the Indian

Language. The corresponding terms in the right hand column were found capable of translation and were used in transmitting messages over the telephone by Choctaw Indians, during the time the 36th Division was in the line.

Regiment	The Tribe
1st Battalion	1 Grain corn
2nd Battalion	2 Grains of corn
3rd Battalion	5 Grains of corn
Company	Bow
Platoon	Thong
Machine Gun	Little gun shoot fast
Artillery	Big gun
Ammunition	Arrows
Grenade	Stones
Rations	Food
Attack	Fight
Patrol	Many scouts
Casualties	Scalps
Gas	Bad air

2. The above table is written from memory but I believe it is approximately correct.
Signed
William J. Morrissey
Lt-Colonel 142nd Infantry.[125]

Only recently have two other newly discovered documents clarified many of the seminal questions and facts regarding the Choctaw communicators in World War I. In September 2018, Erin Fehr located and contacted Kathryn Horner Widder, the daughter of Elijah W. Horner, in Arkansas. Among Kathryn Widder's father's papers were copies of two documents pertinent to the use of the Choctaw in the war and Horner's role in that project. On January 31, 1942, E. M. Kirby, Chief Radio Branch in Washington, DC, wired then Major E. W. Horner:

CAPTAIN E.W. HORNER
183 RD FIELD ARTLY
FTLEWIS WN

PLEASE ADVISE RETURN AIRMAIL IF POSSIBLE FULL STORY OF YOUR ACTIVITIES USING INDIANS TO TRANSMIT CONFIDENTIAL MESSAGES IN THEIR NATIVE TONGUES DURING LAST WAR ARE ANY OF THESE INDIANS

OR THEIR SONS AVAILABLE OF [SIC] SO NAME ADDRESS DO YOU KNOW OF
ANY SUCH ACTIVITY IN PRESENT ARMY TRAINING OR PRACTICE
EM// E M KIRBY CHIEF RADIO BRANCH 645 PM.[126]

On February 10, Horner replied:

Fort Francis W. Warren, Wyoming.
February 19, 1942
SUBJECT: Indian Telephone Operators—Word War.
To: E. M. Kirby, Chief Radio Branch, Washington, D.C.

1. Your telegram of January 31, addressed to Fort Lewis, Washington was forwarded by mail to me at Fort Warren, Wyoming which accounts for delay in answering.

2. During October 1918, the 36th Division was attached to Fourth French Army and participated in the Meuse-Argonne (Champaigne) [sic] Offensive, first on the left flank of the first American Army. One company of the 142nd Infantry was composed almost entirely of Oklahoma Indians, of which thirteen tribes were represented. That was Company "E," and I was in command of the company subsequent to October 8, 1918.

3. Sometime during the last week in October, 1918, I was called to Regimental C.P. [command post], and informed by the Adjutant, Captain Nelson, that apparently the Germans were tapping our telephone wires, since every move was known to the Germans. Captain Nelson asked if I had enough Indians of one tribe to operate the telephone to the three battalions of the Regiment, using their native dialect. I informed him I did, and was requested to furnish eight men for this purpose.

4. Accordingly I selected eight Choctaw boys who had been students at a Government Academy in Oklahoma and who spoke good English. These men were placed two at the regimental C.P., and two at each battalion C.P. Messages were given to them in English, transmitted over the wire in Choctaw, and again translated into English at the battalion C.P.'s. This worked out quite successfully and was not rehearsed beforehand, since there was no time for that.

5. As stated above, this was a very short time prior to the 36th Division's being relieved from front line duty, and this system was in operation for only two days. That was long enough to convince me of the feasibility of the plan, but so far as I know, there has been no follow-up. I did read in some Army Publication last summer that Sioux Indians were being trained at Camp Robinson, Arkansas along

that line, and the article mentioned that I was first to use the system during the World war.

6. There were eight men in the "Telephone Squad" as they later became known, but the names of three of the men have escaped me. The other five were: Corporal James Edwards, Corporal Soleman Lewis [Louis], Privates James [Joseph] Davenport, Mitchell Bobb, and Calvin Wilson. Their homes were in South Eastern Oklahoma, but I have not corresponded with nor seen any of them since 1919. There is a former Lieutenant in Company "E" who I am sure can locate some or all of the men for you. He is Major Highlan Mitchell, Durant, Oklahoma, C/O Post Office Department. Should you desire further information, please call upon me.

E. W. Horner

Major, FA., CASC.[127]

Because Horner's letter clarifies several key issues mentioned in other sources, it is one of the most important documents extant about the Choctaw code talkers. First, Horner was approached by Adjutant Captain David Nelson at the regimental command post to find a number of Native speakers during the last week of October, 1918. Thus, the idea came from the regimental headquarters or higher, while Horner oversaw the recruitment of men and facilitated its implementation. Second, only eight Choctaw were actually used as code talkers at Forest Ferme. Third, no formation of coded terms or practice occurred before the assault. Fourth, pairs of men were placed at the regimental command post and two at each of the three battalion command posts, which total eight men. It is likely that one man at each of the three battalion positions may have been sent to a more forward position, which is suggested by the details in some of the code talkers' own accounts. This would have facilitated a more rapid dispersal of information and increased the transfer of humint intelligence of what was transpiring on the front lines. Fifth, Horner confirms that the Choctaw were used only on October 26–27, 1918, just before the 36th was relieved.

Later, Horner described that "each message sent would be transmitted in Choctaw to be transmitted into English when it was safely off the wire by another Indian stationed at another post. The method proved successful." Horner also noted that all of these Choctaw "had attended government schools and could speak both Choctaw and English."[128]

Horner named five of the eight men (James Edwards, Solomon Lewis, James (Joseph) Davenport, Mitchell Bobb, and Calvin Wilson) who appear with him in the Dixon photos. As the other three are reported to have been from Company E, 142nd Infantry, they are most likely from the remaining named Choctaws who were in the company during the Forest Ferme assault (George Davenport, Tobias Frazier, Noel Johnson, Pete Maytubby, Jeff Nelson, Robert Taylor, and Jonas Durant). Although originally in Company E, Benjamin Hampton does not appear in the list for Company E at the time of Forest Ferme and was likely then in the 142nd Infantry Field Hospital (Barnes 1922:290–297, 363–365).

Some of the earlier, more detailed sources suggest the identities of the other three code talkers. Naming seven individuals, the 1937 *Tulsa World* article pictured Calvin Wilson, Jeff Wilson (Nelson), and Solomon Lewis. Benjamin Hampton's 1939 account states that he served as a code talker.[129] George Davenport's obituary mentions him as "one of a group which transmitted information in the Choctaw language from the front lines back to interpreters in headquarters in a crucial drive against the enemy."[130] The reference to a code talker who did not survive the war is likely Noel Johnson, the only Choctaw identified as a code talker who died stateside before being discharged.

Company E of the 142nd returned to the US in July 1919 on the USS *Pueblo*. The passenger list contains nine Choctaw later reported as code talkers, by name and passenger number: Tobias Frazier (51), Mitchell Bobb (62), Cabin Wilson (91), Robert Taylor (116), George E. Davenport (119), Joseph H. Davenport (134), Solomon B. Lewis [Louis] (181), Pete Maytubby (197), and James Edwards (199). Captain Walter Veach and Noel Johnson, long associated with having been Choctaw code talkers and who were on the company embarkation roster of July 18, 1918, are missing from the return roster to the United States in May 1919.[131] Veach had been transferred, and Johnson was likely already hospitalized for tuberculosis, from which he died that November.

Because Kirby sent his telegraph to Horner less than a month after Pearl Harbor, the communication may have been related to army inquiries regarding the use of Native Americans code talkers, of which they already had small Comanche, Meskwaki, and Chippewa-Oneida groups trained and ready (Meadows 2002:67–72, 2006). Horner was also contacted by news columnist John Hix for his radio program. A 1941 article states:

> The employment of the Indians in this manner was the first time in the history of the US army that such tactics had been used and Captain Horner, commander of the company, has received nation-wide recognition through stories which have been printed concerning the code system. The facts of the incident were recently sent by Horner upon the request of John Hix, author of the newspaper and radio feature, "Strange As It Seems," who said that the story would be dramatized over the air."[132]

First Lientenat John Eddy's Study

Bloor's and Morrissey's letters were written less than two and four months after the war, respectively. They were not written specifically to document code talking but as part of the larger study directed by Lieutenant John Eddy, who was gassed while serving with the 4th Division in the war and evacuated back to the United States. Deeply interested in Native Americans and believing they might best be used as future scouts, Eddy sought to undertake a historical study and assessment of Native American accomplishments in the war (White 1979:16–17; Wise 1931:533–534).

Shortly after the Armistice, Eddy approached Lieutenant Colonel E. Bowditch of the AEF General Headquarters regarding his proposed study. With a letter of introduction, his request proceeded through channels until he was directed to proceed to the chief, Historical Section at the AEF General Headquarters.[133] He soon designed a questionnaire to elicit facts and assess the military performance and value of Native Americans in the war from individual Native American troops and their commanding officers (usually company commanders). The survey was distributed to over 1,500 combat units by Brigadier General Oliver L. Spaulding, chief, Historical Section, G.S., assisted by Jennings C. Wise. Officers in several divisions were solicited to implement the survey, including many in the 36th who had either commanded Indigenous troops or were familiar enough with their performance to judge them as soldiers (White 1979:16–17; Wise 1931:533–534).

The survey focused on existing beliefs of Native American abilities held by non-Natives. In samples of questionnaires given to the 7th, 10th, and 41st Divisions, the first half, labeled "Generally," assessed Native's ability to stand "nervous strain," to be a natural leader in the ranks, and to interact and be popular with whites. The second half, titled "Scouting," focused on issues of "courage, endurance, good humor, keenness of senses and dexterity, judgment and initiative," ability as runners at night, skill with maps and buzzers, and skills in observing and verbal reporting.[134]

The survey assessment of code talker Calvin Atchavit, a Comanche who served in the 357th Regiment, 90th Division (see chapter five) provides an example:

GENERAL HEADQUARTERS
AMERICAN EXPEDITIONARY FORCES

Historical Section, G. S.

Points of inquiry concerning the American Indian as a soldier and more specifically as a scout.

Generally:

1. Does he stand the nervous strain?   YES
   (Medical Corps statistics and observation
   of commanding officer)
2. Does he prove a natural leader in the ranks?   YES
3. Does he associate readily with white men?   YES
4. Is he regarded by the whites as an unusually   YES
   "good" man.
5. Has he demonstrated fitness for any   INFANTRY
   special arm?

Scouting:

6. What capacity has he shown under following heads:
   a. Courage, endurance, good humor.   GOOD
   b. Keenness of senses; dexterity.   GOOD
   c. Judgment and initiative.   GOOD
   d. Ability to utilize mechanical methods;   FAIR
      maps; buzzers, etc.
   e. As night worker, runner, observer,   EXCELLENT
      and verbal reporter."

Jessie, 1489893, Bunnie, Sergt. Co. D. 142nd Infantry.[135]

Eddy's materials and their analysis (White 1976:21–22, 1984:219–220) demonstrate that he believed Native Americans possessed natural or "inherited characteristics" and would best be utilized as scouts in future military service. Commanders in the 36th commended the Native Americans' work ethic, truthfulness, good behavior, patience, athleticism, fearlessness under fire, observational skills, skill at orienting themselves, and willingness to volunteer for hazardous duty. Noting that most Native Americans in his battalion were National Guardsmen and had some education, Captain Ethan A. Simpson stated that he "would rather have a company of educated Indians than an ordinary company of white men." Captain John E. Morley, Company E, 142nd, likewise gave many favorable assessments of Native Americans regarding nervous strain, bravery, firearms use, scouting, sense of direction, and service as observers, runners, and in night work.[136] Believing that their deficiencies (weak in imagination, difficulty in grasping abstract ideas, reversion "to type" in combat, and proneness to using intoxicants) could be overcome with special training, Eddy proposed the formation of all-Native ranger companies after the war. Historians note that Eddy's questions were designed to elicit confirmation of non-Native views and stereotypes of Native American servicemens' behavior (White 1976:21–24, 1990:78–79; White 1984:219–220; Wise 1931:535–536, 540–543).

While scholars repeatedly point out that Eddy's survey was designed to confirm preconceived and racist—even if positive—beliefs regarding Native martial abilities, there is also merit in his findings. Many Native soldiers from more rural, subsistence-based backgrounds often performed out-of-door activities better than some—often urban—non-Natives. Natives often accepted, and in many cases even volunteered for, more hazardous assignments and positions. Some appear to have accepted—and often even embraced—the stereotypical characterizations of their martial capabilities. These observations were reinforced by scores of officers' detailed firsthand reports describing the willingness, lack of complaint, and accomplishments of Native soldiers in combat.

Supported by many accounts of Natives' service from commanding officers, Eddy's study culminated in a seven-page report titled "American Indians as Battalion Scouts" and a recommendation that such units be formed in the US military.[137] While the 1919 memos of Bloor and Morrissey and the briefer accounts from other officers describing the use of the Choctaw Native Americans were a result of Eddy's survey and biologically based assumptions, they nonetheless provided primary sources on the use of Choctaw and other Indigenous languages in World War I. In addition, the five code terms provided by Bloor match those in Morrissey's larger list.

Joseph Dixon

Another primary source on the Choctaw communicators comes from Joseph K. Dixon, who began interviewing and photographing returning Native American soldiers and sailors at military bases and hospitals on the East Coast in 1919.[138] On June 7–8, 1919, Dixon photographed five of the Choctaw code talkers with Captain Elijah W. Horner and Albert Billy in a series of group and individual photographs at Camp Merritt, New Jersey. Dixon also interviewed Horner, and possibly some of the Choctaws, and recorded tribal affiliations, brief biographical information, and post office addresses of the hometowns of Choctaws Mitchell Bobb, Calvin Wilson, James Edwards, Solomon Lewis [Louis], Pete Maytubby, Albert Billy, Robert Taylor, James Davenport, Native Americans of other tribes, and several officers of the 142nd, including Horner and Morrissey.

Titled "Choctaw Telephone Squad," the nature of Dixon's notes makes it difficult to determine exactly whom he recorded some of the information from. While some portions are clearly identified, others are not. Following entries on Mitchell Bobb, Calvin Wilson, James Edwards, and James Davenport, Dixon recorded, "These men all talked Choctaw on the telephone Oct. 24 [26th-27th], 1918, on the Champagne front." James Edwards "was on the battle-line, talking to headquarters. Three men were at the regimental P.C. post of command to receive the messages."[139]

But on the next page, between information on James Edwards and Major Morrissey, Dixon notes:

The telephone work took place in front of St. Etienne, Oct. 8th, Champagne front, working in conjunction with the 4th French Army. They had a code, which they composed because many of the military terms used were not found in the Choctaw tongue.

When they said "one grain of corn," they knew that meant 1st Battalion, and when they said "two grains of corn" that they meant the 2nd Battalion. Advance was the word "run" in Choctaw. The Boche tapped the wires. Colonel put out a fake message that they would attack on a certain cross-road. At exactly that moment, the Boche put down a fearful barrage.[140]

As specified by Bloor, Morrissey, Black, and Horner, the Choctaw language was not implemented until October 26–27 at Forest Ferme, and code terms were not created until after Forest Ferme.

Dixon reported the following testimony from Captain E. W. Horner: "With reference to the organization of the Choctaw telephone Squad: Capt. Horner called the Regimental Headquarters, found seven Choctaws. He put them out on the telephone wires and operated them for several days. Regimental headquarters were at Chufilly on the Aisne front line, or the Aisne completely. We had fourteen different tribes when we started in my Company."[141]

Although Dixon never published his data, he presented it during Congressional testimony that was later published and made public and likely discussed it with others. Dixon's intent to publish a work on Native Americans in World War I is also suggested by the entry "Send book," included with the biography and address entries he recorded for two non-Indian officers.[142]

In 1919, Dixon recorded other insights from Lieutenant Temple Black about the use of the Choctaw, their training, and code formation after Forest Ferme:

[Black] said he was in charge of runners on the line and had indirect control of telephone. A letter was sent by Colonel A. W. Bloor to the Commanding General of the 36th Division on January 23, 1919, which gives the reasons for the use of Indians on the front line for transmitting messages. We felt that there was considerable danger in transmitting messages on the line by the ordinary methods so we made use of some of the more intelligent Indians in the Regiment. The regiment was very fortunate in having an entire company of Indians from which to choose, and these Indians spoke about twenty-six different languages or dialects. There were to [two] Indian

officers in the Regiment who spoke several of these dialects. Indians from the Choctaw Tribe were chosen as best suited to perform
this duty. They were first used on the night of Oct. 26 in ordering a
delicate withdrawal of two companies of the 2nd battalion from Chufilly to Chardeny, which movement was carried out without mishap.
They were afterwards repeatedly [used] in transmitting important
messages on the front line. It was customary to write the messages
in English and they would be transmitted in the Indian dialect and
translated back into English at the other end of the line. It was discovered that the Choctaw vocabulary was limited to the more common words, so it was necessary to substitute expressions for some of
the military terms, such as "Little gun shoot fast" for machine gun,
"Big gun" for artillery, etc. I was in charge of the work of training
these Indians, so I selected three non-coms, and eighteen men to
put through a course of instruction. At first I gave them simple messages to transmit, and inside of a week they could send and receive
messages of any length with accuracy.[143]

George Baconrind (Osage) was likely one of the three NCOs (Lavine 1921a,
1921b:327).

Black's account is the only source that mentions a total of twenty-one
men, three of whom were non-commissioned offices, being trained over
the course of a "week" that could only have occurred after the Forest Ferme
fight, while at Louppy-le-Petit. The mention that the Choctaw were "repeatedly [used] in transmitting messages on the front line" would refer to their
use at Forest Ferme on October 26–27, which Bloor (1919) confirms.

In 1941, James M. Edwards provided the following Choctaw code terms
in an interview.[144]

Field artillery	Big gun
Machine gun	Fast shooting gun
Squad	Eight group
Company	Big group
Battalion	Twice big group

Most of these terms do not match those provided by Morrissey, and
there are several possibilities for the discrepancy. First, Morrissey may not
have remembered all the terms correctly. Second, because the terms were
created less than two weeks before the end of the war but were never used
in combat, they may not have become deeply ingrained in the memory of
individuals. Third, Edwards provides a translation for the term for "squad"
and Dixon states the Choctaw word for "run" was used for advance. Both
are not on Morrissey's list, raising the possibility that other code terms may

have been created that were not documented and are no longer known. Fourth, while Morrissey recorded his recollections less than four months after the war, Edwards did so nearly twenty-three years later. Nevertheless, Morrissey's account is valuable because it gives a sense of the code terms formed and is a second AEF document on the use of the Choctaw in the 36th Division. Both sources report consciously creating code words for combat communications.

Edwards claims to have contributed to the formation of several words used in the Choctaw transmissions, including "twice big group" for battalion, "eight group" for a squad, "fast shooting gun" for machine gun, and "big gun" for field artillery.[145] The fifteen words provided by Morrissey in 1919, as well as additional terms for army, soldier, and code talker (signal speaker), are provided in table 2, which is organized by military term, Choctaw term, phonetic pronunciation in Choctaw, and English translation,.[146] Lieutenant Colonel Morrissey also reported the use of the word "tribe" for regiment.[147]

Although, as Bloor (1919) states, the Choctaw did not have the opportunity to employ the code terms later devised at Louppy-le-Petit, their

TABLE 2   Choctaw Code Terms

Military Term	Choctaw	Pronunciation	Translation
1st Battalion	tanch nihi achaffa	tanch ni-hi-a-chaf-fa	one grain of corn
2nd Battalion	tanch nihi tuklo	tanch ni-hi-tuk-lo	two grains of corn
3rd Battalion	tanch nihi tahlapi	tanch ni-hi-ta-hla-pi	five grains of corn
Company	ititanapo	i-ti-ta-nam-po	bow
Platoon	hlibata	hli-ba-ta	thong
Machine gun	tanampushi	ta-nam-pu-shi	little gun shoot fast
	tushpat tokahli	tush-pat to-kah-li	
Artillery	tanampochito	ta-nam-po-chi-to	big gun
Ammunition	uski naki	is-ki na-ki	arrow
Grenade	tali	ta-li	stone
Ration	ilhpa	ilh-pa	food
Attack	ittibbi	it-tib-bi	fight
Patrol	tikba pisa lawa	tik-ba pi-sa la-wa	many scouts
Casualty	takba pisa	tak-ba pi-sa	scouts
Gas	mahli okpulo	mah-li ok-pu-lo	bad air
Code talker	chito anumpuli	chi-to a-num-pu-li	signal speaker
Army	tvshka chipota	tvsh-ka chi-po-ta	soldier, army, military
Soldier	tvshka chipota	tvsh-ka chi-po-ta	soldier, army, military

Source: Morrissey (1919); Byington (1967:347).

communications in everyday Choctaw sufficed to convey military communications that the Germans were unable to break. Not only did the Choctaws handle military communications by field telephone, they are also reported to have translated radio messages into the Choctaw language and to have written field orders in English—which Lt. Black's account confirms—to be carried by runners between the various companies. While some sources infer that the Choctaws also wrote messages in Choctaw, this seems unlikely, since their position in battalion and regimental command posts necessitated their translating the messages back into English to be handed off to English-speaking non-Native officers.[148] Had the opportunity for use arisen, the addition of coded vocabulary within vernacular Choctaw would have only strengthened the security of voice communications, creating a form of double code of specially coded vocabulary within an unknown language.

Edwards related where some of the code talkers were used. Edwards and Noel Johnson were stationed at division headquarters with the commanding officers. Solomon Louis and Calvin Wilson were placed in front-line trenches, and Joseph Davenport and Mitchell Bobb manned phones at battalion headquarters.[149]

First Lieutenant Ben H. Chastaine had been a newspaper reporter in Oklahoma before the war. Just before leaving for France, the *Oklahoman* arranged with Chastaine to write a series of narrative features chronicling the service of the 142nd in the war, which ran in March and April of 1919.[150] He contributed other articles to the *Daily Oklahoman* from 1917 to 1919, frequently mentioning the service of Native Americans. In chronicling the 36th Division, Chastaine (1920:231–32) described the Choctaws' use of their native language in the late stages of the war:

> In the preparations of the 142d Infantry for the attack a novel scheme of keeping the movements of the troops secret was worked out. The entire country was covered by a network of abandoned German wires which were suspected of having been left purposely in such a condition that the enemy across the river could connect up with them and "listen in" to the messages being transmitted to various parts of the American lines. More than once there had been evidence to indicate that such things were being accomplished. To overcome this condition Colonel Bloor selected some of the most intelligent Indians from Company E, composed almost entirely of redmen from Oklahoma, and stationed them at the telephones. These Indians were members of the Choctaw tribe and when the written messages were handed to them in English they transmitted them in their own tongue and it is reasonably assured that no word of this was picked up by the Huns.[151]

The Choctaw were instrumental in helping the 36th Division win the battle at Forest Ferme. On October 26 and October 27, 1918, the Choctaw proved the usefulness and security of their language. The capture of the German stronghold at Forest Ferme netted 194 prisoners, "only slightly less this number" killed, and "thirty-one machine guns, a large quantity of rifles, grenades, mortars, and trench stores" in approximately thirty minutes (Chastaine 1920:235).[152]

Other Native Communicators

The full extent to which other Native American groups were used for communications service is unknown. Some sources state that other Choctaw in Companies D and E of the 142nd and in the 141st and 143rd were used to transmit orders in their native languages by field telephone throughout the last two weeks of the war. However, documentation is lacking, because Forest Ferme was the last action the 36th Division saw, individuals are not named, and Horner's 1942 account states that those used at Forest Ferme were all from Company E, 142nd.[153]

Although Bloor mentions only Choctaws, General Smith and Major Robinson state that the results were so promising that other Native Americans within the regiment were similarly used for telephone communication purposes, resulting in the use of several of the Indigenous languages and dialects contained within the 36th Division. Unfortunately, these groups and individuals were not identified, and after the 142nd's last combat on October 26–28, 1918, it is not clear to whom this statement refers or when and where the deployment might have occurred. As Major Robinson, then recuperating from being gassed in France, reported at Fort Bowie in January 1919:

> The buzzer phone is an instrument used for the most important messages. No listening-in apparatus can understand the code. It is operated like a radio, but instead of breaks in sound the current is increased and decreased. There were times when messages could not be translated into code, the buzzer phone could not be used. The telephone was the only means of communication.
>
> At such times we would call some Indians. There were many representatives of the various Oklahoma tribes in the 142nd infantry. We would put a couple of Choctaws or Comanches at either end of the phone, give them the message written in English and they would speak over the phone in their own tongue. I expect the Germans had every Chinaman in their army trying to figure out the new language or code."[154]

Likewise, a 1945 source states that "a variety of Indian tongues . . . [were] used by the AEF in the last war."[155] Word of the Native Americans' success and practicality in using their native language undoubtedly spread through the ranks. Other officers may have begun using Native Americans as communications operators, but documentation to this effect is unknown. However, the use of Native American communicators in several different divisions (3rd, 30th, 36th, 90th, and possibly the 41st and 87th) at different times, of which the Hochunk (3rd Division) and Eastern Band Cherokee (30th Division) predate the first use of the Choctaw (36th Division), as well as an absence of any documentation linking these developments, suggests independent invention. Allied knowledge of the German ability to monitor Allied communications was common, as was the presence of Native Americans and the potential use of their languages in respective units. However, as a result of limited documentation, only Choctaws are presently known to have formed intentionally coded vocabulary during World War I.

Other Choctaw

Other Choctaw may have used their language for military communications during the First World War. Carrie Miller Gooding described in a 1977 oral history interview how her husband, Louis Gooding, used Choctaw to send communications during World War I. Corporal Louis Gooding (ASN 2116834) was born in 1887 in Indian Territory and is later listed as being from Valliant, Oklahoma. His mother was an Oklahoma Choctaw. Prior to enlisting, Gooding worked as an electrician for the Valliant Light and Power Company. He and Carrie Miller were married in Little Rock, Arkansas, the day before his unit departed for Europe, most likely at Camp Pike, also known as Camp Joseph Robinson. Mrs. Gooding described what her husband told her of his use of Choctaw in World War I:[156]

> He was in a field signal battalion. . . . They was in the service. They was in the field. He and a partner of his were in the signal corps and . . . they were out in this field. He and this partner were in a haystack and they were sending messages back. Because they used the continental code and they had their instruments and all. And they were sending the messages back to the headquarters and they discovered two enemy soldiers and they was copying their messages down just as fast as they was sending them. . . . They were sending their messages back to headquarters and they discovered that these enemies were copying their messages down. So your dad just thought for a second and said, "Alright brother, see what you can do

with this." So he started sending the message in the Choctaw Indian Language, which he spoke as good as you speak your English. And he started sending the messages in that. And they got so excited, the enemy soldiers, trying to figure that out, that he and his buddy got up, got their instruments up, and they slipped out. They got away. But, they sent all their messages, he sent them all back in the Choctaw Indian Language.[157]

When asked if others at the command post could understand Choctaw, Mrs. Gooding remarked, "[There were] plenty back then that knew. Because in this company there was men from Oklahoma and men from Texas that knew what it was."[158]

While some aspects of the account are lacking, such as how they knew the Germans were "copying their messages," it clearly refers to the use of Choctaw in a military context. Gooding served in Company C, 312th Field Signal Battalion, 87th Division. Drawn from Arkansas, Louisiana, and Mississippi, the 87th Division could have had Choctaw from Arkansas, Oklahoma, and Mississippi. Activated at Camp Pike, Arkansas, August 25, 1917, they went overseas between August 23 and September 13, 1918. In France, the division was assigned to service of supply and ordered to Pons (Charente-Inferieure). There it was broken up, with units placed on various work details in the intermediate section. Gooding returned to the United States in March 1919 (Britten 1997:74–75; White 1979, 1984:40; Wythe 1920:3).[159] A soldier in Gooding's company reports stringing telephone wire between Brest and Coblenz for several months (Laass 1919).

Company E, 142nd Infantry Regiment, 36th Division, at Camp Bowie, TX. Spring 1918. Courtesy of the Texas Military Forces Museum, Camp Mabry, Austin, TX.

Choctaw Telephone Squad at Camp Devons, Massachusetts. Photo W6451, Wanamaker Collection, Indiana University Museum of Archaeology and Anthropology. *Left to right:* Solomon Louis, Mitchell Bobb, James Edwards, Calvin Wilson, James Davenport, Captain Elijah W. Horner.

Colonel Alfred W. Bloor,
142nd Infantry Regiment,
36th Division, WW I.
Courtesy of the Texas
Military Forces Museum,
Camp Mabry, Austin, TX.

```
                              P. C.
                              142nd Inf.,
                              27 October '18. . . . .11:40 O'clock.


Memorandum to C. O. 3rd Bn.

        If upon reaching objective you find the enemy resistance
slight, you will send strong patrols forward to RILLY-aux-OISE
and the river loop in that vicinity will be cleaned up, after
which patrols will return to new line.  Before patrols are
sent out, however, the rocket signal "White Caterpillar" (We
are going to advance, increase range) will be made.  This
information will also be dispatched by runner and, if practicable,
by projector.  See attached plan of liaison between infantry and
artillery.


                         Bloor
                         Colonel

Cys. to -
C. O. 3rd Bn.
C. O. 2nd Bn.
```

Orders of Colonel Alfred W. Bloor that were translated into Choctaw. Forest Ferme,
France, November 27, 1918 (NARA RG-120, Box 14).

Noel Johnson (Choctaw). Courtesy of the Choctaw Code Talker's Association.

George Davenport (Choctaw). Courtesy of the Choctaw Code Talker's Association.

Benjamin Hampton (Choctaw). Courtesy of the Choctaw Code Talker's Association.

Robert Taylor (Choctaw). Courtesy of the Choctaw Code Talker's Association.

Tobias Frazier (Choctaw). Courtesy of the Choctaw Code Talker's Association.

Joseph Oklahombi (Choctaw), 141st Infantry Regiment, 36th Division. Inset of Photo by W. Hopkins, Idabel, Oklahoma. Oklahoma History Center Photo Number 4122.

Otis Leader (Choctaw), Company B, 2nd MG Battalion, 1st Brigade, 1st Division. Otis Leader Collection, Oklahoma History Center.

Company E, 142nd Infantry, June 1919. Postcard of Kathryn Horner Widder. Author's photo.

News clipping on the Choctaw code talkers with Calvin Wilson, Jeff Wilson, and Solomon B. Louis. Tulsa World 1937. Author's photo.

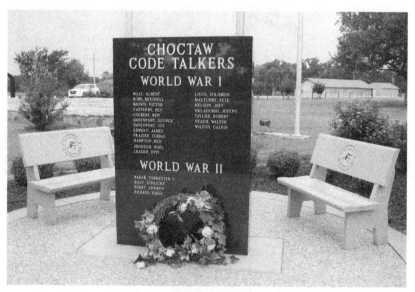

New Choctaw Code Talker Memorial, Tuskahoma, OK. Author's photo, 2016.

George Adair (Cherokee). Company E, 142nd Infantry Regiment, 36th Division, WW I. Adapted from Starr (1926:516).

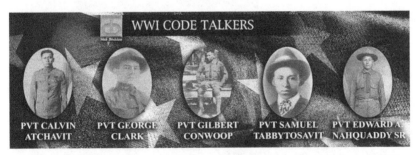

Pvt. Calvin Atchavit, Pvt. George Clark, Pvt. Gilbert Conwoop, Pvt. Samuel Tabby-tosavit, Pvt. Albert A. Nahquaddy Sr. (Comanche). Company A, 357th Infantry Regiment, 90th Division, WW I. Courtesy of the Comanche Indian Veteran's Association and Lanny Asepermy.

ists in suppressing the more hostile Indians of other tribes, though there were times when they too fought the colonists.

In the war of 1812 the Cherokees raised a regiment, joined the forces of General Andrew Jackson, and bore a prominent part in chastising the hostile Creeks.

A number of Cherokees are said to have gone to Mexico as soldiers, but not as an individual military force.

In the civil war three times Cherokee regiments under the command of Colonel William A. Phillips of the Sixth Kansas Cavalry, saw service under the stars and stripes.

In the war with Spain, Cherokees served in Cuba, some being members of the famous Rough Rider regiment. Others served in the Philippines and some in China at the time of the Boxer uprising.—*Columbus* (Ohio) *Journal.*

Winnebago Indians Upheld Record of Ancestors in World War.

Early in 1918, two Winnebago Indians in this city answered the call of their country and enlisted in the army with the hope of seeing early service in France. They were John H. Longtail and Robert Big Thunder and their record at Chateau Thierry shows that they upheld the traditions of their brave and fighting forefathers.

The two men who are cousins were members of the infantry (regulars) Third Division. It is now a matter of history that this division stood against the best of German Chateau Thierry and it was in this battle that both were wounded.

Like so many Indians in the war these men were used for scouts, snipers and telephone operators, and during their seven weeks in the front line trenches had many interesting and exciting experiences. Both went over the top three times and both withstood three attacks from the enemy.

The Indians' natural adaptability to trench warfare was reflected in the work of the men who acted as scouts. They were able to go out and get information and return safely in many cases where white men would fail. Another place where they were invaluable was in transmitting telephone messages, where there was a possibility of messages being intercepted by Germans. In these cases the Indians would transmit the messages in their own tongue.

Private Lontail has been honorably dis-

charged, while Private Big Thunder is still being treated in an eastern hospital.—*Milwaukee* (Wis.) *Sentinel.*

The Poor Indian.

North America suited the Indian exactly. He hunted, fished, fought and bade the squaws scratch up a little patch of ground for maize. One day the bow of a ship's boat crunched on a sandy beach.

It was not firewater that made an end of the Indian. Had every colony been bone dry from the start he must have gone. He vanished because, with all his splendid physique, he was not sufficiently alive. Eyes of the eagle, agility of the panther, cunning of the fox, ability to follow the trail for days on end, availed him not at all. It was a new world and he could not fit himself for a peace in it. Life of man, civilized or savage, repeatedly becomes a state of probation. The red man did not even attempt to meet the required conditions.

Time has made of "the changeless East" nothing but a phrase. China built a wall and settled down behind it to be the same forever. At first the wall seemed to give protection; with it on guard, customs among the Celestials scarcely altered from century to century. But now the wisest men of China see that Japan was right in opening its ports to all the world. The Chinese wall did not forbid the processes to which all life is subject, and the best friends of China are striving to prod her millions to make speed after a procession now centuries ahead.—*Boston Globe.*

Indian Girl Saved from Kidnaping.

At 6 o'clock last night a taxicab drew up to the home of Cyrus C. Mitchell, 1005 South Dearborn street. The driver was admitted to Mr. Mitchell's home, where he remained for twenty minutes. When he emerged he drove directly to the office of State's Atney Hoyne. There, in Assistant State's Attorney Duval's office, H. P. Paris of Oklahoma paid the taxi driver a bill for services.

Thus ended what Mr. Duval and Attorney William Brown later termed "a concerted effort for several weeks" to take to Oklahoma Miss Martha Hope, 18 year old half-breed Indian girl, who is Mr. Mitchell's Ward. Paris has gone back to Oklahoma to inform "certain interests" there that kidnap-

Article on WW I Hochunk code talkers. *Indian School Journal* (1919).

Author testifying before the Senate Committee Hearing on the Contributions of Native American Code Talkers in American Military History. US Capitol, Washington, DC, September 23, 2004. Author's photo.

Choctaw Nation Chief Gregory Pyle and Executive Director of Public Relations Judy Allen, examining materials on the Choctaw code talkers, ca. 2011. Photo courtesy of David Fitzgerald and Choctaw Nation.

Choctaw Code Talkers Association Committee, Tuskahoma, OK. September 1, 2019. Left to right: Chester Cowen, Carole Ayers, Judy Allen, Evangeline Wilson, Cynthia Quellette, Beth Lawless, Nuchi Nashoba (President). Author's photo.

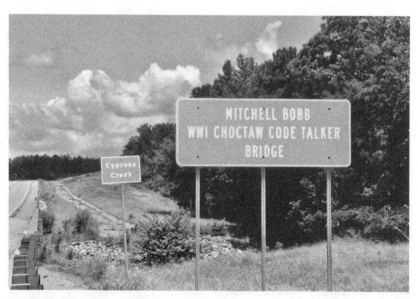

Mitchell Bobb (Choctaw) WW I Code Talker Bridge, State Highway 3, McCurtain County, OK. Photo courtesy of Judy Allen.

Choctaw Contingent with Choctaw Code Talker Congressional Gold Medal, Code Talker Congressional Gold Medal Ceremony, November 20, 2013. Left to right: Tribal Councilman Thomas Williston, Assistant Chief Gary Batton, Lt. General Ret. Leroy Sisco, Chief Gregory E. Pyle, Congressman Dan Boren, Councilmen Delton Cox, Anthony Dillard and Bob Pate. Emancipation Hall, US Capitol. Washington, DC. Author's photo.

4

THE OKLAHOMA CHOCTAW
AFTER THE WAR

According to a 1937 news article in *Tulsa World*, "All of the group who played such a wonderful part by using their native tongue at an opportune time lived to return to their own country, the old Choctaw nation. Here they are living quiet lives on farms or in timbered sections of the state."[1] Several of these men worked in lumber companies and sawmills.[2]

Following the Choctaw's return home in June 1919, word of their language use in the war spread quickly. While the army did not maintain separate records on Native American participation in World War I, their activities and contributions were regularly reported through wire releases, newspapers, and local Native American superintendents. Many articles praised the service of Native Americans soldiers and reported of their wounds, deaths, and decorations. For several months following the war, the Native troops of the 36th Division, and Native American soldiers in general, were praised in news reports and received numerous accolades from their commanding officers, often being noted for excellent service in combat and for complaining less and enduring hardships better than white soldiers.[3]

Captain Charles H. Johnson was promoted to major, appointed commanding officer of the 1st Battalion, 142nd Infantry, and received the French Croix de Guerre. Enlisted Choctaw Joseph Oklahombi, Nicholas Brown, and Bob Carr (aka Marty Beaver) all received the Croix de Guerre, the last two posthumously.[4] While several Native Americans in the 142nd were killed and many were wounded, none was captured. The Choctaw code talkers were praised by their company and battalion commanders, the later reportedly telling the eight Choctaws he was "putting them in for medals." Although Solomon Louis reported that medals were promised to the Choctaw code talkers for their communications contributions in World War I, none was awarded.[5]

An article in 36th Division newspaper, the *Arrow Head* (1919), reports Church War Crosses were awarded to fifty individuals in the 36th, including

"six Choctaw Indians who took charge of the Signal Corps telephone stations at the front and thwarted the Bosche wire tappers by relaying messages in their native language. All are of Company E, 142n Infantry. They
are Corp. Solomon B. Lewis (Louis), Corp. Noel Johnson, Privates Joseph
H. Davenport, Cabin Wilson, Jonas Durant and Mitchell Bobb."

For their performance during twenty-three days of combat, General
John Pershing, American Expeditionary Forces (AEF) commander, wrote
that the 36th's combat record was "one which all ranks may well be proud."
French President Henri Poincaré stated that the division had "proved the
valor and the spirit of discipline of its members." Paul Andre Marie Maistre,
commandant of the French 21st Corps under which the 36th served, also
praised the division's performance (Chastaine 1920:265–266, 273–277).

In public statements delivered in Washington, DC, and Fort Worth,
Texas, in June 1919, General William R. Smith refrained from singling
out any single unit of the 36th for praise, and of the varied ethnic groups
represented in the division, he mentioned the contributions of only one—
Native American. Despite reflecting the racial stereotypes of the era, Smith
noted that the Native soldiers' "hereditary cunning in forest warfare was
a wonderful asset to the Division" and related how the transmission of
messages in Indigenous languages "completely baffled the Huns." He also
noted that although several of "our Indians" were killed in combat, "not
one of them was ever taken prisoner" and that the Germans "did not like
the Indians" and "were afraid of them" (White 1984:219).

When Joseph Dixon asked how the Native Americans of the 142nd
Infantry Regiment stood as to morale in battle, Captain Horner replied,
"This is how they stood. At the battle of Meuse, in the Argonne, Oct. 6
to 29th, the marines relieved the 36th Division, and as they relieved the
Division, the 36th had never been on the firing line before. The hardest
fighting we had. Being fresh troops, the marines remained in support. The
marines never got through talking about how those Indians fought."[6]

Some evidence suggests that many Germans were fascinated, yet somewhat fearful, of Native Americans. German interest in American Indians
had existed for decades through museum displays, popular literature,
and visiting contingents of Natives in Wild West shows performing in
dances, mock battles, and hunting, and in mock villages. These shows
had toured England since 1887 and Germany since 1886, some of which
were stuck in Berlin and Trieste when the war broke out. Other influences
came from the literature of German author Karl May, who published the
first of his popular Western novels on Native American history and culture in 1887, many containing accounts of Native Americans' physical and
fighting abilities and their practice of scalping. Many Germans held the
martial abilities of Native Americans in high esteem but were unaware of

the sociocultural changes that Native peoples had undergone since entering reservations (Britten 1997:107–109; Gaffen 1985:19; Moses 1996:92,
186–188; White 1990:79).

Although unsourced, Farwell (1999:160) asserts that German newspapers tried to conceal the fact that Native Americans were fighting against
them, and during the St. Mihiel offensive, the commander of the German 97th Landwehr reportedly ordered snipers to pick off Native American soldiers when they could be recognized. A *Stars and Stripes* article
describes that "an American officer, captured by the Germans in the Battle
of St. Mihiel, was surprised to find himself interrogated not on his division's movements or objectives, nor yet on its strength, but on how many
Indians there were in the units opposing the Boches in that sector."[7]

Another entry about St. Etienne attributes a retreat by Germans to the
realization they were facing Native Americans:

> It was a genuine surprise for the Prussian Guards when they found
> themselves facing this species of American fighter, intelligence sum-
> maries failed to tell anything about them—but there were certain
> Guards who remembered that American Redskins in past wars had
> been chiefly distinguished by scalping the enemy and wearing paint
> on their faces.
>
> So it happened that when the end of the fight was nearing, Prus-
> sian Guards could be seen running over the hill tops, casting away
> their rifles, knapsacks, canteens—sacrificing everything for speed.[8]

Whether these Germans retreated out of fear of the Native Americans or
the situation of the larger battle is unknown.

During this action, a German sniper was firing at the American line
when a Sioux jumped out of his shell hole and began running toward him.
After firing at the Sioux and missing, the German began to run. The Sioux
was close behind him, yelling and whooping, with his bayonet fixed. When
the German began to head toward his own lines, his comrades began to
fire at him and the Sioux to divert them from their lines. Forced to change
his route down the line, the chase continued for nearly five minutes with
the Germans continuing to fire at both whenever they came close to their
lines, before ending in an old dugout.[9]

Other reports come from the 142nd Infantry. "According to Capt. E. W.
Horner of Company E, his Indians gave the Germans the time of their
lives. They not only scared them to death but gave them the shivers when
they turned up at night in the light of a gray moon on scout duty. The
Boche couldn't make out the red men at all. Scouting, of course, was second nature to them and they were in and out of enemy trenches and dugouts before the Prussians recovered from their scare."[10] Another article

similarly stated that "according to Captain Horner the Indians not only frightened the Germans, but gave them the dull tremors. . . . The Indian is the originator of the scouting method. He employed it in the early days of the Republic and the American Army has used it for many years."[11]

General William Smith (White 1979:16) of the 36th Division maintained that Germans were "afraid" of the Native Americans, and American intelligence reported that German commanders displayed more than a little interest in "the number and disposition of American Indians among our forces." Because Germans had few opportunities to encounter Natives outside of Wild West shows, these values were likely based on stereotypes from literature, early movies, and other media. The use of Native-style whooping or war cries likely reinforced these beliefs. Related to the European romanticism about American Indians and beliefs associated with Indian Scout Syndrome (Holm 1996), the statements and writings of German soldiers and American officers suggest that some Germans were clearly apprehensive about the presence of large numbers of Native American AEF troops, who "through their service as scouts, messengers, and telephone operators, aided the Allied victory and perhaps helped indirectly by demoralizing the enemy" (Eddy 1919; Britten 1997:108–109; Scott 1919:285; Usbeck 2015; White 1979:16). How much Native soldiers actually contributed to the German psychological fears and demoralization is unclear.

Postwar Publicity

Today, both Native and non–Native Americans, including tribal officers and those involved with recognizing code talkers, widely believe that the use of Choctaw and other Native languages used in the Great War was classified until after World War II and that the Natives involved were sworn to secrecy. I regularly encounter these beliefs in newspapers and during my talks across the country in tribal communities, military installations, universities, and civic organizations. While a few scholars have mentioned the plethora of postwar news accounts referencing the use of Native Americans for military communications, none has examined the relationship of these media sources to the use of Native American communicators or its postwar impacts.[12]

As Foreman (1943:212) notes, "Accounts were frequently published during the war concerning the excellent service of Choctaw soldiers, whose language was wholly unintelligible to the enemy, as telephone operators." Much of this popular belief has been driven by three factors. First, some copies of Bloor's (1919) memo were stamped "classification cancelled" by the adjutant general on July 8, 1946. Second, many individuals have indicated in conversations that they assume the restrictions associated with the Navajo code talkers of World War II, for which great efforts were made to keep that program secret, applied to all code talkers. Third, descendants and tribal members have indicated in conversations the assumption that because many of the code talkers did not speak of their service, they were under orders not to.

The declassification stamp on Bloor's memo raises questions. Why are most versions of the memo not stamped with any classification of secrecy? The classification cancellation stamped on the document has two dates, June 27, 1946, and July 8, 1946, representing two stages of declassification. It is also unclear what degree of classification was placed on the document, when it was considered classified, who declassified it, and why—only that it was declassified. It appears that only the copy that ended up in the National Archives RG-120 files became classified and was thus later stamped as declassified in 1946.

Shortly after the war ended, news of the Choctaws' service became public, beginning with statements by Major George Robinson and Colonel Alfred Bloor. No effort to conceal the use of the Choctaw language as a code appears to have been made. Indeed, over twenty public sources on the Choctaw code talkers appeared between 1919 and 1922 in France and the United States in public statements, interviews, and published newspaper accounts, including verbatim reprints of Bloor's (1919) memo. Significantly, most of these accounts are from officers of the 36th Division, including division commander Major General William R. Smith (White 1984:219), Colonel A. W. Bloor (1919, 1922), Major George Robinson, Captain Alexander W. Spence (1919:287–288, 300–301), other officers in the 36th and the 142nd (Barnes 1922:39; Chastaine 1920; Cope 1919:107–108; Lavine 1921a, 1921b; Wise 1931), the division newspaper the *Arrow Head* (1919), newspaper articles, and other sources (Dixon 1919; US Congress 1920:2189–2190).[13]

On January 19, 1919, Major Robinson, commander of the 111th Field Signal Battalion, then in Texas recovering from being gassed in France, reported of the use of Indian languages in an article on the 36th Division in the *Fort Worth Star Telegram*.

INDIANS THWARTED HUNS

When we wanted to give messages quickly and did not have time to translate them into code we put a couple of Indians on the phone. In the Forty-First [141st] Infantry there were a number of Indians of several different tribes. The message would be written out in English and given in the Indian. He would grunt it out in Choctaw, Comanche, or whatever he happened to be. The Indian at the other end would translate it into English.

I expect the Germans had every Chinaman in their army trying to figure out the new language or code.[14]

Two days later, a reworded but essentially similar section of Robinson's statements, cited from an unnamed January 20 Fort Worth newspaper, was reprinted in the January 21, 1919, edition of the *Daily Oklahoman*. Titled "Indian Tongue Used as Code to Dodge Spies. Enemy Listeners Couldn't Translate Army Orders Sent in Choctaw," the article left no doubt as to the nature of their service.[15] At least three versions of Robinson's account were published in three days, preceding the famous January 23 memo of regimental commander Colonel Alfred W. Bloor (1919). Whether Bloor and Robinson were in communication with one another at this time is unknown but unlikely, as these documents were produced almost simultaneously, with Robinson convalescing in Texas and Bloor still in France.

As presented in chapter 3, Bloor's (1919) and Morrissey's (1919) letters provide the earliest sources concerning using Native American languages, naming the Choctaw and detailing the dates, methods, and events that occurred.[16] Bloor's letter was printed in Flogny, France, on February 27, 1919, "told by Co. Alfred W. Bloor, commander of the 142nd, in a detailed report just filed with his commanding officer" and then again verbatim in the article "Choctaw Tongue Gave Surprise to the Germans" in the *Daily Oklahoman* on March 23, 1919.[17]

On April 26, 1919, the *Muskogee Times-Democrat* ran the article titled "Wily Yankees Outwitted Boches. Choctaw Dialect Used for Telegraphic Messages at Front: Wire-Tappers Beaten."[18] This article named the 36th Division, Captain Harner [Horner], and the names and hometowns of six of the Choctaw involved. These accounts ran before the 36th Division had even returned to the United States! While these data suggest a lack of secrecy associated with the Choctaw, even more convincing evidence soon followed.

Any question of secrecy was soon put to rest by a May 1919 article in the official AEF newspaper *Stars and Stripes* titled "Yank Indian Was Heap Big Help in Winning the War" and containing a section on the use of the Choctaw Language:

CHOCTAW CODE FOOLED BOCHE

The code was nothing more than Choctaw—plain, simple, old-fashioned, ordinary, catch-as-catch-can, everyday Choctaw. There was a Choctaw Indian at the P.C. who listened to the order given him by an American officer, and then repeated it, in Choctaw, to a fellow-tribesman at the other end of the wire: and this Indian translated it for the American officer who stood beside him. Shades of Prince

Bismarck! Everything else had the Kaiser taken into consideration when he sprinted into the late unpleasantness but he had failed to teach his soldiers or officers Choctaw.[19]

Dixon's June 1919 interviews with 36th Division officers indicate knowledge of using the Choctaw language was not only widespread, but readily discussed in detail. A Major Moore, intelligence officer; Lieutenant Temple Black, regimental liaison officer, 142nd Infantry; Captain Philip E. Barth, regimental intelligence officer, 142nd Infantry; and First Lieutenant Lucien B. Coppinger, infantry, aide to commanding general Major General Smith, all described the use of Choctaw in conducting telephone communications in their native language.[20] At least seven other accounts followed, including reports from military officers, newspapers, the US Congress, and two Choctaw code talkers.[21]

While one version of Bloor's memo contains a classification cancelled stamp, others contain no stamp, suggesting it was not classified when it was written. The version contained in the SRH-120 Report (USASA 1950) also contains no classification cancelled stamp. The responses to John Eddy's circular #1625 and other documents on the role of Native Americans in World War I also contain no classification stamps.[22] A copy of Bloor's original memo that was originally part of the responses to Lt. Eddy's circular letter #1625 in his study of Native Americans in World War I was possibly later classified as part of Eddy's documents that were eventually deposited in the National Archives as a part of RG-120 records. All of the boxes I examined dealing with World War I in the NARA RG-120 Files were declassified at the same time, with a common declassification stamp of "M. Dobbs, Maj. AGD, AGPA-G 334" and dated June 27, 1946. While we do not know why these documents were declassified at this time, Bloor's memo was not an individual declassification but part of a larger records group.

The second source of military documentation is the letter written by Lieutenant Colonel Morrissey titled "Terms used by Indians over Telephone," described earlier, that lists fifteen Choctaw terms for military terminology that the Choctaw then lacked words for in their language.[23] Both Bloor's and Morrissey's letters were written as part of Eddy's survey of Native Americans soldiers in World War I. Eddy believed that Native Americans possessed natural or "inherited characteristics" and would best be utilized as scouts in future military service. Although based on many racial stereotypes and biologically based beliefs regarding Native American physical abilities, Eddy collected invaluable data on Native Americans' service in the war (White 1976:21–24; White 1984:219–220; Wise 1931:533–536, 540–543).[24]

Division historian Captain Alexander W. Spence (1919:287–288, 300–301), who served as aide-de-camp to Major General William R. Smith and to whom Bloor's memo was written, described the use of the Choctaw and their language in his *History of the 36th Division*. Although not published, his report served as the basis of adjutant general of Texas W. D. Cope's (1919) account of the 36th Division in World War I, a public government document. In his section on Forest Ferme, Cope (1919:107–108) not only included a slightly revised version of Bloor's (1919) memo specifically describing the use of the Choctaw, but also alluded to postwar plans for Native Americans code talkers:

> A very interesting feature of this operation was the outwitting of the German intelligence Service, which had become very proficient in the art of 'listening in' on telephone messages, and thus obtaining advance information of all our movements. Among the Oklahoma National Guardsmen, there was a considerable number of Indians, many of whom were well educated and able to speak several native dialects, besides having a good understanding of English. Preparatory to this attack, Indians of the Choctaw Tribe were detailed to the different headquarters as telephone operators, and all messages were transmitted in their native language. The members of the German intelligence service, well versed in all European languages, apparently had no knowledge of the Choctaw dialects, and were therefore completely baffled. As a result, the attack was seemingly a complete surprise to the enemy. When the Armistice was signed, the American General Headquarters had made plans for the training of a large number of Indians as telephone operators, with the idea of detailing them to all American divisions on the front.[25]

Joseph K. Dixon's photographs and interviews of E. W. Horner and some of the Choctaw at Camp Meritt in 1919 included brief biographical information and post office addresses of their hometowns. Explicitly recording how they were used, his notes and group photos were titled "Choctaw Telephone Squad." That Dixon intended to publish a work on Native Americans in World War I is clear, as the entry "send book" is included in many of the biography and address entries he recorded for both Native American soldiers and their non-Native officers.[26]

Although Dixon never published his data, he clearly shared them with others. On January 28, 1920, he appeared before the Committee on Military Affairs, House of Representatives, as part of a hearing to discuss incorporating one or more divisions of Native Americans in the reorganization of the US Army. In addition to the wealth of data from his work with Native American veterans and the Wanamaker Expeditions, Dixon testified on the Choctaw Telephone Squad and its formation and use, giving a sample of thirteen code terms and naming unit affiliation and officers involved (US Congress 1920:2189–2190). At the end of the session, Mr. C. Kirk, secretary of the Klamath tribe, offered several suggestions regarding the potential use of Indigenous languages for the US military. In particular, Kirk emphasized the large number of Native American languages and their importance as codes for military wireless transmission of orders and suggested developing efforts to ensure tribal languages continued (US Congress 1920:2236):

> The fact is this, in the World War the Indian language and their tactics in warfare has been very essential, and the fact that every Indian tribe all over the United States has a different language from the other tribes on our reservation we have three tribes, and we speak three different, distinct, languages, and if there should be a school created for the benefit of the Indian, principally, I should judge that the various different languages would be a valuable asset to the War department in the transmitting of orders and codes.
>
> We have wireless systems now probably all over the world, and messages transmitted in the Indian languages would not be taken up or picked up by other countries, and for instance, if the War Department wanted to send a message to the pacific coast for a certain purpose, somebody else probably would be on the line, and the consequences are that the message would be known all over the world, because of being picked up some place else. Whereas if the message was sent in Indian, for instance in the language of the Klamath of the Pacific coast, nobody would understand that except a man on the other end of the line in Klamath; and I believe that it would be one of the greatest things for the Indian race to develop the language of all the tribes, practically, in the United States, so that we would have some record of it in history, and it would be an incentive to every Indian to learn the languages of the different tribes and make it an asset that would probably be of great value to the War Department.

Published in 1920, this testimony would have been available in any state and larger university library.

A November 13, 1921, article by Captain Lavine (1921b:326–328) also described how the Choctaw were used:

MESSAGES IN CHOCTAW

The Germans boasted that nothing could happen on the Allied side of the line that they didn't have perfect "dope" on in short order. They had a system of "listening in" on Allied telephone lines that they claimed was infallible. There was a story current in Signal Corps circles during the war concerning a telephone message to the effect that "Petee Dink wishes to talk with Grizzly Bear." A listening German broke in with, "Why don't you say Traub and Bullard instead of 'Grizzly Bear' and 'Petee Dink'? Anyway, Bullard is down the line at a conference."

The German code and language experts boasted that no code or language known to man could "get by" them.

And so one day an American officer treated them to a surprise. What one of these specialists from the land of Kultur heard, with his "listening-in" ear glued to the receiver was this: "ug blupp. Gwnee blkrup pft kowie! Gmrr-klmpp! Hwee-pstoeck!"

"Donnerwetter! Was ist das fur ein verdammten**!!???" The bespectacled Hun was baffled. He puzzled, scratched his head and nearly choked with amazement.

"What kind of language was this anyway?—this strange and incomprehensible gibberish that came dripping, gurgling and bubbling into his ears in a stream of outlandish vowels and consonants."

Perfectly simple if you knew.

In Company E, 142nd Infantry, there were 150 Indian soldiers commanded by Captain E.W. Horner of Mena, Arkansas. Captain Horner simply detailed eight Indians in command of Chief George Baconrind, to transmit his orders in original Choctaw, pure and undefiled. Himmel![27]

The following year, regimental chaplain Charles H. Barnes (1922:39) also explicitly described how and why the Choctaw were used.

In 1928, the Oklahoma City News ran another article describing the use of the Choctaw titled "Officer Who Led Indians in Rout of Germans Now Sets Type—Enemy Fooled by Wires Sent in Language of Red Men." As 1st Lt. Carl Edmonds, Company E, 142nd Infantry, described, "The enemy was tapping our telephone wires when two men from my company, which was an all-Indian company, were detailed to transmit and receive all messages in their own language. This proved a hoo-doo for the Germans as they could not figure out the messages."[28]

In November 1937, Tulsa World published the article, "How the Kaiser's Wire Tappers Were Balked by Oklahoma Indians Using Choctaw at Front." Much of the information appears to have come from an interview with Solomon Louis. The article names six other members of the group, with photographs of three of the men, and details how their language was used. The article also states, "Although not a secret of war, the trick had such far-reaching results in victory for the Allies, that no doubt it will be preserved in military records, to be used again if the need arises in the future."[29] Significantly, this statement points out what many other articles allude to but do not state: that the Choctaw's use was not an existing classified program but an impromptu innovation or "trick" developed in battle. With World War II approaching, the writer likely did not realize how prescient his prediction of using Native American languages in military conflicts again would be. Chastaine (1920:231) dubbed it a "novel scheme." In 1942, Horner, who supervised the Choctaw, referred to it as an "experiment" and a hastily organized activity with no time to rehearse or practice.[30]

In May of 1939, John Hix, author of the syndicated newspaper feature "Strange as it Seems" from Hollywood, California, wrote to the War Department in Washington, DC, on letterhead bearing the design of his column:

> I am told that American Indian telephone operators were used by the Allies during the World War to send important messages in "code"— the Indians using their native language.
>
> Has this information any foundation in fact? If so, I would like to include an item along this line in an early release of STRANGE AS IT SEEMS, my syndicated newspaper feature.
>
> Can you give me some specific instances in which Indians were employed as operators? About how many were used in the service? Which Indian dialect did the Indians speak?[31]

The letter was passed to a Mr. Maley in the "A.E.F. Records," who wrote a May 25 memo to a Miss Lemon, referencing Lt. Eddy's (1919) report and containing Colonel Bloor's (1919) memo on the role of the Choctaw in the 142nd Infantry. The letter continues:

> Your attention is invited to statements made by Major Moore, Intelligence Officer, 36th Division, and Captain Philip E. Berth, Regt'l Intelligence Officer, 142nd Infantry. Attention is also invited to letter from the Commanding Officer, 142nd Infantry, dated Jan. 23, 1919.
>
> If by the statements made by Major Moore and Captain Barth we determine that the transmitting messages in the Choctaw language was a function of G-2, 142nd Infantry, then we may have to deny the data to writer, on a strict interpretation of the memorandum for The Adjutant General dated February 25, 1939 from the Assistant Chief of Staff, G-2.[32]

Another May 25 memo added to the same page from J. E. Lyle, chief clerk, Organization Rec. Section, to a Mr. Dimond noted, "This information is wanted for publication. The data requested is contained in the attached papers. The case appears to come under Colonel Totten's memorandum on G-2 records." A handwritten note reads, "To Colonel Totten. For instructions. AGD."[33]

On May 29, Colonel A. G. D. sent a memorandum stamped "secret" to the assistant chief of staff, G-2, accompanied by Lt. Eddy's report on Native Americans in World War I:

A.E.F. file No. 99–96, A.E.F., Historical Section, G.S. 120303. Memo for Chief Historical Section, G.S. from John R. Eddy, 1st Lieut. Infantry, and papers bound thereto. Subject: The American Indian. Stamped received March 15, 1919. G.H.Q., A.E.F.

This file is classified as SECRET—(A.R. 330–5) in accordance with Memorandum for The Adjutant general of February 25, 1939 from the Assistant Chief of Staff, G-2. Subject: G-2 records retaining to the A.E.F.[34]

On June 2, 1939, Colonel E. R. W. McCabe sent a memorandum to the adjutant general directing "that a letter, substantially as follows, be sent to Mr. John Hix" containing select information regarding the use of such Native Americans in WW I communications.[35] On June 6, 1939, Major General E. B. Adams, by R. M. Fitch, issued the following letter to John Hix:

Dear Sir:

With reference to your letter of May 18, 1939, you are advised that Indians were utilized to a limited extent by one regiment of the United States Army in active operations on the Western front as supplementary telephone operators in order to transmit important messages in their language. In the 36th Division practically every Indian tribe in the Southwest was represented, including Choctaw, Comanche, Chickasaw, and Cheyenne Indians. In the latter part of October 18 [1918], the 142nd of that division made use of eight Indians of the Choctaw tribe, who were placed in important C.P.'s (Command Posts) and transmitted messages in their language. This simple method of coding messages proved to be very satisfactory, and was utilized by the regiment until the cessation of hostilities.[36]

Sources on the Choctaw continued. An August 16, 1939, Durant, Oklahoma, news article stated:

An interesting Durant visitor Wednesday was Benjamin W. Hampton, Choctaw World War I veteran who lives in Bennington. Ben's part in the US battle plan was unique but nonetheless important. High Allied officials had learned that Germans were tapping their communications lines, decoding messages, and using the information to good advantage. There's where Ben and some of his fellow

Choctaw came in. They'd speak only Choctaw over the wire, and then interpret to officers at either end. After the war it is definitely established that the Choctaw lingo defied all efforts of German code experts, which isn't surprising if you've ever heard it spoken."[37]

In 1941, WW I code talker James M. Edwards discussed the use of Choctaw, gave a sample of code terms, and offered the use of his code talking services if needed in the upcoming war.[38]

In his autobiography, Father Gregory Gerrer (1945:190–20) of St. Gregory's College in Shawnee, Oklahoma, recorded how he painted portraits of both Joseph Oklahombi and Otis Leader. Gerrer (1945:20) also noted, "These two men were born and raised in Oklahoma and still live here. During the World War, the Choctaw Indians phoned to each other, here and there and in the trenches; and puzzled the Germans, for they could not understand a word of the Indian language."[39]

Articles on the Choctaw continued for decades. A 1950 obituary for George Davenport reports, "Mr. Davenport was a WW I veteran, serving on combat duty with the famous Thirty-Sixth Division. . . . Of Indian descent he was one of a group which transmitted information in the Choctaw language from the front lines back to interpreters in headquarters in a crucial drive against the enemy."[40] A 1958 interview with Otis Leader described his use of Choctaw in the war.[41] In 1966, the *Antlers American* ran an article titled "Choctaw Tongue Proved Too Tough for German," in which Tobias Frazier related yet another account of the use of the Choctaw language in World War I.[42]

These sources from high ranking military officers, government officials, and code talkers themselves demonstrate that there was in fact no classification of secrecy associated with the Choctaw code. It was an unplanned, opportune discovery that occurred near the end of the war. Initially, its potential future use may not have been considered. The press and even some military personnel describe the use of the Choctaw and other Native languages in an almost kitsch-like fashion, as a slick trick or gimmick that fooled the Germans.

An important point that no one has raised is that the classification of a military document does not necessarily mean individual soldiers were sworn or ordered to keep the associated content—in this case their language use—secret. While a copy of the Bloor memo submitted to Lt. Eddy for his study on the experiences of Native Americans in World War I became classified after the war, it does not infer any other degree of secrecy associated with the Choctaw language or its use as a code.

Several facts suggest that no classification or secrecy was associated with the Choctaw or other codes used during the war or after. Major

Robinson's and Colonel Bloor's news accounts of January 1919 were published in France and the United States before the 36th Division returned home, and they could not have been classified until sometime after this date. Multiple accounts from other officers in the 36th appeared after returning to the United States in June 1919. The use of several tribes' languages was also reported by several individuals in addition to the Choctaw, including George Adair (Cherokee) in the 36th Division and Calvin Atchavit (Comanche) in the 90th Division. Other unidentified individuals reported on the use of Lakota (*Stars and Stripes* 1919a; *American Indian Magazine* 1919), and on Winnebago (*Indian School Journal* 1919) in the 3rd Division.

These sources suggest the brief uses of these languages in World War I were not classified and that officers and men involved were never sworn to secrecy. Otherwise, their postwar proclamations, both by non-Native officers as high as General William Smith and some of the code talkers, would be both illogical and border on treason. What appears to have happened is that a copy of Bloor's letter in Lt. Eddy's larger study was stored in military records and classified until the entire records group was declassified in 1946.

Experiences of the Choctaw Code Talkers

Accounts of some of the Choctaw code talkers' experiences have survived through military records, news accounts, and family oral histories. Military records of individual servicemen indicate that the Choctaw distinguished themselves in service. All the members were honorably discharged, and copies of several of their discharge papers contain commendable comments in several categories such as "Character: Excellent" and "Remarks: No AWOL and no absence."[43]

Sergeant Tobias Frazier, assigned to division headquarters intelligence, stated that he was wounded and sent to a hospital to recover but was recalled to make use of his language skills in an upcoming American assault on Metz, though the war ended before he could do so. This likely refers to the training at Louppy-le-Petit in early November 1918. Frazier was wounded in the fighting at St. Etienne. His discharge record states, "Slight M.G. [machine gun] Bullet left leg, 10–8–18" and that he received the Purple Heart.[44]

Victor Brown was awarded the Purple Heart for wounds received from mustard gas, a broken nose, and head injuries noted on a citation "he received from" (probably signed by) President Woodrow Wilson. As Brown's daughter Napanee Brown Coffman described, "I remember his stories of speaking in Choctaw over the telephone lines." He was pleased to have served in France and to have seen Paris, and he was proud of "fooling the Germans" with the Choctaw language.[45]

Albert Billy was caught during a gas attack without a mask. He quickly dove to the ground, dug a small hole, and placed his face in it. He survived the attack but suffered from its effects the rest of his life. Descendants stated that he turned white before he died in 1959, "whiter than any white man" as one relative described, attributing the change to the effects of the gas (Visonmaker Video 2010). Whether this was caused by gas or by a medical condition such as vitiligo is unknown. Billy apparently did not report the incident or seek aid for it, as he reported no wounds or being gassed in his No. 1625 circular.[46]

Ben Carterby reports having been wounded on the left side on his No. 1625 circular response. His discharge states that he was hit by a machine gun bullet on his left side below the shoulder. Carterby appears in a February 1919 list of Oklahoma casualties under the category "Wounded Slightly."[47]

Little is known about Noel Johnson of Smithville, Oklahoma, whom James Edwards names as one of the Choctaw code talkers in a 1941 interview. Family members and the Choctaw community long believed that he had been killed and buried in France.[48] In discussing the eight Choctaw who used their language, Solomon Louis stated in 1970 that "seven of the eight Choctaws made it through the war," but he does not name who did not.[49] Louis's statement likely refers to Johnson, who is listed in Company E when the Oklahoma and Texas units combined to form the 142nd and in Company E when the company went onto the line (Barnes 1922:249, 364) but not among those killed in action (Chastaine 1920:279–291).

Only recently has Johnson's postwar absence been explained with the acquisition of his death certificate. He returned to the United States aboard a tuberculosis ship, apparently unable to return to Oklahoma. On September 15, 1919, he is listed as a patient at the US Army General Hospital No. 19 in Buncombe County, North Carolina, near Asheville. Johnson had contracted tuberculosis and was being treated for his condition. On November 19, 1919, he died from "pulmonary tuberculosis." Ten days later, he was buried near Cove, Polk County, Arkansas, just across the state line from Choctaw country in eastern Oklahoma.[50] Although all of the Choctaw code talkers survived the war, Johnson was the first to pass.

Joseph Oklahombi

At St. Etienne, one Choctaw participated in an action that would garner him lifetime fame yet remain misunderstood for decades. For over eighty years, Joseph Oklahombi was referred to as Oklahoma's "Greatest Hero of World War I" and compared in newspaper articles as "second only to Sergeant Alvin C. York of Tennessee as America's greatest hero" of the Great War. Oklahombi has also been reported to have received numerous medals and awards for his military service in France, including the Congressional Medal of Honor, the Distinguished Service Cross, and the Silver Star. Records in the National Archives and Oklahombi's own service record show no such decorations awarded to him. Moreover, the American Silver Star award was not created until 1932. Oklahombi's military records indicate that although he performed courageously, earning both French and American awards, he was not Oklahoma's greatest hero of World War I.[51] Some sources report that Joseph Oklahombi was gassed in the Meuse-Argonne campaign, but that he did not appear to have sought treatment. I have found no documentation to confirm this, and an article based on an interview with Oklahombi states he was not wounded.[52]

While it is unclear why publications began reporting Oklahombi as the recipient of numerous military awards, once these media accolades began, a few key statements were reprinted over and over for decades without any examination of their accuracy. Despite numerous errors in the accounts about Oklahombi, the appellation as Oklahoma's greatest war hero appears clearer, most likely extrapolated from the wording in the citation accompanying his Croix de Guerre. The context of his awards and how they have become misinterpreted over time provides clarification.

Lonnie White (1984:220–221) first noticed that the wording on Oklahombi's citation, which suggests a single-handed performance, is misleading and is an excerpt of a longer citation of twenty-four individuals involved in the same combat action. Two later sources investigated the context of Oklahombi's military service and awards.[53] Louis Coleman (2002) reexamined Oklahombi's service record by comparing US and French military records with popular news accounts. His work shows that while Oklahombi performed highly commendable service, he earned only the Croix de Guerre with the French Silver Star Citation from the French, and from the Americans, the American Victory Medal and Silver Star Citation, a small star-shaped pin worn on the Victory Medal. A reexamination of news accounts and military records clarify and contextualize Oklahombi's service while showing the potential dangers that sometimes occur in news reporting.

Oklahombi reportedly walked from Wright City to Idabel to enlist for military service. However, his draft registration recorded by registrar J. W. Dewitt, in Section 1 —"Do you claim exemption from draft (specify grounds)?"—is entered with "Support of Wife." Oklahombi's #1625 circular states that he was drafted. He likely walked to Idabel upon being drafted. Born on May 1, 1895, he was just over twenty-three years of age when he registered on May 25, 1918, at Camp Bowie, Texas.[54]

Following basic training, an officer asked Oklahombi how he liked the army, to which he replied, "Too much salute; not enough shoot."[55] He soon had his opportunity at St. Etienne and Forest Ferme, serving in Company D, 141st Infantry Regiment, 71st Brigade, in the Meuse-Argonne campaign from October 6 to 29, 1918. Upon his return to the US on June 3, 1919, and his discharge at Camp Bowie, Texas, on June 19, a flurry of news accounts soon appeared. Oklahombi visited the office of the *McCurtain Gazette* newspaper in Idabel, Oklahoma, on June 19, with the English version of an extract order and citation. On June 25, the *McCurtain Gazette* ran the article, "Joseph Oklahombi Cited by Gen. Petain and Given Croix de Guerre For Conspicuous Bravery." The article states:

> Upon arrival of the Commander-in-Chief of the American Expeditionary Forces in France, the Marshall of France Commander-in-Chief of the French Armies of the East, cites the order of the Division.
> PRIVATE JOSEPH OKLAHOMBI, 1483609, OF COMPANY D, 141ST, INFANTRY
> Under a violent barrage, dashed to the attack of an enemy position, covering about 200 yards thru barbed-wire entanglements. He rushed on Machine Gun Nests, capturing 171 prisoners. He stormed a strongly held position containing more than 50 Machine Guns, and a number of Trench Mortars. Turned the captured guns on the enemy, and held said position for four days, in spite of a constant barrage of large projectiles and of gas shells. Crossed "No Man's Land" many times to get information concerning the enemy, and to assist his wounded comrades.
> At General Headquarters, the 28th February, 1919.
> The Marshal, Commander-in-Chief of the French Armies
> of the east.
> PETAIN

A copy of the citation from the French government includes the following above the signature: "CES CITATIONS COMPORTENT L'ATTRIBUTION DE LA CROIX DE GUERRE 1914–1918 AVEC E'TOILE D'ARGENT" (these citations include the award of the Croix de Guerre with Silver Star). In addition to several other classes of citation, the Croix de Guerre was commonly awarded to individual French and Allied soldiers cited for a wartime act of gallantry. The silver star reflects the second grade of the Croix de Guerre or individuals cited at the division level. The *McCurtain Gazette* article states that Oklahombi had "killed and captured more Germans than any other man except [Alvin] York, of Tennessee."[56]

The following day, an identical article ran in the *Democrat-Record* at Idabel, Oklahoma.[57] On June 29th, 1919, a brief front-page article in the *Daily*

Oklahoman titled "Indian Yank Helped Take 171 Boches" states, "Sgt. Alvin York, the Tennessean, who has been proclaimed the greatest hero of the world war, has another rival." This article reports that Oklahombi returned home on this day wearing his French Croix de Guerre and recites most of the text in his citation.[58] While correctly stating that Oklahombi "helped take 171 Boches," it included the aforementioned extract of the citation he received that when read in its English translation infers that Oklahombi took the Germans single handedly. If so, he would have qualified for the highest military award that France or America could bestow.

Similar articles followed between June 30 and July 5, 1919, with titles such as "Oklahoma Indian Captured Total of 171 Huns in War," which mistakenly states "participation in fifty successful stormings of enemy machine gun nests," "Hero," and "War Cross to an Indian." These articles, and others printed in 1925, 1932, 1940, and later, mistakenly state that he was awarded the Silver Star, Distinguished Service Cross, and Congressional Medal of Honor.[59]

On October 19, 1919, Oklahombi's photograph appeared in the *Daily Oklahoman* article "Oklahoma's Greatest Indian Hero" with the subtitle "Joseph Oklahombi Captured Single Handed 171 Germans and Silenced Fifty Machine Guns. Many Other of State's Fullblood Indian Fighters Made Wonderful War Records." Reprinting the English wording on his citation, Oklahombi is said to have "almost equaled the record of Sergeant York of Tennessee" and that, "His name has been entered on the government record of the United States Indian Agency here as the greatest Indian war hero of the world's war." This photo and label were widely disseminated.[60] Writers continued reprinting this aspect of the account without confirming it, resulting in over eighty years of confusion regarding Oklahombi's actual contribution in the assault.

While the October 19, 1919, *Daily Oklahoman* article reprints the clause from the citation, it is accurate in reporting that he received "the croix de guerre for his bravery, and a French citation signed by General Petain." Proclaimed as "Oklahoma's Greatest War Hero," Oklahombi's perceived hero status was furthered through news media, during banquets and toasts at the state legislature in Oklahoma City, by fellow Choctaw and state representative James Dyer Jr. and by veterans' groups where he was an honored guest for several months after the war. Dyer appears to have accepted Oklahombi's citation literally and was unaware that it involved a group action. News articles on Oklahombi's accomplishments have continued since 1919, during which the details of the account continued to grow.[61]

In 1987, another component to the Oklahombi story emerged through two identical publications by Barry Plunkett in the September 9 edition of the *Valliant Leader* and the November edition of the Choctaw Nation newspaper *Bishinik*. Plunkett describes that while out alone on patrol during the Meuse-Argonne campaign, "Oklahombi discovered a group of 250 German soldiers having lunch in a cemetery. Blocking the only gate to the high-walled cemetery, Oklahombi methodically killed every German who tried to offer resistance or escape. One hundred and seventy-one completely subdued Germans, all that remained alive, surrendered to him. He had killed a total of 79."[62] As will be demonstrated, this account is highly inaccurate; whether the inaccuracy stems from Plunkett or from the source of his information is unknown. Providing no source for the account, it is difficult to determine how he came by it, and I have been unable to locate him.

Oklahombi's Awards

Exactly what awards did Oklahombi garner in World War I? A review of his military records, photographs, and museum collections indicate that he earned the French Croix de Guerre with the Silver Citation Star and the American World War I Victory Medal with Meuse-Argonne and Defensive Sector Battle Clasps and a 3/16-inch Silver Citation Star.

The Croix de Guerre (Cross of War) is a French military decoration awarded to French and Allied soldiers cited for valor and bravery in battle. Originally intended to be named the Croix la Valuer Militaire (Cross of Military Valor), it was eventually renamed and adopted as the Croix de Guerre in April 1915. Degrees indicate the importance of the award. From lowest to highest, these included a bronze star (individuals mentioned at the regimental or brigade level), silver star (individuals mentioned at the divisional level), silver gilt star (individuals mentioned at the corps level), bronze palm (individuals mentioned at the army level), and silver palm (representing five bronze stars). The cross was worn with the appropriate attachments to signify one or multiple awards of the decoration.[63]

All soldiers who served honorably with the AEF in Europe qualified for the World War I Victory Medal, an American service medal accompanied by a ribbon created by the United States in 1919. Although originally intended to be created through an act of Congress, a delay in the passage of the bill resulted in service departments creating their own awards through general orders. The US Army authorized their medal in April of 1919, and the US Navy that June. This medal was known in the American armed forces as the Victory Medal until 1947 (Laslo 1986).[64]

United States WW I veterans were also issued US Army Battle Clasps, rectangular metal clasps inscribed with the names of campaigns. Many are named for cities or their respective region and are worn on the suspension ribbon of the Victory Medal to denote the campaigns one participated in. Oklahombi earned the Meuse-Argonne and Defensive Sector Battle Clasps.

The US Silver Citation Star is a 3/16-inch star-shaped silver pin that was authorized by Congress on February 4, 1919. It was issued to any member of the US Army who had been cited for gallantry in action between 1917 and 1920. The Silver Citation Star was authorized to be worn on the suspension ribbon of the World War I Victory Medal or its accompanying service ribbon to denote a citation (certificate) for "gallantry in action." The Star was awarded to any soldier or marine (attached to the 2nd Infantry Division, US Army) in the AEF after being officially cited through a general order number.

Approximately six thousand American men were awarded the Silver Citation Star, which was issued by AEF headquarters based on recommendations from lower echelons for an award of the Distinguished Service Cross. When the AEF review board determined that an action did not meet the requirements of the Distinguished Service Cross, it awarded the Silver Citation Star (Coleman 2002:205). On July 19, 1932, the Silver Citation Star was redesigned and renamed the Silver Star, and any individual who had earned a Silver Citation Star in World War I could have it converted to a Silver Star Medal, while any individual cited for gallantry in action back to the American Civil War was retroactively entitled to receive the Citation Star. Additional Silver Citation Stars were replaced by oak leaf cluster devices worn on the Silver Star Medal.

Lieutenant Charles M. Ford, Company D, 141st Regiment, recommended Oklahombi and twenty-three other men for the Distinguished Service Cross for their participation in a group action at St. Etienne. Ford's recommendation details how during the early morning of October 8, his detachment of twenty-four men advanced and attacked in the face of heavy cross fire from twenty-five enemy machine guns. The men advanced to within a few yards of the enemy emplacements when they were confronted with a band of barbed-wire entanglements fifteen feet in depth. Cutting the wire, the men rushed the enemy machine gun nests in the face of severe fire directed at them. Overwhelming the Germans manning the guns, 171 prisoners were taken. The detachment also captured fifty or more light and heavy machine guns, some light mortars, and ammunition, which they quickly reversed and prepared to use in anticipation of a German counterattack. Finding the units to their left driven back by German counterattack and those to the right not yet reaching their objectives, the Company D detachment found themselves in an exposed salient. Over the next four days, the men successfully defended the position, despite a constant barrage of German high-explosive artillery and gas shells, and made many trips into no man's-land during daytime to gather valuable information on enemy positions and to retrieve wounded comrades.[65]

Ford's recommendation for the Distinguished Service Cross was found insufficient, resulting in all twenty-four men receiving the Silver Citation Star for "gallantry in action at St. Etienne, France, 8 October, 1918." Sergeant Bud Henry, Company D, 141st Infantry Regiment, one of the other twenty-three men in the action with Oklahombi at St. Etienne received the same award. The text in his citation (Maxfield 1975:105) is identical to Oklahombi's, confirming that all twenty-four men cited on the award received identical citations and clarifying the confusion stemming from the text in Oklahombi's citation. Assertions that Oklahombi received the Silver Star appear to have confused it with the Silver Citation Star, as the Silver Star medal was not authorized until 1932 (Coleman 2002:205).

Oklahombi was awarded the French Croix de Guerre with Silver Star Citation, and it is the citation associated with this award that appears to have led to the confusion concerning his achievements and hero status. Because the 36th Division was under the operational control of the French 21st Army Corps during the battle at St. Etienne, the French command was entitled to recognize and honor the actions of any American soldier fighting under it. Following a recommendation from the 36th that the detachment from Company D, 141st Regiment, be honored for their heroism in battle, the French army decided to award the men the Croix de Guerre with Silver Star Citation. The significance of the action being awarded with the Croix de Guerre was differentiated with gold, silver, and bronze stars worn on the medal. Although some minor variation between Ford's recommendation and the French document occurs in the spelling of the men's names, all twenty-four men in the detachment are named on the same French order, with a common citation correlating with the actions described in Ford's account (Coleman 2002:207–208).[66]

Ford received the Distinguished Service Cross for the action. His citation provides other details of the group's action:

> For extraordinary heroism in action near St. Etienne, France, 9 October, 1918. After all the officers of his company had been killed or wounded, Lieut. Ford took command of the company, and with about 24 men advanced beyond the main line, over extremely difficult ground, capturing 24 machine guns. Lieut. Ford established his men in a good position, practically isolated from the rest of the line, and manning the captured guns, held the position under heavy machine gun and shell fire for about 60 hours.[67]

Confusion concerning Oklahombi's contributions occurred when each of the twenty-four men were presented with an individual citation extract translated into English from the original French citation and describing the original action. Military citations often use a condensed literary style with reduced articles and pronouns. As Coleman (2002) describes, "It should be noted that the French version of the citation does not include French equivalents of the English pronouns "he" or "his." Instead, a plural French pronoun is used, which would be consistent with the citation applying to several soldiers." In the original French citation, some portions lack pronouns, while others portions imply third person possessive plurals. However, when the individual citations were translated from French into English, singular English pronouns were replaced for the original plural pronouns in French, in particular "he" or an implied singular in place of "they," to make each of the twenty-four citations. Thus, while each of the personalized citations shows only an individual as a recipient, it contained a translated extract of the full citation written for the group that was presented earlier.[68]

A verbatim citation extract also appears in Oklahombi's No. 1625 circular response, received by the superintendent of the Five Civilized Tribes on March 19, 1921, and in a Bureau of Indian Affairs (DOI 1927:2) bulletin on the American Indian in the World War. News article dates show that upon Oklahombi's return in June 1919, the English extract of Oklahombi's citation quickly spread first across Oklahoma and Texas, then across the country. Reprinted for decades, the account has been taken at face value and never questioned.[69] A search on Newspaperarchive.com produced 110 articles on Joseph Oklahombi, most reprinting part or all of the above citation extract and referencing his single-handed capture of 171 Germans.[70]

However, while the original French citation is marked as "Extrait Certifie Conforme" (extract/excerpt certified copy) and is from a longer citation, no one appears to have thought to compare the extract with the original citation prior to Coleman (2002), who discovered the altered wording and context in the extract forms. Without access to the original French citation and not realizing that other verbatim citations existed, anyone examining the English abstract of Oklahombi's citation (or any of the other twenty-three men) would assume that each man performed these actions alone. Extract copies of the award in both French and English are in the Oklahoma History Center in Oklahoma City.[71]

During World War I, the French Croix de Guerre was commonly awarded. In the 36th Division, 415 enlisted men and officers were awarded the medal for exceptionally courageous conduct, including two fellow soldiers from McCurtain County, Oklahoma: Joe E. Prince of Valliant and Corporal Nicholas E. Brown, a Choctaw and member of Company E, 142nd, of Bokhoma. Both were killed in action on October 8, 1918, at

St. Etienne (Barnes 1922:78, 108, 363; Chastaine 1920:277, 283; White 1979:15, 1984:220–221). Many received the award posthumously.

Serving with the French army likely increased their awarding, as their actions were more likely to be observed and the French gave out many of these awards during the war. As White (1984:221) clarifies, "The Croix de Guerre was not, as the American public believed, the 'supreme award' for valor. It might compare to at the least to the Bronze Star and at the most to the Silver Star of later years. Over fifty percent of the French war crosses distributed to the 36th Division went to officers and about one-third of the total number of 36th officers in the Champagne received them." Only four Texans and three Oklahomans, all but one from the 142nd, received the Medaille Militaire, the French equivalent to the Congressional Medal of Honor, the highest authorized French decoration for enlisted personnel, ranking above the Croix de Guerre (Coleman 2002:213; White 1984:221). These seven men were also among thirty-nine men in the 36th to receive the Distinguished Service Cross, first issued in 1918. Twenty-seven of these awards went to members of the 142nd, six posthumously (Barnes 1920:184–185; Coleman 2002:213; White 1984:221).

Only two Oklahoma men in the 36th Division, both in the 142nd Regiment, were awarded the Congressional Medal of Honor, the nation's highest decoration for valor in combat. Corporal Harold Turner, Company H, from Seminole, and Sergeant Samuel Sampler, Company F, from Mangum, Oklahoma, received the Congressional Medal of Honor in recognition of their actions on October 8, 1918, near St. Etienne. These awards were earned the same day and in the same sector that Oklahombi received his Croix de Guerre (Barnes 1920:183–184; Coleman 2002:213; White 1984:221).[72] In terms of military rank, the Distinguished Service Cross and the Congressional Medal of Honor both rank above the Croix de Guerre. These facts are not intended to disparage Joseph Oklahombi or diminish his bravery and accomplishments in any way, but rather to clarify what awards he did earn, in fairness to the other men who earned the Croix de Guerre in the same action or higher awards in other actions. It also provides a valuable lesson in conducting anthropological and ethnohistorical research regarding diligence and comparison of all available sources.

While Oklahombi was clearly involved in the actions of the detachment of Company D, 141st Regiment, at St. Etienne on October 8–11, 1918, his individual contributions are difficult to determine at this point. It is also difficult to decipher exactly where the detachment containing Oklahombi garnered their award. Dated October 8, the citation and details of his action suggest that it involved capturing one of the German dugouts. Chastaine (1920:119, 146–147) and White (1984:127, 131–132) report that the Americans encountered numerous German dugouts at St. Etienne. As Chastaine (1920:146–147) describes:

> Probably in no part of the German lines from the Alps to the Channel were there larger dugouts than those in the village. They were nothing less than caverns. The one into which the relief detachment hurried for shelter had three long passageways opening out from a large central chamber in which there were bunks for 200 men and office space enough for headquarters of a division. . . . In all there were four of these great caverns in the village as well as several smaller ones."

Signs posted in the town and other indications confirmed it had in fact served this purpose. The dugout Chastaine described was located on the east edge of St. Etienne, a quarter mile before reaching the cemetery. With electric lighting, these structures were described as being more comfortable in the winter than local houses.[73]

Chastaine (1920:117–119) describes the capture, on October 8, of one dugout and over a hundred German prisoners just north of Hill 140 by a small detachment of men with grenades in the 142nd. Chastaine (1920:107–109) also notes that two detachments of the 141st pushed so far in advance of their support troops that they were in danger of being cut off from the main body of the regiment and that some elements of the 141st had advanced too far left, becoming mixed with the 142nd. As the assault proceeded and before it stalled, these small groups of the 141st advanced until they closed with enemy machine gunners. Despite threatening enemy counterattacks, one detachment maintained its advanced position, repelling one counterattack with automatic rifle and machine gun fire. The twenty-four men of Company D that Ford cited for bravery was probably one of these units (Coleman 2002:212), and likely the latter.

Chastaine (1920:116–122) mentions the cemetery east of St. Etienne as one of three German strong points that were largely missed by the American artillery barrage prior to their advance on October 8. The cemetery, ditch, and depression were occupied by the 1st Battalion, 149th German Infantry, the 12th Company of the 149th, part of the 4th Reserve Jager Battalion, and the 3rd Machine Gun Company. As Chastaine (1932:18) describes, "In the cemetery the Germans had placed machine guns upon and between the graves to excellent advantage. These guns had a firing range of between 500 and 1000 meters over an effective arc of about 180 degrees from southwest to northeast."

Nearly all of the 71st Brigade's three battalions fought across an area of undulating ground east of the village, with nearly all of the 1st and 3rd Battalions on the line. Only a few elements were held back as support troops.

As these units approached the village, they came under heavy machine gun fire from the German position in the cemetery. After taking out a machine gun in the steeple of the village church, the Americans overran the cemetery from the German's front and flank. After hand-to-hand fighting, many Germans surrendered, while others were driven to the north bank of the Arnes and up the rise toward Machault. While leading many prisoners to the east, German machine gun and artillery from the north began to hit their own men, including those bearing wounded (Chastaine 1920:116–122, 1932:10–15). The cemetery was captured by the 3rd Battalion, 71st Brigade, 142nd Infantry. After digging in and securing their line, a detachment of 2nd Engineers and marine machine gunners were added to the position in the cemetery to bolster against counterattacks (Chastaine 1920:121–129, 139, 152; 1932:15–18).

White (1984:125–126) describes the same cemetery: "The St. Etienne cemetery and the surrounding countryside were well fortified. 'Cunningly situated machine gun nests were connected by tunnels with the cemetery and with each other, and the ravine through which the Arnes brook flowed was utilized to conceal the movement of troops to and from the cemetery.'" After the German resistance on Hill 160 was broken, the 142nd closed in on strongly defended positions at the cemetery. The Germans were finally driven from the cemetery to the northeast-southwest St. Etienne-Semide Road (White 1984:137). White (1984:138) also mentions "utilizing German machine guns and ammunition captured earlier" in repulsing a German counterattack later that day. The details and timeline of these accounts, and the fact that Oklahombi and others were recommended by Lt. Ford for "gallantry in action at St. Etienne, France, 8 October, 1918," suggest that the action involved one of the large dugouts near the St. Etienne Cemetery.

During the fighting between October 8–11, the 141st suffered 194 men killed, including several officers, and 366 men wounded. The French command cited the 71st Brigade for its performance at St. Etienne. Eventually, the 141st consolidated its advance positions, and the 142nd mounted an attack to straighten the Allied line. By the evening of October 9, it became apparent that the Germans were withdrawing. The following day, the 72nd Brigade pressed the attack, pursuing the Germans, who fell back to an entrenched position in a bend in the Aisne River known as Forest Ferme. Sporadic fighting from October 13 to 26 produced few gains.

Aside from officer's accounts, little is known about the action Oklahombi and others participated in on October 8, and no other accounts from the members of the detachment are known. Oklahombi reportedly left no written accounts of the events and was reluctant to discuss the subject. While bits of information are found in news accounts, many of these are inconsistent in places and largely repeat prior accounts of his exploits. Ironically, only after his death in 1960 did a news account refer to the action at St. Etienne as a group effort. The day following his death, a news release from his home town of Wright City, Oklahoma, ran in the *Daily Oklahoman* stating, "During the campaign, he and a few of his comrades were cut off from the rest of the company. They found a German machinegun nest. After four days of holding the Germans down, help came, and 171 German soldiers were taken prisoner."[74] A similar account from the same time states, "For four days the Choctaw Indian and his buddies pinned down a German machine gun concentration. When help arrived, they took 171 German prisoners."[75]

Several sources, mostly secondary newspaper accounts, provide numerous, often contradictory, details of what transpired. A long-time friend of Oklahombi stated that he had told him of holding a number of German prisoners until other fellow soldiers reached him.[76] A similar newspaper account that may refer to the same event reports that Oklahombi discovered a group of 250 German soldiers having lunch in a walled cemetery. Blocking the gate to the walled area, he prevented the Germans from escaping. Later he was told that 171 Germans were taken captive in the cemetery.[77] A variation of this account in other newspaper reports state that after Oklahombi discovered a hole in which several Germans were hiding, he held them for three hours until help arrived to take possession of the 171 prisoners and fifty machine guns. One article describes Oklahombi as "a Choctaw Indian who held 171 Germans entrenched in a shell hole at bay for three hours until his comrades arrived."[78] Copies of this article ran across the country in October and November 1940. This source provides clues in its reference to a "hole" (dugout), and a shorter time in which the position was held. Other news accounts credit Oklahombi with capturing 171 Germans and eighty-eight machine guns, killing dozens of Germans, capturing 125 machine guns, and using a machine gun to kill seventy-nine Germans.[79]

A 1932 interview with Oklahombi, aided by a Native employee at the Veteran's Bureau, reports that he "routed 171 German from their entrenchments, lined them up, and marched them to the rear, about a quarter mile." As Oklahombi briefly described, "The Germans shoot at me. I throw back hand grenades. A lot of them. From about 100 feet. The Germans come out and I take them back. . . . Scared? Sure. That's too much to ask—not to be scared. But I start the fight. Can't do nothing but end it."[80]

The best first-hand account of Oklahombi's actions is a *Daily Oklahoman* feature written by R. G. Miller, who interviewed Oklahombi in his hometown of Wright City in 1937. After Miller found Oklahombi at the local drug store, Oklahombi suggested that they "take a ride, go out in the woods where we can have a good visit." They visited at a spot along the

Little River. Miller asked Oklahombi how he captured such a large number of Germans. The portion of the interview that follows was probably written by hand and subsequently published by Miller:

Q. Well, Joe, tell me about capturing all those Germans, how did you do it?

A. Just out in field as scout, about like this . . . lot of trees and hills . . . guns popping everywhere . . . some big cannons. . . . I see German heads sticking out of ground about far as [from here to the] river. . . . They no see me. . . . I sneak up closer . . . lot of barbed wire in way . . . in little while two, three more Germans come out of hole in ground . . . they set up machine gun . . . then they go back in hole. . . . I get closer . . . two Germans come back out . . . I shoot them . . . then I bounced over to the hole and turn machine gun on them down in hole . . . they no come out, except right by me. . . . Every time German showed his head I pop it. . . . That's all.

Q. Good Work, how long did you hold them that way?

A. Four days.

Q. Were you alone all that time?

A. Yeah, nobody come. No food, no water all that time. Battle go on all time.

Q. Well, when help did come, how many Germans did they find in the hole?

A. I believe 171, and about 50 machine guns down in there.

Q. Did the army give you any medals and things for your bravery?

A. Yes, lots of them, they in Oklahoma City, my gun and uniform, too.[81]

Compared to the wording of the original French citation, some discrepancies arise. If alone, Oklahombi could not have remained at the machine gun emplacement covering the Germans trapped in an underground fortification for four straight days, while crossing no-man's-land several times to collect information and aid his wounded comrades. However, as the French citation was written in the plural, it appears Oklahombi captured and or held the German position while other members of his unit pushed the attack forward, helped hold their position, and performed the other deeds referenced in the citation. If so, this may explain why a review of his service by his company commander was positive in many but not all aspects.[82]

This raises the question of whether Oklahombi's contributions at St. Etienne were associated with the capture of one of the dugouts, the cemetery, or both. First of all, it is highly unlikely that Oklahoma helped kill exactly 79 and capture 171 Germans on two separate occasions, one in an underground hole and another at a cemetery in a four-day assault, and only Plunkett's articles attribute the event to the cemetery. While several dugouts and the cemetery were close to St. Etienne, Chastaine describes a large dugout one-quarter mile east of the cemetery. Available records indicate it was most likely a dugout and not the cemetery that Oklahombi's squad assaulted. Chastaine (1920:117–119) described the capture of one dugout just north of Hill 140 by the 142nd in which over one hundred prisoners were taken. The cemetery at St. Etienne was taken by troops of the 3rd Battalion of the 142nd on the first day of the assault (October 8) and does not correlate with Oklahombi's actions (White 1984:138).

Two other items do not support Plunkett's descriptions. First, only portions of the St. Etienne Cemetery, located just northeast of the town, were walled, and some portions had been heavily damaged by artillery (Cansie're and Gilbert 2008:65–75; Chastaine 1920:122; Franks 1984:28). Second, the fighting to take the cemetery initially involved direct fire on the German positions in the cemetery. When the German machine gun positioned in the steeple of a nearby church in St. Etienne was finally eliminated by 37-mm rifle fire, the American infantrymen closed in on the German position. Making their way to the edge of the village, part of the assaulting troops attacked the Germans from their flank, while others made a direct frontal assault on the cemetery, resulting in close-quarters hand-to-hand combat before several Germans shouted "*Kamerad*," surrendered, and the Americans took the position (Chastaine 1920:121).

Oklahombi's 1937 account describes being "out in the field as [a] scout . . . lot of trees and hills" and the Germans coming from a hole in the ground. After receiving help, the Germans who remained underground were taken prisoner. Oklahombi reported that "I believe 171, and about 50 machine guns down in there" (Miller 1937). The references to being underground clearly indicate a dugout. His account also makes no mention of a cemetery or hand-to-hand fighting in taking it. Dugouts and the cemetery were encountered in the action at St. Etienne from September 8–11, 1918. Oklahombi, who reported maintaining his position for four straight days, could not have been in both sectors simultaneously.

A later news article states that Oklahombi held the German position for three hours rather than four days. A 1940 news release from Oklahombi's hometown, Wright City, Oklahoma, the context of which suggests that it was based on an interview with Oklahombi, states, "He is Joseph Oklahombi, . . . who held 171 Germans entrenched in a shell hole at bay for three hours until his comrades arrived." The article was published in numerous newspapers.[83] While the action at St. Etienne involved four days, how long Oklahombi held the position—four days or three hours—remains unclear, though the disparity may stem from confusion between the number of days of the action at St. Etienne (four) and the time Oklahombi actually held that particular position, as it would be difficult for a single individual to hold such a position for four days. Ford's citation states that the group held their position for sixty hours.

Confusion about where the action occurred appears to have originated with Barry Plunkett's 1987 articles in the *Valliant Leader* and *Bishinik*, describing "250 armed Germans having lunch in a cemetery," "the high-walled cemetery," and 171 Germans captured. Plunkett's article also does not match the account and map of the assault on St. Etienne by Captain Chastaine of the 142nd:[84]

NEXT RESISTANCE AT CEMETERY

The next resistance was at the cemetery. In the village the machine gunner, either because his fire no longer was effective or because he feared to be caught occupying this kind of position, deserted his post in the church steeple. Intelligence men of the second battalion assisted by others from both the first and third battalions made quick work of the jaegers in the graveyard. Advancing over the rolling ground to the right of the village the men in the cemetery soon were outflanked and compelled to desert their weapons which later were used by the Americans to perfect their position for defense.

The accompanying map in Chastaine's account shows the cemetery at St. Etienne on the northeast side of the village. From left to right, the AEF assault forces included the French, the 142nd led by Companies H and E on the left and Companies G and F on the right, and then the 141st, with the overall assault proceeding in a slightly southeast to northwest direction. In the assault, the 142nd advanced faster than the 141st, resulting in the right flank of the 142nd still exposed and subject to counterattack. Some detachments in this area were cut off and forced to retreat, resulting in a thin line of men from Hill 140 to St. Etienne who were ordered to dig in and hold their position for the night. Chastaine also reports the presence of German dugouts in the area: "On the left the same kind of thing was happening. . . . The fire from the automatics and the steady creeping around the flanks brought the Hun boiling out of his holes in the ground 117 strong. Others there were [those] who would never come up out of the ground again." His account also mentions the Americans having little or no food and water by the time they dug in on the evening of October 7 and soon depleting their supplies, having given their canteens to wounded comrades along the way.[85] This appears to have been the area where Okla-hombi and his twenty-three comrades took and held the German position and dugout. To date, I have found no other source linking his action with a cemetery, and thus the association appears to have been a mistake in confusing these two portions of the action at St. Etienne or the result of an inaccurate uncited source. The taking of the German position by Okla-hombi and twenty-three comrades was of a dugout and not the cemetery.

Oklahombi is reported to have distinguished himself in another situation by escorting prisoners back to the reserve lines where he turned them in at a French detention camp. Fellow Choctaw code talker Ben Carterby reported the incident, which was written in a first-hand, albeit stereotypical, form: "An officer saw Oklahombi at a distance coming in with two prisoners. But when he arrived, he had only one man in custody. 'Where's the other prisoner, Oklahombi?' he asked. The stoic Choctaw replied simply, 'I kill[ed] him.' Then before the officer could catch his breath Oklahombi asked, 'Want me to go back and kill him some more?'"[86] Unfortunately no location was reported in this account, and it is thus impossible to determine whether this was associated with action at St. Etienne, Forest Ferme, or other scouting and mopping up actions between these two actions.

Whether Oklahombi ever saw the complete French or English citation naming twenty-four individuals is unknown but unlikely. However, he appears to have received the abridged version of the citation in both English and French, as the aged and worn copies of both are contained in his papers at the Oklahoma History Center, both of which contain his name and army serial number. Once the English extract was published and reprinted, it was taken at face value as an individual award throughout America.

Whether Oklahombi was literate is also unclear, but three sources shed some light on the question. Several Native Americans in the 142nd were discharged in early 1918 before leaving Texas because of their English language deficiency. Although there were plans to teach recruits English as part of their training, fluency in English was not deemed essential for enlistment in World War I (White 1976:17). When R. G. Miller interviewed Oklahombi in 1937, he asked:

Q. You can read and write, can't you?
A. No, no read and write.
Q. Never did go to school?
A. No. Plenty schools to go to when I was boy, but I no go. My people didn't care about that.[87]

Some sources state that Oklahombi attended Armstrong Academy prior to his military service, which would suggest that he had some degree of fluency in English. However, the supplement circular on Oklahombi, filled out by his company commander and containing a line reading "Education (Schools & Colleges and years attended)" bears the entry "NO EDU-CATION."[88] If Oklahombi was illiterate, this might explain why he never

questioned or contested the attention he received based on others' inter-
pretation of the English version of his citation. However, because he spoke
a fair amount of English, it is hard to imagine that he did not know what
was being so frequently printed about him.

Finally, while one descendant remembers him sitting on the family
porch swing reading and singing hymns from a Choctaw hymnal (Visionmaker Video 2010), which typically used roman letters, another individual
reports that Ben Carterby's daughter told her that Carterby had to translate
for Oklahombi.[89] In addition, a 1921 news article states, "When he enlisted
he could not speak English."[90] He clearly learned to speak some English,
as indicated in interviews as early as 1921.[91]

The strongest source suggesting that Oklahombi was literate in English
is a 1925 letter from him to Mrs. Czarina Colbert Conlan of the Oklahoma
Historical Society. When compared, Oklahombi's signatures on his draft
registration card of May 28, 1917, and on the letter to Conlan of March 31,
1925, shows improvement in penmanship but are quite similar. His signatures also differ from the signature of the registrar on the draft card,
J. W. Dewitt. Oklahombi's writing skill may have improved between 1917
and 1925.[92]

If illiterate, Oklahombi would have been able neither to read messages
written in English and translate them into Choctaw nor to receive messages in Choctaw and write them in English. More importantly, Horner
states that Oklahombi was not involved at all in the use of Choctaw as a
code at Forest Ferme, which implies that if he were involved with code
talking at all, it could only have been during the later training at Louppy-
le-Petit, which according to the account of Lieutenant Temple Black, who
supervised the training, required the ability to read and write.[93]

Another story in Choctaw oral history involves Oklahombi's "panther
cry." The account states that Tobias Frazier was laughing at Oklahombi's
mimicry of a panther. One night during the war, Oklahombi decided to
play a trick on the Germans by slipping up near one of their positions and
giving his panther cry. It is reported that not only did the Germans have
the daylights scared out of them, but that since the Germans were on the
telephone, the cry was heard over the lines for some distance.[94]

Although he was frequently sought out to elaborate on his service
record, Oklahombi appears to have been relatively modest about his service after returning home. An article published the week after he returned
and quoting his citation described him as "a very pleasant young Indian
and above the average in point of intelligence. He is 24 years old, and
is very unassuming seemingly considering that his acts were only a
part of his duty."[95] Nevertheless, news accounts of Oklahombi's service
at St. Etienne portrayed him as the Native American equivalent of and

second to Sergeant Alvin York, leading the *Daily Oklahoman* to proclaim him "Oklahoma's Greatest Indian Hero."[96] In May of 1921, Mrs. Czarina C. Conlan of the Oklahoma Historical Society and fellow Choctaw Sol Joel visited with Oklahombi regarding his service and his being ranked as the second greatest WW I veteran. Oklahombi reportedly "saw nothing peculiar in this lack of recognition, he said. He did only his duty, he added, and is now back home with his wife and baby—carrying on as his forbearers carried on."[97] The photograph of the three taken during the visit has been frequently published. Conlan collected a number of items from Oklahombi, including his uniform jacket, helmet, and Croix de Guerre.[98] With Oklahombi's reticence in discussing his service in the war, a lack of first-hand accounts, and his death in 1960, we will likely never know all the details that transpired and the exact role he held in those events. Nevertheless, his service was highly commendable and garnered him the French Croix de Guerre with Silver Citation Star and the American World War I Victory Medal and Silver Citation Star.[99]

Scholars have also never noticed or questioned what awards appear on Oklahombi's uniform in photos taken of him after returning home. Sources commonly refer to his Croix de Guerre and the Silver Citation Star, and Coleman (2002:205) notes that National Archives and Army Military History Institute records list only the Silver Citation Star. As I examined photos of him, I noticed that the awards on Oklahombi's uniform often differed from photo to photo. In several photos, he appears to wear his Croix de Guerre and the small French Citation Star on the medal's ribbon, sometimes on his uniform, and sometimes on civilian clothes. In some photos of Oklahombi where he appears older, the Croix de Guerre is present, but the Citation Star on the ribbon seemed too large and of the wrong shape; pulling out an earlier photo of his uniform I had taken, it appeared to be a US World War I Victory Button. In 2018, I reexamined Oklahombi's uniform and medal again at the Oklahoma History Center in Oklahoma City, and discovered that indeed it was a US World War I Victory Button pinned on his Croix de Guerre.[100] Whether he never received the French Citation Star, or whether he received and lost it, is unclear.

The US Army World War I Victory Button is a five-pointed-star shaped, 5/8-inch diameter pin on a circular wreath, with the letters "US" in the center, all on a solid center backing. The pin was issued in bronze, and for those wounded in combat, in silver. This award required the same eligibility requirements as the World War I Victory Medal denoting service and an honorable discharge in the American Forces in World War I.[101] Officially, this pin was not worn on a service ribbon, but many soldiers wore awards in unofficial arrangements, as indicated in photographs and uniforms. Because the Croix de Guerre was the only award he came home with from the war, Oklahombi appears to have simply added it to the ribbon to display it.

For World War I, the US Citation Star was a 3/16-inch personal valor decoration issued as a ribbon device by the Department of War. The award of a Citation Star was based upon an individual's being officially cited in orders by a general order number. It was first established by Congress on July 9, 1918, though War Department Bulletin No. 43. The Citation Star was typically worn on the ribbon of the World War I Victory Medal to denote a citation for gallantry in action. On July 19, 1932, the Silver Star medal, a large, gold-hue gilt-bronze star containing a 3/16-inch silver star in the center of the medal and hanging from a red, white, and blue ribbon, replaced the 3/16-inch Silver Star.

On the Croix de Guerre, additional ribbon devices indicate the degree of valor associated with the action, in lowest to highest order by a bronze star, silver star, silver gilt star, bronze palm, and silver palm. The French Citation Star is a 7/16-inch-diameter five-pointed star that rises upward along the crests from the ends of the points to the center of the star.

Regarding the US awards, Oklahombi appears to have only received his World War I Victory Button, as in photographs, he does not don the US Victory Medal or a silver US Citation Star. The US World War I Victory Medal was recommended by an inter-Allied committee in March of 1919, but following delays in Congressional passage, it was only approved following general orders of respective military departments beginning in April of 1919 and did not begin to be distributed to army veterans until June 21, 1920 (Laslo 1986). Oklahombi was discharged June 19, 1919, before the US version of the Citation Star was established. Thus, Oklahombi likely never received the US Victory Medal and Silver Citation Star after the war, and like some soldiers may have never tried to obtain them, as they do not appear on his uniform in postwar photographs taken of him over a period of years.

Following the war, Oklahombi resumed life with his wife and son, Jonah, on a small farm near Wright City, Oklahoma, consisting of a small one-room cottage and a few acres. He continued to hunt, fish, raise corn, and help his neighbors at harvest time. In September 1925, he visited the US Veteran's hospital in Muskogee, Oklahoma, for a tumor, for which he was apparently successfully treated.[102] By the early 1930s, Oklahombi was working as a farm laborer, but he was often jobless and financially struggling. In the winter of 1932–33, several Oklahoma news articles describe how Oklahombi was forced to apply to the Veteran's Bureau for relief. By this time, Oklahombi was physically struggling, out of work, and in need of funds. In 1933, he began working on a Native American relief project near his home for $12 a month.[103]

Oklahombi was reticent to talk about his experiences in great detail. According to a 1932 interview, when a reporter from an eastern magazine came to Wright City to interview him shortly after the war, he left town.

In 1935, Oklahombi was still working on the relief project when he was approached by individuals from Hollywood interested in making a movie documenting his life and military service. He declined the offer because it required him to relocate to California for the duration of the project. Oklahombi's wife, Agnes, reports that he adamantly refused all offers, giving various reasons, including that "war was not fun" and he would not be a party to making movies about such activities, that he had to "stay home and catch suckers [fish]" in nearby Horsehead Creek, and that he would go to Hollywood if they could move Horsehead Creek there.[104] Oklahombi is also reported to have said, "Too far from home. I no go."[105]

An article about the film offer in the *Indian Leader* (1935), a weekly publication of Haskell Institute in Lawrence, Kansas, and titled "Indian War Hero Rejects Hollywood," states that Oklahombi turned down $500 a week to act in the picture. He found Hollywood "too far away from home," despite several attempts by producers to persuade him to be in the film. The article went on to repeat the accomplishments that he and twenty-three other soldiers achieved at St. Mihiel (St. Etienne) mistakenly attributed to only him.

According to Leroy Lewis of Muskogee, head of Indian relief work in eastern Oklahoma, Oklahombi "is one of those who would rather live on crusts in his native Kiamichi Mountains than to have the fat of the land and be adored in Hollywood." Lewis reported that Oklahombi received several letters making him handsome offers to work on a film. This source also references a letter from a Hollywood producer promising $500 a week for several weeks to work on the picture. While some might read this as a disparagement, it can also be seen as complementary, as it reflects Oklahombi's modesty, values, and priorities compared to many non-Natives.[106] In a 1937 interview with R. G. Miller, Oklahombi stated, "I was all ready to go, but he never did send me money and railroad ticket," although Miller also reports, "Neighbors told us Joe declined to take the movie job."[107]

In 1936 the US postmaster general planned to depict outstanding World War I heroes on postage stamps. That May, a joint meeting of the Atoka Treaty Rights Association, the Choctaw-Chickasaw League, and the Choctaw-Chickasaw Democrat League passed a number of resolutions including a request to the postmaster general "to place the image of Joseph Oklahombi, a full-blood Choctaw Indian, on future issues of postage stamps as one of the outstanding world war heroes."[108]

By January 1937, his Indian relief job ended and Oklahombi, then forty-two years of age, found himself impoverished, struggling to find work in the local area, and struggling with alcohol. His son, Jonah, was then work-ing at a nearby sawmill for $2 a day. After interviewing Oklahombi, R. G. Miller published an article titled "Our No. 1 War Hero Wants a Job," in which he described Oklahombi's dilemmas as well as his extensive list of manual labor skills. The news articles resulted in several job offers, and Oklahombi took a job at a Wright City lumber company.[109]

On March 9, 1937, the Third District American Legion Convention at Atoka passed a resolution asking the Oklahoma congressional delegation to use its efforts to "care for Oklahombi during the rest of his life." After receiving a copy of the resolution, Oklahoma state representative Wilburn Cartwright of McAlester wrote to the Bureau of Indian Affairs asking for a job for Oklahombi. The Indian Department referred the letter to Vic-tor Brown, a Choctaw code talker and field clerk at Idabel. Several years prior, Cartwright had been unsuccessful in an attempt to get Oklahombi awarded a Distinguished Service Cross for his WW I service.[110]

In 1940, two individuals on a fishing trip picked up a Native American man walking along Kiamichi Mountain to visit his wife in the hospital at Talahina. Along the way, they discovered that it was Oklahombi, then working at a saw mill for $2.56 for a full day's work:

> When asked what battles he fought in, he said, "Just fight 'em like hell all time." Adding "I kill 'em all, but Captain come down hold up his hand and say, no shootum Jo, war all over." . . . In his own way he told us it was hard to understand how a man go to the war and fight hard, kill lots of the enemy, be sly enough to not get wounded himself and now the government not help him and that others go to war, not do much, get wounded and then the government give them a pension. Going several miles out of their way they dropped him at the hospital.[111]

On April 13, 1960, Oklahombi was walking from his home east of Wright City into town along the shoulder of the road and facing traffic. At 3:25 P.M., a half mile east of Wright City on the Wright City-Broken Bow Road, he was struck by a panel truck of the Walsh-Lumpkin Whole-sale Drug Company of Texarkana, Texas, driven by Kenneth Craig Bazil, a thirty-seven-year-old African American. After the left front of the truck struck Oklahombi, the vehicle turned over and came to a stop on its left side in a ditch. The impact threw Oklahombi seventy feet, breaking his neck and both legs and causing other injuries. Oklahombi was killed instantly. He was sixty-five years of age. Bazil was charged with manslaughter in the first degree and held in the county jail while an investigation was under-taken. He was released on $2,500 bond pending a preliminary hearing on May 1; after the incident was determined to have been an accident, charges were dropped. Services for Oklahombi were held in Luksokla Presbyterian Church near Wright City. He was buried in Yaskau Cemetery with full military honors, including a detachment of an escort, bugler, and honor guard from Fort Sill, Oklahoma. Several of his WW I comrades attended his service. He was a member of American Legion Post No. 74, Wright City, Oklahoma, and the Presbyterian Church.[112]

In 1988 and 1989, Jonah Oklahombi wrote to the National Archives and Records Administration at St. Louis requesting a records check and the issuance of any medals and awards that his father, Joseph, may have earned in World War I. The family believed that he had not been recognized by the US Army and that he was deserving of awards for his military service. This belief was likely influenced by an entry in a McCurtain County Historical Society (1982:25) publication depicting the photo of Oklahombi, Conlan, and Jol, repeating his alleged capture of 171 Germans and noting, "Unfortunately, the United States government never in any way recognized Joseph's accomplishments." Jonah Oklahombi attached a copy of this entry with his request.[113]

Over the next seven years, several Choctaw tribal members, veterans, congressional representatives, and photo journalists wrote letters of inquiry and support. One letter from William T. Lee Jr. of Savannah, Georgia, dated June 21, 1989, requested that "Oklahombi should be honored with [a] Congressional Medal of Honor, the Distinguished Service Cross or at very least the Silver Star."[114]

Jonah Oklahombi wrote again asking if his father was eligible for the American equivalent of the French Croix de Guerre he was awarded and included a copy of a discharge and a journal photo from a page in *McCurtain County: A Pictorial History* showing him wearing the French award. At the behest of Oklahombi, Dale Turner of San Antonio, Texas, submitted a January 23, 1989, records search, questioning whether Oklahombi's Croix de Guerre was an individual or group citation. The Oklahombis had already agreed to donate them to the Choctaw Museum in Tuskahoma, Oklahoma.[115]

A card recording this award is contained in Oklahombi's National Archives and Records Administration personnel file, ordered "For gallantry in action at St. Etienne, France, 8 October, 1918" by "Citation Order No. 4, AEF, dated June 3, 1919." The card is stamped "SILVER STAR CITATIONS." Thus Oklahombi was awarded the Silver Citation Star by the United States for the same action that the French had awarded him the Croix de Guerre. A note produced during a review of his records on February 12, 1996, came to the same conclusion. Whether he was never awarded the American Silver Citation Star pin, had lost it, or the family was unaware of the award is unclear. On December 18, 1989, the Silver Star Medal was authorized for reissue to Oklahombi's son, Jonah.[116]

In 1992, the United States military reissued Oklahombi's medals to his son, Jonah. These include the American World War I Victory Medal with two Bar Clasps for the Meuse-Argonne and Defensive Sector Campaigns, the French Croix de Guerre with Silver Citation Star, and the American (post-1932) Silver Star Medal (replacing the American Silver Star Citation), but not the US Army Service Lapel Honorable Discharge Pin for World War I. The reissued medals were displayed at the 45th Infantry Museum in Oklahoma City. Jonah Oklahombi donated the medals to the Choctaw Nation Museum at Tuskahoma, Oklahoma, where they are on display today.[117]

An interview with Oklahombi's son reports, "Jonah said that his father talked very little about the events in France during World War I. Joseph was, like most Choctaws, a very modest man who placed little importance on his own activities."[118] The October 1992 issue of *Bishinik* depicts Jonah and Ruth Oklahombi with a frame of Oklahombi's reissued medals.[119]

Oklahombi's original uniform, wool garrison cap, steel helmet, mess kit, socks, and original Croix de Guerre are in the collection of the Oklahoma History Center in Oklahoma City.[120] Records at the Oklahoma History Center report that Oklahombi's friend and fellow Choctaw Sol Joel donated a copy of Oklahombi's citation to the society in 1928, accompanied by a number of uniform items and other military equipment that Oklahombi had used in the war. Oklahombi had donated his Croix de Guerre to the society sometime after the visit of Sol Joel and Czarina Conlan in May 1921, possibly at the conclusion of her visit, and prior to 1928.[121] News articles indicate that Oklahombi's Croix de Guerre had been on display in the museum at the state capitol since at least 1940.[122] Oklahombi's items were loaned to the Choctaw Nation for a 2005 exhibit about him at the Choctaw Nation Museum at Tuskahoma.[123]

Louis Coleman's (2002) article reassessing Oklahombi's military service and awards initially received mixed reviews in the Choctaw community. Naturally, no one wants to embrace new information that contradicts or diminishes long-held positive beliefs about a local hero. However, Coleman's assessment, which focused on clarifying and not demeaning Oklahombi's service and bravery, which Coleman applauds in the same article, appears very accurate. My own examination of the original award and the extracts of the award in both French and English, the accounts of officers in the 36th Division, the 1937 interview with Oklahombi, the timeline of the assault at St. Etienne, and photographs of Oklahombi support Coleman's reanalysis.

Acceptance of the reanalysis is increasing in both the Choctaw and military communities. In 2000, *Bishinik* released a statement that "Oklahombi and his buddies in Company D, 141st Infantry, 36th Division" accomplished the feat capturing the German position and taking 171 German prisoners.[124] In 2005, *Bishinik* ran an article acknowledging Coleman's (2002) reassessment of Oklahombi's military service and awards.[125] The Texas Military Forces Museum endorsed a similar stance in 2007.[126]

In June 2010, a monument honoring Oklahombi was erected in his hometown of Wright City, Oklahoma, as part of Wright City's Centennial Celebration. A portion of the monument's inscription reads, "On oct. 8. 1918, at St. Etienne, France, Oklahombi and 23 fellow soldiers attacked an enemy position and captured 171 prisoners. They held the position for four days."[127] In the 2016 version of the Choctaw Nation's pamphlet on their code talkers, the section on Oklahombi (CCOO 2016:9) states, "He and 23 of his fellow soldiers are credited with killing 79 German soldiers and capturing 171 others in action at St. Etienne, France from October 8–11, 1918."

Efforts to garner Oklahombi a Congressional Medal of Honor continue. In January 1994, Sergeant First Class (Ret) and Choctaw tribal member Billy Joe Lingo wrote Senator Phil Gram requesting that Oklahombi's Silver Star medal be upgraded to a Congressional Medal of Honor. Lingo based his request on the fact that twenty Medals of Honor had been given to US servicemen for their participation in the Wounded Knee Massacre of 1890, while Oklahombi had "captured 175 Germans in World War I and was given the Medal of Honor from France. He was also awarded the Silver Star by the United States." Although confusing the nature of the French award and Oklahombi's participation in a larger group action, his request was sincere. On October 20, 1995, Maurice Davis submitted a similar request to his congressman, James Cooley, comparing Oklahombi's "singlehandedly capturing 171 Germans and outperformed in another way by killing more Germans than Sgt. York." The comparison, of course, was to Alvin York's taking of 132 prisoners with fellow soldiers. Davis requested Oklahombi's accomplishments be entered into the *Congressional Record* and asked whether a citation or medal might be awarded.[128]

Letters in Oklahombi's personnel file demonstrating efforts to garner him a Congressional Medal of Honor span the years 1988 to at least 1996.[129] Although the outcome of the inquiries is not contained in Oklahombi's personnel files, because the determination of military awards is not determined by their office but by the military, the Congressional Medal of Honor was never awarded. Oklahombi continues to be written about and represents one of the Choctaw's greatest military heroes. Recently, the Choctaw Nation of Oklahoma has renewed efforts to have Oklahombi's Silver Star posthumously upgraded to a Congressional Medal of Honor, which raises the question of whether the other twenty-three men involved in the action will also be reexamined for the award.

Otis Leader

Another of the most memorable Choctaw WW I veterans is Sergeant Otis W. Leader. Born in 1882 near Scipio, Indian Territory, now Pittsburgh County, Oklahoma, Leader was three-fourths Choctaw and Chickasaw and one-fourth Scottish-Irish.[130] After attending local schools and college, he married Minnie Lee, and around 1910, the two moved to a new six-room house located two and a half miles south of Scipio on what he named the X-S Ranch. When the United States entered the war in 1917, Leader was thirty-four years old, the father of three small children, and a widower following the death of his wife on January 4, 1916. Stemming from widespread fear, anxieties, and actual espionage associated with the war, US civilians were sometimes accused by others of being enemy spies. On April 5, 1917, federal agents began following three men around the Fort Worth, Texas, stockyards because they looked and sounded different from the other cattlemen. One of the men followed by the agents was Otis Leader, who, standing 6'3" tall, undoubtedly stuck out in any crowd.[131]

Leader was working as a cattleman on the Arnold Ranch in Pittsburgh County, near Allen, Oklahoma. His employers, Arnold Arn and Karl Marty, were naturalized US citizens from Switzerland who had come to Oklahoma from Chicago to inspect the ranch. The three men were joined by one Nick Koenig. In early April 1917, Arn, Marty, and Leader accompanied a shipment of cattle from the Arnold Ranch to the Fort Worth stockyard and market. There they purchased other cattle and arranged for their transportation to Oklahoma. Arn's heavy Swiss accent was soon mistaken as German, and the tall, dark, handsome Leader was believed to be a Spanish spy. On April 5, 1917, Texas and Oklahoma newspapers ran articles about suspected spies being trailed through the stockyards by law enforcement. Leader was one of those men.[132]

The following day, April 6, the United States declared war against the Central Powers. That same day, the following article ran in the *McAlester News-Capital*:

ACTION OF GERMAN
SUSPECTS WATCHED
SUPPOSED TO BE COMING HERE
TO INFORM BERLIN OF
MILITARY WORK

Three Germans, who have been looking at property in Pittsburg county on the ostensible purpose of investing, are being shadowed by government inspectors on the suspicion that they are spies.

The three men came here in an automobile from some unknown place last Monday night. They are known to have attended the patriotic rally held here that evening.

The next day they disappeared, but returned yesterday. They registered under different names this time, stopping at a different hotel. They were being shown some property near McAlester today by an Indian.

The theory on which the investigation is being conducted is that these men are reporting the military activity here to Berlin by the wireless station said to be located near Mexico City. The Germans are being shadowed constantly. Arrest will follow immediately upon the commission by them of any act on which charges could be placed.[133]

While the publishing and content of the article prior to their apprehension was probably not a good idea, as it could have tipped off real spies, it reflects the views at the time, which in some instances were justified. Many Americans have forgotten that Mexico was considering allying with Germany against the United States during World War I and that many individuals were arrested and held on charges of espionage. In some cases, individuals were cleared and released; in other instances, they were held.[134]

Texas law-enforcement officers wired orders to have the men arrested when they arrived by train at McAlester, Oklahoma, where US marshal Crockett Lee was waiting at the station. When Lee saw his friend Leader and his employer Arnold Arn depart from the train, he realized the enormity of the mistake. Lee quickly straightened out the mistake with officials, but as far as Leader was concerned, the damage had been done.[135]

By April 13, local newspapers were printing a clarification of the incident, assuring the innocence of the men involved:

Now it appears that the three men suspected by government officials as being German spies in a dispatch to Postmaster Lester, are in reality business men of good standing and were coming to this part of Oklahoma with the view of building up a ranch. Carl Marty and Nick Koenig are well known to local men and the Indian named Leader has been working for them on a ranch five miles outside of Stuart for several years.

A Mr. J. S. Yoes reported,

I have known Koenig for three or four years. He is in business in Chicago and he and the other two are interested jointly in a ranch of several hundred acres just across the line in Hughes County. I have met Koenig's family. The three men bought some nursery stock from me for their ranch last week and I returned from there only last night myself ... These men are just as incensed at Germany as we are. Their native country is not at war with the German empire, but the Swiss people have enough grievances against the German rulers to dislike them as much as we do.

Other character witnesses included G. C. Gentry, from whom they had already bought cattle, and H. E. Jones, who delivered stock to the ranch and had stayed an extra day to help brand them.[136]

Years later, an account of the incident was read at the American Legion Post in Colgate:

A cattleman, he was working on the Arnold ranch near Allen where war seemed far away from both the ranch and Otis Leader until he and his Swiss employer Mr. Arnold went on a cattle buying trip to Ft. Worth and Mr. Arnold's heavy Swiss accent was mistaken as German and his tall, dark, and handsome companion was pegged as a Spaniard and a spy. Army intelligence wired orders for arrest of the spies at McAlester when they arrived on the train. Enormity of the mistake was immediately recognized by US Marshall Crockett Lee when he saw his old friend Otis Leader and Mr. Arnold step off the train. Lee straightened out Army intelligence in a hurry; but could not abate the anger of the young Indian father who was appalled at being mistaken for a spy, and immediately hunted up the nearest recruiting office and volunteered for the Cavalry.[137]

Upon learning that he had been mistaken for a spy and that his loyalty to the United States had been questioned, Leader was so infuriated that he headed to enlist a few days later. Nearly two months before the draft began on June 5, 1917, Leader volunteered for the cavalry at McAlester, Oklahoma, and was given two weeks to get his affairs in order. One account reports that he enlisted on April 12. On April 30, 1917, he bid his three children, mother, and sister goodbye and reported to the Oklahoma City recruiting office on May 1.[138]

Fortunately, Leader kept a diary of these events and his subsequent service in World War I, allowing us to understand much about his experiences. Leader had already been considering enlisting for military service. As Leader recorded (DeSpain 2004:6):

I had already been thinking seriously about enlisting for the service should we break with Germany. I had been reading and watching the papers about how the German subs [were] destroying neutral ships and lives. I had considered and summed up everything, that if Germany had conquered England, France, Italy, [and] Belgium, the Allied nation[s], and taken over their naval fleets, [that their] next move would be to make trouble for us [the United States of America]. [If] they conquered our Allies and got their fleet, in connections with what they had of their own, we would have been helpless. People didn't think about those conditions far enough . . .

On April 4th and 5th, 1917, I with my nephew, one of the members of the firm whom I was employed by at that time—[the] FK ranch of Chicago who has large holding[s] in Oklahoma's Pittsburg and Hughes Co. We were in Ft. Worth for the purpose [of] buying cattle off of the stockyards to be shipped to the pastures in Pittsburg Co. and had least expected that any one was on our trail. But after returning back to the ranch we learned that there was some immigration agent [that] had been following us or suspecting us as German spies. The [news]papers came out [with] large headlines about suspected German spies, and [we] discovered that it was us who they had suspected. This [matter] worked on me to a pitched degree so I proceeded to show them that I was 100% American. [So] on or about the 8th or 10th of April, I went to McAlester, [Oklahoma] to enlist and was accepted. . . . [Thus], feeling that it was my duty to answer the call, when they were calling for volunteers, [and] after being accused as a spy previously, I enlisted.

I felt as tho I was defending our rights and [a] just cause to mankind. I went into the service to serve my country under the shadow as a spy, and I knew that right would be corrected, so I went into [the war] with a clear conscious and knew what I was doing . . . I had determined to go through with it [even] if [it] cost my life.

Leader and others in the cattle-buying party may have noticed the immigration agent. In one interview, Leader states, "We were in Fort Worth buying cattle and noticed a man following us around. Later we learned two German spies were believed to be in town and they thought we were them!"[139] Leader later described, "I had already informed my employees that I intended to defend the flag, and when I read the newspaper articles describing me as being a traitor to my country, I took 'French leave,' to come to Oklahoma City, joined the army and June 26, landed in France."[140]

Finding Leader too strong and husky to serve as mounted cavalry, he was placed in the regular army. On May 2, 1917, he was sent to Fort Logan, Colorado, where he arrived on the 3rd. Four days later, he was sent to El Paso, Texas, arriving on May 9, where he was assigned to Company H, 16th Infantry Regiment, 1st Division. He was soon sent to nearby Fort Bliss, then to Socorro and Esillatta, New Mexico, where he participated in patrol duty along the US-Mexican border during the time that American troops were pursuing Pancho Villa (DeSpain 2004:8).[141] Company H was converted to a machine gun company, becoming the 2nd Machine Gun Battalion composed of Companies A, B, C, and D. A new Company H was then formed. Leader's unit left El Paso, Texas, on June 3, 1917, for New York. As he recalled, "We were crossing Texas, heading towards New York City to move overseas when the first men were called by the draft."[142] At Fort Worth, they participated in a thirty-six--hour exercise including marching through the streets. As Leader reflected (DeSpain 2004:9):

> We left Ft. Bliss by the way of Ft. Worth and when we reached Ft. Worth we had to take our usual 36 hour exercise by marching thru the streets which brought back to me the memory of what had happened just a short time before about my being accused as a spy. In 30 days from enlistment, I was on my way to France and wished for this immigration agent to come around and see me while I was there. I felt as though I wanted to give him a piece of him.

The 1st Division sailed from Hoboken on June 14 on the SS *Saratoga* and several banana boats that had been pressed into convoy service. On the evening of June 22, a German submarine attacked his transport, with one shot passing in front of the bow and another behind the stern as it turned lengthwise in the direction from which the shots came. Destroyers nearby launched depth charges at the submarine (DeSpain 2004:10–11). On June 25, they landed at the mouth of the Loir River and marched up the hill at St. Nazaire, France.[143]

On June 6, the 1st reached Gondecourt to begin training under the French 47th Division, the Alpine Chasseres, or "les Diables Bleus" (Blue Devils) from July 8 to October 21, 1917. Gondecourt served as a training ground for several American units prior to entering combat. As the AEF landed in France, French artist Raymond Desvarreux was commissioned by his government to paint portraits of the Allied army and what has been variously described as "the ideal American soldier," "the most typical American soldier," and the "model original American soldier." Because the soldiers of the 1st Division were among the first American troops to land in France in 1917, they immediately drew an assignment to participate in parade duty in Paris on July 4. Watching the parade, Desvarreux saw the model of his choice. Determined to find out who he was, Desvarreux proceeded to Gondecourt to uncover his identity.[144]

At Gondecourt, the slightly built Desvarreux exited from an official car along a street where the machine gun company of the 16th Infantry was located. After a lengthy delay and numerous gestures, he was allowed to enter the regimental headquarters and was taken to an obviously angered American colonel. In broken but enthusiastic English, Desvarreux informed the commanding officer that he wanted to paint a picture

of the "Ideal American soldat." He continued, "I want to paint his picture. Eet will be hung in the Sale des Invalides. I have permission from
the French Government, and I have come." Perturbed, the commanding
officer informed him that the newly arrived doughboys had no time to
pose for portraits if they were expected to help win the war—which was
precisely why they were in France—that none of them was typical, and
that there were two million more on their way. Other officers also exhib-
ited little interest in having their portraits painted. Then Desvarreux produced a small paper that changed the atmosphere of the meeting: written
permission in the form of a request from the French government that
bore the insignia of the American General Headquarters and the signature of General John J. Pershing, making it an order. As the Frenchman
waived his hands and stated, "I have a comeeshun" [commission] they
began to understand. Puzzled, the colonel asked him why he came there
seeking the model for his picture.[145]

Desvarreux explained: "I saw him in Paris on parade with the American
troops on the 4th of July. He was with this regiment, the machinegun com-
panee, I think you call it." When he described the man he wanted as a tall,
dark-skinned soldier parading with the machine gun company in Paris,
the officers decided that it must be Otis Leader he sought.[146]

The artist described Leader as "a half-blood Choctaw Indian from Oklahoma, straight as an arrow and standing over six feet tall; keen, alert, yet with
calmness that betokens strength and his naturally bronzed face reflecting
the spirit that they took across with them, the spirit that eventually turned
the tide." One news source reports that the painting, along with many other
memorials from the war, was hung in the Sale de Invalides in Paris.[147]

In his diary, Leader (DeSpain 2004:18–19) described his experience of
being painted:

> I had the honor to be the one who was selected for the painting from
> among the many. I posed for three days and he said he was only
> getting [an] outline and sketches and [would] touch it up a little, but
> the picture would be finished in Paris. I couldn't see where he could
> improve the painting, from the subject he had to work from, but I
> suppose he knew what he was talking about. The picture hangs today
> in the Art Museum representing the aboriginal American amongst
> other paintings of the Allied nations in the French federal building
> or the Soldats Ivalads in Paris.

Leader was also chosen "by an eminent French sculptor as model for his
statue of 'the American fighting man.'"[148]

Following their training, the 1st Division prepared to enter combat.[149]
The night of October 21, 1917, Leader's unit moved into the front lines

in the Sommerville sector, which he described as "a little town shot all to pieces."[150] On the night of November 2, 1917, the 16th drew relief assignment and moved into the trenches near Bathlemont. Leader's machine gun company defended the flank of the first American unit to enter combat early on the morning of November 3.[151] His company took some of the first German fire to be received by the Americans, killing three of his four man crew, including privates Enright, Gresham, and Hay, who were among the first Americans killed in the war.[152] Leader stated that the Germans "pulled a little raid" and that from his battalion, three men were killed, five injured, and eleven taken prisoner, the first American casualties of the war. Leader describes being gassed in January of 1918 and was moved back to "the gas station for treatment."[153]

Under General Hunter Liggett, the 1st Division was stationed on the south side of the Saint Mihiel salient near the village of Seicheprey when it took part in what many call the first American engagement of the war that could really be called a battle. Leader reported that their trenches were raided by the Germans then retaken by the Americans the following day, April 20, 1918. At Saint Mihiel, the Americans captured over twelve thousand of the enemy on the first day of the offensive, resulting in a steady German retreat toward the Rhine.[154]

The 1st moved into the St. Mihiel sector as a prelude to the battle at Cantigny. On April 25, 1918, the 1st Division formed part of the front line near Montdidier. On May 28, they attacked and captured the town of Cantigny after, according to Leader, beating back more than seven counterattacks. This area is reported to have been the first territory wrested away from the Germans since invading France and fighting at Cantigny, where the Americans established themselves as a significant fighting force. In charge of a machine gun squad, Leader was wounded on the 28th at Cantigny. As he described, "Cantigny was a hot spot. We lost lots of boys there."[155]

After recovering, he rejoined his company in the 1st Division near Soissons three weeks later, where the fighting continued. This led to the Second Battle of the Marne (July 19–August 6, 1918), which began to turn the tide for the Allies. The division fought eastward toward Reims at Soissons in the face of low French morale. French marshal Ferdinand Foch believed that the Americans' presence stimulated the French and British troops who had become somewhat demoralized from the German's constant progress. With five American divisions already on French soil, Foch asked the United States to send even more troops. Every available American soldier was brought up to this sector of the front by motor train to support the retreating French. In July 1918, the Germans were pushing toward Château-Thierry, the gateway to Paris. Leader again saw action near Soissons Château-Thierry in the Second Battle of the Marne as the Germans began a heavy rolling barrage into his unit's advance infantry.

At Château-Thierry one of the artillery blasts killed all of Leader's machine gun crew except him and knocked their gun out of commission. As Leader described:

> When the hottest of the battle was raging I was advancing with fellow members of my company to the enemy's line in the face of hot fire. The members of my particular gun crew were advancing in column hoping to place a gun in such a position that it would command a raking fire along the German defenses. We had progressed without mishap when suddenly a German incendiary bomb landed in the center of the column wiping out every member of the crew but myself and destroying our gun. The explosion left me alone in no man's land suffering from a severe shock from the shell. I have had several experiences in which I figured my last call had come but this one was worth considering when I saw my whole crew blown as it were almost from under my feet.[156]

With several grenades on his belt, Leader picked up two Springfield .03 bolt-action rifles from the dead, slung one across his shoulder, and carried the other. Falling to his stomach, he crawled through a ravine toward a German machine gun nest, continuing through a field of oats to within sixty feet of the enemy. Finding two machine guns in fixed positions and unable to cover the area behind them, Leader flanked them until he reached a position allowing him to cover the enemy position from behind. Taking both positions, he captured eighteen German soldiers manning two machine guns. Leader was awarded the French Croix de Guerre with palm (equal to the American Oak Leaf Cluster) for this action, as well as the Silver Star, then the Silver Citation Star.[157]

Some accounts report this event as occurring closer to Soissons, in the Château-Thierry action, where the 1st Division began their attack on July 18, during the Second Battle of the Marne. Eight American divisions participated in the campaign. During this action, a Polish boy accompanied Leader but was killed by German fire before reaching the German machine gun nest. The eighteen Germans he captured did not know that the automatic rifle he carried would not shoot.[158] As Leader described:

> "We were out on the gun and had been getting fire from some German guns making it hot for us. A couple of the boys came up as our relief, so this Polish boy and I decided to get them." Leader and his assistant gunner grabbed up a couple of weapons ("they were rifles of an automatic sort") from dead French men and "then we took off through the

field, around them," he continued, gesturing to the left, "to get behind them. My Polish boy got hit and fell into a shell hole, but I kept on and got in behind them. I poked the gun over a mound of dirt thrown over the trench and yelled at them. I don't know what I said, just sort of whooped." The Germans turned around. "I waived at them with one hand while keeping the gun pointed at them to get them to put up their hands. And they all went up like this," he gestured.[159]

After motioning the eighteen Germans at the two machine nests out of the trench, Leader marched them back across no-man's-land, despite heavy artillery shelling, to turn them in to a group of astonished marines of the 5th and 6th Regiments. Leader concluded, "Not a one of us got hurt." What made the action more incredible was the fact that Leader accomplished it with an empty weapon. "I had only one shell," he laughed. "And I didn't know how to load it." When his wife interrupted him during the interview to ask him what he would have done if he had needed to shoot, Leader grinned and shrugged his shoulders.[160]

Leader was wounded again on July 18 in the brutal fighting at Soissons Château-Thierry. As he recalled, "I could not tell how many Germans we killed: they fell before our machine gun bullets like wheat before the reaper. We were facing the Prussian guard, the flower of the German army, when a high explosive shell killed eight of my men and I received my second wound." An exploding shell also gassed Leader and hospitalized him for the second time during this campaign.[161] In another account, Leader said, "It was here that the first and second divisions had their hell on earth against all the German resistance. It was here where we captured something more than 33,000 prisoners and killed more than we could tell. The dead men appeared to be falling like wheat before a reaper before our machine gun fire."[162]

Leader is reported as one of the men responding to Archie Roosevelt's (26th Infantry, 1st Division) call to "Come on, and we will clean them out and make them fight." Leader reports when the wave of American troops swept across no-man's-land in the Toul Sector, the "Huns" were unable to resist the onslaught and fled their trenches. "Waiting for the zero hour was the greatest strain I endured," Leader recalled. "We were always told several hours in advance of an impending charge, and the intervening time was spent in serious thought on the part of the Americans, for we did not know whether we would live to see the finish of what the day began. When the signal to advance was given, however, all was changed. Every man forgot his fears and thought only of fighting."[163]

After six months of combat, Brigadier General Frank Parker cited the 1st Division, the first assault division of the AEF, for taking all assignments given on four battlefields, never surrendering an inch of ground to the enemy, and for taking one hundred prisoners for every one lost. Parker attributed the 1st's record to the pride and spirit of each individual in the division who had given his country his entire effort of heart, mind, and body. In turn, each man in the division was reportedly awarded the Croix de Guerre, the second such award for Leader.[164]

Following the Second Battle of the Marne, Leader's unit returned to St. Mihiel and then were sent to the Argonne area. He participated in the Meuse-Argonne campaign that began in September of 1918. As Leader described, "We moved up in dark through canyons. . . . No one knew we were there." His group soon found themselves on top of the German trenches, surprising them. Pulling back, the Americans established positions in an old rock quarry, although they did not discover the nature of the quarry until the following morning. As Leader described it, "In the morning, a scout plane came over and flew circles over us. He must've seen us there, cause the Germans started in shooting at us with everything they had. They weren't too good of marksman tho," he chuckled. "They couldn't put them in the hole with us."[165]

On October 1, 1918, Leader was wounded again by shrapnel and gas and was hospitalized at Vichy. These wounds occurred during artillery shelling and a thick gas attack that inflicted heavy casualties on Leader's position. Out of his unit, only Leader and two others survived. Leader received a second Silver Star (Silver Citation Star) for this action. After he was gassed again and received emergency first aid, Leader was not allowed to return to his regular unit and was sent to Company L, where he remained until the Armistice was signed on November 11, 1918. Leader sailed from France on December 8, 1918, arriving at Hoboken, New Jersey, on December 16, 1918. After receiving treatment in army hospitals, he was discharged on January 6, 1919, at Camp Funston, Kansas. His enlistment record and discharge notes "Excellent" under "Character," "Service Honest and Faithful" under "Remarks," and "No A.W.O.L." As his gravestone lists, "OS CASUAL CONV DET" (casualty convalescent detachment), this is likely the unit he was in at the time of his official discharge.[166] The follow extract describes the action for which Leader received one of two Croix de Guerre awards:

EXTRACT FROM THE ORIGINAL.
DEPARTMENT OF THE INTERIOR.
UNITED STATE[S] INDIAN SERVICE.
CATO SELLS, SECRETARY OF THE INTERIOR.
WASHINGTON, D.C., Dec., 1920.

INDIAN BOY AMONG THE GREATER INDIAN HEROES.

The distinguished service record of the Indians was probably not below that of any other people engaged in the late war.

He bears his honor modestly, which, prevents definite information regarding many cases of individual valor. From instances cited in partial list, it is doubtful if a more brilliant one stands to the credit of any soldier than the achievement of OTIS W. LEADER, a part Choctaw and Chickasaw Indian, who received the CROIX DE GUERRE, under an order of MARSHAL PETAIN, a translation of which follows:

Under a violent barrage, dashed to attack the enemy position, covering about Two Hundred yards through barbed wire entanglements, he rushed on Machine Gun nest, capturing Eight-teen prisoners and killing many. He stormed a strong held position containing more than Twenty Machine Guns and a number of Trench Mortars. Turned the captured Guns on the enemy and held the position for Twenty-Four hours in spite of constant barrage of the large projectiles and of Gas shells. "Crossed no man's land" many times to get information concerning the enemies and to assist his wounded comrades.

(Signed) CATO SELLS, Secy. of the Interior.[167]

The format and wording of Leader's citation closely resembles Oklahombi's award, suggesting a standardized form edited to individual actions was used.

Leader as a Code Talker

It is not known exactly when or with whom Leader spoke Choctaw during the war. One family account mentions that Leader was placed on the phone to use Choctaw while convalescing from wounds in a hospital.[168] A 1958 interview and article on Otis Leader also reports, "For a spell, Leader was used on the signal lines to transmit messages, along with other Indians serving in the U.S. Forces. Leader stated, 'They'd (the Germans) put Russians, Italians to listen in, but they just couldn't understand Choctaw.'"[169]

While this section is described in an article following the Second Battle of the Marne (Aisne-Marne July 18–August 6, 1918), it does not specify when it occurred and thus does not indicate which campaign it involved or with whom he was communicating. The most likely clue is to determine when Leader was hospitalized. He was hospitalized for wounds received in the battles at Cantigny (May 28), Château-Thierry (July 18), and the Argonne (October 1 to the end of the war) in 1918.[170] The latter date is most likely, since the use of other Choctaw code talkers of the 36th Division date to October 26–27, 1918, and were not in theater until September of 1918. However, other Choctaw in other divisions could also have been used since the American 1st and 36th Divisions were not located near one another during the Meuse-Argonne Campaigns, with Leader's 1st Division assigned to the far right of the Allied advance, while the 36th Division was with the French 4th Army on the far left of the advance.[171]

Leader rose to the rank of corporal. He was wounded twice and gassed twice, wearing "two wound stripes and two gas stripes." The wording in some accounts suggests that he may have been gassed a third time, but this is unclear. He was awarded two French Croix de Guerre, two Silver Citation Stars, and the Purple Heart with clusters. During 1918, he took part in the battles of Cantigny (May 28), Soissons Château-Thierry (July 18), St. Mihiel (September 12), Verdun (September 26), and the Argonne Forest (October 1). While some sources state that he earned nine battle stars for Sommerville, Ansauville, Picardy, Cantigny, Second Marne, St. Mihiel, Meuse-Argonne, Mouson-Sedan, and Coblenz-Bridgehead, his personnel file states that he earned the World War I Victory Medal with five stars, with battle clasps for Montdidier-Noyon, Aisne-Marne, St. Mihiel, Meuse-Argonne, and Defensive Sector. His personnel file lists participation by the 2nd Machine Gun Battalion at Sommerville, Ansauville, Cantigny (April–June), Montdidier-Noyon, Cantigny (June–July), Aisne-Marne, Saizerais, Ansauville, St. Mihiel, and two segments of the Meuse-Argonne (September–October; October–November). General Pershing described Leader as one of the war's "greatest fighting machines." Pursuant to General Order 1, 1st Division, dated January 1, 1920, Leader was awarded the Silver Star on February 13, 1936; for wounds received on October 1, 1918, he was awarded the Purple Heart on April 5, 1935.[172]

As early as February 1919, articles on his extensive campaign record and his being chosen as the model American soldier for the Desvarreux painting ran in US papers.[173] Like Joseph Oklahombi, Otis Leader's service record was repeatedly presented in news articles over several decades, including the Chronicles of Oklahoma (Cunningham 1930:437–438). A 2015 search on Newspaperarchive.com produced 247 results for Leader. By decade, these articles include 1920s (19), 1930s (37), 1940s (43), 1950s (64), 1960s (22), 1970s (50), 1980s (1), 1990s (7), 2000s (2), 2010s (2). Since this inventory represents only one collection, there are likely other articles in other newspapers.[174]

After his discharge on June 6, 1919, Leader did special investigative work for the MK&T and Rock Island Railroads and guard duty for the state penitentiary at McAlester, Oklahoma. In 1919, Leader took vocational training and went to work, but he was still undergoing treatment for exposure to mustard gas. In 1922, he contracted tuberculosis as a result of his lungs being weakened by gas attacks during the war. Before he could be treated, he suffered acute appendicitis. Leader was finally sent to Whipple

Barracks in Prescott, Arizona, where his tuberculosis was arrested. After returning to Oklahoma, Leader remarried. In 1924, he joined the Oklahoma State Highway Department, working across the state but primarily out of Oklahoma City. In 1933, Leader, was forced to take time off from the highway department in Hollis, Oklahoma, to fight another round of tuberculosis, but by November, he was improving and "celebrated . . . an armistice of his own" with his recovery.[175]

For many years, Leader belonged to American Legion Post 35 in Oklahoma City, serving as sergeant-at-arms in the late 1950s. In 1935, he was transferred from Hollis to Lehigh, in Coal County, Oklahoma, where he bought a home atop a large hill with a commanding view of the area.[176] The *Oklahoman* reported that Leader was very reticent in speaking about his wartime experiences.[177]

Leader suffered from his war wounds for the rest of his life, reporting that cold wet weather brought back the discomfort.[178] In May of 1948, Leader was hospitalized at Will Rogers Veterans Hospital for a bone infection related to his war injuries. The infection forced Leader, then an auditor, to retire from the Engineering Department of the Oklahoma Highway Commission, where he had worked for over twenty-four years.[179] In April of 1955, he suffered a stroke and cerebral hemorrhage at his home in Lehigh, Oklahoma, and entered the Muskogee Veterans Hospital. The State House of Representatives passed a resolution designating him as the "Outstanding Soldier of World War I" that was signed by Governor Raymond Gary, who expressed sympathy for his recurring illnesses. Although still mobile and described in a June 1955 article as still displaying that "old fighting spirit," his health continued to slowly decline.[180]

Leader's service was never forgotten, in Oklahoma nor in France. On July 24, 1956, the Holmes-Collins American Legion Post No. 242 in Coalgate, Oklahoma, honored Leader with a special program and potluck dinner during Otis Leader Night. He was presented with a citation from Governor Raymond Gary and hailed as the post's first authorized life member. He and his friend Reverend Ed Jenks, a runner in the 1st Division during World War I, gave the benediction.[181]

On April 20, 1958, forty years to the day from when Leader first saw action in France, a French newspaper ran an article on him with his picture. Due in large part to his portrait and lengthy news coverage, the French had viewed Leader as the "most perfect example" of the American soldiers who had sacrificed and bravely served to save their country from tyranny. General Patrick J. Hurley, then in France, saw the article and contacted Leader after returning to the United States. Hurley offered Leader a trip to France, including a letter from President Eisenhower urging him to accept. Although Leader agreed to let Hurley finance the trip, he later had to cancel because of poor health. In turn, Hurley arranged for the funds to buy a new car for Leader and for the remainder to be placed in a bank account for him. However, because such gifts would have compromised his pension, Hurley presented the car to the Colgate Veterans of Foreign War Club, for Leader to use whenever he needed. One might wonder why Hurley, noted for his service as a general and diplomat during World War I and as the US secretary of war from 1929 to 1933 made such offers. Most likely it was because Hurley was not only a life-long friend of Leader from the prewar days when the two lived in McAllister, Oklahoma, but because the two had also served together in the 16th Infantry at Château-Thierry, St. Mihiel, and the Argonne. In 1959, Leader and Hurley dedicated a new building in Coalgate, Oklahoma.[182]

Leader remained active in American Legion activities. On August 11, 1953, he was installed as the sergeant-at-arms at the Holmes-Collins American Legion Post No. 242 in Coalgate, Oklahoma, and was reelected on July 17, 1959. An installation ceremony of the new officers was held on August 11.[183]

Leader was interviewed about his service many times over his life, including several lengthy articles during his last years. In 1919, Leader stated that during his brief career as a soldier, which included many outstanding incidents and honors, his greatest sorrow was when he was suspected of being a German spy in the spring of 1917. However, his "vase of joy was filled" when he was selected as the model original American soldier to have his portrait painted and hung on the walls of the French federal building, where the pictures of all "Allied races" meet.[184] In 1958, when Leader was asked what his toughest battle in the war was, he replied simply, "They were all tough."[185]

Following another stroke, Leader entered the Veteran's Hospital at Sulphur, Oklahoma on May 9, 1960, and was later moved to the Ardmore Hospital that November. He died March 26, 1961, at the Ardmore Veterans Hospital at the age of seventy-nine. His funeral service was held at the American Legion building in Coalgate, and he was buried in Colgate, Oklahoma.[186] The following day, the Oklahoma State Senate issued a resolution expressing regret for his passing.

ENROLLED SENATE BY: TRENT AND BELVIN
RESOLUTION NO. 34
A RESOLUTION EXPRESSING REGRET FOR THE DEMISE
OF OTIS W. LEADER, OKLAHOMA'S VETERAN WITH THE
HONORARY TITLE OF "MR. AMERICAN DOUGHBOY";
EXTENDING CONDOLENCES TO THE BEREAVED FAMILY;

DIRECTING JOURNAL ENTRY AND DISTRIBUTION OF AUTHENTICATED COPIES OF THIS RESOLUTION.

WHEREAS, Otis W. Leader, Oklahoma's veteran with the honorary title of "Mr. American Doughboy," fought his last battle Sunday, March 26, 1961 at Ardmore Oklahoma; and _____

WHEREAS, this Choctaw Indian brought great honor to himself and the State of Oklahoma through his heroic exploits and accomplishments during World War I; and _____

WHEREAS, this beloved veteran received citations from Marshal Ferdinand Foch, of France, and Marshal Douglas Haig, of Great Britain; and _____

WHEREAS, in the course of his military service, he earned two individual awards of the Croix de Guerre, France's highest military honor, two Silver Stars, the Purple Heart with clusters, and battle stars for Sommerviller, Ansauville, Piardy, Cantigny, Second Marne, St. Mihiel, Meuse-Argonne, Mouson-Sedan, and Coblenz Bridgehead and _____

WHEREAS, a monument to his memory stands in Paris France; and _____

WHEREAS, his picture by the French artist Raymond Desvarreux hangs in the French Hall of Fame, the British Hall of Fame, and the Oklahoma State Historical Society Museum, as a tribute to one who served so valiantly in World War I; and _____

WHEREAS, he earned the often cited accolade of "The Best Soldier of World War I"; and

WHEREAS, Otis W. Leader carried his many honors with dignity and modesty: and _____

WHEREAS, his battle of life has transpired. _____

NOW, THEREFORE, BE IT RESOLVED BY THE SENATE OF THE TWENTY- EIGHTH OKLAHOMA LEGISLATURE ENR. S. R. 34 sorrow and regret for the demise of Otis W. Leader. _____

SECTION 2. That condolences are extended to members of the bereaved family from and on behalf of the citizenry of a grateful Oklahoma. _____

SECTION 3. That this resolution be spread at large in the official journal of the Senate of the Twenty-eighth Oklahoma Legislature.

_____

Section 4. That a duly authenticated copy of this resolution be presented or forwarded to Mrs. Myrtle Leader, widow of the deceased, at Lehigh, Oklahoma; Mr. Paul A. Leader, son of the deceased, at Anchorage, Alaska; Mr. James L. Leader, son of the deceased, at 8805 Northeast 25th, Oklahoma City, Oklahoma; and Mrs. Charles H.

DeWeese, daughter of the deceased, at 801 Northeast 32nd, Oklahoma City, Oklahoma. _____

Adopted by the Senate the 27th day of March, 1961.

Bob A. Trent

President of the Senate

*(Certified by Leo Winters, Secretary of the Senate of the State of Oklahoma).[187]

Although the Choctaw lost two of their greatest war veterans, Oklahombi and Leader, within the space of less than a year, the story of the Choctaw code talkers of World War I was far from over.

5

THE OKLAHOMA CHEROKEE, COMANCHE, OSAGE, SIOUX, AND HO-CHUNK

Although the full extent of the use of Native Americans as code talkers in the American Expeditionary Forces (AEF) is unknown, several army units reportedly used them late in the war. These include the Oklahoma Cherokee, Choctaw, Comanche, Osage, Sioux (Hale 1982:4; Britten 1997:107), and Ho-Chunk. Though far less is known about the use of some groups than others—information about the Choctaw and Eastern Band Cherokee is notably more abundant—this chapter presents what is known of these groups and their service.

Oklahoma Cherokee

Company E, 142nd Infantry Regiment, 36th Division

Although Hale (1982:41) reports that "there was also the group of Cherokee soldiers in the telephone service who disconcerted Germans by transmitting orders in their native language," he does not give their unit or location; whether his reference is to Cherokee in the 30th or 36th Division is unclear.

Two sources specifically identify the use of Oklahoma Cherokee in the 142nd Infantry regiment, 36th Division. Cherokee historian Emmet Starr (1921:517) described that George Adair "was taken from the firing line in France, and placed with other full-blood Cherokees in the telephone service, where they foiled the German 'listeners in' by repeating, receiving, and transmitting the military orders in the Cherokee language." Starr includes a picture of Adair in his WW I army uniform. Adair appears in a list of sixty-eight Cherokee in Company E, 142nd Infantry, the same company that the eight Choctaw code talkers came from. Starr's reference and the presence of Adair and other Cherokee in Company E suggest that Oklahoma Cherokee were used in the Meuse-Argonne offensive, where the 36th served, and that they were distinct from the Eastern Band Cherokee who were used in the 30th Division during the Somme offensive.[1] Adair's service is also recorded in a postwar survey of his service, filled out by one of his officers, that lists him as a cook serving at the front with Company E, 142nd Infantry Regiment, from October 6 to 28, 1918.[2]

A second source, the first providing a date, confirms the use of Oklahoma Cherokee in the 36th Division, along with Choctaw, at Forest Ferme on October 26–27, 1918. The 36th Division Services Report states, "The 142nd Infantry . . . employed Cherokee and Choctaw Indians on its phones to send messages in their native tongue. The stratagem worked with entire success."[3]

In 2010, the Cherokee Nation ran a story in local papers mentioning George Adair and seeking information on other Cherokee code talkers. A similar query ran in the *Native American Times*.[4] To date, no other information regarding WW I Oklahoma Cherokee code talkers is known.

Comanche

357th Infantry Regiment, 90th Infantry Division

At least sixty-two Comanches served in World War I.[5] Two oral history accounts from members of the WW II Comanche code talkers and three news releases report the use of the Comanche language for military communications in World War I. When Comanches were recruited for use in the winter of 1940–41, an article titled "The Indian Sign" (1940) described their use in World War I:

An item from Oklahoma City informs us that A. C. Monahan, director of the Indian Service, has received a War Department request to recommend thirty Comanche Indians for work in the Signal Corps. They would be sent to Atlanta, Ga., for training as Army telephone operators.

Our Comanches serving with the A. E. F. in France during the World War caused the Germans quite a bit of confusion. . . . Headquarters discovered that the Germans had tapped our telephone wires from advanced outposts at the front. Instead of laying new lines, the Signal Corps merely sent Comanches to man the instruments. The Comanches have no written language and there are not more than thirty white men who can understand their spoken language. None of these is German. When the Germans heard the Indians talking on the Western Front they naturally assumed, after exhausting all their foreign language experts, that code was being used. Their code experts were called in and worked hard on the problem, but these too gave up in despair. They never did discover what the Comanches were chatting about. Evidently the War Department thinks Comanche would prove a nice line of talk for the next war.[6]

A second source was issued by the Associated Press in Oklahoma City and reprinted in the *New York Times* on December 13, 1940. Titled "Comanches Again Called for Army Service," it also references the use of Comanche communicators in World War I:

> Oklahoma's Comanche Indians, whose strange tongue not more than 30 white men in the world can fathom, will be ready again to defy decoders as they did in the World War.
>
> A. C. Monahan, director of the Indian Service, had a War Department request to recommend 30 Indians, fluent in their language and able to understand each other, for enlistment to train in Signal Corps work. He chose the Comanche who have no written language.
>
> Professor W. G. Becker of the English Department at Cameron Agricultural College, Lawton, and an authority on the tribe, recalled that several Comanche from Southwestern Oklahoma were used for relaying secret messages in the last war and added,
>
> "One would be at a telephone at the front in communication with another back at headquarters. They would relay orders in their native language. The Germans had tapped the wires, and it must have driven them crazy."
>
> The Army plans to send the Indians to Atlanta for training in Signal Corps work, including telephone and radio transmission.[7]

Two of the WW II Comanche code talkers also knew of Comanche communicators in World War I. Haddon Codynah heard Comanche WW I veterans speak of using Comanche and other Native Americans as code talkers in the First World War.[8] Albert Nahquaddy Jr. was told by his father, Albert Nahquaddy Sr., that he and other Comanche used their native language during World War I.[9] Although these sources reference the use of the Comanche language in World War I, they do not indicate whether coded vocabulary was created.

A 1919 *Oklahoma City Times* article identifies one of the Comanche language communicators who served in the 357th Infantry Regiment, 179th Brigade Infantry, 90th Infantry Division.[10] Formed from Texas and Oklahoma, the 90th later contained men from every state in the union. Known as the Texas-Oklahoma, or "Tough 'Ombres," Division, the 90th was activated on August 25, 1917. The 357th Infantry was organized at Camp Travis, San Antonio, Texas, in August of 1917, with regular troops reporting on September 5. The 179th Brigade, composed of the 357th and 358th Regiments from western and eastern Oklahoma, respectively, was designated as the Oklahoma Brigade. Both regiments contained Native Americans. The 358th, with several all-Native companies, was sometimes referred to as "wholly an Indian regiment" and an "Oklahoma Indian Regiment" (Barsh 1991:298n11; Britten 1997:74; US Congress 1920:2168, 2191).

Around one thousand Oklahoma Native Americans—mostly Choctaw, Chickasaw, and Creek—were brought to Camp Travis in 1917. Like Native Americans in the 36th, many had attended Native American boarding schools, included some accomplished athletes, were "most noticeable" in parade review, were described as easy to get along with by non-Native soldiers, and even participated in a circus in Cues, Germany. Those who had poor English or were illiterate were placed beside those who could "interpret orders" for them. English schools were developed for Mexicans, Native Americans, and some whites (White 1979:22, 29, 45, 59, 61, 71). Less is known about Native servicemen in the 90th than the 36th Division. Whether it was because the 36th was a National Guard division and the 90th a draft division, Natives in the 36th received far more press. The 90th was also not included in Eddy's 1919 study (Eddy 1919; White 1996:71, 193–194).

While training at Camp Travis, Texas, the division was notified that it would be sent to France around May 10, 1918. On June 10, the division entrained at Camp Travis for Camp Mills, New York, where they were joined by two hundred men from Camp Upton. The 90th sailed for Europe on June 20, with elements beginning to land at Aigney-le-Duc, France, on July 1, 1918. The 357th first saw combat on the nights of August 21 and 22, when it marched to Froncheville, but they suffered no serious casualties. On August 22–23, the 357th marched to Martincourt to relieve the 1st Division. The 357th later participated in portions of the St. Mihiel (September 12–16) and Meuse-Argonne (October 19–November 11) offensives. The 357th also participated in the engagements at Villers-en-Haye (August 24-September 11), Puvenelle Sector (September 17–October 10), Puvenelle Sector (Preny offensive, September 26), and Fme. Sebastapol offensive (September 23–24), in 1918. The 357th participated in more engagements than any other organization in the 90th Division, suffering 7,549 casualties, with 1,091 killed in action and 6,458 wounded in action. The 90th returned to the United States and was deactivated in June 1919 (CMHUSA 1988:409–417; Smith 1919; Wythe 1920:1–3).

The most specific document identifying Comanches in the 357th using their native language for military communications is a reference to a 1919 *Oklahoma City Times* article on Calvin Atchavit of Walters, Oklahoma:

The Oklahoma City Times of recent date showed the picture of Calvin Atchavit, who has just returned from France with the 142nd Infantry. Calvin's picture is given here because he is one to whom the Belgian Government gave a War Cross in recognition of his service in talking over the phone during fighting times when the Huns were tapping the lines and trying to get the order of our Army. Calvin's Comanche tongue helped the Allied Army send messages which the Germans could not understand. We are glad that Calvin can be in the home land again.[11]

Though slightly reworded, the June 12 edition of the *Oklahoma City Times* contains a picture of Atchavit with the caption, "To their right is a picture of Calvin Atauvich, a Comanche indian, who is wearing the Belgian war Cross. This was given him by the Belgian government in recognition of his service in talking his native tongue when using American wires and thus fooling the Hun wire tappers."[12]

His use of the Comanche language and award is also referenced in Atchavit's card in the Card File Relating to Indians in World War I in the National Archives. Despite some typographical errors, his card reads:

ATAHHAVIT [sic], CALVIN, Kiowa [sic] Indian Draftee.
Record in File.
Wounded Oct. 22 [Sept. 12], 1918.
Was in battles of St. Mihiel, Returned to USA June 5, 1919.

The Oklahoma City Times published his picture and reported that the Belgian Govt. had given him a WAR CROSS, for talking over the lines when they were TRAPPED BY THE ENEMY, His Comache [sic] tongue helped him get messages across that were not understood by the enemy.[13]

Atchavit was also awarded the American Distinguished Service Cross, the nation's second highest award, for gallantry in action while serving in Company A, 357th Infantry Regiment, 90th Division, of the AEF, on September 12, 1918, near Fey-en-Haye, France. The citation reads, "During the attack of his company, though he had been severely wounded in the left arm, Private Atchavit shot and killed one of the enemy and captured another. To date, Atchavit has been the only Comanche to receive the Distinguished Service Cross." He was presented with the Distinguished Service Cross in September 1919 at the Oklahoma State Fair.[14]

Being the only boy in the family, Robert Achavit was close to his uncle Calvin. He remembered visiting his uncle on West Cache Creek, where they took hikes together. He recalled his uncle using a walking stick and that he had a wound in his hip. Although his uncle never talked about the war, Achavit learned that his uncle sustained the wound while on an assignment laying wire and cutting enemy communication lines and barbed wire in no-man's-land, during which he became separated from the group, got into a skirmish, was wounded, and returned after a few days with a German prisoner.[15]

Determining with whom Atchavit communicated when they first used the Comanche language to send messages is difficult. Seargent Major (Ret.) Lanny Asepermy (n.d., 2017) of the Comanche Nation identified three other Comanche serving in the 357th Infantry Regiment with Atchavit and Nahquaddy: George Clark and Gilbert Pahdi Conwoop in Company A and Samuel Tabbytosavit in Company B. It is highly probable that some or all of these Comanche participated in these communications (Asepermy 2011:1–2, 4). These four men have been recognized as code talkers based on their proximity and this inference. All had been drafted into military service, Conwoop on May 18, Tabbytosavit on May 19, and Atchavit and Clark probably around the same time. They trained at Camp Travis, Texas, near San Antonio and were shipped to Europe on June 19, 1918, arriving in London June 30. After changing ships they proceeded to France, landing at Aigney-le-Duc. In addition to smaller skirmishes, they fought in two major actions: St. Mihiel, from September 12–19; and the Meuse-Argonne, from September 26 to November 11, 1918.

It is hard to determine precisely when Atchavit and other Comanche used their native language. A comparison of the 357th's combat and the wounds these individuals received narrows the possibilities. Stallings (1963:377) reports that the 90th Division spent forty-three days in sector and twenty-six days in combat, while Smith (1919) states that the 357th Regiment served sixty-eight days "under fire." While the 357th experienced their first combat on the nights of August 21 and 22, Smith (1919) reports that "during the time spent in trenches, patrolling and the usual trench duties were taken up. No serious casualties resulted and the morale was excellent."

In preparation for the September 12–19 attack on St. Mihiel, the 1st Battalion, which contained Companies A and B in which Atchavit, Clark, Conwoop, and Tabbytosavit belonged, took over the portion of trenches occupied by the 358th Infantry. At 5:00 A.M. on September 12, the 357th was in the assault echelon supported by the 2nd Battalion, with the 3rd Battalion in brigade reserve. The 1st Battalion participated in the assault from September 12 through the raid on the Trench de Grograns and Trench de Pepinier on the night of September 22–23. The 1st Battalion was soon relived for one week by the 3rd Battalion, then returned to the front line. The 357th then participated in the Meuse-Argonne campaign (September 26–November 11, 1918) including assaults on Bantheville (October 23),

Grande Carre Fme. (October 24, which the 179th Brigade helped assault and hold until relieved on the evening of October 30–31), and Sassey and Baalon in early November (Smith 1919).

During these two campaigns, the units in which the Comanche served experienced heavy machine gun and artillery fire, gas, and hand-to-hand fighting, but they never failed to reach their objectives. On November 23, the Comanches, with the exception of Gilbert Conwoop, who was hospitalized and recovering from wounds, marched through reclaimed areas in France and Luxembourg before crossing at Grevenmacher, Luxembourg, into Germany, where they performed occupation duty into May 1919, until elements of the unit were withdrawn from Germany to the port of St. Nazaire, France, for shipment back to the United States (Asepermy n.d.:2; 2012).

Atchavit was severely wounded at St. Mihiel and hospitalized on September 12 during the first day of the AEF's assault on that town. Conwoop was "severely wounded in action" on October 25 during the Meuse-Argonne campaign, around the time that orders were received to take and hold the Grand Carre Fme. Following a fifteen-minute artillery barrage, the 1st and 3rd Battalions jumped off and advanced forward. Although elements of the 1st Battalion reached the outskirts of the farm several times, heavy machine gun and artillery fire prevented them from holding their position. Company K and other elements of the 3rd Battalion advanced past the farm on the right side but were also driven back. On October 25, the Germans attempted their last counterattack, beginning with an artillery barrage at 5:05 P.M. The Americans responded with a barrage at 5:26 P.M., inflicting heavy casualties on the enemy. The 357th repulsed the German counterattack within thirty minutes with rifle and machine gun fire. Mopping-up parties were sent around the area; however, the lines had held and no Germans had broken through. Conwoop was probably wounded during this action. Because the regiment was suffering very heavy casualties as a result of their exposed position in front of the mainline, orders were received to establish a line farther south, which the 179th Brigade organized and held despite terrific shelling and counterattack until relieved by the 180th Brigade on the night of October 30 (Smith 1919). Tabbytosavit is reported as being in an Orleans hospital recovering from "a bad foot" on September 29 (Asepermy 2011:1–2, 4; 2012), but whether from a wound or trench foot is unknown.

Calvin Atchavit	357th, Co. A	Wounded, Sept. 12
Samuel Tabbytosavit	357th, Co. B	In Hospital, Sept. 29
Gilbert Conwoop	357th, ____	Wounded Oct. 25
George Clark	357th, ____	Not wounded

Albert Nahquaddy Jr., who trained with the Comanche code talkers during World War II but did not go overseas, reported that his father told him that he and other Comanche used their language to send military messages during World War I after an officer overheard him and another Comanche conversing in Comanche to sight in an artillery gun.[16] Robert Atchavit also reported that an officer had the idea to use the Comanche language to send messages over landlines that the Germans were tapping after overhearing the men talking to one another.[17]

Edward "Albert" Nahquaddy Sr.'s card in the National Archives states that he was drafted on April 4, 1918, and entered service in the 46th Company, 12th Battalion, 165 Depot Brigade, at Camp Travis, Texas. He went overseas on June 19, 1918, and served at St. Mihiel and the Argonne Forest. He was wounded and gassed but not hospitalized and was discharged in May of 1919.[18] The 165th Brigade Field Artillery was in the 90th Division and correlates with Nahquaddy's statement regarding participating in sighting in an artillery piece.[19]

It is unknown whether the Comanche sent and received any messages with Comanche in other units or if any code terms were created, when any of the three wounded Comanche men returned to their units, and whether they performed telephone service while hospitalized or in the rear echelons, as reported for Choctaws Otis Leader and Tobias Frazier.

The available data suggest that Atchavit could have used Comanche between August 21 and September 12, most likely in the preparations for the start of the St. Mihiel assault on September 12. At this time, none of the four Comanche were wounded. Another possibility is that he used Comanche sometime after September 12, when he was wounded, and before September 29, when Tabbytosavit entered the hospital. Conwoop was wounded on October 25. Clark was not wounded and presumably was present throughout these actions. Unfortunately, we do not know when these individuals returned to their unit following hospitalization, which could narrow the possible dates when most or all could have been used for communications, if they were the recipients. Possibilities appear to have been no earlier than September 12, 1918, and likely occurred at some point thereafter.

The 357th ultimately fought in a total of six engagements during World War I: Villers-en-Haye (August 24–September 11); St. Mihiel (September 12–16); Puvenelle Sector (September 17–October 10); Puvenell Sector (Fme. Sebastapol offensive, September 23–24); Puvenelle Sector (Preny offensive, September 26); and Meuse-Argonne (October 19–November 11) (Smith 1919; Wythe 1920:1–3).

Atchavit was discharged on June 19, 1919, at Camp Bowie, Texas. Conwoop was also discharged in 1919 at Camp Bowie. Clark was discharged on

July 17, 1919, at Camp Travis, Texas. Nahquaddy was discharged on May 24, 1919, at Camp Pike, Arkansas. Tabbytosavit was also discharged at Camp Pike, Arkansas, in 1919 (Asepermy 2011:1–2, 4; Asepermy 2012, n.d.:3).

Osage

Company M, 143rd Infantry Regiment, 36th Infantry Division

Although nearly one hundred Osage served during World War I, little is known concerning the use of their language. A review of service records in the National Archives demonstrates that Osage served in the 28th, 32nd, 35th, 36th, 37th, 77th, 89th, and 90th Divisions, with the largest concentration in the 36th.[20]

From an interview with two non-Native WW I veterans in the 36th, Private Wendell Martin (Company B, 11th Engineers) and Private Alphonzo Bulz (Company M, 143rd Infantry), Berry (1978:292–303) reports that Osage were used for telephone communications in the 143rd Infantry Regiment, a unit that contained a considerable number of Native Americans from Oklahoma.[21] As Bulz (Berry 1978:295) reported, "The ones in my company were mainly the Osage. They used to love to talk on our telephones, and they'd talk in the Osage [language]. We used to wonder if the Germans could ever interpret those calls. If the Germans could, it would have confused the hell out of them." Although this account does not specify how many Osage were used or who they were, it implies that their transmissions were military communications considering their low rank and that unsanctioned access to phones was unlikely.

Bulz (Berry 1978:295) also describes several wealthy Oklahoma Native Americans having oil money and using war whoops in combat, German apprehension of fighting Native Americans, and American admiration of their combat service. Bulz notes that on occasion, while drinking, "they'd do war dances right there in the camp. I don't know if you've ever heard an Indian war whoop, but it is a cross between a scream and a yelp." When non-Native soldiers complained to an officer, the officer told them that the Native soldiers were simply letting off steam and that the complaining troops should bide their time:

> Just wait till they get to France. They'll be the best ones we have. And you know, he might have been right. They were great when we went into the Champagne sector. They'd jump out of those foxholes, screaming those war whoops and yelling in the Cherokee and the Choctaw and all those languages. I think the Germans were scared to death of them. I remember this one officer we captured-he was

petrified, "What kind of men are zeze?" he asked us. "Zey are vild men; ve can't fight wit vild men!"[22]

Captain Lavine mentions the assignment by Captain Horner of the eight Choctaw under "Chief George Baconrind" (Osage) to "transmit his orders in original Choctaw." However, there is no mention of the use of Osage language by Baconrind, any of the other six Osage in Company E, 142nd Regiment (Lavine 1921b:327), or in Bloor's (1919) memo on the Choctaw.[23]

Following the passage of the 2008 Code Talker Recognition Act, the Osage Nation was awarded a Congressional Gold Medal on November 23, 2013, at the Congressional Gold and Silver Medal recognition ceremonies for Native American code talkers in Washington, DC (Meadows 2011, 2016). This award appears to be based on reports of Osage in the 143rd Infantry.

Around 2012, the Osage Nation was contacted by the Department of Defense, which informed them that Augustus Chouteau was a code talker in World War I. This identification is problematic. According to a photo and summary of Private Augustus Chouteau's military service (Welch et al. 1920:313), he never went overseas during World War I: "After receiving his military training at Camp Bowie, Texas, Company D, 1st Oklahoma Cavalry, 36th Division; transferred to 111th Ammunition Train; in regular service; served on the Mexican border; did not go overseas; at camp contracted the influenza, followed by pneumonia, which resulted in his death, Dec. 11, 1919." These records indicate that Augustus could not have been a code talker and suggest that the identification was not verified with military records.

As Choteau was the only "officially" identified Osage code talker, one Congressional Silver Medal was minted and presented to his granddaughter Francis Chouteau Jones. Jones reported that "my grandmother told me that those boys [Osage enlisted] spoke to each other over there in the native language so no one could understand them. It was one of the few things I knew about my grandfather and I made sure to tell all my daughters." The Silver Medal was presented to Jones on November 11, 2016, at the Osage Veteran's Day Dance, hosted by the Hominy War Mothers, at the Wah-Zha-Zhi Cultural Center in Pawhuska, Oklahoma. Augustus Choteau's brother, Charley Chouteau (Army Service No. 1490104), served in Company E, 142nd, and Company D, 143rd Infantry Regiments, embarked overseas on August 3, 1918, and did see action in the Champagne and Meuse-Argonne. He returned to the United States on the USS *Finland* May 31, 1919. However, the nature of his service is not mentioned (Meadows 2002:216; Welch et. al 1920:313).[24]

According to John Henry Mashunkashey, several Osage were taken from Carlisle Indian School and inducted into the US Army, and then served in artillery and infantry units where they spoke to one another on telephones to relate information about incoming rounds.[25] No unit designations are known. According to available data, there were no Osage code talkers in World War II.[26]

Siouan Groups

Members of an unspecified Sioux tribe are also reported to have used their native language to provide military communications against the Germans in World War I. The January 10, 1919, edition of the *Stars and Stripes* describes the Army's use of their language.

BOCHE WIRE TAPPERS RUN INTO NEW CODE

Sioux Observer and Receiver Make Things Easy for Gunners.

Because of the nature of the country over which American troops fought in the Meuse-Argonne offensive, the Germans found it easy at times to cut in on our field telephone wires.

The commander of one brigade of artillery attached to an American division was particularly annoyed by enemy wire-tappers in a heavily wooded section of the Argonne. Code messages from artillery observers were being intercepted by Boche listeners-in, and the commander knew, as all armies know, that no code is impregnable when experts get working on it.

The artillery commander took up with the colonel of one of the line regiments the question of the Huns' wire-tapping activities. And the colonel hit upon an idea.

Two Indians, both of proud Sioux lineage, members of one of his companies, were assigned as telephone operators. One was to go forward with the artillery observer, the other to remain at the brigade receiving end of the wire which the artillery captain was certain the Germans had that day tapped somewhere along the line.

The two Sioux, both intelligent, willing men, were sent for and given instructions. Those instructions were to transmit, in the language of their fathers, all messages given them at their respective posts.

Now, when two Sioux Indians get talking together in their own tongue, what they say sounds very much like code, but isn't. Anyway, it raised hob with the code experts of certain Prussian guard units.

The Sioux stuck on their jobs for three days and nights. They and the artillery commander and their own colonel enjoyed the situation immensely. If the Germans got any fun out of it they kept it to themselves.[27]

Private Paul Picotte, a Yankton Sioux in Battery E, 30th Field Artillery, expressed great pride about Native American contributions during the war, even asserting that Indian telephone operators won the war—single handedly!

> You'll never see it in the histories. But during the First World War all of the various codes of the different nations within that war were ciphered by the Germans, you know that. And to me, that World War was ended by the Indian boys who were in the service, because eventually they were put up to the front as in the, in the communication system, and they talked Indian and then later was transferred to Indians in the commanding officer's quarters and the world war came to an end.[28]

Unfortunately Picotte provides no tribal affiliation, personal names, or unit affiliation. His statement also does not indicate if his knowledge of these activities is first hand, or if he was involved, but rather appears to be hearsay, and may be the source from which some have inferred WW I "Yankton" code talkers.

John Whirlwind Horse, an Oglala Sioux from Pine Ridge in South Dakota serving in Company C, 357th Infantry, 90th Division, described how "they used two Sioux boys on the wire. The Germans were tapping the wires. These boys gave the orders in the Sioux tongue, and thus the German was outwitted."[29] Again, no unit was designated.

Standing Rock Lakota

The Standing Rock Lakota report that Albert Grass and Richard Blue Earth served as code talkers in World War I. Both men originally enlisted in Company I, 2nd Infantry, First North Dakota National Guard, and along with fellow Lakota Joseph Jordan of Standing Rock and Tom Rogers and Joe Young Hawk from Fort Berthold, were reassigned to Company A, 18th Infantry Regiment, 1st Infantry Division in January of 1918 (Grass 2013; Knudson and Knudson 2012a:19–21, 47–48; Welch 1934).

Both Grass and Blue Earth were killed in action in 1918. Grass was killed on July 18, 1918, during the Aisne-Marne campaign while attempting to get water for his fellow soldiers along the Soissons-Paris Road when the 18th Infantry received heavy fire from German troops. The 1st and 2nd Battalions of the 18th had become so depleted that together they barely comprised half of a battalion (Knudson and Knudson 2012a:47–48). Knudson and Knudson (2012a:47–48) cite the unit's regimental history to describe the intensity of the fire that the 18th had been taking when Grass was killed: "Here, as elsewhere, the greatest difficulty was met in bringing up rations and water from the rear. Due to the continuous bombardment only one meal was brought up each day and this invariably was cold. A half canteen of water had to last through an entire day for most of the men. On several occasions ration carts coming up from the rear were destroyed and the men went hungry." Blue Earth was killed on October 9, 1918, during an assault in the Meuse-Argonne campaign (Knudson and Knudson 2012a:19–21, 47–48).

Knudson and Knudson (2012a, 2012b) do not mention that communication work by Blue Earth or Grass could not have occurred later than July 18, the date of Grass's death.[30] They are not likely the Sioux referenced in the January 10, 1919, *Stars and Stripes* article, because Grass was killed before the Meuse-Argonne campaign. However, as the 90th was in the Meuse-Argonne, they could be the Sioux referred to by Whirlwind Horse.

Elements of the 1st Division entered combat on October 23, 1917, when the first American artillery of the war was fired on German forces. Members of the 2nd Battalion, 16th Infantry, suffered some of the first American Army casualties two days later. Grass and Blue Earth are reported as arriving overseas on December 15, 1917 (Knudson and Knudson 2012a:19–21, 47–48). With a window of December 15, 1917, to Grass' death on July 18, 1918, this narrows down the possibilities to two likely periods: the Aisne-Marne offensive of May 27 to June 5, 1918; or the Montdidier-Noyon defensive of June 9 to June 13, 1918, at which both are recorded as having served.

The biggest problem in identifying Sioux code talkers has been the absence of information that might identify which Sioux are referred to and the lack of evidence beyond brief oral history. The only source I have encountered naming Grass and Blue Earth as code talkers is a 2001 letter to the *Lakota Journal* by Blue Earth's grandson Richard Blue Earth III. The letter mentions the announcement recognizing the Navajo code talkers, questioning if WW I code talkers will be recognized.[31]

The Standing Rock Lakota eventually turned in forty-five WW I veterans as code talkers, who were posthumously awarded medals through the Code Talkers Recognition Act of 2008 (Meadows 2011, 2016; SRST 2013). This is not only unlikely but suspect in terms of military structure. First, it assumes that all these men were not only fluent speakers of Lakota, which most probably were, but that they were also sufficiently fluent in English. Many Native Americans were not fluent in English during World War I and did poorly in standardized tests. This is a large number of men to be used without distributing them over many units. During World War I, most companies had one telephone post at each company command post, with lines extending back to larger battalion, artillery, and other units. Other examples, such as the Choctaw, who used eight men in the 142nd

Infantry Regiment and Stanley's (1931) use of Eastern Band Cherokee in the 30th Division in World War I, indicate a smaller number of men at key positions. During World War II, the Navajo often used only six to eight men per regiment, while the 4th, 32nd, and 34th Divisions all used eight to seventeen men per division.

The tribal representative reported that he identified Lakota code talkers by visiting tribal cemeteries to find the graves of all WW I veterans.[32] Nearly half of the men who were reported to have been from Standing Rock Reservation as code talkers do not appear to have even been in the right locations to serve as code talkers. Based on their exit interviews and on service and other records (Knudson and Knudson 2012a, 2012b), at least seventeen of these individuals remained in stateside locations, were hospitalized or discharged for medical issues prior to going overseas, or saw no combat while overseas. One individual did not even join the armed forces until 1920. These seventeen men include Charles Little Chief (stateside), John Brave Bull (stateside), George Molash (stateside), George Sleeps From Home (stateside, hospitalized), Joseph Gray Day (stateside), Benjamin Gray Hawk (stateside), Luke Speaks Walking (no combat), Julius Bear Shield (no combat), Paul Good Iron (stateside), George Many Wounds (served in Philippines), Joseph Pretends Eagle (stateside), George James Red Fox (no combat), George W. Santee (no combat), George Two Bear (enlisted 1920), Richard White Eagle (medical discharge, stateside), Paul White Lightening (stateside), and James Tattooed (1 month, medical discharge, stateside) (Knudson and Knudson 2012a, 2012b).

Based on their service records and unit movements, John Red Bean, Joseph Two Bears, Louis Big Horn Elk, and Frank Young Bear all arrived overseas very late in the war, and with Harry Lean Elk, who arrived overseas on May 3, 1918, and died of pneumonia on June 6, 1918, may not have seen combat (Knudson and Knudson 2012a, 2012b). Yet all were included as medal recipients at the Congressional Gold and Silver Medal ceremonies of November 20, 2013 (Meadows 2016).

Several other issues are also problematic. No one investigated what divisions they served in, their numbers, or their actual service dates in relation to hospitalization. A review of the forty-five Standing Rock Lakota indicate that they appeared in dispersed coast artillery units and in the following divisions and numbers: 1st (4), 3rd (1), 33rd (1), 35th (3), 82nd (2), 88th (2), 90th (1), and 91st (4). Unless there were other unknown Siouan speakers, the low numbers of individuals in some of these units make the likelihood of code talking impossible. While many of the Lakota who participated in the Wanamaker survey describe the nature of their duties and combat experiences, not one mentions any connection to communications work, in contrast to the officers and the Choctaw in the 142nd.

This inclusion of so many Standing Rock Lakota is likely attributable to the verification committee for the Code Talker Recognition Act of 2008 not requiring proof of having served as code talkers or of actually having been in a combat zone at the time. As one member of the committee described, they only accepted the list of names vetted by each tribe as code talkers and had records checked to see that those individuals had actually been in the US armed forces.[33] Their service dates in relation to when and where their respective units served were not checked. At this point, it is very difficult to confirm that many Standing Rock Lakota were in fact code talkers, although it seems that some Siouan speakers definitely served in this fashion, as indicated by the articles in *Stars and Stripes* (1919a), the *American Indian* magazine (1919), and the Paul Picotte (Yankton) interview.

While this does not diminish the honorable service of these men, as the vetting and recognition of them as code talkers came years after their deaths, it represents a serious flaw in the research, vetting, and awarding of these congressional medals. Descendants in many of these Lakota families have stated that they had no idea their grandfather or great-grandfather had served as a code talker in World War I. Unfortunately, for many of these men their military service records indicate that they could not have, which will undoubtedly come as a disappointment to their descendants. What, if anything, will be done regarding the bestowal of these medals, remains to be seen.

Winnebago (Ho-Chunk)

Company A, 7th Infantry Regiment, 3rd Infantry Division

A 1919 article in the *Carlisle Indian School*, reprinted from the *Milwaukee Sentinel*, describes the use of two Winnebago in the 3rd Infantry Division:

WINNEBAGO INDIANS UPHELD RECORD
OF ANCESTORS IN WORLD WAR.

Early in 1918, two Winnebago Indians in this city answered the call of their country and enlisted in the army with the hope of seeing early service in France. They were John H. Longtail and Robert Big Thunder and their record at Château-Thierry shows that they upheld the traditions of their brave and fighting forefathers.

The two men who are cousins were members of the infantry (regulars) Third Division. It is now a matter of history that this division stood against the best of German[y at] Chateau Thierry and it was in this battle that both were wounded.

Like so many Indians in the war these men were used for scouts, snipers and telephone operators, and during their seven weeks in the front-line trenches had many interesting and exciting experiences. Both went over the top three times and both withstood three attacks from the enemy.

The Indians' natural adaptability to trench warfare was reflected in the work of the men who acted as scouts. They were able to go out and get information and return safely in many cases where white men would fail. Another place where they were invaluable was in transmitting telephone messages, where there was a possibility of messages being intercepted by Germans. In these cases the Indians would transmit the messages in their own tongue.

Private Lon[g]tail has been honorably discharged, while Private Big Thunder is still being treated in an eastern hospital—Milwaukee (Wis.) Sentinal.[34]

Big Thunder's Bureau of Indian Affairs card at the National Archives confirms that he used his native language: "Big Thunder, Robert[,] Full-Blood Winnebago Indian, Wounded in France, Over the top three times, also adopted the Indian code signal. Now in U.S. Fort McHenry, Gen. Hospital. Enlisted in Army. Formerly Student At Hampton Institute, Hampton, Virginia."[35]

Family and tribal records indicate that these two men appear to have been among twenty-nine Winnebago who originally enlisted in the 128th Infantry Regiment of the 32nd Division. Big Thunder and Longtail appear to have been transferred to the 3rd Division at some point. Both men appear on the April 6, 1918, embarkation list for Company A, 7th Infantry Regiment, 3rd Division, sailing from Hoboken, New Jersey. A letter that Big Thunder wrote to his father states that he was wounded on June 21 by shrapnel in the face and was hospitalized. The family reports that this was while he was "fighting in a reassigned regiment positioned in the front line." While his name is included on a monument for the 128th Infantry Regiment, his gravestone in the Native American Church Cemetery in Wittenburg, Wisconsin, lists that he served in "A Co, 7th Infantry Regiment."[36]

During the war, the 3rd Division served in the Champagne-Marne, Aisne-Marne, St. Mihiel, and Meuse-Argonne campaigns of 1918. Both Big Thunder and Longtail were wounded on June 21, 1918, at Bois de Belleau in the Aisne defensive. Big Thunder's records list him as participating in the "Aisne Defensive Sector (Bois de Belleau; Chateau-Thierry)" and at "(Soissons; Belleau)." One of Longtail's records lists him at Bois de Belleau. While the date of the use of their native language is not recorded, it appears to have been before June 21, 1918, when Big Thunder was wounded and evacuated. Although the *Indian School Journal* reports that this occurred at Château-Thierry, their service records list their wounds as occurring at Bois de Belleau (Belleau Wood, June 1–26, 1918), where the 3rd Division participated and which correlates with the dates of their wounds. Big Thunder's records also indicate that he served at Château-Thierry.[37] Their use for military communications in June 1918 is the earliest known use of Native American military communicators to date, occurring prior to the Eastern Band Cherokee and Choctaw. These records suggest that they used their native language in the seven weeks leading up to and during the fighting at Belleau Wood.

Private First Class Robert Big Thunder hailed from Wittenburg, Wisconsin.[38] He attended Hampton Normal Institute in Hampton, Virginia. A portion of a letter he wrote to his father in late June 1918 appeared in the *Southern Workman* (1918a:558):

> I was wounded last Friday, June 21, at 5 o'clock in the morning. We made a rapid raid on the Germans early that morning at 3 o'clock, and chased them off a big hill. Our raid was very successful. A piece of bursting shrapnel hit me below my left eye, cutting my skin, and went through my nose. I shall be well again, but am afraid my left eye will be very weak. After being wounded I ran all the way from the front to the first-aid dressing station under heavy artillery fire, but was lucky and was not hit by anything. Another fellow came out with me and we got dressed at the first-aid station, and a[n] auto ambulance hurried us to the field hospital. Then from there I went to two other hospitals, getting the best of care, and finally they shipped us on a U.S. Red Cross hospital train to this base Hospital No. -. I shall be here till I get good and well. It will be some time. Thank God I was not killed. I wish I was home working on the farm, but this is our duty, and we must fight it to a finish, then we can go home.
>
> I've found out what war is now. Gee, it's quite an experience to be in a war like this. I'll never forget the moments I spent at the front. I could hear bullets whistling all around me and big shells from German artillery bursting right behind. Some Germans were up in the trees shooting down on us, and hand grenades coming over and bursting close to us hit some of our boys, hurting them bad. I was with one boy who could shoot well, and he shot down one of the Germans in the tree. One machine gun was only about eight yards from us, but they couldn't see us. I was behind four little trees together, and shooting. We chased them quite a ways and then I was wounded.

Private John H. Longtail was a Winnebago from Winnebago, Nebraska. Longtail enlisted on February 1, 1918. He appears to have served in the

128th Infantry, 32nd Division, later being transferred and serving in Company A, 7th Infantry Regiment, 3rd Division. He was discharged on January 15, 1919, at Camp Grant, Ilinois. His Application for Headstone or Marker, applied for on April 29, 1948, notes that he was awarded the Purple Heart.[39]

While several WW II Ho-Chunk veterans were included in the Code Talker Recognition Act of 2008 (Meadows 2001, 2016), these two WW I veterans were not. Based on the above documentation, they qualify for recognition under the act, and I am in the process of seeking that recognition for them.

First Nations Peoples (Canadian Armed Forces)

Three sources (Aaseng 1992:20; Paul 1973:9; Wright 1986) report that Canadian forces in World War I tried unsuccessfully to use Native languages when they discovered that their telephone lines had been tapped by the Germans. According to Lieutenant Colonel James E. Jones, the Native Americans "had no words in their vocabulary that were exact equivalents for military terms. For example they could find no way of transmitting 'machine gun' or 'barrage.'" The plan reportedly failed because the military had too many terms for which no Indian equivalent then existed. Dempsey (1983:4) states that among First Nations Canadians in World War I, "Language was a common problem among native enlisters since many Indians were unfamiliar with English at first and communication was difficult." Canada's problems in using First Nations soldiers for military communications may reflect a general lack of extensive English fluency among Indigenous Canadians or the Canadian military forces' failure to devise and implement a code instead of looking for direct cognates or vocabulary equivalents in the existing Native languages.

Other Possible Contributions: Cheyenne and Kaw

The earliest reference to Cheyenne using their native language to send and receive messages in World War I is from Britten (1997:107). While a 1939 source issued by Major General E. B. Adams and focusing on the use of the Choctaw code talkers in the 142nd Infantry Regiment mentions the presence of Cheyenne and many other tribes in the regiment, it only refers to the use of Choctaw. "Dear Sir: . . . In the 36th Division practically every Indian tribe in the Southwest was represented, including Choctaw, Comanche, Chickasaw, and Cheyenne Indians. In the latter part of October 18, the 142nd of that division made use of eight Indians of the Choctaw tribe, who were placed in important C.P.'s [command posts] and transmitted messages in their language."[40] One possibility may be Northern Cheyenne from Montana, who served in the 40th Division. The 158th Infantry Regiment contained a predominantly Native American company (Britten 1997:74). In 2017, I was contacted by the Southern Cheyenne in Oklahoma asking if I could provide the names of any Cheyenne code talkers. To date, I have been unable to identify any Cheyenne who served as code talkers in World War I or II. The Cheyenne were initially not included in the Code Talkers Recognition Act of 2008 (Meadows 2011, 2016) but have been added under the Cheyenne and Arapaho in October 2017.

Another claim regarding the use of WW I code talkers involves Moses "Mose" Bellmard, a Kaw (Kansa) Indian from Oklahoma who was born February 16, 1891, and died in March 1948. In 2010, Ken Kirkland presented information regarding the involvement of members of the Kaw Tribe in the use of their native language for military communications. Mose Bellmard, one of the last hereditary Kaw chiefs, attended Wentworth Military Academy in Lexington, Missouri. On September 15, 1915, he joined the US Army, becoming a first lieutenant by June 18, 1916. A 1948 obituary and feature story for Bellmard describes his service in Company E, 1st Oklahoma Infantry (later part of the 142nd Infantry Regiment) starting on July 30, 1918, during World War I in France.

> Bellmard, head of an Indian division [company] . . . is also credited with being the man who originated the use of Indian language in the First World War to battle the enemy's code deciphers. The Germans had been able to unravel every code file Americans could devise and intercepted their plans. Desperate, American officers appealed to Bellmard who offered the suggestion that an Indian sender and receiver be stationed at each dispatch point. Messages were then transmitted in a little-known language which has never appeared in written form. The Indian receivers in turn translated the messages back into English. This method of sending highly secret messages was carried over into World War II and is still believed to defy all attempts to decode it by the enemy. Bellmard was promoted to the rank of captain for his suggestion.[41]

Bellmard served as a first lieutenant in Company D, 1st Oklahoma Infantry, and later as an officer under Captain Charles H. Johnson, in Company C, 142nd Infantry Regiment. Unlike Company E, 142nd, Company C was a largely non-Native company (White 1979:11).[42] The *Kanza Newsletter* (2008) later summarized this report.[43]

These accounts do not suggest that Bellmard or any Kaw tribal members used their Native language for military purposes in the war, but that Bellmard suggested the use of Native American communicators. As discussed in chapter 3, E. W. Horner received a call from Captain Nelson at battalion headquarters, commanded by Major William J. Morrissey, requesting a number of Native Americans of one tribe who could use their language to transmit and receive the messages. Because the date of these accounts (1948) preceded by decades both popular and tribal efforts to garner recognition for Native American code talkers, they would appear reliable. Lieutenant Bellmard could have been consulted by higher ranking officers or been in a group of officers attempting to solve the existing problem. However, there is no evidence he was associated with the battalion headquarters.

While the 142nd Infantry Regiment was training at Bar-sur-Aube, France, in July 1918, a number of rapid changes in regimental personnel occurred among both officers and enlisted men (Chastaine 1920:45–47; White 1984:106–108). Lieutenant Bellmard is listed with Company C, 142nd Infantry (1st Battalion) when it went on the line in early October 1918 (Barnes 1922:344), but an October 19, 1918, report (Spence 1919:543; White 1979:14) states that Bellmard was "on SD at 1st Corps School during engagement." He reportedly led patrols that captured Germans and was severely gassed. In the confusion, he was transferred to a medical facility some distance from his unit and was believed dead for several days. Returning to the United States to recuperate, he saved the news of his return as a surprise only to walk in on his own funeral feast and ceremony in the Kaw community.[44] On July 12, 2010, Senator James Inhofe (2010) entered a record of Mose Bellmard's service into the *Congressional Record*. The Kaw Nation website currently claims the following:

> Mose Bellmard was in the United States Military Services during World War I and World War II. At the end of WWI, the American soldiers began using an Indian code to communicate. It was hoped that this code would confuse the enemy. During the end of WWI until 1939, Captain Mose Bellmard worked with the Defense Department to develop this code for use in the Pacific Theater. Until recently, most of this was classified information. On July 12, 2010, Oklahoma Senator Jim Inhofe entered into the Congressional Record "Remembering Code Talker Mose Bellmard," which recognized Captain Bellmard as the originator of the Code Talking.[45]

The website contains a picture of Captain Horner and five of the Choctaw code talkers in Company E, 142nd Infantry, mistakenly labeled "Mose Bellmard and other members of the WW I Code Talkers." I have not seen any documentation of Bellmard's involvement in any code-talking programs associated with the Pacific Theater of World War II. While his actual contributions are unclear, there is no evidence that the Kaw language was used, and the Kaw were not included under the Code Talkers Recognition Act of 2008 (Meadows 2011, 2016).

Several Tribes have claimed to have and been recognized for having had code talkers in World War I under the Code Talker Recognition Act of 2008. However, for many of these groups that have "World War I" marked on their Congressional Code Talker Medals (Cheyenne, Cheyenne River Sioux, Crow Creek Sioux, Mohawk, Pawnee, Ponca, Sac and Fox Tribe of the Mississippi in Iowa, Meskwaki Nation, Santee Sioux, Standing Rock Sioux, Yankton Sioux), virtually no sources or names of individuals have been made public. The Ponca medal includes both world wars, but only William T. Snake has been named and recognized for World War II. In some cases, an individual is purported to have been a code talker—and may have been—but no actual evidence is provided.[46]

While less is known about some groups, varied levels of data exist for the Oklahoma Cherokee, Comanche, Ho-Chunk, Osage, and some Siouan speakers as code talkers in World War I. Others may have performed similar service but are simply not documented. Although the use of Native languages for secure military communications was a hastily developed experiment late in the war, the accounts of military officers clearly indicate that they proved successful where used.

Chapter 6 focuses on the period since World War II. During this period, a renewed interest in their service, their influence on other code talkers, and a grassroots interest in honoring them for their service in World War I emerged.

6

RECOGNITION

As World War II approached, the Choctaw code talkers of World War I contributed support for the coming conflict in three forms. Their most direct form of support were the offers made by some to reenlist. Less direct but no less significant was the support garnered from their wartime reputations and the stories of their unique contributions; renewed news coverage on the accomplishments of WW I code talkers encouraged others to participate, and the US armed forces used knowledge of their service from World War I to recruit other tribes and to expand the use of code talkers in World War II.

An October 1940 news release from Joseph Oklahombi's hometown of Wright City, Oklahoma, reports that "Oklahoma's outstanding World War hero is ready to fight again for his country if needed." Following the news of events in Europe, Oklahombi also stated, "The United States must prepare and do it immediately . . . [as he believes] the European war is more horrible than the World War."[1] Copies of this article appeared in newspapers across the country. In 1939, James Edwards tried to reenlist but was rejected because he was married (and probably because of his age). Following a divorce and with the start of World War II, Edwards believed he would be more eligible for service and that the use of Choctaw would stump the Germans again. A 1941 news article described his efforts to reenlist: "'They wouldn't take me in 1939, but I've got my divorce now and I'm as healthy as I ever was.' He taps his barrel-like chest with gusto. 'Maybe they haven't learned to talk Choctaw, and they need us now,' he added."[2]

The accomplishments of Leader, Oklahombi, and other Native Americans also appeared during the war in articles praising the accomplishments of Native Americans in World War I and the high rate of voluntary enlistments and resources offered by Native Americans after Pearl Harbor. In particular, Leader's service record and the English version of Oklahombi's citation were frequently reprinted, including at least twenty-four articles on Oklahombi and forty-three on Leader during the 1940s.[3] One article reprinting Oklahombi's citation references the service of Native Americans, albeit related to the American ideals of the Indian Scout Syndrome, while promoting courage against unfavorable odds: "In the last war the Indians were the coolest men to face the enemy. Certainly acts for which Indians received awards indicate that Indian soldiers and scouts were often far ahead of the Allied front; that they fought grimly to win, no matter what the odds. For example, a translation of the order under which Private Joseph Oklahombi . . . received the Croix de Guerre reads as follows."[4]

The Effectiveness of the Choctaw and Other Code Talkers

Historians have tended to focus on four questions related of the role of the Choctaw code talkers in World War I: (1) Why were Native Americans chosen as code talkers? (2) What made them successful? (3) Were they effective, and to what extent did their service contribute to the end of the war? and (4) What impact did they have on the US military?

Bruce White (1976:22) and Lonnie White (1979:17) both conclude that the Choctaws were chosen because it was a "practical" and "logical solution" to the problem of German eavesdropping. Some sources (Britten 1997:106; Callaway 1992) maintain that the choice was based on chance, when Choctaws were heard speaking in their native language, and not a preexisting military plan. This explanation is likely based on news reports, which do not correlate with the accounts of officers in the 142nd.

While Choctaw code talking was used only during two days at Forest Ferme, its success was instant as a result of the obscurity and inaccessibility of their language (Bloor 1919; Kahn 1967:549; Langellier 2000:7; Wise 1931:537–638). Wise (1931:537–538) noted that "the special use made of Indians in the occasion described was possible more by reason of their unfamiliar tongue than of any particular military qualifications which they possessed" and maintained that native speakers of other isolated languages, such as African languages, would have been just as effective as Choctaw. As Kahn (1967:549) described, "The United States raised the latter device to the level of a full-scale system in both world wars by making use of a resource that virtually no other combatant had; pools of tongues so recondite that almost no one else in the world understood them."

Many nonacademic writers have stated that the Choctaw contributed to the end of World War I and saved many lives. Other popular, newspaper, and oral history accounts even maintain that the war was won *because* of the Choctaw and other Native American code talkers, a belief that many individuals, Native and non-Native alike, continue to proudly assert. In discussing the use of eight Choctaw in late October and the surrender of Germany on November 11, 1918, Solomon Louis "said he feels that the action by his company that day, made possible only because of what he and his seven Choctaw companions did, was the 'atom bomb' of World War I."[5]

Naturally, the Choctaw are proud of their ancestors' service in the war. Yet many of these claims have been taken at face value and repeated without question. In spite of the unique nature of their service and the success at Forest Ferme, numerous independent sources of documentary evidence do not support this contention. Although documentary sources indicate that code talkers definitely contributed to the achievements of their respective units, there is no indication that the war was won solely as a result of their efforts. Germany had already retreated in some areas and continued to do so in the early stages of the Meuse-Argonne campaign, and the war would have been won without the use of Native American languages, though it certainly could have taken longer to win and would no doubt have cost more lives, as was borne out by the battle at Forest Ferme, the only documented action in which the Choctaw language was used (Chastaine 1920:229–235; White 1984:167).

While certainly a unique contribution, code talking was a minor part of the larger Meuse-Argonne campaign. However, the contributions of the Choctaw and other code talkers in the Meuse-Argonne campaign did help set the stage for the signing of the Armistice on November 11, 1918. And as the best documented and most well-known example of the practice, Choctaw code talking in World War I established the practicality of using other Native American languages for the same application. The use of the Choctaw language was a great advantage on a local level at Forest Ferme, but in light of the larger theater of the war in terms of several factors involving troops, resources, and logistics, claims of its being the deciding factor of Allied success are unsupported.

During World War I, the United States organized ninety-three combat divisions; forty-two deployed to France and thirty saw combat. United States Army divisions at this time averaged just over 28,000 members, with 979 officers and 27,082 men. British and French divisions normally numbered around 12,000 and 11,000 men, respectively, while German combat divisions averaged a little more than 12,000 men. By the end of 1917, the 1st, 2nd, 26th, 41st, and 42nd US divisions were in France; others arrived throughout 1918 (Lawson 1963:52–54).

The Choctaw were a small part of the 1.25 million Americans from twenty-two US divisions that participated in the forty-seven-day Meuse-Argonne campaign, extending from southeast of Verdun to the Argonne Forest. The Allies engaged and defeated forty-six German divisions, or 25 percent of their entire forces on the Western Front, from late September through November 11, 1918. The 36th Division was one of over forty

American divisions sent overseas, and although twice the size of Europeans divisions, they fought alongside large British, French, Canadian, Belgian, and other forces. Although Germany had already begun seeking terms for surrender, it was the American advance to the heights above Sedan, with machine gun and artillery covering the German rail lines and severing both their transportation and their ability to move mining and industrial resources from the area of Briey and Longwy that was the coup de grâs forcing the German surrender (Freidel 1964:179, 237, 328–139; Lawson 1963:133–134; MacDonald 1996a:33, 1996b:60–61). The 71st Brigade, which bore the brunt of the fighting during the 36th's twenty-three days in combat, had twenty-three officers and 491 men killed, all but eleven dying in the fierce struggle around St. Etienne (Chastaine 1920:277–279, 287; Coleman 2002:213).[6]

The 36th was only one division in a much larger, multinational conflict involving millions of men. Fifteen American divisions in the recently organized First United States Army were commanded by General John J. Pershing and later by Lieutenant General Hunter Liggett. Three US corps, containing twelve divisions, focused on the Argonne, with nine leading the assault and three divisions in reserve. Beside them were thirty-one French divisions in the French Fourth Army under Henri Gourand, and the Fifth Army under Henri Mathias Berthelot. American divisions were normally double the size of European divisions, with sixteen US battalions per division to nine in French, British, and German divisions. Prior to the Meuse-Argonne campaign, Allied divisions had been partly replenished, and both French and US divisions were reinforced as the campaign progressed, bringing considerable numbers of US and French troops to the campaign. Eventually, forty-three American divisions would participate in World War I, with twenty-two American divisions, or the equivalent of two full field armies in the Meuse-Argonne campaign. The largest number of American divisions that saw action at the same time was twenty-nine during the second week of October 1918. By October 12, 1918, the combat strength of the American Expeditionary Forces was 1,078,190 men. Another perspective on the 36th's efforts at Forest Ferme is the total length of the Western Front controlled by American and Allied forces. As of October 30, 1918, a total of 410 miles were being held: 79 by the American, 68 by the British, 248 by the French, and 15 by the Belgians (Freidel 1964:237, 247; Stallings 1963:375–381).

Portions of forty-four German divisions opposed the Allies in the Meuse-Argonne campaign, though not at any one time. During October of 1918, seventeen German divisions were on the frontline in this sector, with six divisions in reserve. In 1918, the average size of divisions on the Western Front were as follows: American (25,500); British (11,800), French (11,400), and German (12,300) (Hallas 2000:277; Stallings 1963:380).

Roughly half the size of American divisions, the German divisions in the Argonne were also under strength and weary, with some estimated to have been at only 50 percent of their normal strength during the attack on Forest Ferme (Chastaine 1920:125; Hallas 2000:277). Chastaine (1920:125) described the German units as "woefully understrength, and the men were fatigued and discouraged."

Because the Choctaw communicators were only used during October 26–27 at Forest Ferme near the end of the war, the best way to examine the extent of their contribution is to survey the results of this action. Although the 36th distinguished itself in the action, Forest Ferme was a minor operation in the larger Meuse-Argonne campaign and resulted in 194 Germans prisoners and slightly less than that number killed (Chastaine 1920:229–235; White 1984:167). Accounts of the Meuse-Argonne campaign rarely even mention Forest Ferme, focusing more on the larger developments of the First United States Army, the incident of the 77th Division's "Lost Battalion" from October 2–7 (Stallings 1963:267–279), and Corporal Alvin C. York's shooting fifteen and capturing 132 Germans on October 8 (Stallings 1963:300–302). As W. D. Cope (1919:105; n.d.:8) characterized, "The taking of Forest Ferme [was] a small but very notable operation" and an important but small part of a much larger offensive. Nevertheless, credit should be acknowledged for the precision with which the offensive was planned and conducted. Although battles rarely follow their plans, Cope (1919:107, n.d.:10) noted, "It has been said that this attack surpassed a maneuver for perfection, the entire operation proceeding, from start to finish exactly according to the field orders."

The use of the Choctaw language at Forest Ferme resolved the problems that developed at St. Etienne when the 71st Brigade could not send orders by telephone because of German monitoring. A quick comparison of the result of the US forces at St. Etienne (over 1,600 casualties, 1,300 on the first day, 298 men and officers killed, and 74 missing) and Forest Ferme (14 killed, 36 wounded, 63 gassed, 5 missing) (Spence 1919:83) show the advantage of using Native American language communications to position and prepare troops prior to an assault. Although both forces were larger at St. Etienne, the ability to surprise the Germans and advance so quickly that the majority of their fire power passed over the US troops poignantly illustrates the value of code talkers. The Choctaw language clearly contributed to breaking this position, capturing and killing a number of enemy troops, and forcing the remaining German forces in the pocket to retreat across the river. As Colonel Bloor (1919) described, "The enemy's complete surprise is evidence that he could not decipher the messages."

It is frequently stated that within twenty-four hours after the Choctaw language was essentially pressed into service and the Choctaws began their communications operations, the German advance in this portion of the front line was stopped. In seventy-two hours, the Germans opposing the 36th Division had been forced into a full retreat with the Americans on full attack. The retreat by these Germans was reportedly precipitated in part by the inability to monitor Allied troop movements because of the inability to break the communications used to implement these movements. However, this seventy-two-hour action refers to St. Etienne, which some news accounts misreport was where the Choctaw language was used.

In reality, much of the German frontline was pushed back in the first days of the Meuse-Argonne campaign and continued to be pushed back until the Armistice, from September 26 to November 11 (Freidel 1964; MacDonald 1996b). Except for the troops at Forest Ferme, the Germans had already retreated across the Aisne River in the sector assaulted by the 36th Division and prior to the use of Choctaw. The German positions were the last remaining salient along that section of the front on the west side of the river.

The question of the impact of Choctaw code talkers on the US military is best answered in terms of two themes: successful experimentation in World War I, and as a model that was greatly expanded upon in World War II. While the use of Indigenous American languages in World War I did not win the war, it is fair to say that the use of the Choctaw language at Forest Ferme and the capture of around two hundred Germans contributed to the larger Allied advance in the Meuse-Argonne campaign and to the end of World War I.[7] That the tactic of using Choctaw code talkers was completely successful was later confirmed when a captured German officer admitted that the attempts by his intelligence personnel to understand the messages through their wiretaps were futile. As Chaplain Barnes (1922:39) of the 142nd described:

> The entire sector was strewn with a network of abandoned Boche communicating wires and from previous experiences it was certain that in some way or other, the Germans were cutting in and getting information as to the movements of our troops. It was during the preparation for the "Forest Ferme" attack, that Colonel Bloor used a novel scheme to baffle the enemy, should he intercept our wires. From Company "E," his Indian company, he selected some Choctaw Indians and placed them on the phones. They transmitted all messages in their own tongue. It proved to be a hoodoo to the Boche as was afterward learned through a captured officer. When being questioned, to gain information, he was asked if he had anything to say. He replied that he had, and would like to know what nationality we used on the phones. However, it is needless to say he never gained his desired information.[8]

This confirmed the Germans monitoring and inability to decipher Allied communications. Albert Billy told his daughter about the capture of a number of Germans the night after the Choctaw language was used to code and transmit messages, which would be October 27, 1918. Choctaw code talker James Edwards reported that word leaked back from the German lines that the German's most expert linguists were stumped.[9]

Although other American units also utilized Native American languages for military communications, there is no indication that a single message sent in any of these languages was ever deciphered by the Germans (Tate 1986:432; White 1979:17–18). However, with enough time and cryptologists, any code can be broken. While the repeated use of such communications for immediate, short-term, front line combat use, where the enemy has little time to decipher them and react to their content, proved effective in both world wars, the military was aware that long-term use for all communications would inevitably be broken. Cognizance of this dichotomy continued during World War II, when groups such as the Navajo and Comanche were used for combat situations but not for mass military communications, and after the war, in Army Security Agency assessments of Native code talker use (USASA 1950).

Recognition

Documentation on the service of Native Americans in World War I consists mainly of archival records and a few primary historical works (Britten 1997; Krouse 2007; Winegard 2012). Although their contributions were acknowledged but largely unrewarded by the American military forces, they did not go unnoticed by French and British officers. Field Marshall Lord Haig praised the Native American soldiers highly. Ferdinand Foch, Marshal of France, wrote, "I cannot forget the brilliant services which the valorous Indian soldiers of the American armies have rendered to the common cause and the energy as well as the courage which they have shown to bring about victory—decisive victory—by attack" (Hale 1982:41). While the British and French recognized the actions of Native Americans in World War I, which was typical as the Americans were serving under their armies, no special American recognition was awarded. According to Choctaw code talker Solomon Lewis, their battalion commander promised that he was "putting them in for medals," but none was ever received, and the type of award was not specified.[10] Nearly sixty-eight years would pass before formal recognition was conferred.

In 1976, the Choctaw newspaper *Hello Choctaw* ran a brief article on the Choctaw code talkers that appears to have been based on the 1938 *New York Sun* article. Next, President Ronald Reagan's Proclamation 4954 on July 28, 1982, designating August 14 of that year as National Navajo Code Talkers Day, noted that other Native American tribes had used their native languages for the good of the United States in both world wars, the first of which mentioned was the Choctaw. In 1986, the National Archives acknowledged the Choctaw as the first code talkers.[12]

In the Choctaw community, this information spread quickly, resulting in an article in the June 1986 edition of the Choctaw Tribal Newspaper *Bishinik* asking for information on Choctaw war veterans. In July, *Bishinik* ran an article titled "D.C. Archives Acknowledge Choctaws as 1st 'Code Talkers.'" Reprinting the body of Colonel Bloor's (1919) memo on the Choctaw, the article also notes the "many responses the *Bishinik* has received since last month's editorial requesting information about Choctaw War Veterans."[13]

It would be the Choctaw Nation that first formally recognized the contributions of their own code talkers. In 1986, Chief Hollis Roberts of the Choctaw Nation and the Choctaw Tribal Council were planning to honor the tribe's veterans in conjunction with the annual Choctaw Labor Day Festival.[11] On August 30, during the 1986 Choctaw Nation Labor Day Festival in Tuskahoma, a special recognition was held for all Choctaw service veterans. In addition, each family of the original eight Choctaw code talkers was presented with the Choctaw Nation Medal of Valor by Chief Roberts and the Choctaw Nation Council. It was also planned to have the names of the eight original code talkers engraved on a marble slab to be erected at the Choctaw Nation Council grounds, also in Tuskahoma. Since this event, the Choctaw Nation has continued to give special recognition to its code talkers at their annual Veterans Day Memorial Service.[14]

That November, seven Choctaw veterans from Ardmore honored the code talkers during the Ardmore, Oklahoma, Veteran's Day Parade by riding in a truck with a driver provided by the Oklahoma National Guard of Ardmore. A member of the Carter County Veterans Council made a poster for the truck, and a large Choctaw Nation seal was placed on the front of the vehicle. The veterans also wore white hats proclaiming "Choctaw Code-Talkers—the Original."[15]

After the summer of 1986, the number of Choctaw reported to have served as code talkers increased, largely through families coming forward to the tribe to report that a relative had been a code talker. These developments are reported in a series of articles in *Bishinik* from 1986 through 1989. The April 1987 edition of *Bishinik* included a nearly two-page article titled "Interest Continues in the Choctaw Code-Talkers" with smaller articles on Victor Brown, Solomon B. Louis, Walter Veach, Ben Hampton, and an article on the use of Choctaw in World War II by Schlicht Billy, Davis Pickens, and other Choctaw in Company K, 180th Infantry Regiment,

45th Infantry Division. An accompanying photo depicts a group of twenty-eight Choctaw in Company K, the "Choctaw Platoon."[16]

As 1987 approached, the French government notified C. Alton Brown, Oklahoma's honorary French consul, of their intention to commemorate the seventieth anniversary of America's entry into the First World War by awarding the French National Order of Merit to a limited number of American veterans who served in France during both world wars. Brown voiced his intention to recommend the Choctaw code talkers for the decoration.[17]

The Choctaw Nation began seeking additional information on each reported code talker.[18] Through late 1986 and early 1987, Mike Wright, a research associate at Scientific Social Research of Norman, Oklahoma, volunteered to collect research on all Native American code talkers in Oklahoma, including the Choctaw. An announcement of the research project, a request to be contacted by family and tribal members with relevant data and contact information for Scientific Social Research was included in the February 1987 issue of *Bishinik*. This issue listed eight Choctaw (Bobb, Carterby, Edwards, Lewis, Maytubby, Nelson, Taylor, and Wilson). Wright collected information from the Choctaw Nation, *Bishinik* and other newspapers, military discharge papers from families, and other publications to compile a list of Choctaws identified as code talkers in both world wars. By February of 1987, preliminary research indicated that the Choctaw, Comanche, Kiowa, and Pawnee Nations all had code talkers. Through telephone calls and correspondences with the Choctaw Nation, C. Alton Brown, and Gerard Dumont, consulate general of France in Houston, Texas, Wright compiled a list of fourteen WW I and four WW II Choctaw who served as code talkers by March of 1987. He also participated in ongoing plans to recognize these men by the State of Oklahoma and the French government.[19]

By October 1989, the Choctaw and Comanche Nations had been notified that their code talkers would be recognized by the French government on the front steps of the Oklahoma State Capitol, known as Flag Plaza, in Oklahoma City.[20] At 3:00 P.M. on November 3, 1989, nearly seventy-one years after the end of World War I, the State of Oklahoma and the French government honored Choctaw code talkers of World War I; Schlicht Billy, the last surviving Choctaw code talker from World War II; and the three remaining Comanche code talkers of World War II. On their behalf, the French government presented to Choctaw chief Hollis E. Roberts and Comanche chairman Kenneth Saupitty the Ordre national du Mérite (National Order of Merit), the highest honor France can bestow on an individual from a foreign nation. At this time, fourteen Choctaw (Billy, Bobb, Brown, Carterby, Edwards, Frazier, Hampton, Louis, Maytubby, Nelson, Oklahombi, Taylor, Veach, Wilson) had been identified by the tribe as WW I code talkers.[21]

Following the folding of the Choctaw and Comanche tribal flags by Native veterans, the medals were pinned on each flag by Pierre Messmer, former prime minister of France under President Charles De Gaulle and the current governor general of French Overseas Territories. Chief Roberts stated, "This recognition is long overdue. This is something you probably won't read about in the history books, but history was made today." He also stated that it was a shame that a foreign government had to be the one to honor the Native American code talkers.[22] Federal recognition from the US government still eluded the Choctaw. John Callaway noted, "Even though the 'Choctaw war cry' has been heard in foreign lands as predicted, it still needs to be heard in the halls of Congress."[23]

On May 6, 1995, the Choctaw War Memorial was dedicated at the Choctaw Nation grounds at Tuskahoma. The memorial reads, "In Honor of Those Choctaws Who Gave Their Lives in Defense of Our Nation. This Memorial Is Dedicated to the Original Choctaw Code Talkers of WW I." The marble marker includes the names of Choctaws killed in action in defense of the United States and a section listing the names of WW I Choctaw code talkers, then eighteen.[24]

In 1996, Rattan, Oklahoma, elementary school teacher Beth Lawless mentioned to her sixth-grade reading class that her grandfather, Tobias Frazier, had been one of the Choctaw code talkers. Enthused, the students bombarded her with more questions than she could answer, setting the stage for her sixth-grade boys' reading class project that took all year. The thirteen students began collecting archival newspaper articles and letters from code talker family members. Next, they visited tribal councilman Bertram Bobb and councilman and tribal historian Charley Jones at the Choctaw national capital at Tuskahoma, and the 45th Infantry Division Museum, Oklahoma State Historical Society, and Oklahoma state capitol building in Oklahoma City. At the state capitol, they met with Senator Rabon and Representative Randall Erwin and were introduced on the floor of the House of Representatives by Erwin. Seeking support to formally recognize the code talkers, the students wrote letters to President Bill Clinton, Governor Frank Keating, Senators Jeff Rabon, James Inhofe, and Don Nickles, Representative Wesley Watkins, and Chief Hollis Roberts. Everyone except Clinton responded. At the end of the school year, the class produced a booklet with their findings, copies of their sources, and sections written by each student on a particular question relating to the code talkers. The students set up a display on the Choctaw code talkers and World War I in the Rattan Public School. Lawless was named the 1997–98 Teacher of the Year for the Rattan Public School.[25]

Other recognitions continued. On November 9–10, 2002, the Choctaw code talkers were honored at the Virginia Nations Veterans Powwow, sponsored by the six Native American nations of that state. The event included recognition of the code talkers, introduction of their descendants in attendance, and presentation of a program that included singing by the Choctaw Nation.[26] Through the efforts of Choctaw Nation judge Juanita Jefferson, who contacted the US Army, a granite marker was placed at the grave of James Edwards at the James-Folsom Cemetery in Whitesboro, Oklahoma, on April 20, 2004. A marker had never been claimed for Edwards, and the US Army was pleased to send one. During the ceremony, Choctaw Nation chief Gregory E. Pyle presented Edwards's son, James M. Edwards Jr., with a Presidential Citation honoring his father.[27]

On April 3, 2003, the Louisiana Army National Guard dedicated the memorial sculpture *Comanche and Choctaw Code Talkers* at Camp Beauregard, Louisiana. Created by artist Jerry Gorum, the statue consists of two soldiers in period uniform, one with a pair of binoculars engaged in conversation with the other, who is operating a WW II tube-type walkie-talkie. The statue is in honor of the Choctaw code talkers of World War I and the Comanche code talkers of World War II. It stands among a collection of military period weapons and machinery near the entrance to the Louisiana Maneuvers and Military Museum at Camp Beauregard, Louisiana.[28]

The Choctaw Code Talkers Association

In November of 1997, descendants of the Choctaw code talkers organized the Choctaw Code Talkers Association (CCTA), an organization focused on identification, education about, and historic preservation of the Choctaw code talkers. Evangeline Wilson, the first association president and a relative of two of the Choctaw code talkers, and a group of families related to the original Choctaw code talkers founded the organization.[29] The association is not an official organization of the Choctaw Nation, but a 501(c)(3) nonprofit entity that raises its own operating funds. It is open to both descendants and collateral relatives of the Choctaw code talkers upon proof of relationship (full members) and to any individual interested in the association (associate members). As its statement of purpose explains:

> The Choctaw Code Talkers Association is dedicated to educating the general public about the Choctaw men who served our country even before they were considered citizens of the United States, to collect and preserve, display and utilize arms, implements, clothing, photographs, documents, medals, citations, and similar materials and artifacts, to document and perpetuate the Choctaw Code Talkers of WW I and WW II through publication of books and articles, scholarships and monetary awards for appropriate recognition of the WWI and WWII Code Talkers and other Indian Veterans.[30]

The association also works to promote the continuation of the Choctaw tribal culture, language, and heritage.[31]

The CCTA adopted a striking logo in the form of the 36th Division WW I military patch, under which the Choctaw code talkers served during that war. The number 36 represents the 36th Division. Resembling lightening striking, eight symbolically electrified arrows represent the original Choctaw Telephone Squad who first used field phones to deliver military messages in the Choctaw language. The letter "T" represents the Texas companies that were consolidated with the Oklahoma National Guard to form the 142nd Infantry. Completing the design is the inclusion of "WW I" and "Choctaw Code Talker Association," all enclosed within an arrowhead—the shape of the original 36th Division crest from World War I. Three Choctaw figured prominently in the development of the association's design. Major General Leroy Sisco suggested the use of the 36th Division patch in which the Choctaw code talkers served. Artist Johnny Bobb was designated by the executive committee of the CCTA board of directors to create a logo for the CCTA. Joe Watkins then contributed a computer copy of the logo designed by Bobb for their convenience and use. On February 9, 2000, the CCTA board's executive committee approved a final copy of the logo.[32] The association holds an annual meeting on the Sunday of Labor Day weekend at the Choctaw Nation Festival at Tuskahoma, Oklahoma. In June of 2012, the CCTA received their 501(c)(3) status as a nonprofit organization.[33]

On November 10, 2006, the Oklahoma History Center in Oklahoma City opened a special exhibit, titled *Hidden Voices, Coded Words*. Focusing on the Choctaw and Comanche code talkers of Oklahoma, the exhibit was named to reflect the inability of the Germans and Japanese to understand the Native American languages they encountered over the telephone and radio waves, while it featured the largely unknown history of Native American code talkers in American history and culture. William C. Meadows presented a PowerPoint lecture on Native American code talkers. Running until January 15, 2007, the exhibit was designed to complement the National Museum of the American Indian and Smithsonian Institution's collaborative traveling exhibit *Native Words, Native Warriors*, simultaneously on exhibit at the museum, and a January 12, 2007, premiere of a twenty-minute documentary on the Choctaw code talkers of World War I, *Telephone Warriors: The Story of the Choctaw Code Talkers*, directed and produced by Valerie Red-Horse. Funded by the Choctaw Nation of Oklahoma, the film was made by Red-Horse Native Productions of Los Angeles from ten hours of video footage shot in Oklahoma, including archival photos and family memorabilia. The film was expanded into a one-hour documentary in 2010.[34]

At the second annual Durant Inter-Tribal Powwow in November 2006, the Choctaw Nation invited the family members of their WW I code talkers to participate in the grand entry, following the color guard, Choctaw Nation chief Gregory E. Pyle, and members of the Choctaw Nation Council. Following the grand entry, a member of each of the eighteen World War I Choctaw code talkers was presented with a cased American flag. Each flag had been flown for a day at the Choctaw capitol in honor of a code talker.[35]

On September 16, 2007, the Texas Military Forces Museum at Camp Mabry in Austin, Texas, honored the Choctaw code talkers of World War I during a dedication ceremony for the opening of a permanent museum exhibit on the code talkers. In 1986, Brigadier General John C. L. Scribner was tasked by the adjutant general of Texas with establishing a museum and archival collection at Camp Mabry dedicated to those who served in the military forces of Texas. Included are ongoing efforts to develop exhibits and written histories of all major Texas National Guard units, with a gallery focusing on the 36th Infantry Division. After several years of planning, the museum formally opened on November 14, 1992, with Scribner serving as founder and first director. The idea to develop a display on the Choctaw code talkers dates back more than ten years earlier, when Ruth Frazier McMillan, daughter of code talker Tobias W. Frazier, proposed such a display to Brigadier General Scribner.[36] His health declining, Scribner made plans to ensure an exhibit on the Choctaw code talkers would reach fruition prior to his passing, hiring retired colonel Pat W. Simpson as the new museum director in June 2005.[37]

Scribner told Simpson that he had a list of ten things he wanted to do in the museum. As Simpson explained, "Before he became ill, he hired me and left me with a laundry list of things he wanted accomplished. At the top was the Choctaw code talker exhibit." Scribner died in May of 2006. During a planning meeting, a list of projects was created, including the need "to build a display to honor the Choctaw Code Talkers." One day, Jared Wayne Harris came to the museum seeking an Eagle Scout project. Examining the museum's list, he came to the code talker listing. Harris had never heard of the Choctaw code talkers, but after researching them, he decided to take on the project. He was soon referred to Carl Deichman, the museum exhibits specialist and a former Boy Scout leader. Jared and Carl created a design for the exhibit, submitted it to the Boy Scout office, and were approved. Over several evenings and weekends, Jared, Carl, members of Jared's family, and fellow scouts in his troop built the exhibit, now in the 36th Infantry Division gallery.

The exhibit contains a life-size replica of a WW I field command post containing mannequins of two soldiers. One is a light-haired corporal standing and holding a pair of field glasses, while the other is a darker haired, darker complexioned private sitting at a small table with a telephone in his left hand (Zambrano 2015). The exhibit represents the use of the Choctaw language during World War I and is open to the public. Harris was awarded his Eagle Scout award in May of 2007 but had yet another contribution to the Choctaw code talkers. Following his project, he asked why the State of Texas could not honor the code talkers by presenting a medal to their descendants. From his suggestion came the awarding of the Lone Star Medal of Merit to the Choctaw code talkers.[38]

On September 16, 2007, the Texas Military Forces Museum at Camp Mabry, home of the current 36th Infantry Division, posthumously recognized the service of the eighteen Choctaw code talkers by awarding eighteen Lone Star Medals of Valor, cased Texas state flags, and certificates from the governor of Texas to their descendants during the opening ceremony. Presented by Lieutenant General Charles G. Rodriguez, the adjutant general of Texas Military Forces, the medals marked the first US military medals from outside of the tribe recognizing the Choctaw code talkers.[39]

The Lone Star Medal of Valor is the second highest decoration the State of Texas can award to a member of the Texas Military Forces. It can be awarded to Air National Guard, Army National Guard, State Guard, state military personnel of other states, or to federal military personnel. The medal is awarded to individuals for conspicuous military valor and gallantry involving the possible loss of life.

> The Lone Star Medal of Valor shall be awarded to a member of the military forces of this state, another state, or the United States who performs specific acts of bravery or outstanding courage, or who performs within an exceptionally short period a closely related series of heroic acts, if the acts involve personal hazard or danger and the voluntary risk of life and result in an accomplishment so exceptional and outstanding as to clearly set the person apart from the person's comrades or from other persons in similar circumstances. Awarding of the medal requires a lesser degree of gallantry than awarding of the Texas Legislature Medal of Honor, but requires that the acts be performed with marked distinction.[40]

Following the presentation of the award, the Choctaw visitors were taken on a tour of the Brigadier General John C. L. Scribner Texas Military Forces Museum.

The formal recognition by the Texas Military Forces Museum in 2007 furthered knowledge of the Choctaw code talkers' contributions and was greatly appreciated by members of the Choctaw delegation, as reflected in their comments. As Tewanna Edwards, a great-niece of Otis Leader, expressed at the event, "We don't have a lot of Indian heroes. Otis Leader was a hero of our people. He represents all Indians."[41] Choctaw Nation chaplain Bertram Bobb, who blessed the museum exhibit, expressed his gratitude: "It is great to see all the code talker relatives here to honor these great Choctaw Soldiers." As Judy Allen, Choctaw Nation executive director of public relations, described, "The reaction has been fabulous. The past years we have been trying to get recognition for the valiant efforts of these Code Talkers, so this is definitely a proud moment. The families are absolutely overwhelmed. Some have told me that to get this much public recognition has been one of the proudest moments in their lives."[42] However, as we shall see, the Choctaw had their sights set on obtaining an even greater form of recognition for their code talkers—a Congressional Gold Medal.

Around 2006, the Choctaw Nation installed a display on the Choctaw code talkers at their tribal museum at Tuskahoma, Oklahoma. Included in the display are several photographs, Otis Leader's cap, and the trunk of Walter Veach, which included an October 27, 1918, letter from their sister, Bird, to their brother, Lieutenant Columbus Veach, then in the 42nd Division, that mentions Walter. Around 2013, the display was expanded to include additional Choctaw code talker awards, a film segment on the code talkers, and other items.[43]

In November 2007, scholar Marie J. Archambeault made a presentation on the Choctaw code talkers of World War I at the Louisiana Indian Hobbyists Association annual fall powwow.[44] The Choctaw code talkers received further recognition from the State of Oklahoma in 2009. Choctaw Nation member and State Representative Lisa Billy presented House Resolution 1031 to recognize "the service, valor and dedication of members of the Choctaw Nation fighting in the American Expeditionary Forces in France" during World War I. The resolution was passed by the State of Oklahoma and was enthusiastically supported by the Oklahoma legislature's Native American Caucus, which Billy initiated in 2005.[45]

In 2010, a quilt designed by Nuchi Nashoba and made by Dianna Powell was donated to the CCTA. The design of the quilt focused on the Choctaw code talkers, their uniform, and a hand-held field-phone bag. Included in the design were a border of diamonds representing the rattlesnake motif used in Choctaw clothing, an American flag, a sun with rays of light shining down on the Choctaw warriors, and purple representing royalty and the Choctaw Nation flag. Also included are eight jagged arrows from the logo of the CCTA, "symbolically electrified" to represent the Choctaw Telephone Squad in World War I and bearing the monogrammed names of the original eight men. The names of the other men are monogrammed in the diamond motifs on the top of the quilt. The quilt was raffled to raise funds for the association. Gary Batton, then assistant chief, won the quilt.

It was later displayed in the Choctaw Tribal Museum for a period. During June 20–23, 2012, the quilt was used as part of a four-day display of the Choctaw Nation during the second annual Choctaw Days at the National Museum of the American Indian in Washington, DC. During the event, members of the Southeastern Oklahoma State University Theater Department performed a short stage production titled "To Us It Wasn't Code."[46]

In October of 2010, coproducers Red-Horse Native Productions, Valhalla Motion Pictures, and Native American Public Telecommunications released the first documentary film on the Choctaw code talkers in World War I, the fifty-seven-minute documentary *Choctaw Code Talkers* (Visionmaker Video 2010). It aired on PBS on October 23, 2010.

On October 23, 2010, the Choctaw code talkers were inducted into the Texas Trail of Fame at the Fort Worth Stockyards in Texas. The ceremony was held on the front steps of the Livestock Exchange Building at the Fort Worth Stockyards National Historic District.[47] On November 1, 2010, the WW I Choctaw code talkers were honored with the Patriotism Award at the inaugural Drum Awards at Durant, Oklahoma.[48]

In 2011, twenty-seven school districts from Delta, Fannin, Lamar, Red River, and Choctaw Counties sponsored a widespread educational program titled "Pennies for Patriots." Studying the soldiers of the Texas Revolution and the Choctaw code talkers of World War I, each fourth-grade class from this region pledged to raise thirty-thousand pennies ($300) to purchase a 1 x 2-foot granite paver for their chosen soldier, to be placed at the Red River Valley Veterans Memorial in Lamar County, Texas. On November 12, 2012, the students presented their pavers, containing the name, branch of service, and war to the committee at the Veteran's Day program at the Love Civic Center in Paris, Texas. Pavers for Mitchell Bobb, Ben Carterby, James Edwards, Tobias Frazier, Otis Leader, Joseph Oklahombi, and Walter Veach were presented.[49]

In early 2012, the Choctaw code talkers were nominated for induction into the Oklahoma Military Hall of Fame by Lanny Asepermy of the Comanche Indian Veterans Association. Asepermy, who has compiled veterans' records for over 1,300 Comanche veterans, and many Kiowa, helped compile those for the Choctaw code talkers. On November 9, 2012, the Choctaw code talkers of World War I and II were inducted into the Oklahoma Military Hall of Fame's thirteenth annual Banquet and Induction Ceremony at Oklahoma City.[50]

World War I Choctaw Code Talkers Highway

Ruth Frazier McMillan, a daughter of Choctaw code talker Tobias Frazier and an executive member of the CCTA, had long dreamed of seeing two honors bestowed on her tribe's code talkers: the official naming of a fifty-five-mile section of Highway 3 through Pushmataha and McCurtain Counties between Antlers and Broken Bow, Oklahoma, in honor of the Choctaw code talkers; and the awarding to the Choctaw code talkers of the Congressional Gold Medal. She lobbied extensively for both projects. McMillan originated the idea to rename the highway as a way to honor the Choctaw code talkers, in large part because fourteen of the WW I Choctaw code talkers resided in the state's 19th district and often walked along this road, and because many of their descendants still reside along this route. State representative R. C. Pruett introduced legislation to have the name changed to World War I Choctaw Code Talkers Highway.[51]

Congressional Lobbying

After several tribes and states began recognizing their own code talkers in the 1980s, efforts to recognize all code talkers on a federal level emerged, especially following the congressional recognition of the Navajo code talkers in 2000 (Meadows 2011).

Interest in recognizing the Choctaw code talkers gained momentum following three events, after which knowledge of their service in World War II grew exponentially: the declassification of the Navajo code in 1968, the recognition of the Navajo code talkers by the US Marine Corps in 1969, and the Navajo code talker reunion and formation of the Navajo Code Talker's Association in 1971 (Paul 1973). Other tribes began efforts to honor Native American code talkers, including the Hopi in 1982 and the Choctaw in 1986.

Like many veterans, the code talkers appear to have viewed their service as simply doing what was needed or asked of them at the time or as fulfilling their role in protecting their people, not as anything special or deserving of merit. They thus did not seek postwar recognition. Typically, it has been the descendants of code talkers or fellow tribal members who have sought their recognition. The emergence of Native American code talkers as iconic figures in American military history and culture is primarily the result of how succeeding generations have viewed them and the symbolism they have attached to their service rather than how the men viewed themselves.

On September 23, 2004, a panel of eleven individuals testified before a Senate committee hearing in Washington, DC, on the contributions of Native American code talkers in the United States armed forces. The panel included Choctaw chief Gregory Pyle, Melvin Kerchee Jr. (Comanche), Don Loudner (Dakota), Brigadier General (Ret.) John S. Brown, John Yellowbird Steele (Lakota), Samson Keahna (Meskwaki), Senator Tom

Daschle, and Professor William C. Meadows of Southwest Missouri State University. Some of the Choctaw code talkers' descendants attended the proceedings.[52]

The day before the Senate committee hearing, a local historian from McCurtain County, Oklahoma, who requested anonymity, "urged caution on not overstating the contributions of Choctaw code talkers in World War I." Quoting material from Bloor (1919) and Chastaine (1920:231–232), the author, who indicated that he meant no disrespect to the Choctaw code talkers, maintained that the claims aimed at recognizing the Choctaw were inflated, pointing out that "only a relative handful of Choctaws actually ever used their code-talking skills." Finding evidence that only eight individuals were used and maintaining that their efforts in the final weeks of the of the war were not crucial to the outcome and probably had little overall effect, the historian related that "they were not a decisive factor in the Meuse-Argonne offensive fought in France in the fall of 1918. And, in fact, German opposition was already crumbling weeks before the Armistice was signed on Nov. 11, 1918, to end the war."[53] While true, these facts negate neither the uniqueness of their service nor the Choctaws' desire to honor them.

During 2004 to 2008, contingents of Native Americans made several visits to Washington, DC, to meet with US representatives and senators in their offices to educate them about the service of the Choctaw and other code talkers and to encourage their support for the House and Senate bills. These efforts were led by Choctaw Nation chief Gregory Pyle, Judy Allen, descendants of the Choctaw code talkers, representatives of the National Congress of American Indians, representatives from the Comanche and Sioux nations, Lieutenant General Leroy Sisco, Major General John T. Furlow, and others. (Bishink 2008b, 2008d). As Chief Pyle described, "My staff and I spent several weeks in Washington, D.C., this year, literally going door-to-door visiting with offices in both the House and Senate, gaining support for the legislation. This honor is very important to our tribe and to us personally. On several trips, we were accompanied by family of Choctaw Code talkers, so they were able to tell first-hand accounts of the men who helped bring about an end to WWI."[54]

Oklahoma 2nd district representative Dan Boren drafted an especially unique letter to solicit cosponsorship of H.R. 4544 from his fellow House of Representatives members. Including a Choctaw expression, his letter began:

CAN YOU READ THIS?
Yakni im aianhli
NEITHER COULD OUR ENEMIES DURING WWI
All Native American Code Talkers Deserve Recognition.[55]

Eventually, the legislation passed, supported by three hundred members in the House of Representatives and seventy-three members in the Senate; 290 House and 66 Senate votes were required, respectively.[56]

Following the passage of the Code Talker Recognition Act of 2008 on October 15, 2008 (Meadows 2011), Choctaw Nation chief Gregory Pyle stated:

> Congressman [Dan] Boren and Senator [Jim] Inhofe both deserve a lot of gratitude from Choctaws for their dedication to memorializing one of the greatest parts of our tribal history. . . . The Choctaw nation is also thankful to the other members of the House and Senate who co-sponsored and voted for this legislation. Most of all, thanks to the Choctaws and friends who rallied to the cause by contacting their representatives and senators with a request for co-sponsoring on HR 4544 and S 2681. This personal touch from people all over the country is what achieved success. This is the greatest example of teamwork I have seen.[57]

Pyle also noted, "Congressman Boren had worked many hours on the passage of HR 4544. Boren's dedication to the military heroes of our tribe is evident. Both Congressman Boren and Senator Inhofe are great Oklahomans and I am proud to know they were the sponsors of such historic legislation. The Choctaw people, especially descendants of the Code talkers, are grateful to them both for this commemoration of a unique use of our language by 18 Choctaw soldiers."[58]

On April 1, 2009, the Oklahoma legislature officially recognized the Choctaw code talkers. Introduced by Representative Lisa Billy, the House Resolution received unanimous approval from both legislative branches.[59] In the summer of 2010, the US Mint began designing the Congressional Gold and Silver Medals for Native American code talkers in collaboration with each respective tribe involved in the Code Talker Recognition Act of 2008. The Choctaw received the preliminary design for their medal in June of 2011. Later that summer, Ruth Frazier McMillan expressed, "It's a long time coming, but as long as it happens, I'll be happy. The main reason is to let our people be proud of their history and their ethnic background . . . to broaden some minds, perhaps. Everybody needs to know what our people did."[60] In 2013, McMillan flew from Seattle to Oklahoma to attend the September 6 dedication of the highway sign she had legislated for at the intersection of Highway 3 and the Indian Nations Turnpike in Antlers. Another sign was placed fifty-five miles away at Broken Bow. The signs were provided through donations from the code talkers' families, state representatives, and the Choctaw Nation and were installed by the Oklahoma Department of Transportation. McMillan passed away soon after returning to Seattle, just weeks before the Congressional Gold Medal ceremony.[61] Choctaw Code Talkers Association member Beth Lawless stated, "I'm excited that they are finally getting the history documented and the recognition that people understand there were Code Talkers in the First World War and not just the second one."[62]

Following almost five years of medal design, all known Native American code talkers included in the Code Talker Recognition Act of 2008 were recognized in the Gold and Silver Congressional Medal ceremonies at Washington, DC, in 2013 (Meadows 2011, 2016). On November 20, 2013, nearly one hundred Choctaw attended the Congressional Gold Medal ceremony at the US Capitol in Washington, DC, for thirty-three tribes, where they received a Congressional Gold Medal for their code talkers. Twenty-three Silver Congressional Medals were awarded later that afternoon at the National Museum of the American Indian for the nineteen Choctaw who provided military communications in World War I and four in World War II. All but one of the silver medals has been placed in the Choctaw Nation Museum in a special display on the code talkers. The gold medal is currently being kept in a bank vault until the new Choctaw Cultural Center in Durant is completed (Meadows 2016). Other tribes are planning similar displays.[63]

Choctaw Code Talker Association president Nuchi Nashoba remarked, "It was a bittersweet moment. The original code talkers never got to see that day and many of their relatives who had campaigned so hard to get recognition for them had also died. But it was also an incredible moment, I can't put into words the joy and pride we felt. Those men deserve to be honoured."[64]

Calvin Atchavit's nephew Robert Atchavit did not hear about his uncle's accomplishments until the early 1980s, when the Comanche Indian Veteran's Association brought their research to his attention. In 2013, he was selected to receive the Silver Congressional Medal for his uncle at Washington, DC.

> I got to go up there you know and represent my uncle. I was the only living relative, so they took me along. It was wonderful, a great experience to go up there and see a lot of the other code talkers [families] and so forth. We were amazed about it, once we found out about his heroism and everything. We were really proud of that and especially when they dedicated that, at the Comanche Nation they got the Court of Honor and you know all the warrior's names are put on the stones. They had a great big ceremony when they put his name on one of the stones.[65]

Each tribe's medal was designed by the US Mint and tribal representatives. The front of the Choctaw medal features a Choctaw soldier in uniform and listening on a field telephone while writing the Choctaw word for "big gun" on a tablet. The reverse side depicts the Great Seal of the Choctaw Nation. This seal features three arrows representing the historic warrior chiefs Apukshunnubbee, Pushmataha, and Moshulatubbee, a smoking-pipe tomahawk that would have been passed in ancient councils of both war and peace, and a bow that the Choctaw keep unstrung in times of peace but are "ready to string in an instant, to protect home and family." The border on the reverse contains a diamond design taken from traditional Choctaw clothing and art and honors their surroundings. The diamonds also symbolize the diamondback rattlesnake, reflecting a conscious recognition of nature and awareness that people must be careful to treat their surroundings with respect, caution, and prudence (Pyle 2012).

Recognition of the code talkers continue. In April of 2014, Kickapoo artist Arigon Starr (2014) published a comic book titled "Tales of the Mighty Code Talkers." Focusing on the Choctaw, it is a narrative loosely based on some of what is known about the Choctaw code talkers' experiences that furthers awareness about their service in a format that is especially popular with youth.[66] That same month, the theme of the annual Air Fest in Durant, Oklahoma, was the Choctaw code talkers.

In 2014, the eighth-grade class of Nellie Garone at Mannsville School in Mannsville, Oklahoma, spent a year studying Joseph Oklahombi, resulting in the focus of a project for the National History Day project. Garone became intrigued when she saw a painting of Oklahombi on a wall during a baby shower. Following her own research, she began to learn more about Oklahombi and presented the topic to her class, who at that time had never heard of him. Struck by his contributions and bravery, they wondered why he had not been awarded the United States' highest military honor, the Congressional Medal of Honor. As Garone explained, "The boys just could not figure out how he did not receive the Medal of Honor. They looked at all of his accomplishments and how he served his country heroically and they felt like he deserved more recognition than he got at the time."[67]

Since then, the students have been compiling records and accounts of Oklahombi's service to seek the Congressional Medal of Honor for him. The students were especially moved by the realization that had he been awarded the Medal of Honor, he would have received more benefits for his family, whom he struggled to support after the war. The students believe that it was his race that prevented his receiving the award. While President Obama requested the military to review records of black, Hispanic, and Jewish veterans, several of whom were upgraded for higher military awards, Native Americans were not included. School Superintendent David Herron described how the students have grown from the project: "We've seen them grow throughout the process as far as public speaking, and the ability to research and present a subject. That's something that's going to help them later on in their careers." Garone reflected on the project in terms of contemporary priorities and learning about people whom they would otherwise not be aware of: "I think in many ways our priorities, as far as who we consider heroes are a little messed up. People admire Spider-man and Superman, but there are plenty of real people who are worth admiring and the more we learn about them, the better off we are." The 2015 eighth-grade class continued the project. These materials and an application were forwarded to the US Army via Oklahoma congressman Markwayne Mullin.[68]

As the hundredth anniversary of World War I approached, the CCTA, the Choctaw Nation, and others worked on a number of projects to acknowledge, honor, and celebrate the history and achievements of the Choctaw code talkers. In 2016, Una Belle Townsend (2016) published a children's book based on the Choctaw code talkers that was illustrated by Choctaw artist Gwen Coleman Lester.

Also in 2016, the CCTA began efforts to have one bridge named for each of the twenty-three Choctaw code talkers of World War I and II in southeast Oklahoma. Each previously unnamed bridge chosen was located near where a code talker grew up. Requiring $800 for two green and white signs per bridge, fundraising was undertaken by the CCTA. In 2016, the Choctaw Nation pledged to cover any costs not raised by the association.[69]

In the 2017 session of the Oklahoma legislature, the House and Senate passed the Choctaw Code Talkers Bridge Naming Act (House Bill 1149) to name twenty-three county bridges in southeastern Oklahoma after the Choctaw code talkers. Signed on May 17, the act took effect on November 1, 2017.[70] Almost one hundred years after the Choctaw code talkers used their language, the first bridge was dedicated in honor of Joseph Oklahombi. On April 19, 2018, a ceremony was held at the Choctaw Nation Community Center in Wright City, in Bryan County, Oklahoma, followed by the unveiling of the sign over Horsehead Creek on State Highway 98 east of Wright City. The sign reads, "Joseph Oklahombi WW I Choctaw Code Talker Bridge." Each sign will be similar, containing the name of the individual code talker honored, and whether they served in World War I or World War II.[71] Students from several schools were bussed to witness the unveiling. Proud of the tribe's legacy, Choctaw Nation chief Gary Batton stated, "We're proud because of our history, our culture. We are resilient. We're strong. We are fighters, we're Tushka[,] . . . the word for warrior in Choctaw."[72] All twenty-three signs were installed in 2018. Table 3 lists all twenty-three bridges by Oklahoma county, nearest highway, and location.[73]

TABLE 3   Bridges in Oklahoma Named for Choctaw Code Talkers

Code Talker	County	Highway	Bridge Location
		WW I	
Albert Billy	Leflore	US 270	Mountain Creek, W. of Wister
Mitchell Bobb	McCurtain	SH 3	1.3 mi. E. of N4495 Co. Rd.
Victor Brown	Pushmataha	SH 3	2,000 ft. W. of Oleta
Ben Carterby	McCurtain	US 259	5.75 mi. S. of Smithville
Ben Colbert	Bryan	US 70	600 ft. W. of N3770 Co. Rd.
George E. Davenport	Pushmataha	SH 3	Beaver Creek Bridge, E. of Antlers
Joseph H. Davenport	Pushmataha	SH 3	Dumpling Creek Bridge E. of Antlers
James M. Edwards	McCurtain	SH 3	Boktuklo Creek Bridge W. of Broken Bow
Tobias W. Frazier	Choctaw	US 70	Raymond Gary Lake Bridge
Benjamin Hampton	Bryan	US 70	Sulphur Creek Bridge / E2078 Co. Rd.
Noel Johnson	McCurtain	US 259	Eagle Fork Creek S. of Smithville
Otis Leader	Pontotoc	SH 1	6 mi. S. of SH 1, in Allen
Solomon Bond Louis	McCurtain	US 259	Yanubbee Creek, N. of Broken Bow
Pete Maytubby	Johnston	SH 7	Pennington Creek Bridge
Jeff Nelson	McCurtain	SH 3	2,300 ft. N. of Little River Bridge, Northbound side only
Joseph Oklahombi	Bryan	SH 98	Horsehead Creek, 1.5 mi. E. of Wright City
Robert Taylor	McCurtain	SH 3	2300 ft. N. of Little River Bridge, Southbound side only
Charles W. Veach	Bryan	US 70	Bridge over old US-70, E. of Durant Bypass
Calvin Wilson	McCurtain	US 70	Just E. of N4750 Co. Rd.
		WW II	
Forreston Baker	Pittsburg	SH 113	1.25 mi. S. of E1368 Co. Rd.
Schlicht Billy	Pittsburg	SH 1	1,800 ft. W. of the Indian Nation Tpk.
Andrew Perry	Pittsburg	SH 1	1.6 mi. W. of the Indian Nation Tpk.
Davis Pickens	Pittsburg	SH 31	Eastern city limits of Krebs

Following the 2013 dedication of highway signs marking the World War I Choctaw Code Talkers Highway from near Antlers to Broken Bow, additional signage was planned, including the creation of two granite markers, one for each end of the sixty-mile section of highway.[74]

In November 2013, the National Security Agency (NSA) and the Central Security Service (CSS) honored all Native American code talkers of both world wars with induction into the NSA/CSS Cryptologic Hall of Honor at Fort Meade, Maryland, and a plaque. This award is unique because it is the first NSA/CSS Hall of Honor induction of a group. The plaque was presented to the code talkers as a group at a ceremony at the National Museum of the American Indian in Washington, DC, in April 2014. It contains the following inscription that speaks to their contributions:

> Native Americans served as secure communicators on the frontiers in two world wars. In that role, they provided protection for tactical voice communications to foil enemy eavesdroppers. Their skillful manipulation of language gave U.S. forces a level of security and a speed of secure communications that otherwise would not have been possible. The actions and innovations of the Native American Code Talkers in combat saved thousands of lives and enabled the success of many operations. The induction of Native American Code Talkers into the NSA/CSS Hall of Honor is intended to remember all code talkers, known and unknown.

Since the establishment of the Cryptologic Hall of Honor in 1999, all prior inductions had been to "individual cryptologists who represented the best of the best in their field and made significant and enduring contributions to American cryptology." On April 8, 2014, the plaque was presented to the National Museum of the American Indian, where Director Kevin Gover received it on behalf of the museum. The plaque will be on permanent display at the National Museum of the American Indian, which Congress charged with maintaining a list of all code talkers.[75] That December, the National Cryptologic Museum updated its display on Native American code talkers, highlighting the Choctaw in World War I and the Comanche and Navajo of World War II.[76]

On November 4, 2017, the Sequoyah National Research Institute at the University of Arkansas-Little Rock opened an exhibit titled *Untold Stories: American Indian Code Talkers of World War I*. The exhibit featured sections providing an overview of Native service in World War I, Native American boarding schools, how Natives were targeted for recruitment, tribes with code talkers, and the legacy of code talkers in World War I. Other sections feature nearby Camp Pike, Arkansas, where many Native servicemen were trained and later discharged, and a list of over 2,300 Native American WW I veterans.[74]

To increase knowledge of the Choctaw code talkers, the CCTA has periodically held booths at arts and cultural festivals throughout Oklahoma. On a national level, in 2017, PBS released *The Great War*, a documentary commemorating the hundredth anniversary of World War I. Included was a segment on the Choctaw code talkers that featured the experiences of Solomon Louis.[78]

In April 2018, a contingent of Choctaw attended an international conference in Reims, France, and toured sites where the Choctaw fought. Tiajuana King Cochnauer presented "Telling Our Own Story: Choctaw Code Talkers" and planted Choctaw Nation flags at sites where the Choctaw fought in World War I. She has started a special collection of Choctaw and family material at the Oklahoma History Center and has donated a quilted wall-hanging containing panels with pictures of the code talkers, military medals, and information about them, titled *Choctaw Code Talkers WW I*. Choctaw author Sarah Elizabeth Sawyer (2018) also participated in the contingent as part of the research for her historical novel on the Choctaw code talkers.[79]

On July 3, 2018, the Choctaw dedicated a Choctaw code talker monument in Antlers, Oklahoma. Recognizing both world wars, the monument is inscribed, "Preserving Our Heritage." The opposite side of the monument lists the names of the twenty-three Choctaw code talkers of World War I and II. The CCTA is currently raising funds for a second monument to be placed at Broken Bow, Oklahoma, at the other end of Chotaw Code Talkers Highway.[80]

On May 15, 2019, Oklahoma legislators approved naming Highway 5 between US 277 and Walters, Oklahoma, Comanche Code Talker Trailway. Following the route to the annual Comanche homecoming held in July at Walters, the highway honors the WW I and WW II Comanche code talkers, several of whom came from that area.[81]

With increased interest in code talkers, recognition of their service is sure to continue.

7

THE LEGACY OF NATIVE AMERICAN CODE TALKERS IN WORLD WAR I

What is the legacy of the Native American code talkers of World War I? To answer this, we must examine their impact on several military and civilian topics. With regard to the US military, these include the origins of the use of Native American language communicators, why Native languages worked as effective codes, types of Native American code talking, efforts to form all-Native military units, the impacts of code talking on US armed forces signals intelligence, secrecy associated with code talkers, the development of the term "code talker," and impacts on World War II. The impact of the code talkers in World War I on the US military came in several forms. It was a new and unique method of secure communications that contributed significantly where it was employed. It contributed to the evolution of military intelligence, which had long been concerned with the need for rapid, secure communications and with enemy abilities to eavesdrop and break codes (Meadows 2002). It also contributed to the positive view of Native American service in the Great War.

But the legacy left by the Native Americans WW I code talkers went beyond military applications alone, with cultural impacts that effected many aspects of Indigenous culture and societies, including dissemination and preservation of Native languages, development of federal policy regarding Native writing systems, formalization of citizenship for Indigenous peoples, and postwar cultural recognition. This chapter addresses many of these subjects while clarifying, and in some instances correcting, a number of popular beliefs or misconceptions regarding Native American code talkers in the First World War.

Military Influences

Near the end of World War I, as American units discovered that their communications were compromised by German forces, they realized that among their numbers were Native American soldiers who spoke languages that were little known, largely unwritten, and not based on mathematical patterns like conventional codes and ciphers. The use of members from several tribes raises the questions of how often this occurred and whether the idea was a centralized plan or represents cases of independent invention.

Another attempt to form a group of Native communicators came from a Cheyenne in the 164th Regiment, 41st Division. Benjamin D. Cloud was born at Fort Shaw, Montana, in 1888 and later resided and was enrolled at Standing Rock Reservation.[1] In 1910, Cloud attended Carlisle Indian Boarding School, where he learned telegraphy. He also attended Dickinson College and worked as a stenographer. In 1914, Cloud enlisted in the North Dakota 1st National Guard, where he served on the Mexican border. Earning the rank of regimental sergeant major, he oversaw of office of the adjutant until being honorably discharged in 1917. During mobilization for the war, Cloud was again called into service in March 1917. On May 26, 1917, he enlisted in the North Dakota National Guard at Bismark. From the rank of private, he was promoted to second lieutenant by October 1917 and served overseas in France.[2]

In January of 1919, Lieutenant John Eddy interviewed Cloud, later submitting the following report to Joseph K. Dixon:

> During his service with the Supply Co., A.B.C., 1st Bn., 41st Div., Cloud came in contact with quite a number of Indians, and endeavored to get them into his battalion, which at that time was a signal battalion. His idea was to show them how they could listen in and make use of their language in outwitting the enemy. In addition to being an attorney, Cloud is an expert telegraph operator (line), and while in charge of the signal battalion he conceived the idea of getting together as many Indians as possible for instruction in telegraphing and signaling. The idea of using Indian language as a code also occurred to him, but he was unable to put his plans into execution."[3]

In 1919, W. D. Cope, brigadier general and adjutant general of Texas, wrote a report on the 36th Division in World War I. Regarding the code talkers, Cope (1919:108, n.d.10) noted, "When the Armistice was signed, the American General Headquarters had made plans for the training of a large number of Indians as telephone operators, with the idea of detailing them to all American divisions on the front." Although these plans did not materialize, they demonstrate an attempt to form groups in another US Army division and the military's postwar awareness of the value and potential use of American Indian communicators.

The use of Native American languages for communications was not an extant military practice but an impromptu adaptation or experiment

TABLE 4 Native American Code Talkers in World War I

Tribe	No.	Unit
Choctaw	(8)	Co. E, 142nd Inf. Reg., 36th Div. Later 18 men and 3 NCOs trained at Louppy-le-Petit.
Cherokee		119th and 120th Inf. Regs., 30th Div.
Cherokee		Co. E, 142nd Inf. Reg., 36th Div.
Comanche	(5)	357th Inf. Reg., 90th Div.
Osage		? Co. M, 143rd Inf. Reg., 36th Div.
Sioux		?
Winnebago	(2)	Co. A, 7th Inf. Reg., 3rd Div.

made near the end of the war. It relied on finding Native Americans with a shared language who also spoke English well enough for translation. Their brief use ceased with the Armistice, the shift to occupation duties, and the return to America. Because the communication tactic of code talking was developed so late in the war, German Forces had no time to identify the languages, collect written sources on them, or attempt to break them. Had their use continued for several months, it is likely that there would have been more documentation and more extensive code formation and training, like that done by Choctaw in the 142nd Infantry Regiment, in addition to more organized German efforts to identify and break these systems.

Statements from officers in the 30th and 36th divisions and from Lieutenant Cloud indicate that there had been no preconceived or official plan to use these languages before the war and that their use emerged in response to US units lacking security in sending voice messages in battle. This led to the realization by military personnel who had Native Americans in their units that these languages could provide potentially undecipherable transmissions for secure communications.

Expanding the use of code talkers was considered during World War I. Of the Forest Ferme action, the 36th Division Service Report notes:

Of interest in connection with this operation is the fact that the 142nd Infantry, which, along with the other regiments of the division, had been greatly troubled by the enemy's ability to listen in on all phone conversation, employed Cherokee and Choctaw Indians on its phones to send messages in their native tongue. The stratagem worked with entire success. Although all directions for the delicate movement executed on the night of the 26th were given over the phone, thanks to the Indians, the movement was completed entirely without the enemy's knowledge and without attracting any artillery fire whatsoever. On reaching the area of reserve, after the withdrawal from the lines, plans were put under way for employing Indians on all front-line phones in the Division, but the signing of the Armistice rendered further steps in the matter unnecessary.[4]

Other factors also suggest that the idea to use Native American communicators resulted from similar but independent ideas by individuals in units containing Native troops. These include dispersed groups (1st, 3rd, 30th, 36th, and 90th Divisions), attempts to form groups by both Native and non-Natives in American (41st Division) and Canadian armed forces, and the dates of their first use in the 3rd, 30th, and 36th Divisions. Dates of unit combat indicate that Native American languages were used by the Ho-Chunk before June 21, 1918, by the Eastern Band Cherokee during September 7–12, and by the Choctaw and Oklahoma Cherokee during October 26–27.

Why Native Languages Worked

Native American languages proved effective against the Germans in World War I for several reasons. First, these languages were largely unknown to the enemy. Second, except for some Native-language religious texts such as Bibles and hymnbooks that were largely confined to local Indigenous communities in the United States, these languages were largely unwritten. Third, because American academic traditions in logic, linguistics, mathematics, and military science derive largely from European cultures, this provided an advantage for the Germans. Because Native American languages were not Latin-based and were unrelated to European languages, they lacked linguistic similarities for comparison. Fourth, Native languages were not mathematical progressions as were used in many code and cipher systems. Finally, the creation of a new Native language–based lexicon for modern military subjects containing terms that tribal languages lacked—the full extent of which is unknown—provided further complexity and security.

The basic premise of using Native American languages was that while codes in known languages could be broken, unknown and largely unwritten languages that were further disguised with encoded vocabulary would be even harder to break. Little-known spoken—not written—Native American languages used as a basis for a crypto-lingual system offered an extremely valuable and difficult to decipher form of communications. The United States made use of a resource that most other countries had not yet employed: Native languages so obscure that virtually no one else in the world knew them. Although developed late in the war, they received considerable, albeit brief, official and public recognition.

Types of Native American Code Talking

Meadows (2002) first defined and classified two distinct forms of Native American code talking (NACT) originating in World War I: those with specially encoded terms (Type 1 NACT), and those without specially designed encoded terms (Type 2 NACT). Because both involve unknown languages, the differentiating factor is the presence or absence of a body of encoded terms. Only the Choctaw are known to have devised specially encoded terminology in World War I. Although others may have done so, there is no known data to confirm this. Thus, all other groups appear to have served as Type 2 code talkers. Both forms provided secure, expedient, tactical communications, and none are known to have been compromised.

Some writers contend that Native American military communicators were only "code talkers" if they used a set of prearranged and formally organized, encoded terms in sending messages. While the generic definition of a code (a formula for secret messages) conjures up images of creating new forms of encoded writing based upon an existing language, can the intentional use of another unknown oral language serve the same purpose? I suggest that this too qualifies as a code in that the basic US armed forces definition of a code (a system of secret message transmission) is not specifically limited to writing or speech to achieve the same goal of secret communications.

All-Native Units

Related to their accomplished military service, efforts to form all-Native military units in the US Army continued after the war. A 1920 *New York Times* article, "Indians for the Army," discusses congressional legislation that included a proposal to form one or two all-Native army divisions. General John J. Pershing and other officers supported the proposal, praising the excellence of Native American service in the war. Major Thomas Reilley, 165th Infantry, 42nd Division, asserted that "they are expert in rifle fighting, game, strong, brave, resolute. They were superior in scouting and patrol work. They were unexcelled in every phase of every fight."[5]

Other officers indicate that Natives in their units performed exceptionally and demonstrated an esprit de corps (Krouse 2007; US Congress 1920:2167, 2185, 2205). Major Reilley, who took twenty of the men and added them to the Intelligence Department, also stated, "I hold all of these Indians in the most enthusiastic regard. I advocate the segregation of Indian troops, for I noted that when they were sent out as a distinct Indian force they did their best work" (US Congress 1920:2185). Colonel Morrissey (US Congress 1920:2167) also noted that Native Americans performed better in "their own company, massed together as Indians." Taking note of Indigenous populations, the proposal suggested that perhaps one wartime division (then around twenty-five thousand men) or two peace-strength divisions could be manned by Native Americans.[6] Although these efforts continued into World War II, because of desires to continue Native American assimilation and concerns of sufficient numbers of replacements, they never materialized. While based in part on stereotypes of the Indian Scout Syndrome (Holm 1986:88–89), these efforts reflect positive views and respect for the courage and martial ability of Native servicemen that continues today (Meadows 2017).

The US Armed Forces and Signals Intelligence

World War I code talkers also affected future US military communications. Following the war, US military intelligence grew largely dormant. Few language and cryptographic specialists were retained in the military, and American signals intelligence was greatly weakened. Army leadership did not realize the importance of maintaining professional intelligence personnel and that a viable intelligence effort was crucial for maintaining contingency plans during peacetime. The signal corps assumed responsibility for securing the army's communications. Between 1930 and 1935, then civilian William F. Friedman helped revive security measures in the US Army by reassembling former personnel, enlisting new recruits, and helping establish a training school for officers under the Signal Intelligence Service. Army cryptographers shifted from simple codes to machines, and finally to electromechanical devices. Code and cipher officers were placed in all army and general headquarters and personnel trained in radio intelligence work. Just before World War II, other advances were made in organizing intercept units in the United States and its territories and in aerial photography, which sought to keep the United States at the forefront of military communications (Spector 1998:6; Gilbert 2012:218–220).

Prior to World War I, the American military devoted little effort to collecting secret intelligence. While intelligence played a crucial role in the planning and conducting of operations in World War II, Vietnam, and the Middle East, much of the fighting in World War I and Korea occurred along stalemated lines where neither side dominated in military intelligence. Intelligence on troop strength, type, location, and offensive and defensive capability were primary needs in World War I, and the ability of artillery to reach behind enemy lines led to accelerated efforts to pinpoint and counter enemy artillery batteries (Gilbert 2012:199). Ferrell (2007) maintains that artillery was a major cause of troop deaths in World War I, especially in the Meuse-Argonne campaign.

Another issue in World War I was a divide in communications during combat between the corps level and above and between the division level and below. Timely intelligence reports from the US General Headquarters and Army Headquarters rarely made it past the corps level in time to be of use. This was especially problematic during the Meuse-Argonne campaign when the analytical base at General Headquarters was far from the front line of battle. Subsequently, division and lower unit-level commanders were forced to rely on their organic intelligence systems, consisting primarily of humint forms of observation and scouting. These methods continued on division levels in both World War II and Korea, where commanders often had to rely on their organic intelligence collection and security resources. Not until Vietnam would improved, secure communication links allow timely delivery of accurate military intelligence from corps and army levels to ground commanders (Gilbert 2008:199–200). This is precisely the type of situation in which local commanders emphasized using Native Americans as scouts and eventually as code talkers to foil enemy listeners.

A greater focus on intelligence gathering and technology-aided intelligence (phone and radio transmission, aerial photo imagery, air intercept, flash and sound ranging, direction finding, mobile map printing, counterintelligence) contributed to the growth in military intelligence. While these advances produced significant intelligence changes and clear benefits, just as tanks, planes, gas, and the machine gun changed ground warfare, they were only briefly maintained. Despite the burst of activity in World War I US military intelligence, postwar advances were relatively small and short lived. Following the war, the US military maintained few career opportunities for communications personnel, resulting in an exodus of most of the linguists and intelligence individuals responsible for the successes in the conflict. Consequently, a small number of scattered efforts in military communications remained. Only twenty years later, the United States would find itself having to reestablish a military communications force on a far greater scale with the advent of World War II (Gilbert 2012:199–201, 220).

Many new devices and methods were developed between 1917 and 1918, and World War I is often considered the beginning of military intelligence. As James Gilbert (2012:220) summarizes, a more accurate assessment of US military intelligence during the First World War is that it represented a turning point in the history of US military intelligence, "having created a clear demarcation with the past and having established a precedent upon which the next generation of intelligence professionals could draw as they faced the challenges of World War II and the Cold War." Native American code talkers represent one advance in US military communications that would also be deactivated, largely forgotten, reestablished, and increased in World War II.

Secrecy

Another widespread misconception about code talkers is the belief that little is known about them because they were all sworn to secrecy following the war. It is also widely maintained that the US military believed that their languages might again be of use in a future war. This can be attributed to the misconception, based on the declassification date on one version of the Bloor (1919) memo, that code talking was classified as secret until 1946.[7] Many sources cite the date of secrecy for all code talkers as 1968, when the Navajo code was officially declassified.

In 2007, the *Fort Worth Star-Telegram* reported, "Just two weeks after the Choctaws became code talkers, World War I came to a close. . . . In the next few months, as the Choctaws rejoined their line units and word of what they had done reached higher levels of the Army, they were told to keep it to themselves."[8] A woman related to two of the Choctaw code talkers reported (Archambeault 2008:14), "The original group of WW I Choctaw code talkers honored this pledge of secrecy so fervently that some of their own families were not even aware that they had provided such an important service to the United States. . . . It is believed that even today, some descendants still do not know if their fathers or grandfathers were code talkers in WW I."

Other factors offer a more plausible explanation for the lack of knowledge about World War I code talkers and expose some of the myths about code talking. An examination of the nature of using Native languages as codes, existing federal policy towards Native languages, postwar publications, and how Native American veterans view military service offer more credible explanations.

While many descendants sincerely believe that the Choctaw code talkers were sworn to secrecy, this appears to be largely based on assumption, as numerous documentary sources prove otherwise. As demonstrated in chapter 3, following publication of Robinson's public statements and Bloor's (1919) official letter in France, over twenty-five public sources on the Choctaw code talkers appeared in the US between 1919 and 1922. Most came from officers' writings or interviews in the 36th Division, from the division commander down.[9] Joseph Dixon's interviews with other 36th Division officers in June 1919 demonstrate knowledge of the Choctaw was widespread, detailed, and freely discussed.[10]

Several newspaper articles detail using the Choctaw language against the Germans.[11] On May 31, 1919, the *New York Evening World* ran the article,

"150 Indians Back after Fooling Foe by Choctaw Talk. Redmen Arriving To-Day on Pueblo Furnished Puzzle and Terror for Germans," and a similar *New York Times* article outlined how Horner employed the Native Americans: "They talked over the wire in their native language. This 'stumped' the Germans." The following day, the *Arkansas Gazette* published "Arkansan Led Company of Indian Braves in France. Captain Horner of Mena Lands in New York With Redskin Scouts, Who Outwitted Germans by Talking in Their Native Tongue."[12] More sources followed between 1928 and 1941, including Choctaw code talkers Benjamin Hampton in 1939 and James Edwards in 1941. Other sources describing the use of Cherokee, Comanche, Sioux, Osage, and Winnebago reinforce this trend.[13]

Later interviews and articles focusing on E. W. Horner further detail the Choctaws' use in World War I, including "Capt. Horner Put Indian Sign on Germans in War. First Man to Use an Indian Language in Sending Code."[14] An article on the 142nd's return on May 31, 1919, in New Jersey highlighted the Choctaws' use: "Much interest on the part of army officers at the port, and newspaper writers in the Indian contingent, owing to its accomplishments in preventing the Boche from invading the secrecy of the order."[15] Another article states, "Much attention was attracted by 150 Indian soldiers in command of Captain E. W. Horner of Mena, Ark. These Indians solved the problem of how to prevent the Germans from listening in on the telephone of communication. They talked over the wire in their native language. This 'stumped' the Germans."[16]

Frequent accounts from high ranking military officers suggest that no effort was made to keep the use of Indigenous languages for military communications secret. Aside from the classification of one copy of Bloor's (1919) already widely published memo in the RG-120 records, no further efforts to secure knowledge of Native American language use is known.

Use of the Term "Code Talker"

Individuals continue to debate whether the term "code talker" is appropriate for all Native American language communicators. Most detractors maintain that it applies only to the Navajo in World War II, not recognizing the presence of specially encoded vocabulary (Type 1 NACT) among other Native communicators (Meadows 2002) in both world wars. While the term "code talker" first appears in reference to the Navajo code talkers, recognition of using Native American languages as a code clearly dates to World War I and is a legacy whose effects continue to be felt today.

Some army personnel and reporters viewed these men as using their native language as a code and as serving as code transmitters if not code talkers. The January 10, 1919, *Stars and Stripes* article on two Sioux soldiers sending messages in their native language in the Meuse-Argonne campaign was titled "Boche Wire Tappers Run into New Code."[17] The men transmitted messages "in the language of their fathers" and while "talking together in their own tongue, what they say sounds very much like code, but isn't."[18]

A subsequent *Stars and Stripes* article on May 30th, 1919, used the subheading "Choctaw Code Fooled Boche."[19] A January 21, 1919, *Daily Oklahoman* article was similarly titled: "Indian Tongue Used as Code to Dodge Spies."[20] Although not using the term "code talker," Colonel Alfred Bloor's (1919, 1922) description, "to code every message of importance and coding and decoding took valuable time," infers that the use of Choctaw was a faster form of code. Referring to E. W. Horner and the Choctaw, Lieutenant John Eddy reported that the Native American languages provided "nearly absolutely safe code for important intelligence transmission."[21] From interviews on the Choctaw Telephone Squad, Dixon wrote, "They had a code, which they composed because many of the military terms used were not found in the Choctaw *tongue*."[22] A 1919 *New York Evening World* article describing Choctaw stated, "All reports were sent over the line in the Choctaw dialect, and what those Germans must have thought of that language can be left to the imagination. They found a new code which they couldn't break in on."

United States Army Signal Corps historian Rebecca Raines (1996:266) noted, "Perhaps the most unusual procedure practiced during the war was the use of American Indians as 'code-talkers.' Because few non-Indians knew the difficult native languages, which in many cases had no written form, they provided ideal codes for relaying secret operational orders." Although code talkers accounted for only a brief part of her study, her recognition of the use of their language in both wars as actual "codes" supports my classification of Type 1 and Type 2 code talking (Meadows 2002). Although the war ended before the Choctaw code terms could be used in combat, the idea of using Indigenous American languages as codes and creating and inserting specially encoded vocabulary for military subjects was set. These sources demonstrate that military officers and reporters commonly viewed the use of Native American languages in World War I as a form of code no later than January 1919.

The Choctaw represent the best documented case of Native American communicators in World War I and laid the foundation for what later become known as "code talking." Drawing from World War I, the use of Native American languages as military codes appeared again prior to World War II. While the terminology describing the use of Native Americans as military communicators varies, many continued viewing and describing the practice as "code." In 1939, Major General E. B. Adams described using

Choctaw in World War I: "This simple method of coding messages proved to be very satisfactory, and was utilized by the regiment until the cessation of hostilities."[23]

As new groups of Native communicators were recruited, their languages were referred to as codes. The February 9, 1941, article "Pima Indians Have Own 'Code'—Aboriginal Language Helps 158th Infantry" further describes the use of the Pima language as "a system of field communication that defies decodification," and that "there's no key to the army's new 'code.'"[24] A series of articles on the use of Chippewa and Oneida in the 32nd Infantry Division appeared in 1941. The August 31, 1941, article "Indians' Code Upsets Foe[.] They Speed Dialect Messages by Radio in War Games," notes that "the Thirty-second Division will use seventeen Michigan and Wisconsin Indians to send radio messages in "code," their own Indian dialects, in the big Louisiana war games starting Monday."[25]

A September 2, 1941, article in the *Niagara Falls Gazette* titled "Indian Languages become 'Code' in Army Maneuvers. Classic World War Trick Again Being Employed by American Troops" emphasized the use of the Chippewa and Oneida languages as code. A nearly identical version titled "Indian Languages become "Code" followed in *El Palacio* (1941), and a verbatim copy appeared in the November issue of the *Masterkey* (1941:240). Labeled "Indians As Code Transmitters," it states, "The classic World War I trick of using Indians speaking their own language as 'code' transmitter, is again being used in the Army." A sample of Native terms and translations created and assigned to convey military terms were provided, while adding, "The Indian 'coders' work in pairs." Identifying Native Americans from Michigan and Wisconsin in the 32nd Division, these articles describe them as "code transmitters" and "Indian coders" even though the term "code talker" had yet to be used.

Similar articles on the recruitment and training of Comanche from Oklahoma and Meskwaki from Iowa to use their native languages for military communications followed. A February 1941 *New York Times* article announced, "Indians Volunteer for Defense Army" and notes in subtitles, "Will Have Unique Task. Some, Assigned to 'Walkie-Talkie' Radio, Will Use Language to Baffle Enemy." An article on a Comanche unit states, "They are to be part of a special detachment to make use of the Comanche language, because it is so little known, for code purposes in communication."[26] Another article on the same page about eight Sac and Fox in the 18th Iowa Infantry, titled "To Speak Another Dialect," describes the same purpose without using the word code: "They will speak their own dialect, so that an enemy would be unable to understand their reports even if their messages were intercepted."[27]

Four other sources in the early 1940s describe the use of Native American languages for military transmissions in World War I, while another source announced the recruitment of the Comanche for training in coded radio transmissions nearly a year before Pearl Harbor.[28] The *New York Times* December 13, 1940, article "Comanches Again Called for Army Code Service" reflects the army's classification of the Comanche as "code" communicators in both wars. In 1941, at least five sources described the recruitment of Native Americans and their native language training for military communications.[29] Although the terminology describing these groups just prior to America's entering World War II is inconsistent, the term "code" is commonly used to describe this form of transmissions.

Other sources on the prewar training of Native American language communicators include June 1941 news articles on Captain E. W. Horner from the *Fort Warren Sentinel* in Wyoming and the *Weiser Signal* in Idaho. "The use of Indians in transmitting secret messages in time of war may again take place if the United States enters the war. Experiments of this kind are being carried on in New Mexico as well as with Sioux Indians at Camp Robinson."[30]

A 1943 *New York Times* article described "Indian communications men" on Guadalcanal.[31] The term "code talker" began to be used to refer to Native American men who used their Native languages for military communications during their US military service, in particular the Navajo.[32] During World War II, the marines initially referred to the Navajo as "talkers" or "Indian talkers," and by late 1944 as "code talkers." The first such reference to the Navajo as "code talkers" I have encountered is a December 1, 1944, letter from General Lemuel C. Shepard Jr., 6th Marine Division, who wrote, "In addition to their value as code talkers, the Navajo Indians have shown themselves to be good Marines and are efficient in the field."[33] A September 18, 1945, *Washington Post* article referred to Navajo men using their language in the marine corps as "Navajo talkers." The next day, a *New York Times* article by marine corps correspondent Murray Marder referred to these men as "code talkers" as did an additional work by Marder.[34] Following Marder's (1945a, 1945b, 1945c) articles, the expression "Navajo code talkers" became ubiquitous.

The marine corps seem to have originated the term "code talker" during World War II. However, the aforementioned articles referencing the army's training and Native Americans using their native language in "code" for military "code" purposes; and the presence of the status of "radio operator" and "code talker" on the discharge papers (DD-214) of some of the Hopi code talkers, reflects the same concept as the marine corps' "code talker."[35]

Many individuals still believe that only Navajo were code talkers and that other Native American soldiers who communicated via telephone, radio, or walkie-talkie in their everyday vernacular were simply conversing. This issue is quickly clarified by examining what constitutes a code and by defining more precisely the role and activities of the code talkers. The term "code" derives from the Latin *caudex* (trunk of a tree), through Middle French, to fourteenth century Middle English, in reference to a document formed originally from wooden tablets. A code may be defined as (1) a system of signals or symbols for communication or (2) a system of symbols (as letters or numbers) used to represent assigned and often secret meanings.[36] For Type 2 NACT, using existing, unknown languages, the first definition of code is most applicable. For Type 1 NACT, using unknown languages with additional coded vocabulary, the second definition is most applicable. All languages, spoken and written, are symbol based. Thus, both are forms of coded communications (Types 1 and 2 NACT), distinguished by the presence or absence of specially coded vocabulary. While the formation of a code from an existing language (such as codes and ciphers based on English letters and roman numerals) represents a newly created language for communication, an unknown spoken language, both in its vernacular form and when further encoded, can serve the same purpose.

Several factors support recognizing all of these groups as "code talkers." The Comanche, Meskwaki, and Chippewa-Oneida were recruited in 1940–41, before the Navajo program began in April 1942, and the Hopi group was formed in the 81st Division in 1943. The Comanche had an extensive coded vocabulary of approximately 250 terms (Meadows 2002), and the Chippewa-Oneida and Hopi devised similar coded terminology. All groups, including the Navajo, were speaking their vernacular language, differentiated by the extent of the coded vocabulary developed and the alphabetic spelling systems for proper names mixed into the languages. Realizing that a single word for each letter in English was susceptible to frequency analysis, especially for commonly used letters, the Navajo later developed three words (extra or substitute homophones) for each letter.[37]

Comparing the service of army code talkers in both world wars with the US Marine's definition of code talker during World War II is also similar. The United States Marine Corps Manual of Military Occupational Specialties defines classification 642 "Code Talker" as "Transmits and received messages in a restricted language by radio and wire. Sends and receives messages by means of semaphores and other visual signal devices. May perform field lineman, switchboard operator, or other communications duties."[38] Finally, H. R. 4544 (The Code Talkers Recognition Act of 2008), defines "code talker" as "a Native American who served in the Armed Forces during a foreign conflict and who participated in military communications using a native language." Compared with the marine's definition, all of the non-Navajo groups discussed here transmitted and received messages in a restricted language by radio and wire. Those in the signal corps, such as the Comanche in World War II, were also trained in all signal corps communications including Morse code, semaphore, line construction, switchboard operation, mail delivery and other duties (Meadows 2002).

Cultural Influences

Military service had important impacts for Native communities. For many Native Americans, World War I provided the first large-scale opportunity to regain veteran status since entering a reservation, or for some since the Civil War. While some individuals served as US Marshals, army scouts, or in the Spanish-American War, this was more regionally based and did not affect Native Americans on a national level. Some individuals questioned citizenship, draft status, and treaty obligations and resisted the draft, but the overall Native response to World War I produced high levels of voluntary enlistment, patriotism, and tribal and national devotion. Joseph Dixon's interviews of returning Native American servicemen recorded several instances in which noncitizen Native Americans desired to fight, in part seeking equal rights and citizenship (Grillot 2018; Krouse 2007:17–34, 154–164).[39] This was significant because at the time of World War I, nearly one-third of all Native Americans lacked US citizenship and the constitutional rights for which they were willing or drafted to fight and die for. Representing a return to acquiring veteran status, servicemen in World War I were frequently given protective religious rites and farewell celebrations to the accompaniment of military society, war journey, and other forms of ritual songs and dances prior to leaving and upon returning received related cleansing rituals and homecoming celebrations .

Native Americans were widely lauded by the military and their commanding officers for their service. Many exemplary comments about the service of Native Americans are found in Lieutenant John Eddy's surveys. As Joseph Dixon (US Congress 1920:2190) reported, Colonel Morrissey was asked if he had to fight the war over again and were given command of a regiment, would he like to have any Native Americans in it? He replied, "I would make every effort to fill my regiment with Indians." When asked, "Do you think that the Indian has in him the capabilities of becoming an officer?" Morrissey replied, "I know of men who are Indians who made very efficient officers; there is no question about it in my mind. Altogether the Indian possessed sterling qualities as a soldier. It is only just now to give him the privilege of citizenship."

In another instance, Morrissey reported the following (US Congress 1920:2189):

I was in a position to closely observe the Indians during all the fighting, and found them absolutely fearless and loyal in every aspect.
Their ability as fighters is beyond a question of doubt. In addition
to their fighting ability, they were extremely valuable as scouts and
runners, which was probably due to their ability to find direction
under any circumstances, both in the daytime and at night. They
never complained about lack of food or any other of the hardships
that were necessarily incident to battle conditions. . . . As to his initiative in battle, I have this to say, he absolutely set out to lick Germany alone.

When asked, "If it were necessary to go back to France and fight, would
you take any Indians with you?," Captain John N. Simpson, 90th Division replied, "I would not take anybody else. They are not afraid of hell
itself . . . . If we had had more Indians we would have killed more Germans. They did not believe in taking prisoners" (US Congress 1920:2183).
Similarly, Colonel F. A. Snyder, commander, 103rd Engineers, 28th Division, remarked, "If I had only been in command of a few regiments of
Indians, we could have driven the Boche out of the Argonne Forest very
much sooner and with less loss of life "(US Congress 1920:2191).

Major Frank Knox, 90th Division, similarly lauded the Native Americans' service in his unit: "Personally, I shall always regret that the War
Department refused the Indian his chance—a chance given so freely to
the black man. If I could have had the proposed regiment of Indian cavalry
in the drive to the Meuse, the orderly retreat of the Germans would easily
have been forced into a rout. It was lack of cavalry that permitted their
orderly withdrawal" (US Congress 1920:2191).

Sergeant Thomas E. Fitzsimmons, commander, Stokes Mortar Platoon, 165th Infantry, 42nd Division, commanded a mortar crew of five
Oklahoma Native American replacements from the 36th Division who
stopped a German counterattack in the Argonne, routing them into a
retreat. Fitzsimmons was awarded a Distinguished Service Cross in the
action, while commanding officer Colonel Davidson commended the
crew with saving the regiment (US Congress 1920:2186).

While returning Native American servicemen encountered popular
praise for their service, little changed in government-Native relations
or the everyday views that non-Natives held about Indigenous Peoples.
Native veterans were expected to return to their respective reservations
and tribal communities. Some were no longer physically able to perform
the strenuous labor that they had before the war. Others were forced to
sell their allotments and seek work in the Indian Service, in local trades
and industry, or as common agricultural laborers. For the wounded and

disabled, reduced federal funds, which had been depleted from wartime spending, forced some veterans and their families to return to diminished levels of medical and educational services. Geographical isolation and racism added to problems in receiving veteran's benefits (Grillot 2018; Lynn-Sherow and Bruce 2001:95–96), and some Native Americans still lacked US citizenship.

On the positive side, military service prompted the revival of numerous songs, dances, men's warrior society rituals, naming ceremonies, and gift giving (give-away ceremonies) to honor individuals. Several tribes formed their own American Legion posts in honor of fallen tribal members, erected monuments in memory of tribal members who died in the war, and developed Armistice Day ceremonies with ritual observations just prior to 11:00 A.M. at the flag pole.[40]

Returning Native servicemen necessitated recognition of a new generation of warriors according to traditional cultural forms. Families and crowds met incoming servicemen at local train stations, and family and tribal celebrations were held to honor veterans. Throughout the summer of 1919, numerous Plains and Prairie tribes sponsored traditional homecomings with large community or tribal encampments where scalp and victory dances and powwows of a social nature were held. New songs were composed to honor returning veterans, some becoming tribal flag songs among the Cheyenne, Comanche, Kiowa, Naishan Apache, and Ponca.[41]

During this period, tribal martial ideology was reinvigorated and elevated to that of ethos in support of their young veterans, as the focus of many Native community's attention and daily news focused on the war (Britten 1997:84, 149–151; Krouse 2007; Meadows 1995, 1999; Parman 1994:62–63). Although federal government attempts to stamp out Native practices continued, postwar celebrations were generally seen as expressions of patriotism and became harder to condemn. Because veteran's celebrations contained dancing, singing, and giving-away ceremonies, many were still technically illegal and disdained by Indian agents attempting to eradicate them. In 1919, Cato Sells, Bureau of Indian Affairs (BIA) commissioner, complained that many Native American veterans had returned from the war in France where they had "counted coup" in modern form, only to take part in victory dances, watch as their sisters and mothers performed scalp dances, and been ritually cleansed from the taint of combat by tribal medicine people.[42] Celebratory dances, naming ceremonies, and warrior society initiations occurred in many communities. The increased ceremonialism and outpouring of celebration among numerous tribes associated with the war rekindled past traditions on such a widespread basis that the BIA could not counter them and gradually acquiesced to not opposing them (Britten 1997:84, 149–51; Parman 1994:62–63).

The distinguished military service of Native Americans in World War I facilitated widespread Native reacquisition of the traditional role of the warrior, and the culturally appropriate means of honoring them were revived and experienced by younger generations. Although the positive postwar cultural impact of Native American service during World War I was short lived, it revived symbols, ideology, ethos, and community gatherings associated with traditional forms of honoring veterans. Blended with US armed forces service, tribal military expressions became a syncretic form acceptable to both Native communities and the larger American society (Meadows 1995, 1999). Whites increasingly viewed Native servicemen as an asset instead of a threat. The use of their languages as a military strategy brought further respect as a unique and valued resource.

Citizenship

Another widespread misconception associated with Native Americans involves blanket assertions that all Native Americans were not US citizens during World War I and did not receive citizenship until 1924. This belief is still common today, even in Native communities.[43] Although the citizenship status of Native Americans differed greatly in the early twentieth century, it was often determined by allotment and treaty specifications, and after the Burke Act of 1906, citizenship was granted to Indigenous Americans at the discretion of the US government and the BIA. Often this came through forced fee patents (government assigned individual land titles) based on assessments of literacy and self-sufficiency under the label of "competency." Because of the quagmire of determining a Native American's citizenship and draftabilty, the BIA turned over the determination of citizenship during the war to local draft boards, which typically responded to local needs and were often inconsistent in policy. Native Peoples living on allotted reservations normally received US citizenship at the time of allotment (Britten 1997:51–58, 147–149).

For the Choctaw, passage of the Curtis Act in 1898 forced allotment upon them in 1901. The Five Civilized Tribes in Indian Territory, later Oklahoma, became US citizens on March 3, 1901 (ARCIA 1919:6–8; Britten (1997:176); DOI 1922), and citizens of the State of Oklahoma upon statehood in 1907 (Morris 2006:12–27). *Caddo Herald* editor G. A. Crossett (1926:115–116) referenced the status of Choctaw citizenship: "With the coming of the World War, the Choctaws had become much more civilized; had become educated in the schools, had taken their places with their white brothers as citizens on an equal footing. Their tribal government had [been] dissolved, and they were all equal citizens of Oklahoma and

The United States." By this time, Choctaw had also served as members of congress and in the Oklahoma House of Representatives.

Draft registration cards of individual veterans also provide evidence of citizenship. On page one, question four states, "Are you (1) a natural born citizen, (2) a naturalized citizen, (3) an alien, (4) or have you declared your intention (specify which)?" Albert Billy, Mitchell Bobb, Ben Carterby, Joseph Davenport, Pete Maytubby, Joseph Oklahombi, and Calvin Wilson, who all registered on June 5, 1917, but at different county precincts, wrote "natural born" or "natural born citizen" in the space for this question.[44] Allotment records provide additional proof of citizenship as with Peter P. Maytubby.[45]

In Oklahoma Territory, the Kiowa, Comanche, and Apache were allotted in 1901. Comanche code talker Calvin Atchavit, who could write, recorded "U.S.A. Citizen" on his draft registration card on May 5, 1917.[46] Parker McKenzie (1897–1999), a Kiowa allotted in 1901, related how he was three days from reporting for military service when the war ended and how prior to World War I, he had voted as a US citizen in the 1916 presidential election.[47] As Nabokov (1992:281) notes, "While participation in World War I and accepting allotments earned citizenship for about two-thirds of America's Indians, citizenship was still not their birthright."

The service of Native Americans soldiers in World War I furthered existing efforts by reformers such as Joseph Dixon and the Wanamaker Expeditions to gain citizenship for all Native Americans. This scenario is perhaps best exemplified by a statement from John Whirlwind Horse (Lakota), who received several wounds at St. Mihiel (US Congress 1920:2168–2169, 2187): "Are you a citizen of the United States?" "No." "How did you come to get into this fight?" "They drafted me. They said, 'You are a ward of the Government; you have no rights. . . . You must go and fight. . . . I said to them, 'All right. I will go and fight for the rights of a country that will not give me any rights.'"

Service in World War I was a primary factor in seeking citizenship for Native Americans veterans. In 1919, around 125,000 Native Americans still did not possess US citizenship (Britten 1997:176). As a result of service in World War I, all Native American veterans were offered US citizenship on November 6, 1919, contingent on individuals petitioning for it. Few did, as governmental bureaucracy, geographic isolation, and difficulties in applying discouraged and prevented many from seeking it. With the recognition of the exemplary service record of Native Americans, larger reform and assimilation-oriented politics finally resolved the citizenship question, albeit with residual issues concerning land and property restrictions. With the Indian Citizenship Act of June 1924, citizenship was finally given to all Native Americans born in the United States and its territories (Britten 1997:176–180; Krouse 2007:12).

Holm (1996:100) notes that "the conferring of American citizenship on American . . . Indians . . . was not necessarily a reward for Indian loyalty. Rather it simply was acknowledgement that Indians were no longer threats to American policy." Scholars still debate whether this act was a reward given to Native Americans for their service in World War I or a larger politically motivated action.[48]

An accurate timeline of the granting of US citizenship to Choctaw and tribes is slowly coming into focus. Discussing the question of citizenship during World War I, one Choctaw Nation official stated that many older tribal members were unclear of their citizenship status and believed that they were not citizens prior to the 1924 Indian Citizenship Act. This official stated that allotment made all Native Americans in southeast Oklahoma US citizens.[49]

Joseph Dixon continued to press for the creation of all-Native military units. His efforts culminated in the presentation of numerous testimonials from Native American soldiers and army officers before the House Committee on Military Affairs during hearings on the reorganization of the army on January 28, 1920, including proposals for the formation of one or more all-Native army divisions. Despite these efforts and additional legislative efforts by Julius Kahn, no provisions were made to create all–Native American units (Britten 1997:178–179; Krouse 2007:11–12; Tate 1986:434–435; White 1976:22).

Native Language Use and Federal Indian Policy

Following World War I, federal policy regarding Indigenous American languages did not change until 1934. At the request of Hubert Work, secretary of the interior, and under the auspices of the Brookings Institute, a group of ten professionals from different civic fields were charged with examining the state of affairs on Indian reservations in 1928. Visiting every federally recognized Native American community in the lower forty-eight states during a six-month trip, the party discovered that virtually all Indigenous communities were below the national poverty level in almost every area examined (education, income, housing, health, etc.).

Published as *The Problem of Indian Administration* and popularly known as the Meriam Report (Meriam et al. 1928), their work produced a scathing review of BIA policy over the previous seventy years and called for massive reform. John Collier, the new commissioner of Indian affairs under President Franklin D. Roosevelt, enacted legislation that became the Indian Reorganization Act in 1934. This act was designed to reverse many suppressive BIA policies, stop allotment of reservations, reorganize tribal government, create business committees, and restore freedom of Native cultural practices, including religion and languages. Yet use of Native American languages continued to be discouraged and or inhibited in public and BIA schools until well after World War II. Interviews with elders of several Oklahoma tribes born between 1897 and 1925 who attended schools prior to both world wars reported that the degree of Native language and culture prohibition varied from one school to another, often depending on the superintendent's beliefs and personality.[50]

Ironically, despite the languages of several tribes aiding the American Expeditionary Forces through code talking during World War I, schools in Native American communities maintained the "superiority" of English, discouraging and in some instances banning Indigenous languages. The very languages that provided Allied advantages in some sectors of the war were not to be embraced at home. The use of Indigenous American languages in World War I also demonstrates that military objectives do not necessarily correlate with larger civilian government, religious, and cultural goals. This can perhaps be attributed to limited knowledge of their contributions during the war; more likely, its source was the continuing efforts of the federal government and the BIA to assimilate Native Americans into mainstream society.

Despite the provisions of the Indian Reorganization Act, it would be several more decades before legislation aimed at preserving Native languages appeared. In 1985, tribes such as the Choctaw who lost control of their local schools to the federal government in 1898 regained control from the State of Oklahoma through the Tribally Controlled Schools Grant Act.[51]

Finally, the Native American Languages Act of 1990 (Public Law 101-477) was passed. Section 102.3 of this law notes that "the traditional languages of Native Americans are an integral part of their cultures and identities and form the basic medium for the transmission, and thus survival, of Native American cultures, literatures, histories, religions, political institutions, and values." Section 104.1 of this law provides support for the survival of Native American languages, making it the policy of the United States to "preserve, protect, and promote the rights and freedom of Native Americans to use, practice, and develop Native American languages."[52]

Passage of the Native American Languages Act of 1992 (Public Law 102-524) provided funds to assist Native Americans in maintaining their languages.[53] Many high schools, tribal colleges, and universities with significant Native American populations began offering tribal language courses. Native Americans who served as code talkers in both world wars demonstrate that the attempts of the BIA and others to forcefully assimilate them into mainstream American culture was not completely successful. However, by this time, many individuals no longer spoke their native languages. Those with whom I consulted for this book indicated that boarding and public schools contributed to a lengthy psychological process of making Natives feel shame and doubt in retaining Native American cultural practices, languages, and identity.[54]

Another significant factor affecting the retention of Choctaw language involves its relationship with foreign governments. In the pre-settlement era, the Choctaw resided in what is today the state of Mississippi. After interacting with the Spanish, French, and English, the Choctaw came under US protection with the Treaty of Hopewell in 1786 and the Treaty of San Lorenzo in 1795. With the aid of missionaries, Choctaw became a written language in 1827. After losing much of their lands through treaties with the United States between 1801 and 1830, most of the Choctaw were removed to an approximately 31,000-square-mile area within Indian Territory under the 1830 Treaty of Dancing Rabbit Creek. In 1838, the Choctaw adopted their first constitution in Indian Territory and soon reinstituted their education system, with neighborhood or day schools, reservation boarding schools, and Sunday schools. Sunday schools typically instructed adults in reading and writing Choctaw. By 1844, the Choctaw maintained nineteen neighborhood schools and eight boarding schools (Morris 2006:17).

According to Angie Debo (1961:62), the Choctaw became literate within a generation of reaching Indian Territory, and "the quality of written English used by the Choctaws both in their official and private correspondence is distinctly superior to that of the white people surrounding them." The Choctaw maintained control of their government and educational systems until they were dissolved under the Atoka Agreement in 1897 and the Curtis Act of 1898, placing them under federal control. With Oklahoma statehood in 1907, federally run Native American day schools were gradually replaced with state-ran county schools. While some boarding schools remained, a liberal arts focus was replaced or supplemented with vocational work (Jackson 1951:207).

In the US government's effort to assimilate Native Americans, US Commissioner of Indian Affairs Thomas J. Morgan (1889–93) implemented several orders prohibiting Native cultural forms. In 1889, Morgan ordered that native languages not be allowed in federally funded Native American schools, that English be spoken exclusively, and that English-speaking teachers be employed in such schools (Morgan 1889:179). Reflecting the BIA's focus on assimilation, in 1887, J. D. C. Atkins, then Commissioner of Indian Affairs (1887:175), remarked, "Nothing so surely and perfectly stamps upon an individual a national characteristic as language. . . . When they take upon themselves the responsibilities and privileges of citizenship their vernacular will be of no advantage."

Jessica Morris (2006:10–11, 28–29) describes the experience of the Choctaw code talkers as a triumph in resisting the constant struggle with the US government to eradicate their native language and culture. She maintains that because the Choctaw, like the other Five Civilized Tribes, "had developed their own educational system, they were able to avoid, or at least postpone," the US government's efforts to assimilate Native Americans and eradicate native languages through government-run education. The Choctaw's control of their own educational system, hiring of Choctaw speaking teachers, everyday use of Choctaw, and emphasis on funding and promoting education undoubtedly aided the longevity of their spoken language. However, comparison with other groups experiencing similar periods of external control but without control of their own educational system is needed to test Morris's thesis.

Other factors bearing consideration regarding language survival include geographical isolation and tribal population size. Many Plains tribal members who served as code talkers in both world wars came from much smaller tribes than the Choctaw that had no control over their educational systems in the reservation system, had no written language, and underwent a much shorter period of US control and acculturation on reservations. Even though most of the World War I Choctaw code talkers were under the age of six when federal control over Choctaw schools was implemented in 1907 and were thus products of federally controlled schools, the legacy of the tribally controlled school system produced a largely bilingual population that allowed many World War I–era Choctaw to remain fluent (Morris 2006:36–37). For the Choctaw, Morris (2006:49) maintains that "they retained control of their language and culture because of the priority they placed on education." During World War I, members of several tribes demonstrated the same shortsightedness that Commissioner Atkin had shown in his statement and that was displayed in the American emphasis on monolingualism. Their languages, after all, had saved lives during the war, Native and non-Native alike.

Native Writing Systems

Another factor of language retention involves writing. While no North American Indigenous group developed fully written pre-Columbian languages, many orthographies were developed prior to World War I through church, missionary, and ethnological publications. Choctaw and Cherokee became written languages in the early 1800s before removal in the 1830s. Choctaw accounts tell of individuals praying and singing hymns from books prior to and during the Trail of Tears (Visionmaker Video 2010). Alfred Wright and Cyrus Byington (1825, 1848) published a Choctaw-language primer and a Choctaw version of the Bible, while Byington (1870, 1915), a missionary for nearly fifty years who came to Mississippi in 1820, left a grammar and a bilingual Choctaw-English dictionary that were published after his death in 1868. Ironically, Byington's Choctaw dictionary was published as a Bureau of American Ethnology bulletin in 1915, which German institutions subscribed to but lacked sufficient time to associate as one of the languages used against them. Chief Allen Wright, Choctaw principal chief (1880), also published a Choctaw dictionary. In 1833, missionary Jotham Meeker established Shawanoe Mission Press in Indian Territory in what is present-day Kansas. Using English (roman) letters, the press printed over fifty books and pamphlets in Indigenous languages including Choctaw in 1835. Choctaws also published newspapers in their language, such as the *Choctaw Intelligencer,* which began June 20, 1850, in Doaksville, Choctaw Nation.

Cherokee was recorded and published by Congregationalist missionary Daniel Sabin Buttrick and Cherokee assistant chief David Brown in a spelling book (Buttrick and Brown 1819) and in a grammar by Pickering (1820:15; 1830). The Sequoyah syllabary, created about 1821, superseded earlier orthographies and resulted in widespread literacy and publications by both Cherokee and early scholars (Goddard 1996:31–33; Walker 1996:168). Similar prewar sources existed for other tribal languages used by code talkers, including Dakota (Riggs 1852, 1890, 1893), Osage (Walker 1996), and Comanche (García Rejón 1866), although they were "obscure and relatively inaccessible" (García Rejón and Gelo 1995:xi). Goddard (1996) provides other examples.

Several factors inhibited the Germans from using these sources to their advantage. The publications focused on obscure languages, some possibly not even known to Germans, and were difficult to obtain as they were printed for use in small local communities. In the 1880s, significant scholarly works on tribal languages increased through the work of the Bureau of American Ethnology bulletins. While Germany and Japan subscribed to these publications, some of the languages used in both world wars were not contained in these works. More importantly, because they were used late in World War I, the Germans did not have time to identify, learn, and break them. Eastern Band Cherokee was used in the last thirty-five days of the war, Choctaw and Oklahoma Cherokee in the last seventeen.

The full impact of boarding schools on native language retention varies. While their widespread prohibition on native languages is frequently and often patently blamed for the decline and loss of native languages, the actual impacts are more complex. Some boarding school graduates were no longer fully fluent in their native languages. This is especially prevalent with more distant boarding schools where students remained for years with little or no family and community contact. Many others remained fluent, such as those in local boarding schools where students had more regular contact and language use with their tribal communities. I interviewed many tribal elders born between the 1890s and 1930s who attended boarding schools but remained fluent speakers of their language. Geographic isolation, the degree of homogeneity or heterogeneity in ethnic-linguistic demography, opportunities for language use (vis-à-vis nonspeakers and different ethnicities), intermarriage, and enculturation factors also affected language retention or loss.[55]

What impacts have World War I code talkers had on native language retention? The extent to which World War I code talkers encouraged the retention of the language in their families is unclear because most of their children have also passed. Speaking of her father, Choctaw code talker Tobias Frazier, Ruth Frazier McMillan provides an example of how Choctaw was not passed on: "I thought it was very patriotic to go to war and not even be a U.S. citizen. Even though Papa used Choctaw in the war, he wouldn't let us speak it, because he wasn't allowed to speak it" (Austin 2011), inferably at school.

In 1966, Tobias Frazier reflected on the decline of the Choctaw language: "It's not like it used to be. When I was a small boy, there were more Choctaws than white men in the area and interpreters were needed for the Indian and his white brother to carry on a conversation. But today there's no need for this. My niece, for instance, who attends Rattan school, will have no need for the old tribal language. Why should she learn it?" Frazier believed the Choctaw language would soon be "dead."[56] In light of Frazier's life experiences well before language retention legislation and funding began, it is not difficult to understand his view. Most of the World War I code talkers passed before formal language classes were implemented in tribal communities. Factors of ignorance, racism, and stereotyping of Native cultures and languages as backward contributed to federal policy aimed at promoting Native American assimilation into the mainstream American culture and language. Despite family orientation regarding language retention, boarding schools clearly disrupted and undermined normal enculturation and Native language use, contributing to their decline and loss in some families. The code talkers' greatest impact for tribal languages is likely more symbolic in cultural and historical importance than efficacy in language maintenance. One legacy has been the reinforcement of an appreciation of tribal languages within their communities, both by speakers and nonspeakers and despite language decline, while fostering a deep historical pride in knowing that they contributed to winning World War I.

In 2004, approximately four thousand fluent Choctaw speakers remained; in 2019, the tribe estimated that that number had shrunk to one thousand. The number of speakers fluent in Comanche is now estimated to be under two hundred. For several years, tribal language departments have offered language revitalization programs. Classes in Choctaw have been offered in at least eighteen communities in Oklahoma and over the internet, and high school and college students are able to take classes through the University of Arkansas, the University of Oklahoma's Indian Languages offerings since 1991, and Oklahoma's OpeNet telecommunications system.[57] Gregory Pyle, Choctaw Nation chief, reported that "the language is so important to the tribe today that there are classes offered in 43 public schools, two colleges, and three universities, as well as on the Internet and in many community centers."[58] However, tribal members frequently express concern for the overall decreasing fluency in the language throughout the tribe. In 2018, Faith Jacob Parra, the Choctaw language coach at Broken Bow, acknowledged, "It's dying out and we need to keep it revived and so hopefully these kids will use it and continue the legacy. The kids are incredible, they love to learn more about the Choctaw language and their culture and their ways."[59] As in most Native American communities today, the number of fluent speakers in the Cherokee, Choctaw, Comanche, Ho-Chunk, Osage, and Siouan groups continues to decline. While language programs and immersion schools have been implemented, only time will tell whether these languages can survive. Regardless of how these languages fare in the future, the enormous pride espoused by tribal communities in their use by the code talkers has become an important part of tribal histories and will likely continue.

Research and Family Oral History

One of the largest problems in documenting World War I code talkers is the time that has elapsed since their service. A century later, little is known regarding who served in this capacity and details of their individual service. Before interest in recognizing them developed in the mid-1980s, all known World War I code talkers had passed, the last Choctaw in 1975. Family members, who said that they rarely inquired about their relative's military service, indicate that the men themselves rarely talked about the war and their experiences and use of the Choctaw language. In hindsight, many of their descendants lament not asking more. In 2007, Reverend Bertram Bobb, a nephew of Choctaw code talker James Edwards, explained, "I knew four of the code talkers personally. I regret not having talked to them [about it]. I had opportunities. I never did."[60]

Ruth Frazier McMillan remarked that her father, Tobias W. Frazier, never talked much about his military service, although she knew that he was very proud of his service. She reflected, "I didn't ask the right questions." In asking others about what they know about their family's code talker, she noted that rarely did they know any detailed information.[61] Other descendants have told me the same.

Frazier's son, T. W. Frazier, expressed his own recollection—and regret—in 1997: "I'm sorry I didn't take him more seriously when he talked about it, but here is what I remember. Him and his Choctaw friend were talking Choctaw outside their tent when an officer overheard them and got the company commander to listen and they put them on the line telephones and radios. Then the headquarters commander put them on the radios. The code [Choctaw language] could not be broken."[62]

Kathryn Hooker remembered her grandfather George Davenport as "a very quiet person. . . . He wasn't like an outgoing person. . . . He was just real quiet and stern and he didn't talk a lot. . . . My grandmother is the one who told us that he was [a code talker]. And, she said when asked what he did, she said that he translated. She said, you know, in one language and he would tell'em what it said. But that's all she ever said."[63]

Cultural modesty, especially regarding military service, is common in some Native societies, further limiting knowledge of their accomplishments. As described by Nuchi Nashoba, Choctaw Code Talker Association president and great-granddaughter of code talker Benjamin Carterby, "It is not Choctaw belief to talk about your own achievements, it's up to others to praise you. The code talkers would not have told many stories about themselves, they regarded what they had done as just doing their duty. When my great grandfather was interviewed for a local publication after he returned from the war, he simply said, 'I went to France, I saw the country and I came back alive.' Just that."[64] Joseph Oklahombi also spoke little of his experiences in World War I. Few people knew that his medals were on display in the Oklahoma State Historical Society and later in the state capitol. Oklahombi's son Jonah related, "He never talked about the things he did. He wasn't interested in bragging about the things he did, and none of us [who knew him] knew to ask."[65] Many veterans do not talk about their combat experiences unless among other veterans.

Other Choctaw code talkers appear to have spoken more openly about their service, at least within family contexts, and some family members did inquire about it. Benjamin Hampton's granddaughter, Delores Marshall, stated that she grew up hearing how her grandfather "participated in using his mother tongue to fool the Germans" and provided a copy of a 1979 article in the *Daily Durant Democrat* on his participation.[66]

In 1987, Napanee Brown Coffman wrote of her father Victor Brown:

He told me that he was one of the Indian telephone operators who spoke Choctaw and that the Germans could not break the code. He served in the Meuse-Argonne Offensive and was wounded (as his citation from President Wilson states)—gassed (mustard gas), broken nose, and head injuries. My father seldom talked about the War, but I used to ask him and he would tell me about his service and experiences. I remember quite well about his speaking in Choctaw over the telephone lines as he was very proud and pleased that they had "fooled the Germans."[67]

Although not all shared their experiences, or did so in great detail, an ethnohistorical research method combining archival and ethnographic research has facilitated the reconstruction of many aspects of their service and code talking in general during World War I.

While numerous postwar news articles mentioning the Choctaws' unique service demonstrate that many military officers remembered the men, one example reflects a more personal connection. Despite organizing the Choctaw code talkers in World War I, Elijah W. Horner spoke little about the war with his family. His daughter, Kathryn Horner Widder, stated, "Well, he was interested in the code talker business. He talked about that. That's about all." Horner's grandson John Widder recalled:

He was shot in the arm in the trenches in World War I. It was a grazing shot to his left arm, right up here [points] and he always had that scar and he always talked about actually getting shot in the trenches, the medics coming and wrapping him up and I don't think he went to the hospital for several days . . . . He showed me the scar and talked about it. . . . He was very quiet about things. He didn't want any fanfare about being shot in the war.

Daughter Kathryn added, "And he wouldn't take a Purple Heart. He wouldn't let them give him a Purple Heart. We used to have the trench coat that had the hole in it."[68]

Horner was proud of his involvement with the Choctaw code talkers, saving several newspaper articles about them and his role in their use that the family still has. His daughter Kathryn remembered the photo of Horner and the Choctaw code talkers that hung in their home: "It was in the bedroom, beside the door to the bathroom. Oh yeah, it was always there. And those cut outs were on my mother's dresser." The photo was a framed copy of the well-known Dixon photo of Horner with five of the Choctaw. Today she keeps that same framed photo and two wood-backed photographic cutouts of her father in his World War I uniform in her bedroom.[69]

Following the war, Horner and his wife went on their honeymoon to visit his sister in Weiser, Idaho. Horner partnered with Westley Oakes to establish a successful insurance company and remained there for forty-two years. After returning to Arkansas in 1962, Mr. and Mrs. Horner traveled to Oklahoma to visit one of the Choctaws. As his daughter Kathryn described, "After they moved to Fayetteville, they went over to see one of them, over in Oklahoma. . . . My mother was so impressed with the furniture in his home which was made of [cattle] horns." She reported it was Solomon Louis whom they visited.[70]

CONCLUSION

Code talkers in World War I reflect the larger patterns and experiences of other Natives in the US armed forces, with the addition of using their native languages for communications. For many Native Americans, military service is a logical extension of the earlier traditional warrior role whereby men were expected to protect and provide for those who could not protect and provide for themselves. Military service is also intimately linked to the history and cultural aspects of male gender roles and part of what it means to be a warrior and a leader for many Native communities. In turn, veterans have traditionally received very high respect and social status in their respective communities, which continues (Meadows 2017).

While many tribes had World War I veterans, the presence of code talkers represent a small, unique group. They are now posthumously and regularly honored and remembered in tribal observances, plaques, veteran and memorial statues, documentary films, men's society ceremonies, organizations such as the Choctaw Code Talker's Association and the Comanche Indian Veteran's Association, state military halls of fame, museum exhibits, children's books, novels, and numerous internet sites and publications.

Their impromptu creation and limited documentation preclude identifying all groups and individuals who served as code talkers and the exact nature of their service. Their formation appears to have resulted from independent invention to similar circumstances rather than any centralized plan. At least seven groups are known to have been used. Two types of code talking emerged in World War I. Although several tribes used their everyday language during the war (Type 2 Native American code talking; see chapter 7), only the Choctaw are known to have developed specially encoded vocabulary (Type I Native American code talking) for military communications just before the Armistice. The US Army considered expanding the use of code talkers near the war's end, but this was not pursued following the Armistice.

Code talkers set the important tactical precedent of further disguising unknown languages with the insertion of specially coded vocabulary. Their legacy continued as the model, cited in numerous military and news sources, for recruiting and using code talkers on an expanded basis throughout World War II. Without the documentation of World War I code talkers, especially the Choctaw, the US Army may not have continued their use, which also directly led to the US Marines' Navajo program. Despite popular beliefs, their service was neither classified nor kept secret. Their wide coverage in military and news media began even before returning home and contributed to using other tribes in World War II, some recruited as early as 1940. Beyond saving lives in World War I, the greatest contribution of WW I Native American code talkers is arguably the precedent that they set and the expanded use of the strategy in World War II. At least six groups of type 1 code talkers (Comanche, Meskwaki, Chippewa-Oneida, Hopi, Navajo, and Pima) were formed, while many other groups provided type 2 code talking (Britten 1997:114; Meadows 2002, 2007, 2016; Paul 1973:7; White 1979).[1]

Although the scarcity of relevant military records prevents a full accounting of the number and contributions of Native American code talkers in World War I, two wartime engagements exemplify the extent of their impact. At Forest Ferme, Choctaw and Cherokee contributed to a complete surprise of the enemy, with Americans suffering far fewer casualties than the Germans (Barnes 1922:39; Chastaine 1920:229–235; White 1979:15, 1984:167). At Montbrehein, the use of Cherokee was also successful (Stanley 1931). The groundwork laid by at least seven documented groups of code talkers in World War I and the success in their efforts was well recognized by United States armed forces, which greatly expanded code talker tactics in World War II.

A 1962 news article mentioning the Choctaw code talkers notes their importance in establishing their use in World War II:

> Ben Locke's Choctaws in World War I, recruited around Push [Pushmataha] county, started a precedent used in the 45th Infantry Division from World War II on. That was to put Indians on communications networks, talking in their own language, which was a "code" no enemy was ever able to break. It is recorded that this mystified the German high command to the extent that after the war they asked to have the "code" explained.[2]

Recognition of World War I code talkers began in the 1980s and culminated over two decades later in the Code Talker Recognition Act of 2008. Vetting for this recognition does not appear to have entailed extensive military records research, which this work shows resulted in some individuals who could not have been code talkers being improperly recognized as such. Others with solid documentation (Eastern Band Cherokee, Ho-Chunk) have yet to be recognized.

For many, Native American code talkers are an intriguing human-interest story. Emerging from the cultural and linguistic suppression of boarding schools, Native Americans willingly used their Native languages during World War I to defend their tribal lands and peoples—and those of Europe and the United States—when called upon to do so. That they did this despite government efforts to eradicate their Native languages and cultures, and forewent seeking recognition for doing so, should serve as a lesson in cultural perseverance, grace, dignity, cultural pride, and patriotism. It also highlights the value of multilingualism for cultures. Languages that were long deemed primitive, backward, detrimental to maintain, and prohibited contributed to the defense of America and several European counties. This unique contribution would be expanded in World War II. Yet perhaps the greatest legacy left by the Native American code talkers is the immense pride they instilled in their respective Native communities. Using perhaps the simplest and most human of expressions—language—their obscurity proved a valuable weapon. More than a century after their unique service in the Great War, Native American code talkers have become iconic figures and an important part of many intersecting cultures and histories. We owe them a profound debt of gratitude.

APPENDIX A

US Army Campaigns in World War I

Cambrai	November 20–December 4 1917
Somme Defensive	March 21–April 6, 1918
Lys	April 9–April 27, 1918
Aisne	May 27–June 5, 1918
Montdidier-Noyon	June 9–June 13, 1918
Champagne-Marne	July 15–July 18, 1918
Aisne-Marne	July 18–August 6, 1918
Somme Offensive	August 8–November 11, 1918
Oise-Aisne	August 18–November 11, 1918
Ypres-Lys	August 19–November 11, 1918
St. Mihiel	September 12–September 16, 1918
Meuse-Argonne	September 26–November 11, 1918
Vittoria Veneto	October 24–November 4, 1918

Source: US Army 2014.

APPENDIX B

World War I Code Talker Biographies

The following biographical data are from personal military papers of the Choctaw code talkers (courtesy of Judy Allen, Choctaw Nation of Oklahoma; the Choctaw Nation Public Relations Office; the Choctaw Tribal Newspaper *Bishinik*; DO (1917); the *Code Talker Handout* (CTH 2012); Choctaw Code Talkers Association (CCTA 2013); USDRC (1917); US military personnel files (NARA-PF); US Army discharge papers (USADP 1919); Meadows (2002); and grave markers. Other sources are cited in text. While birth and death dates vary slightly in sources, I have used the dates on individual tombstones. The biographies are sequenced alphabetically by tribe and individual's last name.

Cherokee (36th Infantry Division)

George Adair was born at Braggs, Indian Territory, on May 24, 1887, and educated in the Cherokee public schools. He married Edna F. McCoy in 1907 at Nowata, Oklahoma. Adair enlisted for military service on September 19, 1917 (Army Service No. 1490079), at Nowata and served as a cook in Company E, 142nd Infantry Regiment, 36th Division in France. He was discharged June 16, 1919, at Camp Bowie, Texas. Following the war, he farmed near Nowata and was a member of the Adair School Board. He was struck from behind and killed while driving by another driver on October 8, 1947, and is buried in the Nowata Memorial Cemetery. His grave marker reads "Oklahoma / Cook 142 INF 36 Div" (NARA-PF George Adair; Starr 1921:517; D.O. November 18, 1917; NDS 1947). Whom Adair communicated with is unknown.

Choctaw (36th Infantry Division)

1. Private First Class Albert Billy was born October 8, 1885, at Howe, Indian Territory. He is reported as a full blood Choctaw (Choctaw Roll #6799).

He is listed as being from Poteau, Oklahoma, in LeFlore County, and in some instances Jove, Indian Territory. Billy (Army Service No. 1491485) was drafted, entering service on September 22, 1917 (his NARA-PF and AHM form states September 19, 1917), with Company B, 358th Infantry, 90th Division. He was transferred to Company E, 142nd Infantry, 36th Division on October 27, 1917. On November 21, 1917, he was again transferred to the Headquarters Company, 142nd Infantry. He was discharged on June 17, 1919, at Camp Bowie, Texas. Mozelle Dawson reported that her father suggested the idea to use Choctaws on the phone to his commanding officer to confuse the Germans listening to American communications. Dawson also stated that her father told her that during the night, Germans were captured, and a general of the German Army said he would like to ask a question: "What nationality was on the phones that night?" The only reply the German officer received was that it was Americans on the phone. Albert Billy died May 29, 1959. He is buried at Vaughn Memorial Cemetery in Gilmore, Oklahoma (USAFPR 1919; NARA-PF Albert Billy; NARA RG-75, Box 3, Response to Circular #1625 for Albert Billy; AHM Albert Billy; Bishinik 1986c; CCTA 2013, CNOO 2013:3).

2. Private Mitchell Bobb (Choctaw Roll #3581) was born January 7, 1895, at Fowlerville or Rufe, Indian Territory. He is reported as a full blood Choctaw. He was registered on the Choctaw tribal rolls in 1902 as age four. His father, Jackson, was then deceased. His mother, Ellen (Aalin), died September 17, 1902. Orphaned, he became a ward of Hosea L. Fowler until his enlistment. Bobb (Army Service No. 1490094) entered service on September 19, 1917, at Idabel, Oklahoma, and later served in Company E, 142nd Infantry, 36th Division. He reportedly used a field phone to deliver the first Choctaw code message to Ben Carterby, who then translated it back into English for the battalion commander (who would have been Major William Morrissey). He was discharged on June 16, 1919, at Camp Bowie, Texas. Bobb was married to Agnes Wallace. He died in 1922 at the age of twenty-seven (CNOO 2013:3). His daughter's birth certificate (Nora Bobb, born February 24, 1917) lists Mitchell Bobb as dead in 1922, 34 [sic] years of age at his last birthday, and as a farmer (USAFPR 1919; NARA-PF Mitchell Bobb; Bobb 2001).

3. Corporal Victor Brown (Choctaw Nation Roll #3251) was born March 15, 1890, near Goodwater, Indian Territory. His mother was the daughter of a French trader and a Choctaw woman. He became an orphan at an early age and was sometimes looked after by pro-assimilation Choctaw leader Gabe Parker. He attended Armstrong Academy and Tyler Commercial College and graduated from Haskell Institute in Lawrence, Kansas. Later he attended Southeastern State College in Durant, Oklahoma. Brown (Serial No. 1483614) entered service on May 30, 1918, and served in the Headquarters Company, 143rd Infantry, 36th Division. He

was discharged June 14, 1919, at Camp Pike, Arkansas. Brown's daughter Napanee Brown Coffman of Bartlesville, Oklahoma wrote, "He was wounded in the war, being gassed (mustard gas), and suffering a broken nose and head injuries, which is noted on a citation he received from President Woodrow Wilson." As Coffman described, "I remember his stories of speaking in Choctaw over the telephone lines." Napanee also stated that he was pleased to have served in France, to have seen Paris, and was proud of "fooling the Germans" with the Choctaw language. After the war, Brown worked as a field clerk for the Choctaw Nation and as an auditor for the Internal Revenue Service. During World War II, Brown served as a deputy state examiner and inspector for the State of Oklahoma and finished his government service at Fort Sill. Coffman reports that he was three-quarters Choctaw and one-quarter French. Brown died July 22, 1966 (Brown 1919; USADP 1919; USAFPR 1919; NARA-PF Victor Brown; Bishinik 1987d, 2000d; Milligan 2003:253; CTH 2012; CNOO 2013:4).

4. Private First Class Benjamin Carterby (Choctaw Nation Roll #2045) was born December 11, 1891 (some sources state September 25, 1891), in Ida, Indian Territory, to Ebon and Taboll Carterby. Some reports list his birth as December 11, 1891, at Ida, Indian Territory, and others at Bethel, Indian Territory, near Battiest, Oklahoma. In 1917, he was serving as a US Indian policeman at Bethel and Smithville, Oklahoma. He is reported to have been a full blood Choctaw. Carterby reports attending five years at Jones Academy and one year at Armstrong Academy in Oklahoma. His NARA service report and discharge papers state that he was drafted (Army Serial No. 1483743), entering service at Camp Bowie, Texas, on May 28, 1918. Although he is often reported as serving in Company E, 142nd Infantry, 36th Division, his NARA data lists him as serving in Company D, 141st Infantry of the 36th. Carterby was assigned at Company Headquarters. Private First Class Mitchell Bobb used the first field phone to deliver the first Choctaw code message to Ben Carterby, who then transposed it back into English for the Battalion Commander. He was discharged on June 16, 1919, at Camp Bowie, Texas.

In a rare interview (IPP 1937), he stated, "I served in the World War, went to France with the other boys over there, saw a new country and came back alive." Remarks on his discharge states, "No AWOL no absence under GO [General Order] 31 1912, on 4S, 1914." Carterby's NARA-PF file and discharge papers report that he was wounded in the left side by a machine gun bullet. Carterby died February 6, 1953, and is buried at Nashoba Indian Cemetery in Pushmataha County, Oklahoma (NARA RG-75, Box 3, List of Indians in the World War, Responses to Circular 1625 report, Ben Carterby; Ben Carterby Service Report, NARA RG-120, Box 1200, File 21125;

NARA-PF Ben Carterby; USADP 1919; USADP Ben Carterby 1483743; CNOO 2013:4).

Carterby is noted for being reluctant to speak about his experiences in World War I. Great-Grandson Floyd Alexander, a former US Marine, said in an interview, "I wasn't a code talker; but like my grandfather I wanted to do what my country asked of me." Alexander didn't think it strange that Carterby's involvement was kept secret. "It's not the Choctaw way to brag or boast about your accomplishments. When I returned from Vietnam, I didn't want to talk about what went on over there. I just wanted to pick up where I'd left off and live my life" (CCTA 2012).

5. Benjamin Colbert Jr. was born September 15, 1900, at Durant, Indian Territory. His father, Benjamin Colbert Sr., served as a Rough Rider in Troop F during the Spanish American War (Roosevelt 1990:252). Colbert Jr. died in January 1964. If he served as a code talker, he was the youngest of the Choctaw code talkers in World War I. In the NARA personnel files, at least three individuals named Benjamin Colbert appear. One Benjamin Colbert (Army Serial No. 979885) is reported as being born September 16, 1891, in Haskell, Oklahoma, entering service on May 29, 1918, and being discharged August 20, 1919, at Camp Pike, Arkansas. This individual appears on the roster of the Evacuation Hospital No. 19 (1918, 1919) rosters on its embarkation to France in August 1918 and its return to the United States in August 1919. A Benjamin Colbert (born September 13, 1892, died May 5, 1964) is buried at Haskell Cemetery in Muskogee County, Oklahoma. This individual is listed as being from Arkansas, a private in rank, and as serving in the Evacuation Hospital 19 during World War I. These details are confirmed on his service card and final payment roll in the NARA Personnel Files (CCTA 2012; CNOO 2013:5; NARA-PF Benjamin Colbert). Although several Choctaw accounts reference this individual as Benjamin Franklin Colbert, no middle name is given in his NARA-PF. However, his signature on the final payment roll appears to be Benjamin James Colbert. The other two individuals, Private Benjamin Franklin Colbert (Serial No. 3023762) from New Orleans, LA, and serving in the a private in the "Gd Company Med Dept.," and Private Benjamin Horrace Colbert of the 1st US Cavalry, do not appear to be the correct individuals. Colbert's assignment in Evacuation Hospital No. 19 (1918, 1919) and his late departure to Europe, leaving New York on August 31, 1918, make his association with the 142nd Infantry and involvement with the code talkers logistically questionable.

6. Private First Class George Edwin Davenport (Choctaw Nation Roll #5002), was born April 23, 1887, in Antlers, Indian Territory (some sources say Finley, where his half-brother Joseph H. Davenport was born). George may also have been called James. His military personnel records are one

of the most complete of the Choctaw code talkers, but they were damaged by fire. He underwent a medical exam on August 8, 1917, in Antlers, Oklahoma. He enlisted into the armed services (Serial No. 1484283) with his brother Joseph H. Davenport at his hometown of Antlers, Oklahoma, on September 17, 1917. Davenport was married to Maggie L. Davenport, and they had two children at the time. He reported his occupations as farmer and pipe fitter. On September 22, 1917, he was assigned to the Machine Gun Company of the 358th Infantry at Camp Travis, Texas. He was transferred to Company E, 142nd Infantry, in October 1917 (dates of both the 18th and the 27th are contained in his file). He was hospitalized with influenza on February 16, 1918, at Camp Bowie. On March 9, 1918, he passed through gas at the 36th Division Gas School. Davenport served in 142nd Infantry, 36th Division. He sailed from the United States for Europe on July 17, 1918, arriving at port on July 31, 1918. He was promoted to Private First Class on January 21, 1919. On May 19, 1919, he sailed from port in France arriving at Hoboken, New Jersey, on May 31, 1919. Davenport was reported AWOL from December 31, 1917, to January 29, 1918, and again on February 18, 1918. While the reasons for his absences are unknown, he was honorably discharged on June 19, 1919, at Camp Bowie, Texas.

Davenport lived his entire life near Finley, Oklahoma, where he farmed. He belonged to the Methodist Church and the American Legion Post in Antlers. On August 29, 1934, he was examined for medical disability but appears to have been declined the following day. He died April 17, 1950, in the veteran's hospital in Muskogee, after nearly three weeks of treatment for a heart ailment. He is buried in Darwin Cemetery in Antlers, Oklahoma (NARA-PF George E. Davenport; AA 1950; CCTA 2012; CNOO 2013:5). His obituary reads, "Mr. Davenport was a WW I veteran. . . . Of Indian descent he was one of a group which transmitted information in the Choctaw language from the front lines back to interpreters in headquarters in a crucial drive against the enemy"(AA 1950).

7. Private Joseph Harvey Davenport (Choctaw Nation Roll #5012) was born February 22, 1892, at Finley, Indian Territory. He entered service (Army Serial No. 1484381) with his half-brother George E. Davenport at Antlers, Oklahoma on September 19, 1917, and served in Company E of the 142nd Infantry. He was honorably discharged on June 16, 1919, at Camp Bowie, Texas. He died April 23, 1923, and is buried at the Davenport Family Cemetery on the Tucker Ranch (NARA-PF Joseph H. Davenport; Barnes 1922:292; CCTA 2012; CNOO 2013:5; USAFPR 1919).

8. Corporal James (Jimpson) Morrison Edwards (Choctaw Nation Roll #2739) was born October 6, 1898, at Golden (Glover per 1902 Choctaw Nation Census; Edwards Jr. 2004), Indian Territory, to Morrison and Lena Carney Edwards. Edwards attended Armstrong Academy in Caddo and

the Folsom Methodist Training School in Smithville, Oklahoma. Edwards served in Company H, 1st Oklahoma National Guard, and enlisted for service in Oklahoma City, Oklahoma (Army Serial No. 1490047). During World War I, he served as a corporal in Company E, 142nd Infantry, 36th Division. He is described as "A member of the Choctaw language 'relay team' for messages and helped with the code words used in transmissions." He was known for his laughter, sense of humor, and joking with buddy and fellow code talker Ben Carterby. He was discharged at Camp Bowie, Texas, on June 16, 1919. Edwards reenlisted in the US Army on August 14, 1920, at Oklahoma City, served in the Quartermaster Corps, and was discharged as a corporal August 13, 1921, at Camp Eagle Pass, Texas.

During World War II, Edwards tried to enlist again but was turned down for being married. After the war, he worked for the Bureau of Indian Affairs and served the Choctaw people as pastor in Indian Methodist Churches. He loved to sing Choctaw hymns and Gospel songs and was an avid sports fan. He was a member of the American Legion, Lock Sanders Post in Hugo, Oklahoma. Edwards retired in Denver, Colorado, and died there on October 13, 1962. He is buried in the James-Folsom Cemetery, near Whitesboro, Oklahoma. A special ceremony commemorating his life and installing a new grave marker was held there on April 20, 2004. Edwards was issued a Presidential Citation, which was received by his son James M. Edwards Jr. (Edwards 1921; TO 1941; Edwards Jr. 2004; Bishinik 2004b, 2004c; CCTA 2012; CNOO 2013:6; NARA-PF James M. Edwards).

9. Corporal Tobias William Frazier (Choctaw Nation Roll #1823) was born August 7, 1892, in Golden (Spencerville, according to his Army discharge and his daughter Ruth Ada Frazier McMillan), Indian Territory, to Reason John and Susan Payne Frazier. His military discharge and NARA personnel file indicate that he was born in 1895. His father was a Choctaw Nation ranger or light horseman (Indian Territory Police). Frazier is reported to have been a full blood Choctaw and attended Armstrong Academy. He enlisted in the army May 19, 1917, at Fort Sill, Oklahoma (Army Serial No. 1490055), and became a corporal on December 17, 1917.

Frazier served in Company E, 142nd Infantry, 36th Division. Frazier helped break the Hindenburg line in 1918. Daughter Ruth Frazier McMillan stated,

Papa volunteered to defend our country on May 19, 1917. Deployed to Camp Bowie, near Fort Worth, Texas, the Native American soldiers were disappointed not to have their own regiment. They were combined with the Texas National Guard and became the 36th Division. Comments were made about the small structure of the Native men, and their ability to keep up with marching due to their small feet.

They proved to be exceptional soldiers. Papa sailed for France on July 18th, 1918. I asked about his journey from Oklahoma to the east coast by train. He said it was a huge world and his eyes were big, looking at the sights. Papa received a flesh wound in the left leg from a sniper's bullet and received a purple heart. He told us the sniper was killed by his buddies, when he saw the sniper, it looked like it was a woman. I would look at the scar and wonder if it were painful. He always said it was more painful playing football at Armstrong Academy than getting his war wound" (VNVPW 2002; CNOO 2012; CCTA 2013).

On October 8, 1918, Frazier was wounded in the left leg by a "slight M.G. [machine gun] Bullet." He was discharged at Camp Bowie, Texas, June 16, 1919. On his discharge, completed by Col. A. W. Bloor and company commander E. W. Horner, his vocation states "student," the entry for character reads, "Excellent"; and under remarks, "No AWOL of record, No absence for duty under G.O. 31, No. 12 or G.O 45 No. 1914" (NARA-PF Tobias Frazier; USADP 1919 Tobias W. Frazier). Tobias Frazier died November 22, 1975, the last surviving WW I Choctaw code talker, and is buried in the Rattan Cemetery, at Rattan, Oklahoma. His NARA personnel file states that he qualified for the American WW I Victory Medal with Champagne-Marne and Meuse-Argonne Battle Clasps, and the Purple Heart. An October 18, 1974, letter in the file states that he was honorably discharged as a private on June 16, 1919. His discharge marks his rank as corporal since December 17, 1917 (USADP 1919; NARA-PF Tobias Frazier).

A hand-written note in Frazier's personnel file with the name "Private Frazier" states that he was drafted at Camp Bowie, Texas, on May 26, 1918, assigned to Company M, 141st Infantry, arrived in France on August 6, 1918, and served in Company M, 141st Infantry, in the Meuse-Argonne section (NARA-PF Tobias Frazier). His US Army discharge and Barnes (1922:205, 292, 363) lists him with Company H, 1st Oklahoma, arriving at Fort Sill in April, 1917, and Company E, 142nd Infantry, upon consolidation of the 1st Oklahoma and 7th Texas to form the 142nd Infantry and on entering combat in France.

10. Private Benjamin Wilburn Hampton (Choctaw Roll as #10617) was born May 30, 1892, at Bennington, Indian Territory. He was inducted on October 3, 1917, at Durant, Oklahoma. Hampton (Army Serial No. 1490133) served in the 142nd Infantry Field Hospital, 36th Division, with the grade of Private M.D. F.H. 142 (Medical Detachment, Field Hospital, 142nd Infantry). He was discharged June 19, 1919, at Camp Bowie, Texas. A *Durant Daily Democrat* (1979) article describes a visit with Benjamin W. Hampton on August 16, 1939, naming him as one of the Choctaws who

used their language in the war. Hampton died April 15, 1963, and is buried at the Old Church Cemetery (Presbyterian) in Bennington, Oklahoma (Bishinik 1987f; CCTA 2012; CNOO 2013:7; USADP 1919; NARA-PF Benjamin W. Hampton; AHM Benjamin W. Hampton).

11. Corporal Noel Johnson (Choctaw Nation Roll #3796) was born August 25, 1894, at Smithville, Indian Territory. The 1902 Choctaw Nation Census lists him as full-blood Choctaw born in 1896. He attended Dwight Indian Training School. Johnson (Serial No. 1484284) served in Company E of the 142nd Infantry. His draft registration states that he had "weak eyes." Surviving the war, he does not appear to have returned to Oklahoma. Having contracted tuberculosis, Johnson was hospitalized at US Army General Hospital No. 19 at Oteen, near Ashville, North Carolina, where he died of "pulmonary tuberculosis" on November 19, 1919. His Report of Death form lists November 9 as the date of death and the nature of his illness and cause of death as "Tuberculosis, Chronic, pulmonary, active, all lobes, both lungs." His remains were sent to his brother E. J. Johnson in Cove, Arkansas. Ten days later, he was buried near Cove (CNOO 2013:7; Report of Death, NARA-PF Noel Johnson).

12. Corporal Otis Wilson Leader (Choctaw Nation Roll #13606) was born on March 6, 1882, to Mr. and Mrs. James Leader near Citra (some sources say Calvin), Indian Territory, now Oklahoma. Leader was Choctaw, Chickasaw, Irish, and Scottish. He lived with his parents. He attended local schools in Hughes County. Later he attended Oklahoma Presbyterian College at Durant, Oklahoma, and Texas A&M College at College Station, Texas, playing both football and baseball. He married Minnie Lee, daughter of Citra rancher James Lee and his wife, the daughter of Caleb and Malina Folsom Impson, and around 1910, he moved to Scipio. Leader's wife died in 1916. He worked as a foreman on a cattle ranch prior to enlisting on May 4, 1917, at Oklahoma City (Army Serial No. 105473). He is listed as serving in Company H, 16th Infantry, 1st Division and in Company B, 2nd Machine Gun Battalion, 1st Brigade, 1st Division. Upon his arrival in France, he was chosen to pose as the model representative of the American soldier. French artist Raymond Desvarreux was commissioned to paint portraits of the Allied army by the French government. His portrait and statue are in Paris and London. General Pershing described Leader as one of the "war's greatest fighting machines." On November 2, 1917, Leader's company drew the first relief assignment, moving into the trenches at Bathlemont. His company defended the flank of America's first engagement in World War I. On May 28, 1918, Leader was wounded and gassed during the American offensive at Cantigny. After recovering, he rejoined his division in July, then still in combat near Soissons. On October 1, 1918, he was wounded again and hospitalized at Vichy, where

he remained when the Armistice occurred, on November 11. He returned to the United States at Hoboken, New Jersey, on December 16, 1918, and was honorably discharged on January 6, 1919, at Camp Funston, Kansas.

Tewanna Anderson-Edwards recalled that as a young girl, she would eat raisins, scrunch her nose in disgust, and repeat the action, just to hear her great-uncle's laugh. "His smile just radiated warmth. It just makes you so proud his blood runs through your veins." After the war, Leader remarried a woman named Myrtle. He worked for the Oklahoma Highway Department for twenty-five years, much of it near Altus. He later lived at Stuart, Oklahoma. In 1955, the Oklahoma House of Representatives recognized Leader with a resolution designating him as the "Outstanding Soldier of World War I" and expressing sympathy for his recurring illnesses. Leader enjoyed hunting and fishing. Well-liked by the community, his neighbors described him as never having much to say, just going about his business, and being a great fisherman. Leader enjoyed attending state and national American Legion conventions and visiting with former comrades. He was a member of Oklahoma City American Legion Post 35, and later the Colgate, Oklahoma, Post, as well as the "40 et 8" society at McAllister. The "40 et 8" was la Société des Quarante Hommes et Huit Chevaux (The Society of Forty Men and Eight Horses), an honor society and charitable organization formed in 1920 for certain members of the American Legion that took its name from the railway cars used to transport troops in World War I that were stamped "40 et 8" (40 and 8) for the number of men or horses each car could hold (LSFE 2017). Suffering from a stroke, Leader entered the veterans Hospital at Sulphur, Oklahoma, on May 9, 1960, and that November, he moved to the Ardmore Hospital. Leader earned the Croix de Guerre, two Silver Citation Stars (later the Silver Star), and two Purple Hearts. Some sources state that he earned the Distinguished Service Cross, but his military records do not indicate this award. Leader died March 26, 1961, and is buried in the Colgate Cemetery in Colgate, Oklahoma. His tombstone lists his unit as OS Casual Conv. Det. (OS Casualty Convalescent Detachment), reflecting his hospital location upon the Armistice. At the war's end, seriously wounded men were often given the unit affiliation of the hospital they were recovering in. Leader was thirty-six years of age when the war ended (DO 1919p, 1959; DOI 1927; TO 1936; AEN (1958); MD 1961; MN 1961; CCTA 2012; CNOO 2013; NARA-PF Otis W. Leader; AHM Otis W. Leader; Otis Leader, grave marker, Coalgate Cemetery, OK).

13. Corporal Solomon Bond Louis (Choctaw Nation Roll #1755) was born April 22, 1899 at Hochatown, Indian Territory. He is later reported as coming from Brown [probably Bryan] County, Oklahoma. Louis was enrolled as a full blood Choctaw. He attended Armstrong Academy and

seeing his schoolmates enlist in the armed services, Louis, who was underage, pretended to be 18 in order to enlist. One source (HC 1976) states that he joined with six others; Ben Cartaby (Carterby) (1891), Robert Taylor (1894), Calvin Wilson (1895), Pete Maytubby (1891), James Edwards (1898), and Jeff Wilson (Nelson). The fact that not everyone started school at the same age or graduated at eighteen, and the cluster of their birthdates makes their simultaneous attending of school and enlistment likely, however their enlistment dates and locations involved varied locations and different dates. Although enrolled as Louis in the Choctaw Rolls, his name became misspelled in the military as Lewis. Louis enlisted May 10, 1917 at Fort Sill, Oklahoma (Serial No. 1490041). After receiving basic training at Ft. Sill, he was sent to Ft. Worth, Texas where he joined the nearly all-Indian Company E, 142nd infantry, 36th Division. Louis reportedly met his wife at a football game at Southeastern College while he attended Armstrong Academy. When the war began he was too young to enlist but being an orphan, no one objected when he exaggerated his age. With no family member to name as the beneficiary of his insurance, he sent for his girl-friend to meet him at the training camp near Fort Worth, where they were married on November 30, 1917. In July 1918, the 36th embarked for France (NYS 1938; HC 1976). Some sources credit Louis as the organizer of the Choctaw Code Talkers during the war. In France, Louis was stationed at Division Headquarters with James Edwards on the other end of the telephone line towards the front line. Edwards reported to Louis in Choctaw what the Germans were up to. He was discharged June 16, 1919 at Camp Bowie, Texas. After the war Louis worked as a farmer and carpenter. He was elected Justice of the Peace in Bennington, Oklahoma, four times and was serving as a preacher when he died February 19, 1972 in Bennington, Oklahoma. He is buried in the Homers Chapel Cemetery at Boswell, Oklahoma (NARA-PF Solomon B. Lewis; DH 1970; CCTA 2012; CNOO 2013; HC 1976; Bishinik 1987c).

14. Corporal Peter P. Maytubby (Chickasaw Roll #4685) was Born September 26, 1891 (1892 per his draft card), at Reagan, Indian Territory. Prior to military service he lived near Lester, Oklahoma (142nd Infantry register). He entered service on September 19, 1917 and served in Company E, 142nd Infantry (Army Serial No. 1490159). Although enrolled as a Chickasaw Indian by the Dawes Commission, Maytubby was part Choctaw and spoke fluent Choctaw. He was honorably discharged June 16, 1919 at Camp Bowie, Texas. Maytubby died January 24, 1964 and is buried in the Tishomingo City Cemetery in Tishomingo, Oklahoma (USAFPR 1919; USADP 1919; CCTA 2012; CNOO 2013).

15. Jeff Nelson or Wilson was from Kullituklo, Oklahoma. He served in Company E, 142nd Infantry, 36th Division (CCTA 2012; CNOO 2013). He

is identified as a code talker (TW 1937) as "Jeff Wilson," with a photograph in uniform.

16. Private First Class Joseph Oklahombi was born May 1, 1895, at Bokchito (some sources state near Alikchi, Indian Territory), Choctaw Nation Roll #3389). Around 1910, he moved to Bismark, Oklahoma, later renamed Wright City. Oklahombi became an orphan at an early age. His NARA record reports he attended no schools or universities, noting "No Education." Under the heading #7 of his draft registration card, "What is your present trade, occupation of office?," it states, "Farmer (in Jail)." He was married at the time of his enlistment. He walked from his home to enlist at Idabel, Oklahoma. His official enlistment date is given as May 25, 1918, at Idabel, Oklahoma (Army Serial No. 1483609). He was sent to Camp Bowie, Texas.

During World War I, Oklahombi served in Company D, 141st Infantry, 36th Division (Joseph Oklahombi Service Record, NARA RG-120, Box 1200, File 21125). He left the United States for Europe July 26, 1918. During combat on October 8, 1918, Oklahombi and twenty-three fellow soldiers were ahead of their company. Coming across a German machine gun emplacement, Oklahombi shot two Germans setting the gun up, rushed the machine gun nest, and captured the gun. He and the other soldiers turned the weapon on the enemy and held the position until support allowed the surrender and removal of 171 German prisoners from a dugout. The twenty-four men were cited in General Orders for bravery for their actions and awarded by General Pershing the Silver Citation Star to be worn on the Victory Ribbon. A card recording this award is contained in Oklahombi's NARA personnel file ordered "For Gallantry in action at St. Etienne, France, 8 October, 1918" by "Citation Oder No. 4, AEF, dated June 3, 1919." The card is stamped "SILVER STAR CITATIONS." He was also awarded the French Croix De Guerre with Silver Star from Marshal Pétain. Several postwar pictures show Oklahombi wearing the French Croix de Guerre with a US WW I Victory Button pinned to its ribbon.

Oklahombi returned to the United States on May 30, 1919, and was discharged June 19, 1919 at Camp Bowie, Texas. He returned to his home near Bismark with his wife, Agnes, and son, Jonah. During the war, Bismark was renamed Wright City because of the German origins of the name of Bismark and in honor of William Wright, the first soldier from McCurtain County killed during World War I. Oklahombi farmed for several years then worked intermittently as a sawmill worker in Wright City Lumber Company from January 18, 1937, to March 3, 1941, when poor health forced him to stop. Oklahombi's employment on January 18 began the day after R. G. Miller's article on Oklahombi described his financial problems and lack of employment. With Oklahombi being reluctant to talk about his war experiences, most information comes from the reports of close friends. Refusing to even speak English in public, Oklahombi spoke in his native Choctaw language at a reception honoring him at Southeastern State College. His actions received much press in newspapers in Oklahoma, where he was frequently lauded as Oklahoma's greatest WW I hero. His medals, displayed at the Oklahoma State Historical Society and later at the State Capitol, are now in the Oklahoma History Center in Oklahoma City. He was active in the Luksokla Presbyterian Church. On April 13, 1960, Oklahombi was walking from his home east of Wright City into town when he was accidentally hit and killed by a truck driver. He is buried in Yashau Cemetery near Broken Bow, Oklahoma. In 1992, his medals were reissued to his son, Jonah, and are now displayed at the Choctaw Capitol Museum at Tuskahoma (NARA-PF Joseph Oklahombi; Bishinik 1987h; CCTA 2012; CNOO 2013, 2016:9).

17. Private First Class Robert Taylor was born January 13, 1894, in Idaville (? Idabel), Indian Territory (some accounts report 1895 at Bokchito). Enrolled as a full blood Choctaw (Roll No. 916), Taylor reports attending one year in the Idaville Public School. He enlisted September 19, 1917, at Idabel, Oklahoma, and served in Company E, 142nd Infantry (Army Serial No. 1490194). The history of 142nd lists him as coming from Idabel. Taylor served at the front from October 6–28, 1918. He was discharged on June 16, 1919, at Camp Bowie, Texas. Gertrude (West) Beene, daughter of James Taylor and Jenny (Taylor) Biggs, reported Taylor as a relative and code talker, stating, "Another relation of our family is Robert Taylor, one of the Code Talkers." His date of death in presently unknown (Robert Taylor Service Survey, March 15, 1919, USAFPR 1919; NARA-PF Robert Taylor; NARA RG-120, Box 1200, File 21125; CCTA 2012; CNOO 2013, 2016:9; RCCTA 2013).

18. Captain Charles Walter Veach (Choctaw Roll No. 10021; Army Serial No. 448184106) was born May 18, 1884, to Horatio and Sophina Veach in Blue County, Indian Territory, near present day Durant, Oklahoma. Veach lived most of his life on the outskirts of Durant, Oklahoma, and attended Armstrong Academy. Prior to Oklahoma statehood, Veach was among the youngest members ever to serve in the Choctaw legislature. He joined Company H, Oklahoma National Guard, in August of 1908, and by 1910, he was a first lieutenant. His daughter, Jeanette Veach Brinkerhoff, states that Veach helped organize Company H, 1st Infantry, Durant's first National Guard Unit. His steady, continued efforts resulted in a promotion to captain and later to company commander. Veach led Company H in putting down the Crazy Snake uprising near Henryetta, Oklahoma. In 1915, the 1st Oklahoma National Guard was mobilized at Fort Sill, Oklahoma, and on July 22, 1915, was at San Benito, Texas. There they formed a

brigade with the 4th South Dakota and the 2nd Louisiana Infantry. Company H was later detailed to patrol the US-Mexican border and contributed in stopping Pancho Villa's incursion into Texas. In February 1917, Company H was ordered to Fort Sill to be mustered out of service. Veach reenlisted on April 1, 1917, and by April 4, with the changes occurring in Europe, joined the mobilized at Fort Sill.

Later in 1917, the company merged with the 36th Division and was sent to France. Veach served as a captain with the nearly all-Indian Company E, 142nd Infantry. Although seminal in forming the largely all-Indian Company E in the 142nd, Veach was discharged as company commander at Bar-sur-Aube, France, and was transferred prior to their entering combat (DO 1919i:B1; White 1984:107). He was not with the unit when the idea to use Choctaw for voice communication developed on October 26, 1918. A 1919 news article also states that Veach was discharged and sent home before the 142nd entered combat in France (DO 1919i:B1; White 1984:107). Veach's personnel file states that he was discharged on October 14, 1918, which would have been in the United States, prior to the 142nd's assault on Forest Ferme on October 26–28, 1918 (NARA RG-75 Card File; NARA-PF Captain Walter Veach; DO 1919i:B1; White 1984:107). White (1979:14, 20) states that Veach was transferred to the 42nd Division after the Armistice, which had to have occured earlier. He was a charter member of the Five Civilized Tribes Intertribal Council and served this organization for many years as an elected Choctaw delegate. Veach died October 13, 1966, age eighty-two, and is buried in Highland Cemetery in Durant, Oklahoma (DO 1917b; Bishinik 1987e; CTH 2012; CNOO 2013:10).

The belief that he was a code talker may come from his obituary and gravestone inscription. His obituary (DDD 1966) states, "His men were credited with confounding Germans by use of the various Indian languages over field telephones–the lines were often tapped by the enemy." The first part of this statement is inscribed on the reverse side of his gravestone (CCTA 2012; CNOO 2013:10). The reverse side of his gravestone reads (CCOO 2016:10), "Captain Walter Veach organized Company E, 36 Div. an all Indian company, composed of all Indian tribes in Okla. His men confounded the Germans by using Indian languages over field telephones. The gallant record of Company E, in World War I influenced the granting of full citizenship to the Indians by Congress in 1924. Captain Veach was a charter member of the Inter-tribal Council of the Five Civilized Tribes, an elected delegate of the Choctaws."

On October 27, 1918, Bird Seely wrote to her brother, Lt. Columbus Veach. Addressed to the 142nd, 36th Division, it was crossed out, presumably by a postmaster, who wrote "42nd Div"[ision] and forwarded. In the letter, Seely writes, "I hope this will find you and Walter well," which suggests Seely did not know of her brother Columbus's transfer and possibly of Walter's location (Bird Seely to Columbus E. Veach, October 27, 1918. CNA, Walter Veach File).

In 1966, Choctaw Chief Harry J. W. Belvin described Veach as follows: "His great interest in Indian affairs never waned as the years came and went. This abiding interest kept him alert and in search of the Indian problems that continue to plague and confound the U.S. government today. . . . He possessed a keen knowledge of Indian affairs and was an assiduous student of the Indian's nature of which he was a true representative; quiet, retiring, and modest" (DDD 1966). Veach studied Choctaw history and often told wonderful family stories. When his daughter Janet wanted to record his words, Walter would not allow it, stating, "When I die, my voice goes with me" (Swink n.d.:4).

19. Corporal Calvin Wilson (Choctaw Nation Roll #14564) was born June 25, 1895 (1894 per his draft registration card). He was from Eagletown (sometimes reported as Goodwater), Indian Territory. His first name is listed as Cabin on Choctaw roll books and military records. He served in Company E, 142nd Infantry (Army Serial No. 1483461). After returning to McCurtain County, Oklahoma, he donated land for the Panki Bok Presbyterian Church near Eagletown. Wilson died February 8, 1972, and is buried in the Panki Bok Cemetery, Oklahoma (NARA-PF Calvin Wilson; USADP 1919; CCTA 2012; CNOO 2013:10; Allen 2018).

20. Jonas Durant of Stigler, Oklahoma (Dawes Roll number 7081), served in Company E, 142nd, Infantry. He (Army Service No. 149011) is cited as being a code talker in two sources and as receiving a Church War Cross for doing so (MTD 1919a; TAH 1919).

Comanche (357th Infantry, 90th Infantry Division)

1. Private Calvin Nahoto Atchavit (June 20, 1893–October 9, 1943) was born in Indian Territory, later Cotton County, Oklahoma, near Randlett and west of Temple along West Cache Creek. Orphaned while young, he and his brother were raised by their aunts. Atchavit was married when he registered for the draft in June 1917. Atchavit (Army Service No. 2806696) was also known as Nahoto. He was drafted April 25, 1918, at Walters, Oklahoma, and assigned to the 19th Company, 5th Battalion, 165th Depot Brigade. On May 18, 1918, he was transferred to Company A, 357th Infantry, at Camp Travis, Texas. He arrived in France on July 7, 1918. On October 22, 1918, the *Oklahoman* reports that he was wounded in the battle of St. Mihael [*sic*]. On September 29, 1918, he is reported with a "sprained arm" and as recovering in hospital 202 Orleans, France, and improving. He is listed in service at St. Mihiel on August 10, 1918.

Atchavit earned the Distinguished Service Cross, Belgian War Cross, and Purple Heart. His headstone application form (AHM Calvin Atchavit) states that he also earned the "Silver Star" (Silver Citation Star). He was awarded the Distinguished Service Cross, the nation's second highest award for gallantry, for service near Fey-en-Haye, France. His citation reads:

> The President of the United States of America, authorized by Act of Congress, July 9, 1918, takes pleasure in presenting the Distinguished service Cross to private Calvin Atchavit (ASN 2806696), United States Army for extraordinary heroism in action while serving with Company A. 357th Infantry Regiment, 90th Division, A.E.F. near Fey-en-Haye, France, 12 September, 1918. During the attack of his company, though he had been severely wounded in the left arm, Private Atchavit shot and killed one of the enemy and captured another. General orders 87 (1919): War Department.

He was later transferred to Company A, 142nd Infantry, 36th Division, with whom he returned to the United Stateson June 5, 1919, was sent to Camp Merrit, New Jersey, and then to Camp Bowie, Texas, where he was honorably discharged June 16, 1919. Atchavit had no children. He died on October 9, 1943, at age fifty and is buried at Highland Cemetery in Lawton, Oklahoma (NARA-PF Calvin Atchavit; Robert Atchavit to the author, November 25, 2018; WFTRN News 2018:3B).

On Atchavit's card file entry (NARA Card File, Atahhavit [sic], Calvin states, "Wounded, Oct, 22, 1918. Was in battles of St. Mihiel. Returned to USA June 5, 1919. The *Oklahoma City Times* published his picture and reported that the Belgian Govt. had given him a WAR CROSS, for taking over the lines when they were TRAPPED BY THE ENEMY. His Comanche tongue helped get messages across that were not understood by the enemy."

Atchavit's NARA Service Survey lists his birth as December 15, 1894, at Faxon, Oklahoma (then Indian Territory), that he attended eight years in grade school, and that he lived in Walters, Oklahoma. He was then a mechanic, and in order of preference, he liked football, baseball, and basketball. He was drafted April 26, 1918. Remarks by Captain Ben Chastaine state, "Able to perform duties of average soldier well but not able to express himself well and not ambitious and displays little initiative." These remarks apply to Atchavit's post-Armistice service with the 36th Division, prior to returning home, as he was with the 90th Division in combat (Calvin Atchhavit [sic] Service Survey, NARA RG-75, Box 68; NARA RG-120, Box 1200, File 21125; AHM Calvin Atchhavit; Asepermy 2011:1–2; CNN 2013; Robert Atchavit to the author, November 25, 2018).

2. Private George Clark (January 2, 1896–August 6, 1944) was drafted on May 18, 1918, and assigned to the 357th Infantry at Camp Travis, Texas.

His NARA personnel file states he entered service on September 19, 1917. Clark (Army Service No. 2215844) left Camp Travis on June 10 for Camp Mills, New York. He sailed for England on June 19, 1918, then continued on to France. During the war, he was involved in two campaigns in France, the Argonne and St. Mihiel. He was sent to Germany around November 20, 1918. Following occupation duty, he departed Germany on May 26, 1919, arriving in the United States on June 22, 1919. He was discharged on July 17, 1919, at Camp Pike, Aransas. He is buried at Deyo Mission Cemetery west of Lawton, Oklahoma (NARA-PF George Clark; NARA RG-75, Box 68; Asepermy 2011:2; CNN 2013).

3. Private Gilbert Pahdi Conwoop (June 4, 1895–Feb. 2, 1962), from Lawton, Oklahoma (Army Service No. 2806489), was drafted on May 18, 1918, and assigned to Company A, 357th Infantry at Camp Travis, Texas. His NARA personnel file lists him entering service on April 26, 1918. On September 29, 1918, Calvin Atchavit mentions him as being in the same battle approaching Metz, but did not know whether he was killed. A December 2, 1918, wire from Adjutant General Harris of the War Department states that Conwoop was "severely wounded in action, in the arm, on October 24, 1918, during the Battle of Meuse-Argonne." He partially recovered from his wound at Hospital 202 in Orlean, France. On January 10, 1919 he arrived at Camp Steward, Virginia. He was then transferred to Camp Logan, Texas, and to the hospital at Camp Travis, Texas. He was discharged at Camp Bowie, Texas, in 1919. Conwoop died on February 2, 1962, and is buried at Deyo Mission, west of Lawton, Oklahoma (NARA-PF Gilbert Conwoop; NARA RG-75, Box 68; Asepermy 2011:2; CNN 2013)

4. Private Edward Albert Nahquaddy Sr. was born in October 1891 or 1894 and was from Walters, Oklahoma. Nahquaddy (Army Service No. 2249674) was one of the first Comanches to enlist in World War I, on February 24, 1918. His card file entry states that he enlisted at Camp Travis. He trained at Camp Travis, Texas, Camp Gordon, Georgia, and Newport News, Virginia. He served in Battery C, 319th Field Artillery, 90th Division. He was sent overseas June 19, 1918. Nahquaddy served at St. Mihiel and the Argonne Forest. He was wounded and gassed, but he was not hospitalized. The Comanche Nation reports that he received a Purple Heart. After occupation duty in Germany, he returned to the United States on May 11, 1919, and was discharged on May 24 at Camp Pike, Arkansas. He is listed as serving in the 46th Company, 12th Battalion, 165 Depot Brigade (NARA Card File, Nahquaddy, Edward; NARA RG-75, Box 68). He died December 12, 1974, and is buried at the Walters Cemetery in Walters, Oklahoma.

5. Private Samuel Tabbytosavit was born May 25, 1896. Tabbytosavit (Army Service No. 2806854) was drafted May 18, 1918, and assigned to

Company B, 357th Infantry, at Camp Travis, Texas. His NARA personnel file lists his entry into service as April 26, 1918. On September 29, 1918, Calvin Atchavit reports him recuperating in a hospital from a bad foot (trench foot) at Hospital 202 in Orlean, France. The Comanche Nation reports that he received the Purple Heart. Tabbytosavit participated in the Meuse-Argonne Campaign. After occupation duty, he returned to the United States on June 10, 1919, and was later discharged at Camp Pike, Arkansas, on June 21, 1919. His daughter Ida Valdez stated that he remained very patriotic and marched in the Fourth of July parades at Walters, Oklahoma, until physically unable to do so. His military items were kept in a trunk in the family cellar for many years. After the cellar fell in, they were not retrieved. He died March 20, 1970, and is buried at the Walters Cemetery, west of Walters, Oklahoma (NARA-PF Samuel Tabbytosavit; NARA RG-75, Box 68; Asepermy 2011:4; CNN 2013).

Lakota (Company A, 18th Infantry Regiment, 1st Infantry Division

1. Corporal Richard Blue Earth (45,907) was born at Cannon Ball, North Dakota, on October 30, 1893. Then a rancher and working for the Northern-Pacific Railroad, he enlisted in Company I, 2nd Infantry, North Dakota National Guard, on August 2, 1917, at Bismarck, under Colonel A. B. Welch. On January 9, 1918, he was assigned to Company A, 16th Infantry Regiment, 1st Infantry Division. He saw action in the Aisne-Marne, St. Mihiel, and Meuse-Argonne offensives and in the Ansauville and Saizerais (Lorraine and Cantigny [Picardy] Defensive Sectors). After arriving in France in December 1917, he was sent up to the 1st Division, where he became a noted sniper. On October 9, 1918, during the Meuse-Argonne Campaign, he was killed when a German shot him between the eyes south of Sedan in the Argonne Forest. He was buried in Grave No. 97, Section No. 97, Plot No. 2 in Cemetery No. 1232, in the Argonne-American Cemetery, at Romange-sous-Mountfaucon, at Meuse, France. His body was returned to Cannon Ball on September 19, 1921; two days later, services for him were held in Cannon Ball and attended by several members of the Albert Grass American Legion Post of Fort Yates, North Dakota, after which he was buried in the Indian Cemetery at Holy Hill in Cannon Ball, North Dakota. Blue Earth received the French Four-ragère, which is similar to a unit citation award. Blue Earth was cited in General Orders No. 1, Headquarters, 1st Division, Camp Zachary Taylor, Kentucky, on January 1, 1920, for gallantry in action and especially meritorious services. He was entitled to wear a Silver Citation Star (later the Silver Star Medal). The Richard Blue Earth American Legion Post at

Cannonball, North Dakota, was named in his honor. On March 14, 1934, Lieutenant Colonel Welch participated in an event honoring Blue Earth at Mandan, North Dakota (SCP 1921; Knudson and Knudson 2012b:19–21; Welch 1934).

2. Private Albert Grass was born February 7, 1896, on Standing Rock Reservation, North Dakota, to John and Annie Grass Jr. His father died while he was young. He was the grandson of noted Lakota Chief John Grass. On July 17, 1917, Captain A. B. Welch met with John Grass and other elders at Standing Rock Reservation. Chief Grass stated, "Go, my son, and do thy duty by the Great White father in Washington." With his grandfather's permission, Albert Grass, then a farmer, and Joseph Jordan became the first men from Standing Rock to volunteer in Company I, 2nd Infantry, North Dakota National Guard, on July 22, 1917 (his gravestone states that he was the first Lakota to enlist). In January 1918, Grass (Service No. 45,935) was assigned to Company A, 16th Infantry Regiment, 1st Infantry Division. He saw action in the Aisne-Marne offensive, Montdidier-Noyon defensive, and the Ansauville (Lorraine) and Cantigny (Picardy) Defensive Sectors. Grass was killed in action at the Soissons-Paris Road on July 18, 1918, near Soissons, France. Grass was killed when he volunteered to try to get water for his fellow soldiers. He was buried in the Romange Cemetery in France. In 1921, his body was returned to North Dakota. On May 18, 1921, a detail of American Legion members, including Tom Gray Bull, Alphonse Bear Ghost, and Frank Zahn, met the body at Mandan Station and escorted it to Cannon Ball. The White Cavaliers (Sunk'ska akan'yanka), directed by Thomas Mertz, oversaw a final tribute and honor to Grass. Major A. B. Welch, Reverend A. T. Tibbets, and Claude Kill Spotted gave the address, attended by over three thousand Standing Rock Lakota and many non-Indians. Grass was interred on Holy Hill in Cannon Ball, North Dakota. On January 1, 1920, Grass was cited in General Orders No. 1, Headquarters 1st Division, Camp Zachary Taylor, Kentucky, for gallantry in action and especially meritorious service, earning a Silver Citation Star. American Legion Post #173 in Fort Yates, North Dakota is named for Albert Grass (Knudson and Knudson 2012a:19–20; 2012b:47–48; Grass 2013). Grass (2013) shows his grave and states he is buried at Saint Elizabeth Catholic Cemetery in Sioux County, North Dakota.

Winnebago (Ho-Chunk)

1. Private First Class Robert Big Thunder was born in 1892 in Hatley, Wisconsin. He enlisted in the 128th Infantry Regiment, 32nd Division (Army Serial No. 540657), and was inducted at Camp Green, North Carolina, on February 1, 1918. He was later reassigned to Company A, 7th Infantry,

3rd Division, where he served until the war's end and where he conveyed messages in Winnebago with his brother-in-law Robert Longtail. He sailed from the United States on May 27, 1918, and served overseas from May 27, 1918, to May 24, 1919. His engagements include Aisne defensive (Bois de Belleau [Belleau Wood], Château Thierry), and Soissons (Belleau). He was severely wounded by shrapnel to the face and left eye on June 21, 1918, and received the Purple Heart. He was honorably discharged on June 12, 1919, at Camp Grant, Illinois, and is listed as residing at Wittenburg, Wisconsin. He died in 1954 and is buried in the Native American Church Cemetery in Wittenburg, Wisconsin (ISJ 1919:351; NARA-PF Robert Big Thunder; WVM Robert Big Thunder; Garvin 2018).

2. Private John H. Longtail was born in Portage, Wisconsin, on May 29, 1894. He later resided in Winnebago, Nebraska, and Wittenburg, Wisconsin. Longtail (Army Serial No. 540725) was inducted on February 1, 1918, at Camp Greene, North Carolina, listed as being "24–4/12" (twenty four years, four months) years old. He served in Company A, 7th Infantry Regiment, 3rd Division, through December 28, 1918, serving overseas from April 6 to December 23, 1918. His battles and engagements include Bois de Belleau, France, June 15 to 21, 1918, where he conveyed messages in Winnebago with his brother-in-law Robert Big Thunder. On December 28, 1918, he was transferred to Company 16-4, Battalion 153, Depot Brigade, until discharged. He appears on a passenger list for the Chemical Warfare Service Casual Detachment Number 1 in 1919. He was honorably discharged on January 15, 1919, at Camp Grant, Illinois. Longtail died December 18, 1944, and is buried in Mission Cemetery in Wittenburg, Wisconsin. His Application for Headstone or Marker, applied for on April 29, 1948, notes that he was awarded the Purple Heart (ISJ 1919:351; NARA-PF John H. Longtail; WVM Nathaniel H. Longtail).

APPENDIX C

World War I Messages Sent in Choctaw

The following document from the Choctaw Nation Archives contains Colonel Alfred Bloor's orders sent in Choctaw at Forest Ferme on October 27, 1918 (NARA RG-120, Box 14, 142nd Inf. 71st Brigade Operations Folder. Memorandum to C.O. 3rd Bn., P.C. 142nd Inf., 27 October '18. . . . 11:40 o'clock; Spence 1919:appendices), with more recent Choctaw translations added.

1. Post of Control, 142nd Infantry
   Holitah kallo apelichi
   Tahlepa chuffa pokoli ushta micha tuklo
   Akka nowa Tushka chipunta
2. 1140 hours 27 October 1918
   Hvshi kanvllit tahlepa sipokni achvffa tahlepa chvffa micha pokkoli ushta
   Pokkoli tuklo micha untuklo
   Aktoba tahlepa sipokni achvffa chakkali auah untuchina
3. Memorandum to CO 3rd battalion
   Holissot KO Batalin im anumpuli aianhle
4. If upon reaching objective you find the enemy resistance slight, you will send strong patrols forward to RILLY aux OISE (RIIE-OH-WAZ) and the river loop in that vicinity will be cleared up, after which patrols will return to new line.
   Pakko achi- Yakni ma hash onakma tanap ittinsanali ahlehat kallo hosh ittibit ik lawok ma, Tushka Chipunta ahoyochi ma pit isht chafachi chike, ikma lale oh wahis micha bok itatakla ma koshofit taha hinla, koshofit tahlikmvt okla falamvt okla aiyula chike.
5. Before patrols are sent out however, the rocket signal 'White Caterpillar—'we are going to advance, increase range'—will be made.

No hoyochi tikbanli kan, na oktanichi katapila tohbi e pila chin, yakni achakali chin kvt it ia chin acha chin.

6. Signals: White caterpillar is the signal to advance. Red Stars means 'I need Artillery fire.' Green Stars means 'I have reached my objective.'
   Oktanichi: Katapila tohbi akosh tinkba ihinya. Ikma fichik homma ato tanapo chito tokaffi, anonti fichik okchamali at, il atahli.

7. From Bloor, Colonel
   Minko Bloor amiti.

APPENDIX D

Code Talker Timeline, 1918–2020

World War I

1918	Wisconsin Ho-Chunk used as code talkers, 1st Division, before June 21
1918	Eastern Band Cherokee used as code talkers, 30th Division, October 7–12
1918	Choctaw used as code talkers, 36th Division, October 26–28
1918	Comanche used as code talkers, 90th Division
1919	Articles describing the use of Choctaw, Comanche, Ho-Chunk, and Sioux languages in World War I published in French and US newspapers

World War II

1940	Oneida and Chippewa recruited for code talking, autumn
1940	Comanche recruited for code talker training, December 1940–January 1941
1941	Meskwaki recruited for code talking, January
1941	Code talkers used in Louisiana maneuvers, August–September
1942	First Navajo recruited for code talker training, April
1942	Meskwaki code talkers first enter combat in North Africa
1942	Navajo code talkers first enter combat, Guadalcanal
1943	Hopi code talkers formed
1943	US Army, Navy, and Marine Corps representatives begin discussions of using and expanding Native American code talkers, September
1943	Canadian Cree recruited for code talking, England
1944	Comanche code talkers land at Utah Beach, Normandy, France, June 6

1946	Colonel Alfred Bloor's 1919 Memo on Choctaw code talkers and American Expeditionary Force records declassified
1950	Special Research History (SRH-150) "Utilization of American Indians as Communications Operators" compiled by US Army Security Agency discusses future use of code talkers in the US armed forces
1955	The Oklahoma House of Representatives names Otis Leader (Choctaw) as Outstanding Soldier of World War I
1968	Navajo code declassified
1969	Navajo code talkers honored at twenty-second annual reunion of the 4th Marine Division Association, Chicago, June 25–28
1971	Navajo code talker reunion and formation of Navajo Code Talker Association, Window Rock, AZ, July 9–10
1973	Doris A. Paul publishes *The Navajo Code Talkers*
1981	United States Army Security Agency Report SRH-150 declassified, May 27
1986	Choctaw Nation posthumously awards the Choctaw National Medal of Valor to their WW I code talkers
1989	French Government honors the Choctaw and Comanche code talkers with the Chevalier de l'Ordre National de Merit (Knight of the National Order of Merit); State of Oklahoma recognizes the Choctaw and Comanche code talkers at the Oklahoma State Capitol, Oklahoma City, OK, November 3
1993	Hopi Tribe honors five surviving Hopi code talkers on September 24 Native Heritage Day Program, Polacca Day School, Polacca, AZ
1995	Choctaw War Memorial is dedicated by the Choctaw Nation at their capitol building in Tuskahoma (Tvshkahomma), OK; a large section is dedicated to the Choctaw code talkers
1997	Choctaw Code Talkers Association is formed
1999	Department of Defense presents Charles Chibitty (Comanche) with the Knowlton Award for outstanding military intelligence work on behalf of the Comanche code talkers, Pentagon, Washington, DC, November 30
2000	Honoring the Navajo Code Talkers Act (Public Law 106-554, 114 Stat 2763) signed into law
2000	Hasbro Toys introduces the Navajo Code Talker GI Joe doll
2001	Original twenty-nine Navajo code talkers receive Gold Congressional Medals Washington, DC, July 26
2001	Other Navajo code talkers receive Silver Congressional Medals Window Rock, AZ, November 24

2002	Professor William C, Meadows publishes *The Comanche Code Talkers of World War II*
2003	Louisiana Army National Guard dedicates a life-sized monument of two Indian code talkers at Camp Beauregard, Louisiana, in honor of the Choctaw code talkers of World War I and the Comanche code talkers of World War II, April 3
2003	Comanche Indian Veterans Association and the Comanche Nation dedicate the life-size statue memorial *Spirit Talker* honoring the Comanche code talkers, Comanche Nation Complex, Lawton, OK, September 26
2004	Senate Committee hearing on the contributions of Native American code talkers in the United States armed forces, September 23, Washington, DC
2006	Smithsonian traveling exhibit *Native Words, Native Warriors* opens. Originally designed for three years, it continued for several years.
2006	Oklahoma Museum of History opens the exhibit *Hidden Voices, Coded Words*, November 10, 2006, to January 15, 2007, which featured the Choctaw and Comanche code talkers of Oklahoma and complemented the Smithsonian Institution's *Native Word, Native Warriors* exhibit
2006	Documentary film *Telephone Warriors* is released by Red-Horse Native Productions of Los Angeles, CA
2007	Documentary film *The Language of Victory: American Indian Codetalkers of WWI and WWII* is released by Tribal Eye Productions
2007	Lone Star Medal of Valor is presented to the Choctaw code talkers by the State of Texas at a ceremony at Camp Mabry in Austin, TX, September 16
2008	Code Talkers Recognition Act (Public Law 110-420) signed into law by President George W. Bush, October 15, awarding congressional medals to all Native American code talkers
2009	Oklahoma State Legislature presents the Citation of Valor on behalf of the Choctaw code talkers
2010	First documentary on the Choctaw code talkers of World War I aired on PBS, October 23
2010	Code talker star is placed on the Texas Trail of Fame at the Fort Worth Stockyards
2010	Choctaw code talkers receive the Patriotism Award at the inaugural Drum Awards, Durant, OK, November 1

2011	Navajo code talker Chester Nez and Judith S. Avila publish the book *Code Talker*
2011	Fourteen WW II Comanche code talkers are inducted into the Oklahoma Military Hall of Fame, November 11
2012	Hopi Tribe holds their inaugural Code Talker Recognition Day, Kykotsmovi, AZ, April 23
2012	Choctaw code talkers are featured during Choctaw Days in Washington, DC, June
2012	Choctaw code talkers of World War I and II are inducted into the Oklahoma Military Hall of Fame, November 9
2013	Navajo code talker Samuel T. Holiday and Robert S. McPherson publish the book *Under the Eagle: Samuel Holiday Navajo Code Talker*
2013	Hopi Tribe holds its first annual Code Talker Recognition Day, April 23, Kykotsmovi, AZ.
2013	World War I Choctaw code talker highway signs unveiled and dedicated on State Highway 3 at Antlers and Broken Bow, OK, September 6
2013	Congressional Gold Medal Ceremony in Honor of Native American Code Talkers, US Capitol, Washington, DC, November 20
2013	The National Security Agency and Central Security Service induct all Native American code talkers as a group into the Cryptologic Hall of Honor with a plaque at Fort Meade, Maryland, November. On April 8, 2014, the plaque was presented to the National Museum of the American Indian (NMAI), where Director Kevin Gover received it on behalf of the museum. The plaque will be on permanent display at the NMAI, which Congress charged with maintaining a list of all Native code talkers.
2014	Edmund Harjo (Seminole), the only code talker able to attend the November 2013 Congressional Gold Medal Ceremony, dies, March 31, age 96
2014	Code talker Gilbert Horn Sr. is named chief of the Fort Belknap Assiniboine Tribe in May, the first tribal chief since 1890
2014	Fourteen Comanche code talker descendants visit Utah Beach, France, for the seventieth anniversary of D-Day. On June 9, the French government present George Red Elk, on behalf of the fourteen Comanche code talkers who served in Europe in World War II, with the French Legion of Honor during a ceremony at Utah Beach.

2014	Arigon Starr (Kickapoo Tribe of Oklahoma) publishes *Tales of the Mighty Code Talkers, Number One*, a comic book featuring the Choctaw code talkers, April
2014	Chester Nez, last of the original 29 Navajo code talkers, dies, June 4, age 93
2014	The Native American code talker exhibit at the National Cryptologic Museum is updated, Washington, DC, December
2014–2015	The Comanche Tribe and Comanche Indian Veterans Association place bronze military markers on the graves of their twenty-two code talkers of World War I and II, identifying them as code talkers, Congressional Gold Medal recipients, and Oklahoma Military Hall of Fame inductees
2015	Central Issue Facility Building at Fort Sill, Oklahoma, is renamed Code Talker Hall in honor of Comanche, Kiowa, and Cheyenne code talkers of Western Oklahoma, March 20
2016	The US Mint releases the Native American $1 coin featuring code talkers
2017	Oklahoma State Legislature passes the "Choctaw Code Talkers Bridge Naming Act" to name twenty-three bridges in southeast Oklahoma after WW I and II Choctaw code talkers, May 17
2017	The exhibit *Untold Stories: American Indian Code Talkers of World War I* opens at the Sequoyah National Research Institute, University of Arkansas–Little Rock, November 4
2018	First bridge named in honor of the Choctaw code talkers is dedicated in honor of Joseph Oklahombi, east of Wright City, Oklahoma, April 19. Twenty-three bridge signs are erected throughout the year.
2018	Choctaw dedicate a black granite Choctaw code talker monument in Antlers, Oklahoma, recognizing the Choctaw code talkers of World Wars I and II, July 6
2018	Sarah E Sawyer (Choctaw) releases *Anumpa Warrior: Choctaw Code Talkers of World War I—A Novel*, October
2018	William C. Meadows interviews Ruby Kathryn Horner Widder, daughter of Elijah W. Horner on the hundredth anniversary of the assault on Forest Ferme, October 27
2018	Several tribes hold ceremonies honoring their code talkers and veterans commemorating the hundredth anniversary of the end of World War I, November 11
2019	Comanche code talker descendants visit Utah Beach, France, in remembrance of seventy-fifth anniversary of D-Day

2019   Oklahoma legislators approve naming Highway 5 between
            US 277 and Walters, Oklahoma, Comanche Code Talker
            Trailway, May 15. Ceremony held November 20.
2020   National Native American Veterans Memorial dedicated,
            Washington, DC, November 11

NOTES

Introduction

1. *Arizona Republic* (2001:A12). See also Code Talkers.info (2005).
2. *USA Veterans* magazine (2006).
3. Archives.gov (2007).

Chapter 1

1. This chapter is an expanded version of chapter 1 from my book *The Comanche Code Talkers of World War II* (Meadows 2002).

2. Carroll's (2008) work on Native veterans must be used cautiously. It relies on many secondary sources, makes broad sweeping assessments, does not consult several seminal works, and fails to recognize the context of cultural diffusion, borrowing, and variation within even single Native communities. His Southern Plains material (2008:123–130, 140–145, 151–152) contains numerous errors regarding military societies, their relationships to one another, and Native American family names, and in several instances he mis-cites my own works in content and context. Data on recent conflicts center more on politics, controversy, and political correctness than Native military service and objective documentation.

3. At least fourteen books, two novels, a master's thesis, ten children's books, ten documentary films, over forty sections in books, chapters, articles, and pamphlets, seven bodies of archival sources, and dozens of news articles exist on the Navajo code talkers. Most primary sources used in these works can be found in the bibliographies of McClain (1994); Meadows (2002); Nez and Avila (2011); Holiday and McPherson (2013); and (Gorman 2015). Many of these works, both academic and popular, are heavily based from Paul (1973) and on limited primary archival sources, and they only briefly mention other groups with code talkers. Some works have pursued new research foci (Riseman 2007, 2012; Ross 2014), published portions of more recent interviews with other code talkers (Mack 2008; Tohe 2012), or produced memoirs of actual Navajo code talkers (Holiday and McPherson 2013; Nez and Avila 2011). Zonnie Gorman (2015), daughter of Carl Gorman, one of the original twenty-nine Navajo code talkers, has recently written a master's thesis on the original twenty-nine Navajo code talkers.

4. This work is based primarily on secondary sources, with no citations even for quoted material. It fails to incorporate other publications on the subject, identify other known code talker units, and misspells several Native veterans' names.

It does provide brief interview transcripts with seven code talkers, although some accounts of the same material are already published.

5. FWST (1918d).

6. *Indian Record* (1970). See also Holm (1996) and Britten (1997:59) for discussion of the accuracy of these estimates.

7. The Indian's War Activities, December 1, 1918:4. NARA RG-75, Box 1, World War I Folder. Although not signed, the wording and context of the twenty-two-page document infers that it is by the commissioner of Indian Affairs, then Cato Sells.

8. *Stars and Stripes* (May 30, 1919b:3); Hale (1982:40). Lieutenant John Eddy's materials on Native American service in World War I lists seventy-eight tribes. While the context of the list is not provided, it appears to correlate with his larger study, suggesting some members of all of these tribes served. See NARA RG-120, Box 3471, Folder 2.

9. GDMC letter of April 18 and April 20, 1898.

10. JJPC. Letter of April 16, 1900.

11. Barsh (1993) gives a scathing review of Dixon's efforts and motivations. Following the 1913 Citizenship Expedition, Barsh (1993:108) reports that Dixon became more of a realist, publicizing the social and health conditions of reservations and championing unconditional Indian suffrage. Despite questionable actions, Barsh (1993:111) acknowledges that Dixon's efforts likely contributed to the level of Native American participation in World War I, the legacy of returning Native veterans in postwar reservation politics, an increased Native use of the American flag in everyday life, and increased support for Indian citizenship.

12. Dixon (US Congress 1920:2176) later received a September 3, 1918, letter from General John J. Pershing embracing his effort "to enlist 10 or more regiments of American Indians on the grounds of giving them citizenship."

13. US Department of the Interior, Bureau of Indian Affairs, ARCIA, 60th Congress, 1st Session (Washington, DC: US Government Printing Office, 1918).

14. DO (1918b:1, 10); FWST (1918b).

15. Hugh L. Scott (1928:168–169) who commanded Troop L at Fort Sill from 1891–97, maintained that the "failure" of the Indian Cavalry Program was more through the lack of support and undermining of the program by high ranking official than through the failure of the Native Americans' service. The Indian's War Activities, December 1, 1918: 1–2. NARA RG-75, Box 1, World War I Folder.

16. Scott's view was likely influenced by his success as commander of Troop L, 7th Cavalry, an all-Native cavalry company from 1891 to 1897 at Fort Sill (Meadows 2015:57–65).

17. Sells (1918); NA (1918a:170); White (1979:13, 1984:45).

18. Benjamin Cloud to Lt. John Eddy, 1919, IUMAA.

19. DOI (1922); ARCIA (1919:6–8).

20. *Indian's Friend*, January 1918; ARCIA (1920:8–10. See also Haynie (1984:7); Holm (1985:151); Bernstein (1991:22); Parman (1994:60); and Britten (1997:58–60, 73, 84).

21. "Chilocco Indians in Army Service." DO (1918e:B-3); HINU (2018); *Southern Workman* (1918b:608).

22. John R. Eddy to Brigadier General Spaulding, February 15, 1919 (Eddy 1919).

23. *Stars and Stripes* (1919b).

24. FWST (1918d).

25. NA (1918a); Parker (1918); DO (1918c, 1918d). Gabe E. Parker presented a detailed plan encouraging Native American citizenship, sales of surplus lands, continuation of Native American boarding schools, and better hospitals to eradicate disease. Parker also encouraged and oversaw Native American purchases of Liberty Loan Funds and War Saving Stamps.

26. NYT (1918).

27. AIM (1917b:198).

28. *Stars and Stripes* (1919b). See also Lynn-Sherow and Bruce (2001:86, 96).

29. Cf. Hallas (2000:261–262).

30. *Stars and Stripes* (1918b).

31. Dixon (1919:33, WW-33-01:33/42). See also US Congress (1920: 2189–2190).

32. *Stars and Stripes* (1919b); Lieutenant Colonel Wm. J. Morrissey, Captain Philip E. Barth, Captain M. A. Simpson, Lieutenant Ray H. Duncan, First Lieutenant Lucien B. Coppinger, Captain M. D. Steen to Joseph K. Dixon (1919 WW-75-09:3–6).

33. Dixon (1919:40–41, WW-33-01p.40–41/42).

34. Dixon (1919:37–39, WW-33-01p.37–39/42).

35. FWST (1918a).

Chapter 2

1. Cf. *Bishinik* (1986a, 1986d, 1994b).

2. Around seventeen Eastern Band Cherokee also served in the 3rd Battalion, 321st Regiment, 81st Division, most in Company I (Finger 1986:288, 297).

3. These unit assignments and review of individual veterans within the 30th Division demonstrate that these were Eastern Cherokee from Qualla Boundary in North Carolina rather than Oklahoma Cherokee.

4. Lt. John W. Stanley, Co. C, 119th Infantry, to Commanding General, 30th Division (Thru channels), Camp Sevier, S.C., October 19, 1917. 1st Ind. Colonel Frank B. Meeks, Headquarters 119th Infantry to Commanding General, 30th Division (Thru commanding general, 60th Brigade), October 17, 1917. NARA-RG 120, Box 97, File 201.

5. 2nd Ind. Major G. L. Van Deusen, Major, Signal Corps, to Headquarters, 105th Field Signal Battalion, Camp Sevier, S.C., Nov. 4, 1917. 3rd Ind. Major Gayton, National Army, Division Signal Officer, to Division Signal Office, 30th Division, Camp Sevier, S.C., Nov. 4, 1917. NARA-RG 120, Box 97, File 201.

6. Extract, Special Orders No. 61. Headquarters, 30th Division, Camp Sevier, S.C., Nov. 6, 1917. NARA-RG 120, Box 97, File 201. In July–August 1917, First Lieutenant John W. Stanley is listed in Company C, 1st Battalion, 2nd Infantry Regiment, North Carolina 1st Infantry Brigade. He is listed as a commissioned officer in Company C, 1st Battalion, 119th Infantry Regiment, 60th Infantry Brigade, 30th Division between August 1, 1917, and March 1, 1919 (Murphy and

Thomas 1936:156, 176, 188). He transferred to the 105th Field Signal Battalion in November 1917. NARA-RG 120, Box 97, File 201. NARA-RG 120, 105th Field Signal Battalion, Box 214, Officers of the Signal Corps; Box 216, Special orders N. 14, November 12, 1917.

7. Stanley's (1931) account is available on line: http://www.benning.army.mil /library/content/Virtual/Donovan papers/wwi/.

8. Dixon (WW-33-01:4/42).

9. IL (1917). Similar to Holm's (1996) findings of motivations behind Native enlistment in the US military, Principal Chief Robert S. Youngdeer (Eastern Band Cherokee) told historian John Finger (1986:306) "that some Cherokee found the service attractive because they were familiar with the semi-military regimen of schools like Carlisle, Haskell, Hampton, and the Cherokee boarding school."

10. Ragan's (2012) research included data from cemetery markers for her doctoral dissertation and as Post 143 historian.

11. USDRC (1917). In the section entitled "Ability to utilize mechanical methods, maps, buzzers, etc.," on a questionnaire on Crow's service notes, the officer recorded "None." NARA RG-120, Box 3472, 30th Division File. In addition to Chippewa, Osage, Sioux, and three individuals who appear to be Lumbee based on surname and home in Pembroke and Robeson County, North Carolina, some are listed as Indian by blood quantum, but without tribal affiliation.

12. NARA RG-120, Box 3472, 30th Division File; Conway (1919:76); Erin Fehr, Sequoyah National Research Center, emails to the author, July 23 and July 26, 2018.

13. NARA RG-120, Box 3472, 30th Division File.

Chapter 3

1. Mike Wright, Scientific Social Research, to Mr. Bob Gann, Director, Oklahoma Indian Affairs Commission, Oklahoma City, Ok., November 18, 1986; Hollis Roberts, Chief, Choctaw Nation of Oklahoma to Mr. Gerard Dumont, Consulat General de France, Houston, Tx., February 25, 1987; Mike Wright, Scientific Social Research, to Dr. C. Alton Brown, Honorary French Consul March 3, 1987; Mike Wright, Scientific Social Research, to Gerard Dumont, Consulat General de France, Houston, Tx., March 10, 1987; Mike Wright, Scientific Social Research, to Persons Involved in Code-Talker Research February 18, 1987, copies courtesy of Judy Allen and the Choctaw Nation Archives; Eddy (1919). Biographical materials on the Choctaw code talkers: US Army discharge papers of Victor Brown, Ben Carterby, James Edwards, Tobias Frazier, and Benjamin Hampton, Solomon Louis, Pete Maytubby, and Calvin Wilson courtesy of Judy Allen and the Choctaw Nation of Oklahoma. Individual discharge papers and copies of military pay rosters confirm the presence of these Choctaw in Company D, 141st Infantry; Company E, 142d Infantry; and the Headquarters Company of the 143d Infantry.

2. *Bishinik* (1986a, 1986b, 1987a, 1987b, 1989a, 1989b, 1992a, 1992b, 1994a, 1994b, 1996, 2008a, 2008b, 2008c).

3. FWST (1918d).

4. NARA (2013a).

5. Armstrong Academy was located 3.5 miles northeast of Bokchito, in Bryan County, Oklahoma (Section 12, T 5N, R 11E). It operated from December 2, 1845, to February 1921, when fire destroyed it. The federal government refused to rebuild it, and operations ceased (BCHAI 1983:53–54; TW 1937; DH 1970; *Bishinik* 2000c).

6. Author's fieldnotes 2016.

7. BCHAI (1983:53–54); TW (1937); DH (1970); *Bishinik* (2000c).

8. HC (1976).

9. DO (1918j, 1919g); White (1979:11, 1984:43).

10. DO (1917a).

11. Ibid.

12. Ibid.

13. FWST (1918d); DO (1918j), DO (1919i:B1); White (1979:11, 1984:44).

14. DO (1917b); White (1979:9–11, 1984:44–45).

15. DO (1917b:2a-c). Although titled "Fifteen Tribes Represented in Indian Company," members of only fourteen actual Native American populations were present. The fifteenth was Corporal J. Sullivan, a non-Native member of the "so-called Irish Tribe." Corporal Sullivan served under Choctaw Captain Veach and was being transferred to the headquarters of Brigadier General Roy Hoffman at the time of this article (FWST 1918d).

16. Cope (1919, n.d.:5).

17. DO (1918a); FWST (1918d).

18. Harold Mahseet (Comanche-Ottawa), born March 2, 1896, was from Cyril, Oklahoma. He attended one year at Haskell and two years at Oklahoma A&M. He played football and baseball and was the right guard on the 36th Division team (Harold Mahseet Service Survey, NARA RG-120, Box 1200, File 21125). Other sources mistakenly report him as Maseet and Muskeet and that he was Seminole (AG 1919; NYEW 1919). Two Comanche, Carl Mahseet (Company B, 142nd) and Lee Mahseet (California Coast Artillery), also served in World War I (NARA RG-75, Box 68). I have not found a tribal affiliation for Richards.

19. *Bishinik* (1987b, 1987g, 2000c, 2000d); Phillip Allen (2007).

20. Unsourced photocopy, author's fieldnotes.

21. Service Reports for Ben Carterby, Robert Taylor, and Joseph Oklahombi, NARA RG-120, Box 1200, File 21125.

22. Brown (1919); *Bishinik* (1987d, 2000d); CTH (2012); Milligan (2003:253).

23. TO (1941).

24. DH (1970); *Bishinik* (1987c, 1987d, 2000c, 2000d); Morris (1977:229).

25. DO (November 17 and 18, 1917), in White (1979:12–14); DO (1918f, 1918g, 1918h, 1918j); FWST (November 18, 1917) in White (1979:13, 1984:44–45, 79). Tobias W. Frazier, Honorable Discharge, June 16, 1919.

26. DO (1918f).

27. DO (November 17 and 18, 1917, in White (1979:12–14); 1918f, 1918g, 1918h, 1918j); FWST (November 18, 1917) in White (1984:44).

28. DO (November 17 and 18, 1917), in White (1979:12–14); DO (1918f, 1918h, 1918i, 1918j); FWST (November 18, 1917), in White (1979:13, 1984:45, 1918d).

29. Ibid.

30. FWST (1917a, 1917b, 1917c), November 29, in White (1979:12–14), (1918d).

31. FWST (1918c).

32. TW (1937); Louis (n.d.).

33. DO (1918h, 1918i); Chastaine (1920:23–25); White (1978:17); White (1979:14, Photo 4).

34. Company E, 142nd Infantry (1918).

35. CNA, James Edwards File.

36. Cope (1919, n.d.:5–6); DO (1919f).

37. DO (1919f); Chastaine (1920:51–52).

38. Spence (1919:33–34); White (1984:107); DO (1919f, 1919i:B1); NARA-PF Walter Veach; NARA RG-75, Card File, Walter Veach. Another article by Chastaine (DO 1919d) also reflects Veach's removal. His hometown, rank, and unit and his dates of birth, enlistment, and death all match in his personnel file, NARA-PF Walter Veach.

39. DO (1919f, 1919i:B1). The latter account states that Bellmard remained the only Native American lieutenant in the 142nd.

40. DO (1919i:B1). The major was Washington Grayson, a Creek, who commanded the 336th Machine Gun Battalion, 84th Division. Another Native American, Major Victor M. Locke, was assigned to a southern army camp where he was retained throughout the war.

41. Cope (1919, n.d.:6); DO (1919f).

42. *Bishinik* (1996:4, 2000f:4); Milligan (2003:249). For York's feats, see Perry (2010:25, 42–56).

43. Cope (1919, n.d.:6–7); Lt. Temple Black, Regimental Liaison Officer, 142nd Infantry, NARA RG-120, Box 3471, Folder 2.

44. Cope (1919, n.d.:6–7).

45. DO (1919j, 1919k); Horner (1942).

46. Imon (1977:86–87) reports that Choctaw communicators transmitted orders for a preemptive attack against the "Prussian Guards Division" during the St. Mihiel offensive on October 7 and 8 of 1918. The 36th Division was not engaged at St. Mihiel, as Oklahomans in the 357th and 358th Infantry Regiments of the 90th Division undertook this assault (Franks 1984:33–35. 120–121). Imon likely refers to the 142d's attack down the northern slope of Mont Blanc toward and along the sunken road to Saint-Etienne-a-Arnes (Franks 1984:29–30, 118–119). Bloor (1919) clearly indicates that the Choctaw were only used as code talkers on October 26 and 27 of 1918 at Forest Ferme, and no primary sources reference their use before this time. Imon (1977:87), probably citing the *New York Sun* (NYS 1938) article, also refers to the unit being under the command of a Colonel Brewer, which should be Colonel Bloor. See also CNOO (1986); NYS (1938:30); Lavine (1921a, 1921b); NYA (1921); Chastaine (1920:82–83); and White (1979:16).

47. Bloor (1922:66–69); White (1979:15, 1984:123–145, 157–159, 169); Franks (1984:118–119); Stallings (1963:280–289).

48. While General Smith reported 548 prisoners in one document and 813 in another, the discrepancy is from the 71st Brigade's only being officially credited with taking 381 prisoners when they actually captured over 600 (White 1984:169).

Many German prisoners were disarmed and sent to the rear without guards, where they were received by the 2nd Division, who did not credit their capture to the 36th. Bloor reported 520 prisoners and 50 machine guns by 10:30 that morning, while White reports that it was actually more than 600 (Bloor 1922:66–69; White 1979:15, 1984:123–145, 169). Coleman (2007) reports 711 casualties for the 141st and 681 for the 142nd.

49. *Stars and Stripes* (1918a:8).

50. White (1979:15; 1984:159–166); ABMC (1944:8); Scribner (n.d.).

51. "Observations and Experiences at the Front, By Capt. E.W. Horner, 142nd Inf." NARA RG-120, Box 14, ARC ID 30164, Entry NM-91 1241. The date of Horner's letter is either November 9 or 10, 1918. Horner appears to have originally written "November 9th," then corrected it by writing "10" over the "9." Horner first served in Company H, 1st Oklahoma Infantry, Oklahoma National Guard, from June 16, 1916, to August 1, 1917, including service against Pancho Villa in 1916. He then served in the 1st Oklahoma Infantry, Oklahoma National Guard, from August 2, 1917, to October 15, 1917, which after becoming part of the 142nd Infantry, 36th Division, continued from October 16, 1917, to July 29, 1919. Horner later served in the 116th Cavalry and 83rd Field Artillery in the Idaho National Guard from February 11, 1926, to July 10, 1941. He served again in the US Army as a lieutenant colonel from July 11, 1941, through April 8, 1945, including three years in France, then in the US Army Reserve from April 15, 1946, to June 30, 1949. Horner served in the US Army Honorary Reserve from July 1, 1949, to May 19, 1953, retiring with thirty years' service. Born May 19, 1893, Elijah Witt Horner died January 19, 1984, at the age of ninety-one (HUa 1942, HUb 1953, HUc 1953; HARB 1953; Kathryn Horner Witter, to the author, October 27, 2018).

52. Cope (1919, n.d.:9).

53. 71st Infantry Brigade (1918).

54. Chastaine (1920:217–223); White (1979:15, 1984:159–166, Map 6); ABMC (1944:8, 16–18); Scribner (n.d.). Kahn (1967:550) states that the Choctaw were in Company D, 141st Infantry, but Bloor's letter specifically states the 142nd in two instances. Most of the men are also listed in Company E when the 36th went on the front line (Barnes 1922:290–297; *Bishinik* 1986a; Bloor 1919; Eddy 1919; White 1976; White 1979:20).

55. Gilbert (2012:122) lists "French *telegraphie par sol*, known simply as TSP" and again as "TSP" while Bloor (1919) lists it as "T.P.S." Gilbert apparently transposed the letters in the acronym.

56. USASS (n.d.); Cameron (1919).

57. Bloor (1919); Greely (1919); Morris (2006:42).

58. Greely (1919:7–8).

59. Bloor (1919); Greely (1919); Chastaine (1920:231–232); White (1984:164).

60. Greely (1919:8). Of Sergeant 1st Class Virgil C. Mottern, Company C, 105th Field Signal Battalion, Greely (1919) describes, "He lost his life while personally laying a telephone line over exceedingly dangerous ground, under continuous artillery fire which caused a great loss among the runners." Mottern was awarded the Distinguished Service Cross posthumously.

61. *Bishinik* (1986b). This source does not cite where this statistic was obtained. Accounts of the 36th Division reference several instances of a high loss of runners.

62. Greely (1919:7–8).

63. Greely (1919:8).

64. Ibid.

65. Bloor (1919).

66. FWST January 19, 1919, in White (1979:18); DO (1919a). Bloor (1919) reports this as a "rumor" within the division.

67. Gilbert (2012:190) states that "13 enlisted men and two officers from the Choctaw tribe" were selected and used in the withdrawal of the two companies from Chufilly to Chardeney on October 26, 1918. Although Gilbert (2012:202n22, n23) consulted Bloor's (1919) memorandum, unit records from the USA Center of Military History, and a letter from the Oklahoma Historical Society, he does not provide a source for this statement or name any individuals.

68. Franks (1984:29) states that the attack occurred in the early morning, with the artillery barrage beginning at "0410," or 4:10 A.M. However, officers' accounts (Chastaine 1920:223–225; Barnes 1922:343–344; White 1984:164) report that it started at 4:30 P.M., correlating with the twenty-minute barrage begun at 4:10 P.M. and the timing to maximize inhibiting the German's use of their observation posts by the approaching nightfall.

69. RG-120 36th Division, 142nd Infantry, Box 14, Personnel Experiences, Steve Lillard Folder:2–3.

70. Chastaine (1920:227); White (1984:164–165); ABMC (1944:8).

71. Cope (1919, n.d.:9–10).

72. Spence (1919:317, 322–324); ABMC (1944:8, 17–18). Approximately forty-nine Germans, including the battalion commander, were killed, over two hundred taken prisoner, and others wounded. Chastaine (1920:235) reports 194 German prisoners and slightly less that number killed. See also (Maxfield (1975:116–117).

73. Cope (1919, n.d.:10).

74. Spence (1919:326); DO (1919f:D1).

75. DO (1919f:D1).

76. The Services of the Thirty-Sixth Division with the American Expeditionary Forces:25. NARA RG-120 Box 2, History July 1918-May 1919 Folder. White (1982:167) lists fourteen killed, thirty-six wounded, sixty-three gassed, and five missing, and German losses of forty-nine killed, two hundred prisoners, and an unknown number wounded.

77. DO (1919k:D4).

78. *Observations and Experiences at the Front*, by Capt. E. W. Horner, 142nd Infantry. NARA RG-120, Box 14, ARC ID 30164, Entry NM-91 1241.

79. Captain Byron S. Bruce, M.C., U.S.A. Supplemental to History of Actions in 36th Division, January 5, 1919. NARA RG-120, Box 14, ARC ID 301641.

80. Chastaine (1920); Bloor (1919).

81. Camp Merritt (1919).

82. Dixon (WW-33-01:33/42); WS (1941).

83. Dixon (1919:29, WW-33-01:30/42).

84. NYEW (1919); NYT (1919); Camp Merritt (1919); Co. E, 142nd Inf. (1919).

85. NYS (1938); TO (1941); AA (1966); Bishinik (1986b, 1986c, 1997b, 2000a, 2000f); DO (1948).

86. Wanamaker Collection, Photo W6451, Indiana University Museum of Archaeology and Anthropology. Evangeline Wilson states that Horner signed his name on the back of the Wanamaker photo (NMAI 09-243 Box 5:136), although I have not been able to confirm this.

87. TW (1937).

88. DH (1970).

89. DH (1970). See also TO (1970) and NYS (1938).

90. *Bishinik* (1986b). With more than ninety Choctaw in the battalion (DO 1917b), only eight fluent speakers seems very low. Maytubby (Barnes 1922:364) is listed in Company E, but he could have been moved to the Headquarters Company. Carterby was in Company D, 141st Infantry Regiment (Ben Carterby File, NARA RG-120, Box 1200, File 21125).

91. This information was reported in 1979 by Len Green, who obtained it from Solomon Louis (often misspelled as Lewis). Louis, the last surviving WW I Choctaw code talker, died February 19, 1972. Tobias Frazier and his relatives claim that he originated the idea to use the Choctaw as code talkers (AA 1966; *Bishinik* 1986a, 1986b). See also NYS (1938:30). White (1984) contains no Lawrence. Barnes (1922:342–346) lists no Captain Lawrence among the "Roster of Officers of the 142nd Infantry on Going Into the Line."

92. Judy Allen, Choctaw Nation, to the author, 2015.

93. For other Choctaw, see Durant (1919); for James Edwards, see Edwards (1937), TO (1941); for Solomon B. Louis, see Lewis (1979), TW (1937); Antlers American (1966). See also NYS (1938). Author's fieldnotes (2015).

94. NARA RG-120, Box 3471, Folder 2.

95. Lt. Temple Black, Regimental Liaison Officer, 142nd Infantry, Indian War College Data 1920, Folder WW-75-09:2–3; NARA RG-120, Box 3471, Folder 2; NARA RG-120, Box 3471, Folder 2.

96. MTD (1919a). Durant appears in Company E, 142nd (Barnes 1922:292).

97. Dixon (WW-33-01). A photo and address of Emerson Jackson (Choctaw), Company A, 142nd Infantry, of Ardmore, Oklahoma, appears in this group, but there is no indication that he was a code talker.

98. TW (1937). Solomon Louis states that the Choctaw "recall the approach of armistice and the suffering of the dreadful day, with no water or food. Many of the boys were so thirsty they took canteens from the dead Germans." Similar statements appear in other 1970 accounts, emphasizing that the last two weeks before the Armistice were harsh. "We were out of food and water," recalled Louis. "And we took canteens off the bodies of Germans to quench our thirst. If they hadn't of signed the armistice when they did, we might have lost a lot more men through sheer starvation" (DH 1970; TO 1970). Like the NYS (1938) article, several

discrepancies appear in these articles, confusing actions at St. Mihiel with those at Forest Ferme. As the 142nd was relieved after Forest Ferme and at a rest area, they would not have experienced this situation.

99. NYS (1938); TO (1941); *Bishinik* (1986b:2–3; 1996; 2000F); CNOO (ca. 1990); Langelier (2000:7). Gregory E. Pyle to the Attendees of the Six Nations of Virginia Pow Wow, Oct. 2, 2002 (VNVPW 2002). Judy Allen, email to the author July 21, 2005.

100. *Bishinik* (1994b:3); Evacuation Hospital No. 19 (1918, 1919).

101. Judy Allen to the author, August 5, 2015.

102. Author's fieldnotes, Tuskahoma, OK, August 4, 2015.

103. *Bishinik* (2000e); TMFM (2014); TO (1941).

104. AA (1966).

105. AA (1950); Visionmaker (2010).

106. AEN (1958).

107. Two sources (*Bishinik* 1986b; Unknown 1986) report, "Of the eight Choctaw involved," one was from Bryan County, one from Choctaw County, and six from McCurtain County, Oklahoma. These appear to be the first eight reported.

108. Horner (1942).

109. Code Talkers Recognition Ceremony, Oklahoma State Capitol, November 3, 1989, author's copy. TO (1941); *Bishinik* (1986a, 1994b:3); TT (1991).

110. NYS (1938:30); Kahn (1967:550). Lavine (1921a, 1921b) states that the code talkers came from Company E, 142d Infantry, and were led by Chief George Baconrind, not Solomon Lewis [Louis]. See also CNOO (1986). Imon (1977:87) states that Soloman Louis was requested by commanding officers to select several Choctaw as communications operators.

111. Bloor (1919); NYS (1938); *Bishinik* (1986b; 1994b).

112. DO (1917b:2a–c). These may have been Captain Columbus E. Veach (Choctaw) of Company E and 1st Lt. Moses Bellmard (Kaw) of Company C. Captain Charles H. Johnson of Company C, Pawnee, Oklahoma, may also be one of these individuals (Barnes 1922:344–345). A 1919 source (Camp Merritt 1919) mentions Captain Bellmard and a Captain Seran, both Natives, and implies that they were involved with the use of the Choctaw. First Lieutenant Walter L. Seran of Company F was from Wewoka, Oklahoma (Barnes 1922:344)

113. NYS (1938).

114. *Stars and Stripes* (1918a); FWST (December 1, 1918, in White 1979:16); Wise (1931:532–536). See also White (1979:16, 20n30). Newspaper accounts of the Choctaw contain several errors. Lavine (1921a, 1921b) and the NYS (1938) appear to describe the same event, with Horner having the idea to use the Choctaw, setting up the program, and using eight Choctaw. Lavine (1921a) states that, Captain Horner detailed the men under Chief George Baconrind, while the NYS (1938) article states that "they had been selected by Solomon Lewis who was told to choose seven trustworthy men who wouldn't flinch." The NYS (1938) maintains the Choctaw Native American language communicators were used to transmit orders against the "Prussian Guards Division" during the St. Mihiel offensive. However, the anonymous writer appears to have confused St. Mihiel for St. Etienne, since the

36th Division did not fight at St. Mihiel and the Choctaw only used their language for military communications at Forest Ferme. Chastaine (1920:90, 120, 122–124) identifies the German units that the Americans faced at St. Etienne, which included some of the 3rd Prussian Guard, the artillery barrage shortly after 5:00 A.M., and the heavily defended cemetery. The NYS (1938) statement that one of the Choctaw reported a forthcoming attack by Prussian Guards that was preempted by a 5:55 A.M. artillery barrage and an infantry advance "over the top" at 6:00 A.M. also confuses the St. Etienne and Forest Ferme fights, since troops advanced on Forest Ferme at 4:40 P.M. The NYS (1938) article also references "General Gribble" (Greble), and "Col. Brewer" (Bloor). While the article names eight Choctaw who transmitted messages, only Oklahombi's unit is given (Company D, 141st Infantry). See also Bloor (1919).

115. WS (1938). This is Captain David R. Nelson (Barnes 1922:188, 342, 344). See note 127, below.

116. NYS (1938:30). Another account (FWST 1919b:6) reports 813 prisoners captured from four German Divisions. Imon (1977:87) and Stallings (1963:288), who likely based their accounts on the NYS article, report the use and immediate result of the Choctaw communicators.

117. Bloor (1919).

118. TO (1941). This list of Choctaw differs from the NYS (1938) article. Only Edwards, Lewis, and Wilson appear in both.

119. Eddy (1919).

120. When the 1st Oklahoma and 7th Texas consolidated, then Lieutenant Spence was attached to Company G, 142nd Infantry (Barnes 1922:246).

121. Presumably, this refers to Captain Johnson and Lieutenant Charles Walter Veach. The latter was transferred to the 42nd Division after the Armistice (White 1979:20). Captain Veach, a Choctaw commanding Company H of the Oklahoma National Guard prior to the American entrance into World War I, was requested in 1917 to form an all-Native company composed of all tribes in Oklahoma. DDD (1966).

122. P.C. refers to the French *poste de commandement*. American armed forces now commonly use C.P. for command post. Major General Hugh F. Foster Jr. to the author, March 3, 1996.

123. Eddy (1919), Peterson (1986). Temple Black of Weatherford, Texas, was a second lieutenant in Company I, 3rd Battalion, 142nd Infantry Regiment (Barnes 1922:345). Britten (1997:106) reports that "several Indian soldiers received instructions in how to transmit messages over the telephone," under supervision of Lieutenant Black, a liaison officer, and Lieutenant Ben Cloud attached to the 41st Division. Bloor (1922:75) used Black earlier at St. Etienne to establish "an advance information center" to facilitate telephone contact between himself and his battalion commanders. Winegard (2012:124, 194n52) states, "On 28 October a training school was opened for Indian radio and telegraph operators. During the last two months of the war, various units of the 36th and 41st Divisions employed Indians as telephone operators." Citing Bloor's letter as the source, this likely refers to the training at Louppy-le-Petit by the 142nd after November 3. I have found no source for code talkers in the 41st Division.

124. J. W. Wright, Colonel, Infantry, Army War College, Washington D.C., to Col. S.P. Collins, Acting Chief, Signal Security Branch, A.S.F., Arlington, Virginia, September 29, 1943, NARA; Peterson (1986).

125. Morrissey (1919).

126. Kirby (1942).

127. Horner (1942). At the time that the 142nd entered combat, Highlan Mitchell from Company H, 1st Oklahoma Infantry, under Captain Walter Veach, is listed as a first lieutenant in Company E, and Captain David R. Nelson is listed with the Regimental Headquarters (Barnes 1922:188, 342, 344). Another source states that Horner was asked "to supply 12 Indians to transmit secret messages"; however, this may be an error, as another reference to "12 Osage tribal members" in Company E who were very wealthy appears in the same article, and Horner states that eight Choctaw were used (WS 1941; Horner 1942). See note 115 above.

128. WS (1941).

129. DDD (1979); TW (1937); TMFM (2014).

130. Unknown (1950).

131. Co. E, 142nd Inf. (1918, 1919).

132. WS (1941).

133. NARA RG-120, Box 1200, File 21125.

134. Lynn-Sherow and Bruce (2001:96). Their assessment is based on Eddy (1919, Box 3471). The following are the questions on page two of this questionnaire:

GENERAL HEADQUARTERS
AMERICAN EXPEDITIONARY FORCES
Historical Section, G. S.
A. P. O. No. 706.

Points of inquiry concerning the American Indian as a soldier and more specifically as a scout.
Generally:
1. Does he stand the nervous strain?
   (Medical Corps statistics and observation of commanding officer)
2. Does he prove a natural leader in the ranks?
3. Does he associate readily with white men?
4. Is he regarded by the whites as an unusually "good" man.
5. Has he demonstrated fitness for any special arm?
Scouting:
6. What capacity has he shown under following heads:
   a. Courage, endurance, good humor.
   b. Keenness of senses; dexterity.
   c. Judgment and initiative.
   d. Ability to utilize mechanical methods; maps; buzzers, etc.
   e. As night worker, runner, observer, and verbal reporter.

135. Calvin Atchavit RG-75, NARA Box 1, World War I Folder; Responses to Circular Letter #1625. Entry Number 998 E.

136. Captain John E. Morley, Co. E, 142nd Infantry to 1st Lt. John R. Eddy. NARA RG-75, NARA Box 1, World War I Folder; Responses to Circular Letter #1625. Entry Number 998 E.; "American Indians as Battalion Scouts" and "Summary of Incidents and Comments Recently Gathered Evidencing the Superior Fitness of American Indians over the Average Soldier for Scout Service," NARA RG-120, Box 3471, Folder 2.

137. "American Indians as Battalion Scouts" and "Summary of Incidents and Comments Recently Gathered Evidencing the Superior Fitness of American Indians over the Average Soldier for Scout Service," NARA RG-120, Box 3471, Folder 2; Lt. John R. Eddy and Lt. Sewell. "Ranger Service. Proposed effectively use of North American Indians." 3 pages. NARA RG-120, Box 1200, File 21125. ca. 1919.

138. Originally organizing his materials into eight volumes aimed at a single, final volume, he expanded this collection in 1920, eventually collecting on 1,672 men with an additional 1,174 records compiled by the US Army's Historical Section.

139. Dixon (1919:29, WW-33-01p.30/42).

140. Dixon (1919:29, WW-33-01, p.31/42). Drawn from his interviews, Dixon repeated the same mistakes regarding the date and action in his congressional testimony (US Congress 1920:2190).

141. Dixon (1919:29, WW-33-01:33/42).

142. Dixon (1919), WW-33-01:32/42.

143. Lt. Temple Black, Regimental Liaison Officer, 142nd Infantry, Indian War College Data 1920, Folder WW-75-09:2–3. See also NARA RG-120, Box 3471, Folder 2.

144. TO (1941).

145. CTH (2012).

146. CCTA (2013). Choctaw Language Department director Richard Adams provided the following list of terms in 2001. Whether these terms were developed in 1918 or are simply modern translations of the English names for these items is unknown: tank (*tali tanamp chito shali*), gun (*tanapo*), battleship (*peni isht ittibi*), code talker (*anumpa aluhmiehit anumpuli*), warrior/soldier (*tushka chipota*). Because the term "code talker" was not associated with World War I, this term is likely a later creation. Richard Adams to Keevin Lewis, October 26, 2001. NMAI 09–243, Box 3, Choctaw Folder.

147. Morrissey (1919).

148. Bishinik (1986b, 1994b); TT (1991). McCoy (1981:68) states that the Choctaw transmitted "uncoded messages" in World War I. Bloor's (1919) memo shows that the Choctaw composed code terms after Forest Ferme but were unable to use them before the war ended. See also AIM (1919:101).

149. TO (1941).

150. DO (1919d:C1).

151. White (1979:19n5) states that Chastaine signed only those articles that he wrote after the 36th left Camp Bowie, but he provides evidence suggesting that Chastaine also authored several unsigned 1917–18 articles from Fort Sill and Camp Bowie in the *Daily Oklahoman*.

152. Franks (1984:29–30) assesses the Choctaws' effectiveness in capturing Forest Ferme in October 1918, by the 36th Division (US) after the French 73rd Division had been "brutally repulsed" attempting to take the position. Though not citing Bloor (1919), Frank lists the 3rd Battalion, 142nd Infantry, as the assault unit on October 27, 1918. See also Barnes (1922).

153. White (1979:17); Paul (1973); LC (1989:4b). US Army discharge papers and additional records courtesy of Judy Allen, Choctaw Nation of Oklahoma.

154. DO (1919a); FWST (1919a, 1919b). Major General A. W. Greely (1919) provides a detailed account of signal corps communication forms used during World War I.

155. FWST (1919a, 1919c); Marder (1945b).

156. Louis L. Gooding, USDRC, 6/5/1917.

157. The Goodings later lived in Ontario, California, from 1943 to 1965, then moved to Ventura, California, probably to live near their son Jack. Louis Gooding worked as an aircraft worker, an electrician, and at the Armstrong Nursery in Ontario. He died in 1967 at the age of eighty. Their son Jack Gooding recorded this account in November 1977 at the City Library in Ontario, California. Gooding (1977); Blackstock (2009).

158. Gooding (1977); Blackstock (2009).

159. Co. C. 312th FSB (1918, 1919).

Chapter 4

1. TW (1937). This article refers to Lewis, Carterby, Taylor, Wilson, Maytubby, Edwards, Nelson, and Oklahombi.

2. Ibid.

3. DO (November 17 and 18, 1917) in White (1979:12–14, 1918f, 1918j, 1919a, 1919e); FWST (November 18, 1917), in White (1979:13, 1984:45).

4. *Bishinik* (1986b:3).

5. Ibid.

6. Dixon (1919:34, WW-33-01:35/42).

7. *Stars and Stripes* (1919b:3).

8. *Stars and Stripes* (1918a:8).

9. *Stars and Stripes* (1918a:8).

10. NYEW (1919).

11. Camp Merritt (1919).

12. White (1979:18–20) mentions Bloor's report and that "the utilization of Indian troops as telephone operators in World War I, albeit near the end of the war, received considerable official and public attention," but he did not elaborate on the subject.

13. For Robinson, see FWST (1919a) and DO (1919a, 1919b); MTD (1919a); FWST (1919a, 1919b); *Stars and Stripes* (1919b:1).

14. FWST (1919a).

15. DO (1919a).

16. Lieutenant Spence was attached to Company G, 142nd Infantry, when the 1st Oklahoma and 7th Texas were consolidated to form the 142nd. Eddy (1919), Peterson (1986).

17. DO (1919a, 1919g); Bloor (1919), Morrissey (1919).

18. MTD (1919a).

19. *Stars and Stripes* (May 30, 1919:1).

20. IWCD (1920), Folder WW-75-09:2–6. These statements are also contained in NARA RG-120, Box 3471, Folder 2.

21. Eddy (1919), US Congress (1920), OCN (1928), Wise (1931), NYS (1938). For accounts from Choctaw code talkers, see Benjamin Hampton in 1939 (*Bishinik* 2000e; TMFM 2014) and James Edwards (1941).

22. NARA RG-75 Boxes 1–3.

23. Morrissey (1919).

24. First Lieutenant Eddy was a former superintendent of the Crow Indian Reservation in Montana. He was gassed while serving with the 4th Division. Deeply interested in Native Americans, he believed that they might best be used in the future as scouts. Evacuated back to the United States, he transferred to the General Staff's Historical Section to collect data concerning the service of Native Americans in the war. He designed a questionnaire to elicit facts of military value that was distributed to over 1,500 combat units by Brigadier General Oliver L. Spaulding, the chief of the section, and Jennings C. Wise.

25. See also Cope (1920). A portion of Cope's report is on line through the Texas Military Forces Museum (Cope n.d.).

26. Dixon (1919); Krouse (2007:210n30).

27. While an imitation of how Choctaw sounded to Germans unfamiliar with the language, the point is well made. Lavine was formerly of the Air Service, AEF, and author of *Circuits of Victory*, a book on the code system used by the army in World War I. Lavine (1921b:327) reports that the story was "current in Signal Corps circles during the war" and that H. Blair-Smith, assistant vice president of the American Telephone and Telegraph Company and brother to the 36th Division commander, Major General William R. Smith, related that "Captain Horner detailed eight Indians, in command of Chief George Baconrind . . . to transmit the orders in Choctaw." Greely's (1919:8) account is similar. See also DO (1919a). The *Native American* (NA 1918b) cites American folk sayings of the Choctaw language, including "It was Choctaw to me," a remark said to date back to the Elizabethan period, and "I could no more understand what he said than I could understand Choctaw." The article ethnocentrically maintains that "Choctaw, in short, has the reputation of being a mere confused jumble of indistinguishable sounds, signifying nothing." The American expression "It's Greek to me" is essentially no different and reflects a group's lack of knowledge with the language rather than an accurate assessment of its linguistic structure.

28. OCN (1928). Edmonds received a citation from Marshal Petain of France. From Antlers, Oklahoma. He served in Company L, 142nd, and was in Company E, 142nd, when it entered combat (Barnes 1922:189, 314).

29. TW (1937).

30. AGZ (1919); Horner (1942); Eddy also uses the term "experiment" (NARA RG-120, Box 3471, Folder 2).

31. John Hix, Hollywood, California, to the War Department, Washington, D.C. (May 18, 1939).

32. Mr. Maley, A.E.F. Records, to a Miss Lemon (May 25, 1939), and J. E. Lyle, Chief Clerk, Organizational Rec. Section to Mr. Dimond, May 25, 1939. G-2 refers to the military intelligence staff of a unit in the US Army, in contrast to other sections including; G-1 (personnel), G-3 (operations), G-4 (logistics), and G-5 (civil-military operations).

33. Ibid.

34. Colonel A. G. D., Officer in Charge, World War Division, The Adjutant General's Office, Memorandum to the Assistant Chief of Staff, G-2, American Indian in World War (May 29, 1939).

35. E. R. W. McCabe, Colonel, General Staff, Assistant Chief of Staff, G-2, Memorandum to the Adjutant General, American Indians in World War (June 2, 1939).

36. E. B. Adams, Major General, the adjutant general, to Mr. John Hix, Hollywood, California (June 6, 1939). Courtesy of Ken Kirkland.

37. DDD (1979) reprinted the article chronicling Hampton's 1939 visit. See TMFM (2014). This microfilm is missing at the Oklahoma History Center.

38. TO (1941).

39. Gerrer (c.1945:19–20; Phillips 2010) was involved in the Catholic Church's collection and curation of art, teaching summer art school at Notre Dame University for twelve years, and was commissioned to paint at least seventy-nine portraits for the St. Gregory's College art gallery.

40. Unknown (1950).

41. AEN (1958).

42. AA (1966).

43. USADP (Joseph Oklahombi, Benjamin Hampton, Solomon Lewis, Tobias Frazier, and Victor Brown).

44. AA (1966); Unknown-3, courtesy of Judy Allen, Choctaw Nation. Barnes (1922:174) lists Frazier's wound.

45. Bishinik (1987d); CTH (2012).

46. NARA RG 75, Box 3, Albert Billy, Encl. No. 39926.

47. NARA RG 75, Box 3, Ben Carterby, Encl. No. 20663; USADP Ben Carterby (1483743); ADA (1919:2).

48. Great niece Christine Ludlow reported that her grandmother, Johnson's sister-in-law, stated that he was killed in France and that his body was not returned to the United States (TO 1941; CCTA 2012). Johnson is not listed as killed in action (Barnes 1922).

49. DH (1970).

50. Noel Johnson, Smithville, Oklahoma, Death Certificate. North Carolina State Board of Health, Bureau of Vital Statistics, Standard Certificate of Death. Register 873. November 19, 1919. Copy courtesy of Judy Allen, Choctaw Nation.

51. MG (1932); MSGN (1996).

52. LS (1932); MDNR (1932); DO (1937:D1).

53. MSGN (1996); Coleman (2002).

54. MG (1919, 1960); DR (June 26, 1919); NYS (1938). NARA RG-120, Box 1200, File 21125. Oklahombi's #1625 circular states that he was drafted. Joseph Oklahombi, draft registration, June 5, 1917; Joseph Oklahombi, Encl. No. 39926, NARA RG-75, Box 3. Some sources state that he was under age when war was declared, that he lied about his age to enlist, and that because he was an orphan, he was not questioned. This confuses the circumstances of Solomon B. Louis's enlistment.

55. MG (1919, 1960); DR (June 26, 1919); NYS (1938). This statement is attributed in different articles to at least three different instances. See also AEN (1921) regarding Oklahombi's comment.

56. MG (1919). York and seven other men captured 132 German prisoners on October 8, 1918, near Hill 223 (Perry 2010:47–52, 59), while Oklahombi was incorrectly credited with single-handedly capturing 171 prisoners.

57. DR (June 26, 1919); NYS (1938).

58. DO (1919L, 1919p).

59. BB (1919); CR (1921); LN (1921); YD (1921); AEN (1925); AWN (1925); MG (1932, 1935); SP (1940).

60. DO (1919p).

61. DO (1919L, 1960; TO (1937; NYS (1938); Co-Operator (1960); Coleman (2002:209–210); Bishinik (2005:1).

62. VL (1987); *Bishinik* (1987h).

63. MSGN (1996).

64. French Marshal Ferdinand Foch, supreme commander of the Allied forces during World War I, suggested that several Allied and associated countries involved against Austria and Germany should receive Victory Medals. Each country adopted a standard ribbon (double rainbow) and a 36-mm round bronze medal, but with distinct national designs representing a winged victory (Laslo 1986).

65. Memorandum of Lieutenant Charles M. Ford, no date, Records of the A.E.F., NARA RG 120. Ford was "killed by a bursting shell" on October 27, 1918, at Forest Ferme (Maxfield 1975:117).

66. Chastaine (1920:69); Order No. 13.910 "D," (February 28, 1919).

67. 2nd Lt. Charles L. Ford, November 30, 1918. NARA RG-120, Box 2, Commendations and Decorations Folder, 236–11.4

68. Order No. 13.910 "D" Extract (February 28, 1919); NYS (1938); VL (1987); Unknown (1986), Tuskahoma, Oklahoma, ca. 1987. Ironically, Oklahombi's ancestral surname translates as "Man or People Killer." The suffix *hombi* or "killer of," is a common suffix in Choctaw names and has correlates in several southeastern tribal naming systems. Unfortunately, a lack of detail leaves several aspects unanswered. The action at Forest Ferme lasted less than three full days, and as previously demonstrated, Oklahombi was awarded for his action on October 8, at St. Etienne.

69. Cf. MG (1919, 1960); DO (1919L, 1937); *Bishinik* (2005:1); NARA RG-75, Box 3, Joseph Oklahombi, Encl. No. 39926; NARA RG-120, Box 1200, File 21125, Joseph Oklahombi Supplemental Circular, Captain H. E. Stone, 141st Infantry.

70. Most articles at Newspaperarchive.com focused on the text of Oklahombi's citation and capture of Germans. Fewer focus on a 1925 illness, his appeal for veteran's assistance in 1932–33, his willingness to fight in World War II if needed in 1940, his exploits as motivation for servicemen in 1942, and his death with reference to his wartime accomplishments. By decade, these article number are as follows: 1910s (5), 1920s (27), 1930s (41), 1940s (24), 1950s (0), 1960s (8), 1970s (0), 1980s (3), 1990s (1), 2000s (1). More articles likely exist in other papers.

71. OHC. Joseph Oklahombi Papers, February 28, 1919; Record No. 97.32.03, 97.32.04.

72. MSGN (1996).

73. Chastaine also describes these dugouts in one of his news articles (DO 1919j:D-4).

74. MG (1932, 1935; 1940, 1960); DO (1919L, 1919p, 1960); LC (1960); *Bishinik* (1987h); Coleman (2002:210).

75. LC (1960).

76. Joe Slater to Louis Coleman, September 4, 1978 (Coleman 2002:210).

77. See Coleman (2002:210, 215n22); MG (1940, 1960); DO (1919L).

78. Coleman (2002:210, 215n22); MG (1940, 1960); DO (1919L); SCT (1940).

79. MG (1932, 1935); Bishinik (1987h); DO (1919L); Coleman (2002:211).

80. OKN (1932).

81. TO (1937:59); MD (1961); Coleman (2002:210).

82. In the two categories of the questionnaire, Oklahombi's company commander, Captain H. E. Stone, characterized him as follows:

Generally: 1. Does he stand the nervous strain, "Yes. Very well"; 2. Does he prove a natural leader in the ranks, "No"; 3. Does he associate readily with white men, "Yes"; 4. Is he regarded by the whites as an unusually "good" man, "Yes"; 5. Has he demonstrated fitness for any special arms, "Yes, automatic rifle."

In Scouting he was described as follows:

a. Courage, "average," endurance, "average," good humor, "average"; b. Keenness of senses, "average"; dexterity, "normal"; c. Judgment and initiative, "Average"; d. Ability to utilize mechanical methods, maps, buzzers, etc., "Poor"; e. As night worker, runner, observer, verbal reported, "Good."

Stone also noted, "This man is only an average soldier. He did good work with an Auto Rifle but nothing more than many others have done." NARA RG-120, Box 1200, File 21125, Joseph Oklahombi supplement. Captain H. E. Stone, 141st Infantry.

83. HT (1940); OT (1940); AG (1940).

84. DO (1919h).

85. DO (1919h:D-4).

86. TW (1937); VL (1987); Unknown (1986); NYS (1938:30).

87. DO (1919p); TO (1937); OHC (2013); Coleman (2002:209).

88. TO (1937); Coleman (2012:213–214).

89. Evangeline Wilson to Tim Jones and Keevin Lewis 2002. NMAI 09–243, Box 5:147.

90. AEN (1921:4).

91. Ibid.

92. OHC-Joseph Oklahombi Papers. Joseph Oklahombi to Mrs. Czarina Conlan, March 31, 1925. Record No. 97.32.01.

93. WS (1938).

94. Judy Allen to the author, August 18, 2015. This account is from a grandchild of Tobias Frazier.

95. DR (1919:8).

96. VL (1987); Unknown (1986); MG (1935, 1960); NYS (1938:30); Coleman (2002:210, 215n18). Some of these sources state Oklahombi called for a girl he had met to come to the training camp and was married shortly before the 36th sailed for France. Oklahombi was already married and had a son. This account relates to Solomon Louis (TW 1937).

97. AEN (1921:4).

98. Conlan conducted interviews, solicited donations, and purchased items for the Oklahoma Historical Society (OHS), and she frequently published articles in the *Chronicles of Oklahoma*. In 1926, she was the supervisor of the Indian Department (Conlan 1926). Oklahombi's uniform jacket is a 1911-pattern uniform coat of summer-issue cotton duck, commonly issued to returning WW I veterans to replace previously issued uniforms. Although collected earlier, Conlan accessioned Oklahombi's items in 1928, either from memory or another accession register that is no longer in the OHS collection. Other items recorded by Conlan match the date of accession. Matt Reed, Oklahoma Historical Society, to the author, August 7, 2015. *The Ada Evening News* (AEN 1921:4) account indicates that the visit occurred in 1921. Oklahombi's Croix de Guerre is reported to have been obtained by the OHS in 1921. The photo of Joel, Conlan, and Oklahombi is in the Oklahoma History Center (OHS Photo No. 4122), see Colman (2002:211). Czarina Colbert Conlan was a sister of Benjamin Colbert (Choctaw), who served in the Spanish-American War and later had a son by the same name. She served as a field agent for the OHS when she visited and collected Oklahombi's Croix de Guerre and later served as a curator. Michael W. Bell, curator, Oklahoma History Center, to the author, November 7, 2018.

99. Four Croix de Guerre and several other Church War Cross awards for gallantry were awarded to members of the 142nd Infantry (Bucholz et al. 1996:2). Although a special report on Native Americans as soldiers, in which the 36th Division figured prominently, was written in 1919, it was based only on "divisions . . . within easy reach of Chaumont" and did not include the 90th Division, which had a comparable number of Native servicemen. However, intra-divisional assessments of Native American soldiers and their combat service with the 90th Division were very positive. See Eddy (1919), White (1996:193–194).

100. CFR (2007). My thanks to Matt Reed and Michael W. Bell, Oklahoma History Center, for showing me Oklahombi's items.

101. CFR (2007).

102. AEN (1921:4, 1925:3); AWN (1925:4).

103. LS (1932); MDNR (1932); MG (1932); OKN (1932); ADTT (1933); DO (1937); LC (1960).

104. OKN (1932); VL (1987); Unknown (1986); MG (1935, 1960); NYS (1938:30); Coleman (2002:210, 215n18); Mrs. Joseph Oklahombi to Louis Coleman, September 4, 1978, February 27, 1979; Joe Slater to Louis Coleman September 4, 1978. Some people later compared the offer to Oklahombi with the film *Sergeant York* (Warner Brothers 1941).

105. MG (1935).

106. Ibid.

107. TO (1937).

108. ADA (1936).

109. DO (1937); LC (1960). Miller (TO 1937) also stated, "At this time Oklahombi reported having a difficult time. After the war he received $450.00 in bonus money, which he used to pay off debts. For a number of years he received $12.00 a month until it was discontinued in 1933 when the Economy Act was enacted. He also reported problems associated with alcohol and irregular work habits."

110. AEN (1937).

111. SP (1940).

112. DOI (1927); TO (1937); Oklahombi (1949); DO (1960); LC (1960); MG (1960); Co-Operator (1960); Coleman (2002).

113. NARA-PF Joseph Oklahombi.

114. Ibid.

115. Ibid.

116. Ibid.

117. *Bishinik* (1992c); TMFM (2014); William T. Lee Jr. to Deborah L. Haverman, Chief, Army Reference Branch. Military Personnel Records Center, St. Louis, Missouri, June 21, 1989, CNA; Hollis E. Roberts, Chief Choctaw Nation of Oklahoma to William T. Lee Jr., October 6, 1992, CAN; Milligan (2003:252).

118. *Bishinik* (1992c).

119. *Bishinik* (1992c).

120. Matt Reed, Oklahoma History Center, to the author, October 10, 2014. Bill Pitts, Oklahoma State Museum of History, to Judy Allen, October 6, 1991. Accession Cards, Items #1697, 2153–2156, 2165, 2167, 3075, CNA.

121. Oklahoma Historical Society, Accession Records, Nos. 2153–2156, 2167, 2544; Coleman (2002:209, 211).

122. HT (1940); OTH (1940).

123. *Bishinik* (2005:1); TMFM (2014); Milligan (2003:252).

124. *Bishinik* (2000f).

125. *Bishinik* (2005:1).

126. TMFM (2007:9).

127. *Biskinik* (2010a). Wright City, Oklahoma, was formerly named Bismarck.

128. NARA-PF Joseph Oklahombi.

129. Ibid.

130. AT (1948); CRR (1956).

131. DO (1919b, 1919p); TO (1936); DOI (1927:2); CRR (1956). Millie Lee Leader was born August 6, 1885, and died January 4, 1916. She is buried in the Citra, Oklahoma, cemetery.

132. MNC (1917a, 1917b); TO (1936); CRR (1956). Some sources state that the agents were either secret service or immigration agents.

133. MNC (1917a).

134. Many American newspapers in 1917 detail these events. For other cases of suspected spies in Kansas and Oklahoma, see the TDW (1917a, 1917b).

135. DO (1919b, 1919p); TO 1936; DOI (1927:2); CRR (1956); MNC (1961).

136. MNC (1917b).

137. CRR (1956).

138. DO (1919b, 1919p); TO 1936, 2010; DOI (1927:2); CRR (1956); Archambeault (2008:13); CTH (2012). One account reports that the incident occurred at Fort Worth, Texas (TO 1936). Another article (DO 1919b) that appears to have interviewed Leader states that it occurred at McAlester, Oklahoma. These articles confuse Leader being followed at Fort Worth with his learning of the government's suspicion upon arriving at McAllister from Marshall Crockett Lee.

139. AEN (1958:1).

140. DO (1919b).

141. AEN (1958:1); MNC (1961).

142. TO (1936); CRR (1956); OCT (1958); AEN (1958:1,3); MN (1961); Tewanna Edwards to Larry Zander, February 21, 2000 (NMAI 09–243, Box 3, TEP).

143. Ibid.

144. MTD (1919b); TO (1936). "Diables Bleus" (blue devils) was the nickname of the Chasseurs Alpins, the elite mountain infantry regiment of the French army. See also DeSpain (2004:17, 21n19–20).

145. TO (1936); AT (1948); MSPTD (1955); DO (1959).

146. TO (1936); AT (1948); DO (1959).

147. The Sale des Invalides is an institution founded by Louis XIV for disabled veterans that now houses military offices and an army museum in Paris. Accounts differ as to sites where his portrait was to have been hung, among them the art department of the French Federal Building in Paris, in a display of "types of all the allied races." Another account was that a portrait and statue were to be sent to the British Hall of Fame in London (DO 1919b, 1919p, 1959; DOI 1927:2; TO 1936; OCT 1958). Reverend Guerrer also painted a three-fourths length portrait of Leader after the war in the home of Mrs. Czarina C. Conlan, paid for by Chickasaw and Choctaw friends. For many years, it hung in the Memorial Room of the Oklahoma Historical Society Museum in Oklahoma City, but it was later transferred to the Mabee-Gerrer Museum in Shawnee, Oklahoma. Guerrer 1945; Phillips 2010; OHC–Otis Leader, Federal Writer's Project, Biographies; Lacy-Leflore. Box 21, FF 6. Record No. 81.105: Biography, Otis Leader; Elmer L. Fraker to Sybil Miracle, June 6, 1953; Otis W. Leader to Overton Colbert, Paris France, February 1, 1924; Undated note on painting of Otis Leader. This painting was made in 1922 (TO 2010).

148. NN (1920).

149. DO (1919b, 1919p); MTD (1919b); DOI (1927:2); OCT (1958); Tewanna Edwards to Larry Zander, February 21, 2000. TEP, NMAI 09–243, Box 3.

150. AEN (1958:3).

151. CTH (2012); MN (1961); MD (1961).

152. TO (1936); OCT (1958); MD (1961); MN (1961).

153. AEN (1958:3).

154. AEN (1958:3); MSPTD (1955); DO (1959).

155. DO (1919b, 1959); TO (1936); MSPTD (1955); CRR (1956); OCT (1958); MD (1961); CTH (2012). Some of these accounts state that Leader was both wounded and gassed in this engagement. Another source who interviewed Leader (AEN 1958:3) states that he was gassed in January 1918 and only wounded at Cantigny.

156. OCT (1919b).

157. TO (1936); MSPTD (1955); OCT (1958); DO (1959); MN (1961); MD (1961). Accounts vary, reporting sixteen to eighteen prisoners.

158. CRR (1956); DO (1959).

159. AEN (1958:3); DO (1959); MD (1961). See also TT (1991).

160. AEN (1958:3); DO (1959); MD (1961). See also TT (1991). Most sources, as well as his official military citation, state that he took eighteen German prisoners in the action.

161. DO (1919b).

162. OCT (1919b).

163. Ibid.

164. CRR (1956).

165. AEN (1958:3).

166. CRR (1956); AEN (1958); DO (1959); TO (2010); CTH (2012); NARA-PF, Otis W. Leader; Otis Leader grave marker, Colgate, OK.

167. Sells (1920).

168. Visionmaker Video (2010).

169. AEN (1958:3).

170. DO (1919b, 1919p); CRR (1956); AEN (1958:3); MD (1961).

171. Stallings (1963); CMHUSA (1988:1–19; 222–229). Despain (2004:5) mistakenly states that Leader was in the 36th Division.

172. DO (1919b, 1919p, 1959); DOI (1927:2); MSPTD (1955); MD (1961); MN (1961); Phillips (2010); TO (2010); Visionmaker Video (2010); NARA-PF, Otis W. Leader.

173. DO (1919b); MTD (1919b); NN (1920).

174. Newspaperarchive.com, accessed July 24, 2015.

175. MTD (1919b); AEN (1933, 1958:3); TO (1936); CRR (1956); OCT (1958); MNC (1961). In 1924, Leader donated a complete set of the AEF *Stars and Stripes* newspaper in France to the Oklahoma Historical Society. AEN (1924).

176. MTD (1919b); TO (1936); CRR (1956); OCT (1958); MNC (1961).

177. TO (1936).

178. Ibid.

179. AT (1948); OCT (1958); DO (1959:8E).

180. OCT (1958); AEN (1958:3); DO (1959:8E); TT (1991:7).

181. CRR (1956).

182. OCT (1958); ADE (1958:3); MNC (1961).

183. AEN (1953, 1959).

184. DO (1919b).

185. AEN (1958:3).

186. MD (1961); MN (1961); MNC (1961).

187. Oklahoma Senate Resolution (1961); MD (1961).

Chapter 5

1. DO (1917b).

2. George Adair (1490079) Survey, NARA RG-120, Box 1200, File 21125.

3. DO (1919c); The Services of the Thirty-Sixth Division with the American Expeditionary Forces:25. NARA RG-120 Box 2, History July 1918–May 1919 Folder. Sergeant William Adair (Oklahoma Cherokee), born in the Braggs-Fort Gibson area in Indian Territory (later Oklahoma), served as a telephone operator in Company C, 315th Field Signal Battalion, 90th Division. Already awarded the Distinguished Service Cross, Adair was awarded the Medal of Honor, the citation for which reads, "After being severely gassed, Sergeant Adair stayed at his post and ran his telephone lines. Through a terrific artillery barrage, he remained on duty, though he was blinded and could hardly talk, until his organization was relieved." While the 90th Division contained many Native Americans, we do not know whether Adair used Cherokee or English or if other Natives were involved.

4. Cherokee Nation (2010); CGL (2010); NAT (2010).

5. Asepermy (2017). Asepermy has identified sixty-two Comanche WW I veterans. Sergeant Major (Ret.) Lanny Asepermy to the author, November 11, 2018.

6. The Indian Sign (1940). How they determined the German's efforts is unknown.

7. NYT (1940).

8. Haddon Codynah to Joe Todd, April 8, 1987. OHC.

9. Albert Nahquaddy Jr. to the author, July 24, 1996. Mr. Nahquaddy stated that an officer overheard his father and another Comanche conversing in Comanche to sight in an artillery gun and that this resulted in using the Comanche language for military communications by other Comanche in World War I. Based on a single interview with Charles Chibitty, Walker (2000:564) states that Comanches were not used in World War I as code talkers. Chibitty may not have known of their use.

10. NARA RG-75, Box 68, Asepermy (2017).

11. Ibid.

12. OCT (1919a).

13. NARA RG-75, Card File, Box 1, Special Medals Section. OCT (1919a article, cited in NARA RG-75, Box 68). Atchavit was Comanche, but from the Kiowa Agency in Oklahoma.

14. Calvin Atchavit (USDRC 1917); DMN (1919); WP (July 22, 1919:6); OCT (1919a article, cited in NARA RG-75, Box 68 and Asepermy 2017); CNN (2013).

15. WFTRN (2018:3B).

16. Albert Nahquaddy Jr. to the author, July 24, 1996. See also Meadows (2002:29, 247n37).

17. WFTRN (2018:3B).

18. NARA RG-75, Card File.

19. Lieutenant J. A. Soles, the 3rd Battalion Headquarters information officer, 358th Infantry, reported, "I know of only one case where Indians were put in this line of work. This Indian had been a telegraph operator in civilian life and made an excellent buzzer man." His tribal affiliation and whether he performed voice communications was not stated. Lieutenant J. A. Soules, I.O., H.Q., 3rd Battalion, 358th Infantry, March 27, 1919. NARA GR-120, Box 3473, 90th Division File.

20. Ninety-eight Osage are listed. NARA RG-75, Box 25, Osage Service Records in World War I Folder. Another source lists forty-six Osage and their tribal roll numbers, for whom service data were collected. Superintendent, Osage Indian Agency, to the Commissioner of Indian Affairs, May 13, 1921. NARA RG-75, Box 3.

21. Bulz's unit assignment is unclear. Bulls Alphonzo Buls, Gilmer, Texas, appears in the Company M, 359th Infantry (1918), 90th Division. Company M, 143rd, had only fifteen Oklahomans, not from the Osage area. "Awall H. Buls" (480503) of Rosewood, Texas, appears in a June 18, 1918, Company M, 143rd Infantry (1918) embarkation list.

22. In the 1970s, Martin and Bulz frequently spoke to public schools about their experiences in World War I. While their account contains some colloquial slang and stereotypes of the period, it appears to be firsthand and credible and is supported by other accounts (White 1979, 1984).

23. DO (1917b); Bloor (1919).

24. ON (2016); Company D, 143rd Infantry (1919).

25. ONO (2013); John Henry Mashunkashey to the author, August 21, 2017. Charley Choteau is listed in Company E, 142 Infantry, in November 1917 (DO 1917b:2B).

26. In 2012, the Osage Nation Chief's Office, three Osage WW II veterans, and the Osage Tribal Museum announced that they knew of no Osage code talkers in World War II. World War II veteran Bill Mashunkashey stated, "I served with Kenneth Jump, Russel Warrior Jr., and only those two could speak Osage, beside myself. They weren't code talkers." Osage WW II and Korean War veteran Richard Lutrell also stated that he did not know of any Osage code talkers. Luttrell also related that although he served with other Osage in Korea, he did not serve with any in World War II and that most Osage entered service as individuals and not as groups, unlike other Natives who were code talkers who went in as a group (ON 2012). John Henry Mashunkashey also reported that to the tribe's knowledge, there were no WW II Osage code talkers. John Henry Mashunkashey to the author, August 21, 2017.

27. *Stars and Stripes* (1919a:5). A near identical version of this article also appeared in AIM (1919) cited from the Steubenville, Ohio, *Gazette*.

28. Paul Picotte (Yankton) to Joseph Cash, August 16, 1968. Interview No. 0067:45–46 DDIOHC, South Dakota Oral History Center, IAIS, University of South Dakota, Vermillion. Paul Picotte, Circular #1625 Response, NARA RG-75, Box 3. Picotte's account may be secondhand, as the 30th F. A. was constituted on July 6, 1918, and assigned to the 10th Division, organized August 10, 1918, at Camp Funston, Kansas. Influenza and numerous deaths delayed their training and deployment. Although an advanced party departed for Europe on October 27, 1918, the remainder of the regiment did not complete training and embark prior to the Armistice. The 30th was demobilized on February 5, 1919, at Funston.

29. Dixon (1919, *American Indian Book* 3:8).

30. Their deaths (Grass in July 1918 and Blue Earth in October 1918) require that their communications service had to have occurred before July unless at least one other unnamed individual was involved. See also Hunhoff (2007).

31. LJ (2001:B5). The letter states that both were in the Meuse-Argonne campaign. Grass was killed during the Aisne-Marne campaign; Blue Earth during the Meuse-Argonne.

32. McLaughlin (2014). Several sources describe the wide range of English language fluency among Native American soldiers in World War I and the discharge of some Native American recruits for their lack of English fluency. DO (November 17 and 18, 1917, in White 1979:12–14; 1918a, 1918f, 1918g, 1918h, 1918j); FWST (November 18, 1917) in White (1979:13, 1918d); *Bishinik* (1987:b, 2000c, 2000d); Phillip Allen (2007); White (1979:13, 1984:44–45, 79); Scott (1919:314); Britten (1997:74).

33. William Norton, US Treasury Department, to the author, August 2013; Rob Dalessandro, US Department of Defense, emails to the author, September 25, 2013, and October 24, 2013.

34. ISJ (1919:351).

35. NARA RG-75, Card File.

36. Garvin (2018); ISJ (1919:351); NARA-PF Robert Big Thunder.

37. WVM–Robert Big Thunder, Nathaniel H. Longtail.

38. ISJ (1919:351); NARA-PF Robert Big Thunder.

39. ISJ (1919:351; NARA-PF John H. Longtail; WVM Nathaniel H. Longtail.

40. E. B. Adams, Major General, the adjutant general, to Mr. John Hix, Hollywood, California (June 6, 1939). Documents courtesy of Ken Kirkland.

41. Ken Kirkland, email to the author, March 19, 2010; PCN (1948a, 1948b); DO (1948); Meadows (2011:35n.63).

42. First Lieutenant Moses Bellmard, service questionnaire. NARA RG-75, Box 1.

43. This account added that Kaw elder Houston Taylor told his daughter Naomi Wright that Kaw WW II veterans Tom Conn, Theodore Sumner, Harry Stubbs, Dan Test, and Jim and Henry Wynoshie had used "this method of confusing enemies trying to intercept conversation." This suggests Type 2 NACT.

44. DO (1948); PCN (1948a, 1948b).

45. KN (2011).

46. AL (2016); Holman (2018).

Chapter 6

1. HT (1940); OTH (1940); AG (1940).

2. TO (1941).

3. ASV (1932); HI (1942); SDA (1943); Newspaperarchive.com, accessed July 24, 2015.

4. HI (1942).

5. DH (1970). Many such claims are found in newspaper articles, including the Choctaw Nation newspaper *Bishinik*.

6. Stallings (1963:377) reports nineteen days of front line combat service for the 36th division.

7. Bishinik (1986b); Moseley (1988).

8. See also TT (1991; Wigginton (1992).

9. CTH (2012); TO (1941); *Bishinik* (2000a, 2000f); Archambeault (2008:12). Another version states that the officer was told simply, "They were only Americans."

10. *Bishinik* (August 1986b).

11. *Bishinik* (1986a).

12. *Bishinik* (1986a); HC (1976).

13. *Bishinik* (1986a).

14. *Bishinik* (1986a; 1994b:3; 2004e:3); Unknown (1986); Moseley (1988), TT (1991); Milligan (2003:256).

15. *Bishinik* (1986d).

16. *Bishinik* (1987b:8–9).

17. *Bishinik* (1987a:2,7).

18. Evangeline Wilson to Tim Jones and Keevin Lewis, 2002. NMAI 09–243, Box 5:133, 140–141; Judy Allen to the author, January 16, 2014.

19. *Bishinik* (1987a:2,7); Mike Wright, Scientific Social Research, to Mr. Bob Gann, Director, Oklahoma Indian Affairs Commission, Oklahoma City, Ok., November 18, 1986; Hollis Roberts, Chief, Choctaw Nation of Oklahoma, to Mr. Gerard Dumont, Consulat General de France, Houston, Tx., February 25, 1987; Mike Wright, Scientific Social Research, to Dr. C. Alton Brown, Honorary French Consul March 3, 1987; Mike Wright, Scientific Social Research, to Gerard Dumont, Consulat General de France, Houston, Tx., March 10, 1987; Mike Wright, Scientific Social Research, to Persons Involved in Code-Talker Research February 18, 1987. Copies courtesy of Mr. Mike Wright, Judy Allen, and the Choctaw Nation.

20. *Bishinik* (1989a:1,5).

21. *Bishinik* (1986a, 1989b); MG (1989).

22. *Bishinik* (1989b).

23. *Bishinik* (1996).

24. CCTA (2013); *Bishinik* (2008c). Benjamin Colbert Jr. is not included on the marker.

25. *Bishinik* (1997); AA (1997).

26. VNVPW (2002).

27. CLJE (2004); *Bishinik* (2004b:2, 2004c:1); TA (2004).

28. CBVF (2003); Asepermy (2017).

29. *Bishinik* (2004b:2, 2004c:1); CCTA (n.d.); NMAI 09–243 Box 5:150; Allen (2018:13).

30. CCTA (n.d., 2012). For the association's objectives, see Choctawcode talkersassociation.com.

31. CCTA (n.d.).

32. CCTA (n.d., 2012); "The Logo of The Choctaw Code Talkers Association," copy courtesy of Nuchi Nashoba, CCTA.

33. Nuchi Nashoba to the author, October 9, 2015.

34. *Bishinik* (2006a, 2006b, 2006c); Telephone Warriors (2007); Telephone Warriors Draft (2007); MG (2007).

35. *Bishinik* (2007).

36. FWST (2007); Scribner (n.d.).

37. TMFM (2007:10–11); Scribner (n.d.).

38. FWST (2007); TMFM (2007:10).

39. FWST (2007); Gregory Pyle, letter to the Choctaw Nation (2007); *Bishinik* (2008c); Archambeault (2008); GX Magazine (2007:38). Benjamin Colbert Jr. was not included in the Choctaw awarded on this day.

40. Texas Government Code, Title 4, Subtitle C, Chapter 431, Subchapter J. Awards, Sec. 431.132.

41. FWST (2007).

42. GXM (2007:38).

43. Bird Seely to Columbus E. Veach, October 27, 1918. CNA, Walter Veach File. Regina Green, Choctaw Nation Museum, to the author, March 25, 2019.

44. Archambeault (2007).

45. BN (2009).

46. *Biskinik* (2011); Choctaw Days (2012); Regina Green, Choctaw Nation Museum, to the author, March 25, 2019. Quilt design (written description) and copy of "To Us It Wasn't Code" program courtesy of Nuchi Nashoba, CCTA.

47. TTF (2010).

48. *Biskinik* (2010b).

49. Pennies for Patriots Campaign packet, 2013. Copy courtesy of Nuchi Nashoba, CCTA.

50. TO (2012); OMHF 2012a, 2012b. Copies courtesy of Choctaw Code Talkers Association.

51. *Biskinik* (2013); Judy Allen to the author, January 16, 2014.

52. Senate Testimony (2003: DL., JB., JYS., SK., TD., WL.). See Meadows (2011) regarding this event and the efforts leading to the Code Talkers Recognition Act of 2008. See also *Bishinik* (2004d:1,3); TO (2004); TW (2004:A15).

53. MG (2004). The article indicates that the author knew that the Choctaw planned to seek the Congressional Gold Medal for the code talkers. I have always suspected that the local historian was Louis Coleman, who investigated Joseph Oklahombi's service record (Coleman 2002).

54. *Bishinik* (2008b).

55. Boren (n.d.).

56. *Bishinik* (2008b, 2008d).

57. *Bishinik* (2008d).

58. *Bishinik* (2008d).

59. *Bishinik* (2009).

60. Austin (2011).

61. *Bishinik* (2013); Judy Allen to the author, January 16, 2014, March 11, 2019.

62. Durant Democrat.com (2013).

63. Author's fieldnotes, Congressional Gold Medal Ceremony for Native American Code Talkers. US Capitol, Washington, DC, November 20, 2013; Choctaw Nation Museum, August 4, 2015. Judy Allen to the author, March 11, 2019. Currently, only Davis Picken's family has not loaned their silver medal for display.

64. *BBC News* (2014).

65. Robert Atchavit to the author, November 25, 2018.

66. Several historical errors exist regarding unit membership, length of language use, date of declassification, citizenship status, etc. The value of the work is in spreading knowledge of the code talkers to youth.

67. TO (2015). In the accompanying photo, students mistakenly hold a poster of Otis Leader.

68. Ibid.

69. Nuchi Nashoba to the author, September 4, 2016.

70. *Biskinik* (2018a); CNOO (2018a); Nuchi Nashoba to the author, April 20, 2018.

71. CNOO (2018b).

72. KXII (2018).

73. Nuchi Nashoba to the author, April 20, 2018.

74. DurantDemocrat.com (2013); *Biskinik* (2018a).

75. NSA/CSS (2014); NCMF (n.d.).

76. NCMF (n.d.).

77. CP (2017).

78. Nuchi Nashoba to the author, September 4, 2016.

79. *Biskinik* (2018a:4, 2018c); Sarah Elizabeth Sawyer to the author, April 5, 2018.

80. *Biskinik* (2018b); Allen (2018).

81. Lanny Asepermy to the author, August 3, 2019.

Chapter 7

1. Born in Montana and listed as Cheyenne in his 1919 interview with Lieutenant Eddy, Benjamin Dog Cloud appears to have been Northern Cheyenne, and possibly part Lakota. He spent much of his youth at the Standing Rock Reservation and appears on the Standing Rock census. 2d Lt. Benjamin Cloud, 164th Inf., to Lt. John Eddy, Tuesday, Nov. 17, 1919. IUMAA; Knudson and Knudson (2014:29–30).

2. 2d Lt. Benjamin Cloud, 164th Inf., to Lt. John Eddy, Tuesday, Nov. 17, 1919. IUMAA; Knudson and Knudson (2014:29–30).

3. Ibid.

4. The Services of the Thirty-Sixth Division with the American Expeditionary Forces:25. NARA RG-120 Box 2, History July 1918-May 1919 Folder.

5. NYT (1920:10).

6. NYT (1920:10).

7. Archambeault (2008:14) reports 1948.

8. FWST (2007:B6).

9. See Smith (in White 1984:219); Bloor (1919, 1922:39); Robinson (FWST 1919a); DO (1919a); TAH (1919); Spence (1919:287–288, 300–301); Chastaine (1920); Lavine (1921a, 1921b); Cope (1919, n.d.); Dixon (1919); Eddy (1919), and US Congress (1920).

10. Dixon (1919); IWCD (1920), Folder WW-75-09:2–6.

11. For newspaper accounts, see DO (1919a, 1919g); AGZ (1919); MTD (1919a); FWST (1919a, 1919b); Camp-Merritt (1919); NYEW (1919); *Stars and Stripes* (1919b:1).

12. NYEW (1919; NYT (1919); AGZ (1919).

13. AIM (1919); *Stars and Stripes* (1919a); DO (1919a); ISJ (1919); Starr (1921); DOI (1927); NYS (1938); MTR (1941b); NYT (1940, 1941b); NFG (1941); TO (1941). Code talkers' accounts include Benjamin Hampton in 1939 (TMFM 2014) and James Edwards (1941).

14. WS (1938, 1941); HUa (1942).

15. Camp Merritt (1919).

16. NYT (1919).

17. *Stars and Stripes* (1919a:5).

18. AIM (1919) reprinted this article.

19. *Stars and Stripes* (1919b:1).

20. DO (1919a:3).

21. Eddy, NARA RG-120, Box 3471, Folder 2.

22. Dixon (1919 WW-33-01:31/42).

23. NYEW (1919); E. B. Adams, Major General, Adjutant General, to Mr. John Hix, Hollywood, California (June 6, 1939). Courtesy of Ken Kirkland.

24. AR (1941).

25. NYT (1941b:21).

26. NYT (1941a:32).

27. Ibid.

28. "Played Joke on Huns" (AIM 1919:101); Chastaine (1920); "Amazing Code Machine That Sent Messages Safely to U.S. Army in War Baffles Experts: Warfare Tricks That Puzzled Germans (Lavine 1921a; NYA 1921); "Choctaws Stopped War Wire Tappers: Germans at St. Mihiel Finally Circumvented by Indians of the U.S. Forces" (NYS 1938); "Comanches Again Called for Army Code Service" (NYT 1940).

29. Sources include Masterkey, "Indians as Code Transmitters" (1941:240); MTR, "Original Americans" (1941a); MTR, "Enemy Will Have Tough Time Decoding Messages of 168th" (1941b); NYT (1941a) "Indians Volunteer for Defense Army"; NYT (1941b) "Indians' Code Upsets Foe."

30. AGZ (1919); FWS (1941).

31. NMAI (2007).

32. Ibid.

33. Lemuel C. Shepard Jr., Commanding General, Sixth Marine Division, to The Commanding General, Fleet Marine Force, December 1, 1944. NARA, Record Group 127, Box 59, Folder 3, Intelligence.

34. Murray Marder, "Navajo Code Talk Kept Foe Guessing: Indians with Marines, Using Rare Native Tongue, Insured Secrecy of Messages" (NYT 1945); Master Sergeant Murray Marder (1945a), "Navajo Code Talkers."

35. Hopi Veteran's Service Office, Kykotsmovi, AZ, author's fieldnotes, August 2016.

36. *Meriam-Webster*, s.v. "Code," accessed March 3, 2010, http://www.merriam-webster.com/dictionary/code.

37. Meadows (2002, 2006:188).

38. USMC-MYP (2009–2017).

39. Dixon's (1919) books contain other accounts as well.

40. I attended several of these observances from 1990 to 2018.

41. Author's field notes; DO (1919m, 1919n, 19190).

42. ARCIA (1919:16).

43. Among the Choctaw, see *Bishinik* (1989b:1, 3).

44. USDRC (1917).

45. Maytubby (Chickasaw Roll #4685) was allotted on March 18, 1904 (Choctaw-Chickasaw Allotment Deed Records #8807, 1904, Book 14, p. 385). Copy in Pete Maytubby File, CNA. He was Chickasaw and Choctaw and spoke Choctaw.

46. Calvin Atchavit, Registration Card. 518, No. 9. 35–2-24-A. June 5, 1917.

47. Parker McKenzie (Kiowa) to the author, 1991–98.

48. Cf. Franco (1999:190–191).

49. Author's fieldnotes, Choctaw Nation, 2015.

50. Author's fieldnotes 1989–2019.

51. 25 U.S. Code, Chapter 27. See also Bishinik (2005:1).

52. NALA (1990).

53. NALA (1992).

54. Author's fieldnotes 1989–2019.

55. Author's field notes, 1989–2019. I have recorded instances of tribal elders choosing not to teach their native language to their children as a result of the discrimination that they themselves had experienced in schools, believing that their children had a better chance of economic success with English. I have also recorded cases where children decline to learn or use the language.

56. AA (1966).

57. TO (2004); James Parrish, Choctaw Nation, to the author, March 22, 2019.

58. CNOO (n.d.).

59. KXII News (2018).

60. *Bishinik* (2007).

61. FWST (2007:B-6).

62. T. W. Frazier, letter dated April 3, 1997, RES 1997.

63. Kathryn Hooker to the author, October 4, 2015.

64. *BBC News* (2014); Nuchi Nashoba to the author, October, 6 2016.

65. *Bishinik* (1987h:6).

66. Delores Marshall to Mike Wright, February 16 and March 5, 1987, copy courtesy of Judy Allen, Choctaw Nation; DDD (1979).

67. Napanee Brown Coffman to Mike Write, February 26, 1987, copy courtesy of Judy Allen, Choctaw Nation.

68. John Widder and Kathryn Horner Widder to the author, October 27, 2018.

69. Kathryn Horner Widder to the author October 27, 2018.

70. Ibid.

Conclusion

1. Others appear to have been considering using Navajo, such as linguist Robert Young. However, after reading news reports on the testing of Chippewa-Oneida, Comanche, and possibly others in the 1941 Louisiana war games in December 1941, Philip Johnston considered using the Navajo and brought their attention to the US Marine Corps (Johnston 1964:131). The Navajo in World War II became the largest use of code talkers ever.

2. DO (1962). Captain Benjamin Davis Locke helped form and command Company L of the Oklahoma National Guard, organized at Antlers, and was in its service on the Mexican Border in 1916. When the 142nd Infantry Regiment absorbed Company L, Locke was relieved of command and reassigned to the 61st Depot Brigade in November 1917 (Houston 1975; White 1979:9–11, 1984:44). His reassignment, his not serving overseas, and the idea to use the Choctaw language having not developed until late October 1918 in France preclude any role in his forming the Choctaw code talkers.

SOURCES CITED

Interviews

Allen, Judy (Choctaw)
    2014   Phone Interview with the author, January 16. Durant, OK.
    2019   Phone Interview with the author, March 13. Durant, OK.
Atchavit, Robert (Comanche)
    2018   Phone interview with the author, November 25. Wichita Falls, TX.
Coddynah, Haddon (Comanche)
    1987   Haddon Codynah to Joe Todd, April 8. Oklahoma History Center. Oklahoma City, OK.
Garvin, Ona (Ho-Chunk)
    2018   Phone Interview with the author. Wisconsin. February 5.
Gooding, Carrie Miller
    1977   Oral History Interview, November 22. California Audiovisual Preservation Project. Ontario City Library, Robert E. Ellingwood Model Colony History Room. Ontario, CA. http://archive.org/details/con_00098. Accessed August 24, 2017.
Hooker, Kathryn (Choctaw)
    2015   Phone Interview with the author, October 4.
Mashunkashey, John Henry (Osage)
    2017   Phone interview with the Author, August 21. Wichita, KS.
Nahquaddy, Albert Jr. (Comanche)
    1996   Interview with the author, July 24. Oklahoma City, OK.
Nashoba, Nuchi (Choctaw)
    2016   Interview with the author, October 6. Blanchard, OK.
Widder, John
    2018   Interview with the author, October 27. Fayetteville, AK.
Widder, Ruby Kathryn Horner
    2018   Interview with the author, October 27. Fayetteville, AK.

Bibliography

Aaseng, Nathan
    1992   *Navajo Code Talkers*. Walker Publishing Co., New York.

ABMC (American Battle Monuments Commission)

1944 *36th Division Summary of Operations in the World War.* US Government Printing Office, Washington, DC.

Allen, Judy

2018 "Choctaw Code Talkers: Telephone Warriors. They Served, They Sacrificed." Choctaw Nation Historic Projects. Choctaw Nation of Oklahoma, Durant, OK.

Allen, Phillip

2007 "Choctaw Indian Code Talkers of World War I." Choctaw Nation Tribal Website. http://choctawnation.com/history/people/code-talkers. Accessed August 13, 2013.

Archambeault, Marie J.

2007 "Acknowledging Contributions: World War I Code Talkers of the 36th Division of the National Guard." Louisiana Indian Heritage Association's 41st Annual Fall Powwow Booklet. November 23–25, Robert, LA.

2008 World War I Choctaw Code Talkers: 36th Division of the National Guard. *Whispering Wind* 38(1):9–15.

Archives.gov

2007 "The 1973 Fire at the National Personnel Records Center (St. Louis, Mo)." National Personnel Records Center, National Archives and Records Administration, College Park, Maryland. http://www.archives.gov/st-louis /military-personnel/fire-1973.html. June 19. Accessed September 9, 2013.

Arthur, Anthony

1987 *Bushmasters: America's Jungle Warriors of World War II.* St. Martin's Press, New York.

Asepermy, Lanny G.

n.d. *The Comanche Code Talkers of World War I and World War II: Recipients of the Congressional Gold Medal.* Copy courtesy of the author, March 2017.

2011 *Comanche Warrior Monuments—1,008 Names.* Updated August 31. Copy courtesy of Lanny Asepermy.

2012 World War I Code Talkers. *Comanche Nation News,* July. www .comanchenation.com/TCNN/TCNN%20July%202012%20PDF.pdf. Accessed August 1, 2012.

2017 *From Warrior To Veteran: A Written and Pictorial History of Modern-Day Comanche Veterans That Served in the United States Military.* Intertribal Visions, Lawton, OK.

Atkins, J. D. C.

1975 Annual Report of the Commissioner of Indian Affairs 1887. In *Documents of United States Indian Policy,* edited by Francis Paul Prucha, pp. 174–176. University of Nebraska Press, Lincoln.

Austin, Brenda

2011 Heroes in Word and Deed. IndianCountryTodayMediaNetwork.com. August 10:20–25. Accessed September 5, 2011.

Ball, Gregory Wayne

2010 "Soldier Boys of Texas: The Seventh Texas Infantry in World War I." PhD dissertation, University of North Texas, Denton.

Ballou, James L.

2000 *Rock in a Hard Place: The Browning Automatic Rifle.* Collector Grade Publications, Ontario, CA.

Barnes, Charles H.

1922 *History of the 142nd Infantry of the Thirty-Sixth Division October 15, 1917, to June 17, 1919. Including a Sketch of First Oklahoma Infantry and Seventh Texas Infantry.* Blackwell Job Printing Company, Blackwell, Oklahoma.

Barsh, Russel L.

1991 American Indians in the Great War. *Ethnohistory* 38(3):276–303.

1993 An American Heart of Darkness: The 1913 Expedition for American Indian Citizenship. *Great Plains Quarterly* 13(Spring):91–115.

2001 War and the Reconfiguration of American Indian Society. *Journal of American Studies* 35(3):371–411.

BCHAI (Bryan County Heritage Association, Inc.)

1983 "Armstrong Academy." In *The History of Bryan County, Oklahoma.* Vol. 1, pp. 53–54

Bernstein, Alison R.

1991 *American Indians and World War II. Toward a New Era in Indian Affairs.* University of Oklahoma Press, Norman.

Berry, Henry

1978 *Make the Kaiser Dance.* Doubleday, Garden City, NY.

Bixler, Margaret T.

1992 *Winds of Freedom: The Story of the Navajo Code Talkers of World War II.* Two Bytes Publishing Company, Darien, CT.

Blackstock, Joe

2009 Choctaw Soldier Thwarts German Eave[s]droppers During WW I. *Inland Valley Daily Bulletin, California,* October 6. http://www.nativetimes.com /index.php/life/commentary/2472-choctaw-soldier-thwarts-german -eavedroppers-duringww1. Accessed October 24, 2014.

Blanton, Deanne, and Lauren M. Cook

2002 *They Fought Like Demons: Women Soldiers in the Civil War.* Vintage, New York.

Bloor, Alfred W.

1922 "Report of Operations of 142nd Infantry, October 5th to 11th, 1918." In *History of the 142nd Infantry of the Thirty-Sixth Division October 15, 1917, to June 17, 1919. Including a Sketch of First Oklahoma Infantry and Seventh Texas Infantry,* edited by Charles H. Barnes, pp. 60–71. Blackwell Job Printing Company, Blackwell, OK.

Brager, Bruce L.

2002 *The Texas 36th Division: A History.* Eakin Press, Austin, TX.

Braun, Captain Harold

2005 Braun's Battlin' Bastards. The Bushmasters of Company B, 1st Battalion, 158th R.C.T. Sea Bird Publishing, Melbourne, FL.

Britten, Thomas

1997 *American Indians in World War I: At War and at Home.* University of New Mexico Press, Albuquerque.

Bruce, Norman

    1973   *Secret Warfare: The Battle of Codes and Ciphers.* Acropolis, Washington, DC.

Bucholtz, Rodger, William Fields, and Ursula P. Roach

    1996   *20th Century Warriors: Native American Participation in the United States Military.* Prepared for the Department of Defense by CEHIP Inc., Washington, DC: Department of the Navy, Naval Historical Center, Washington Navy Yard.

Buttrick, Daniel S., and David Brown

    1819   *Tsvlvki Sqclvclv, A Cherokee Spelling Book.* F. S. Heiskell and H. Brown, Knoxville, TN.

Byington, Cyrus A.

    1967 [1870]   Grammar of the Choctaw Language: Edited from the Original MSS. In *The Library of the American Philosophical Society,* edited by Daniel G. Brinton, Kraus Reprint, New York. Original 1870 edition published by McCalla and Stavely, Philadelphia.

Cameron, A. D.

    1919   Military Radio Communication: Co-ordination of Army Operations Depends upon Communication by Radio-Goniometric Stations Serve Important Purpose in Locating Enemy Units, While Telephone and Telegraph Systems at Listening Posts Intercept and Report Enemy Messages. *Electrical World* 73(11):521–525.

Cansiére, Romain, and Ed Gilbert

    2018   *Blanc Mont Ridge 1918: America's Forgotten Victory.* Osprey Publishing, New York.

Carroll, Al

    2008   *Medicine Bags and Dog Tags: American Indian Veterans from Colonial Times to the Second World War.* University of Nebraska Press, Lincoln.

Chastaine, Ben H.

    1920   *Story of the 36th: The Experiences of the 36th Division in the World War.* Harlow Publishing Company, Oklahoma City, OK.

    1932   Operations of Company A 142nd Infantry (36th Division) in the Champaign Offensive, October 7 to October 12, 1918. The Infantry School, Fourth Section, Committee "H," Fort Benning, Georgia. Advanced Course 1931–32. http://www.benning.army.mil/library/content/Virtual/Donovanpapers/wwi/. Accessed September 1, 2016.

Chinn, George M.

    1951   *The Machine Gun. History, Evolution, and Development of Manual, Automatic, and Airborne Repeating Weapons,* Vol. 1. Bureau of Ordnance, Department of the Navy. Government Printing Office, Washington, DC.

CCTA (Choctaw Code Talker Association)

    2012   The Official Website of the Choctaw Code Talkers. http://choctawcodetalkersassociation.com/index.php. Accessed December 10, 2012.

    n.d.   *Choctaw Code Talker Association.* Association Pamphlet, Choctaw Nation Archives. Choctaw Nation Headquarters, Durant, OK.

CFR (Code of Federal Regulations)

2007   Title 32—National Defense. Vol. 3. Title: Section 578.63—Lapel Buttons. Government Printing Office, Washington, DC.

CMHUSA (Center of Military History, United States Army)

1988 [1931]   Order of Battle of the United States Land Forces in the World War. American Expeditionary Forces: Divisions. Vol. 2. Government Printing Office, Washington, DC.

Coleman, Louis

2002   Oklahoma's "Greatest" Hero? A Review of the Military Record of Joseph Oklahombi. Chronicles of Oklahoma 80(2):204–215.

2007   "Thirty-Sixth Infantry Division." Encyclopedia of Oklahoma History and Culture. http://digital.library.okstate.edu/encyclopedia/entries/T/T003 .html. Accessed July 12, 2014.

Collier, John

1942   The Indian in a Wartime Nation. Annals of the American Academy of Political and Social Science 223 (September):29–35.

Conlan, Czarina C.

1926   Annual Report of Czarina C. Conlan, February 2, 1926. Chronicles of Oklahoma 4(1):70–73.

Conway, Coleman B., and George A. Shuford

1919   History of the 119th Infantry, 60th Brigade, 30th Division U.S.A. Operations in Belgium and France 1917–1919. Wilmington Chamber of Commerce. Wilmington, NC.

Cooper, Jerry, and Glenn Smith

2005   Citizens as Soldiers; A History of the North Dakota National Guard. University of Nebraska Press, Lincoln, NE.

Cope, W. D.

1919   Annual Report of the Adjutant General of Texas for the Year Ending December 31, 1918. Von Boeckmann-Jones Co., Printers, Austin, TX.

1920   Biennial Report of the Adjutant General of Texas—From January 1, 1919 to December 31, 1920. Knape Printing Company, Austin, TX.

n.d.   36th Division in World War I. Texas National Guard in World War I. Texas Military Forces Museum. http://www.texas militaryforcesmuseum.org /gallery/wwi/cope.html. Accessed July 14, 2014.

Crossett, G. A.

1926   A Vanishing Race. Chronicles of Oklahoma 4(1):100–115.

CTH (Code Talker Handout)

2012   They Served. They Sacrificed. Telephone Warriors—Choctaw Code Talkers of WWI. s3amazonaws.com/choctaw-msldigital/assets/512/ codetalkerhandout. Accessed December 11, 2012.

Cunningham, Hugh T.

1930   A History of the Cherokee Indians. Part III, The Protest. Chronicles of Oklahoma 8(4):407–430.

Daily, Robert

1995   The Code Talkers. American Indians in World War II. Franklin Watts, New York.

Davis, Goode, Jr.

1990 Proud Tradition of the Marines' Navajo Code Talkers: They Fought with Words—Words No Japanese Could Fathom. *Marine Corps League* 46(1):16–26.

Debo, Angie

1961 *Rise and Fall of the Choctaw Republic.* University of Oklahoma Press, Norman.

Dempsey, James

1983 The Indians and World War One. *Alberta History* 31(3):1–8.

1988 *Persistence of a Warrior Ethic Among the Plains Indians.* Alberta History 36(1):1–10.

1999 *Warriors of the King: Prairie Indians in World War I.* Canadian Plains Research Center, Regina, Saskatchewan.

2006 Aboriginal Soldiers in the First World War. National Library and Archives of Canada, Ottawa. http://www.collectionscanada.gc.ca/aboriginal-heritage /020016–4001-e.html. Accessed February 24, 2015.

DeSpain, Matt

2004 The Horrors of the Western Front Part I: Original Journal by Otis Leader. Edited with an introduction by Matt Despain. *Journal of Chickasaw History and Culture* 10(2):4–21.

Downing, Taylor

2014 *Secret Warriors: The Spies, Scientists, and Code Breakers of World War I.* Pegasus Books, New York.

Dunlay, Thomas W.

1982 *Wolves for the Blue Soldiers: Indian Scouts and Auxiliaries with the United States Army, 1860–1890.* University of Nebraska Press, Lincoln.

El Palacio

1941 Indian Languages Become "Code," 48(9):212–213.

Farwell, Byron

1999 *Over There: The United States in the Great War, 1917–1918.* W. W. Norton, New York.

Feaver, Eric

1975 Indian Soldiers, 1891–1895: An Experiment on the Closing Frontier. *Prologue* 7:109–118 (Summer).

Ferrell, Robert H.

2007 *America's Deadliest Battle: Meuse-Argonne, 1918.* University of Kansas Press, Lawrence.

Finger, John R.

1986 Conscription, Citizenship, and Civilization: World War I and the Eastern Band of Cherokee. *North Carolina Historical Review* 63(3):283–308.

Fisher, George A.

1947 *The Story of the 180th Infantry Regiment.* Newsfoto Publishing Co., San Angelo, TX.

Foreman, Carolyn Thomas

1943 *Indians Abroad, 1493–1938.* University of Oklahoma Press, Norman.

Franco, Jere' Bishop

1986   Loyal and Heroic Service: Navajos and World War II. *Journal of Arizona History* 27(4):391–406.

1990a   Patriotism on Trial: Native Americans in World War II. PhD dissertation, University of Arizona.

1990b   Bringing Them in Alive: Selective Service and Native Americans. *Journal of Ethnic Studies* 18(3):1–28.

1999   *War and the Southwest Series: 7. Crossing the Pond: The Native American Effort in World War II.* University of North Texas Press, Denton, TX.

Franks, Kenny

1984   *Citizen Soldiers: Oklahoma's National Guard.* University of Oklahoma Press, Norman.

Freidel, Frank

1964   *Over There: The Story of America's First Great Overseas Crusade.* Little, Brown, Boston, MA.

Gaffen, Fred

1985   *Forgotten Soldiers.* Theytus Books, Penticton, British Columbia.

García Rejón, D. Manuel

1866   Vocabulario del Idioma Comanche. Sociedad Mexicana de Geografia y Estadistica. Imprenta de Ignacio Cumplido, Mexico.

García Rejón, D. Manuel, and Daniel J. Gelo

1995   *Comanche Vocabulary Trilingual Edition.* Compiled by Manuel García Rejón. Translated and edited by Daniel J. Gelo. University of Texas Press, Austin.

Garvin, Ona M. White Wing

2018   Ona M. Whitewing Garvin Speech for Veterans Day. November 11. Copy courtesy of Harald Prins.

Gawne, Jonathan

1998   *Spearheading D-Day: American Special Units of the Normandy Invasion.* Histoire and Collections, Paris, France.

Gilbert, Ed

2008   *Native American Code Talker in World War II.* Osprey Press, Oxford, UK.

Gilbert, James L.

2012   *World War I and the Origins of U.S. Military Intelligence.* Scarecrow Press, Lanham, MD.

Goddard, Ives

1996   The Description of the Native Languages of North America before Boas. In *Handbook of North American Indians: 17. Languages,* edited by Ives Goddard, pp. 17–42. Smithsonian Institution, Washington, DC.

Grass, Albert

2013   Albert Grass (1897–1918). Find A Grave. http://www.findagrave.com/cgi-bin/fg.cgi?page=gr&Grid=112383767. Accessed January 9, 2013.

Greely, A. W.

1919   The Signal Corps in the Great War. The Wires it Operated Would Have Five Times Girdled the Earth and Losses in Action Ranked in

Proportion Next to Those of the Infantry. *New York Times Magazine* May 25: 7–8.

Grillot, Thomas

2018   *First Americans: U.S. Patriotism in Indian Country after World War I.* Yale University Press, New Haven, CT.

Grotelueschen, Mark

2007   *The AEF Way of War: The American Army and Combat in World War I.* Cambridge University Press, Cambridge, UK.

Hale, Duane K.

1982   Forgotten Heroes: American Indians in World War I. *Four Winds* 3(2):38–41.

1992   Uncle Sam's Warriors: American Indians in World War II. *Chronicles of Oklahoma* 69(4):408–429.

Hallas, James H.

2000   *Doughboy War: The American Expeditionary Force in World War I.* Lynne Rienner, Boulder, CO.

Harmon, Alexandra

1999   *Indians in the Making: Ethnic Relations and Indian Identities around Puget Sound.* University of California Press, Berkeley.

Haynie, Nancy Anne

1984   *Native Americans and the Military: Today and Yesterday.* U.S. Army Forces Command Public Affairs, Command Information Branch, Fort McPherson, GA.

Hertzberg, Hazel W.

1971   *The Search for an American Indian Identity.* Syracuse University Press, Syracuse, NY.

Holiday, Samuel T., and Robert S. McPherson

2013   *Under the Eagle: Samuel Holiday Navajo Code Talker.* University of Oklahoma Press, Norman.

Holm, Tom

1978   Indians and Progressives: From Vanishing Policy to the Indian New Deal. PhD dissertation, University of Oklahoma, Norman.

1985   Fighting a White Man's War: The Extent and Legacy of American Indian Participation in World War II. In *Plains Indians in the Twentieth Century*, edited by Peter Iverson, pp. 149–168. University of Oklahoma Press, Norman.

1992   Patriots and Pawns: State Use of American Indians in the Military and the Process of Nativization in the United States. In *The State of Native America*, edited by M. Annette Jaimes, pp. 345–370. South End Press, Boston.

1996   *Strong Hearts, Wounded Souls: Native American Veterans of the Vietnam War.* University of Texas Press, Austin.

2007   *Code Talkers and Warriors. Native Americans and World War II.* Chelsea House, New York.

Houston, Donald E.

1975   The Oklahoma National Guard on the Mexican Border, 1916. *Chronicles of Oklahoma* 53 (Winter 1975–76):447–462.

Imon, Frances
  1977   *Smoke Signals from Indian Territory*. Hennington, Wolfe City, TX.
Inhofe, James
  2010   Remembering Code Talker Mose Bellmard. *Congressional Record*, Proceedings and Debates of the 111th Congress, 2nd Session, 156, Number. 102. Monday, July 12.
Iverson, Peter
  1985   *The Plains Indians of the Twentieth Century*. University of Oklahoma Press, Norman.
  1990   The Navajos. In *Indians of North American Series*, edited by Frank W. Porter III. Chelsea House, New York.
Jackson, Joe C.
  1951   Survey of Education in Eastern Oklahoma From 1907–1951. *Chronicles of Oklahoma* 29(2):200–227.
Jevec, Adam
  2001   Semper Fidelis, Code Talkers. *Prologue* 33(4): 270–277.
Johnson, Broderick H. (editor)
  1977   *Navajos and World War II*. Navajo College Press, Tsaile, AZ.
Johnson, Hubert C.
  1994   *Breakthrough! Tactics, Technology, and the Search for Victory on the Western Front in World War I*. Presidio Press, Novato, CA.
Johnson, Thomas M.
  1929   *Our Secret War: True American Spy Stories 1917–19*. Bobbs-Merrill, Indianapolis.
Johnston, Philip
  1964   Indian Jargon Won Our Battle. *Masterkey* 38(4):130–137.
Kahn, David
  1967   *The Codebreakers: The Story of Secret Writing*. Macmillan, New York.
Kidston, Martin J.
  2004   *From Poplar to Papua: Montana's 163rd Infantry Regiment in World War II*. Farcountry Press, Helena, MT.
Knudson, Michael J., and Ann G. Knudson
  2012a   *Warriors in Khaki: Native American Doughboys from North Dakota*. Robertson, Fenton, CA.
  2012b   *Warriors in Khaki: Native American Doughboys from North Dakota*. 2nd ed. Robertson, Fenton, CA. Released ca. 2016.
Krouse, Susan Applegate
  2007   *North American Indians in the Great War*. University of Nebraska Press, Lincoln.
LaBarre, Weston
  n.d.   Autobiography of a Kiowa Indian. Unpublished manuscript, copy in author's possession.
Langellier, John
  2000   *American Indians in the U. S. Armed Forces, 1866–1945*. Chelsea House, Philadelphia.

Laslo, Alexander J.

  1986   *The Interallied Victory Medals of World War I*. Dorado, Albuquerque.

Lavine, Abraham Lincoln

  1921a   Amazing Code Machine That Sent Messages Safely to U. S. Army in War Baffles Experts. *New York American* November 13:L-9.

  1921b   *Circuits of Victory*. Country Life Press. Doubleday, Page & Company, Garden City, NY.

Lawson, Don

  1963   *The United States in World War I*. Scholastic Book Service, New York.

Lynn-Sherow, Bonnie, and Susannah Ural Bruce

  2001   "How Cola" From Camp Funston: American Indians and the Great War. *Kansas History* 24(2):84–97.

MacDonald, Charles B.

  1996a   World War I: The First Three Years. In *American Military History: 2. 1902–1996*, edited by Maurice Matloff, pp. 18–38. Combined Books, Conshohocken, PA.

  1996b   World War I: The U.S. Army Overseas. In *American Military History: 2. 1902–1996*, edited by Maurice Matloff, pp. 39–62. Combined Books, Conshohocken, PA.

Mack, Stephen

  2008   *It Had to Be Done: The Navajo Code Talkers Remember World War II*. Whispering Dove Design, Tucson, AZ.

Marder, Murrey

  1945a   Navajo Code Talkers. *Marine Corps Gazette*, September:10–11.

  1945b   Navajo Code Talk Kept Foe Guessing. Indians With Marines, Using Rare Native Tongue, Insured Secrecy of Messages. *New York Times*, Wednesday, September 19.

  1945c   "Navajo Code Talkers." In *Indians in the War*, pp. 25–27. Bureau of Indian Affairs, US Department of the Interior, Office of Indian Affairs, Chicago.

Marshall, R. Jackson, III

  1998   *Memories of World War I: North Carolina Doughboys on the Western Front*. Division of Archives and History, North Carolina Department of Cultural Resources, Raleigh.

Maslowski, Peter

  1995   Military Intelligence: Unmasking Those Fearsome Apparitions. In *War Games Again: Comparative Vistas on the Civil War and World War II*, edited by Gabor Borritt, pp. 51–82. Oxford University Press, New York.

Maxfield, Bernice B.

  1975   *Camp Bowie Fort Worth 1917–18: An Illustrated History of the 36th Division in the First World War*. B. B. Maxfield Foundation, Fort Worth, TX.

McClain, Sally

  1994   *Navajo Weapon*. Books Beyond Borders, Boulder, CO.

  2012   *Search for the Navajo Code Talkers*. Rio Nuevo, Tucson, AZ.

McCoy, Ron

1981   Navajo Code Talkers of World War II. *American West* 18(6):67–73, 75.

Meadows, William C.

1991   Tonkonga: An Ethnohistory of the Kiowa Black Legs Society. Master's thesis, Department of Anthropology, University of Oklahoma, Norman.

1995   Remaining Veterans: A Symbolic and Comparative Ethnohistory of Southern Plains Indian Military Societies. PhD dissertation, University of Oklahoma, Norman.

1999   *Kiowa, Apache, and Comanche Military Societies: Enduring Veterans, 1800 to the Present.* University of Texas Press, Austin.

2002   *The Comanche Code Talkers of World War II.* University of Texas Press, Austin.

2006   "North American Indian Code Talkers: Current Developments and Research. In *Aboriginal Peoples and Military Participation: Canadian and International Perspectives,* edited by P. Whitney Lackenbauer, R. Scott Sheffield, and Craig Leslie Mantle, pp. 161–213. Canadian Defense Academy Press, Kingston, Ontario.

2009   They Had a Chance to Talk to One Another: The Role of Incidence in Native American Code Talking. *Ethnohistory* 56(2):269–284.

2010   *Kiowa Military Societies. Ethnohistory and Ritual.* University of Oklahoma Press, Norman.

2011   Honoring Native American Code Talkers: The Road to the Code Talkers Recognition Act of 2008 (Public Law 110–420). *American Indian Culture and Research Journal* 35(3):3–36.

2015   *Through Indian Sign Language: The Fort Sill Ledgers of Hugh Lenox Scott and Iseeo 1889–1897.* University of Oklahoma Press, Norman.

2016   An Honor Long Overdue: The 2013 Congressional Gold and Silver Medal Ceremonies for Native American Code Talkers. *American Indian Culture and Research Journal* 40(2):91–121.

2017   Native American "Warriors" in the US Armed Forces. In *Inclusion in the American Military: A Force for Diversity,* edited by David E. Rohall, Morten G. Ender, and Michael D. Mathews, pp. 83–108. Lexington Books, Lanham, MD.

2018   Text for "Native American Code Talkers of World War I." The United States World War One Centennial Commission. Sequoyah National Research Institute, University of Arkansas at Little Rock. https://www.worldwaricentennial.org/index.php/american-indians-in-wwi-code-talkers.html.

Medicine Crow, Joseph, and Herman J. Viola

2006   *Counting Coup: Becoming a Crow Chief on the Reservation and Beyond.* National Geographic, Washington, DC.

Melton, Brad, and Dean Smith

2003   *Arizona Goes to War: The Home Front and the Front Lines During World War II.* University of Arizona Press, Tucson.

Meriam, Louis, Ray A. Brown, Henry Roe Cloud, Edward Everett Dale, Emma Duke, Herbert R. Edwards, Fayette Avery McKenzie, Mary Louise Mark, W. Carson Ryan Jr., William J. Spillman.

    1928   *The Problem of Indian Administration: Report of a Survey Made at the Request of Honorable Hubert Work, Secretary of the Interior and Submitted to Him, February 21, 1928.* Johns Hopkins University Press, Baltimore.

Mihesuah, Henry

    2002   *First to Fight.* University of Nebraska Press, Lincoln.

Milligan, James C.

    2003   *The Choctaw of Oklahoma.* H. V. Chapman, Abilene, TX.

Mooney, James

    1898   *Calendar History of the Kiowa Indians.* 17th Annual Report of the Bureau of American Ethnology, 1895–96, Part I. Smithsonian Institution Press, Washington, DC.

Morgan, Thomas Jefferson

    1975 [1889]   "Supplemental Report of Indian Education 1889." In *Documents of United States Indian Policy*, edited by Francis Paul Prucha, pp. 178–180. University of Nebraska Press, Lincoln.

Morison, Samuel Eliot

    1953   *History of the United States Naval Operations in World War II: 8. New Guinea and the Marianas, March 1944–August 1944.* Little, Brown, Boston.

Morris, Jessica

    2006   The Choctaw Code Talkers of World War I: A Study of the Survival and Validity of the Choctaw Language in the Early Twentieth Century. Master's thesis, Department of Historical Studies, Southern Illinois University, Edwardsville.

Morris, John

    1977   *Ghost Towns of Oklahoma.* University of Oklahoma Press, Norman.

Morrison, Robert H., and Eugene B. Graham Jr.

    1961   *History of the Charlotte, N.C. Machine Gun Company in World War I. Company D, 115th Machine Gun Battalion, 30th Division.* S.I.:S.N. [Unnamed Publisher]. Available through Worldcat; University of North Carolina, Chapel Hill. OCLC# 5260266.

Moses, Lester G.

    1996   *Wild West Shows and the Images of American Indians, 1883–1933.* University of New Mexico Press, Albuquerque.

Murphy, Elmer A., and Robert S. Thomas

    1936   *The Thirtieth Division in the World War.* Old Hickory, Lepanto, AR.

Nabokov, Peter

    1992   *Native American Testimony.* Penguin. New York.

National Park Service

    1995   Hopi Prisoners on the Rock. Wendy Holliday, Historian, Hopi Cultural Preservation Office. http://home.nps.gov/alca/learn/historyculture/hopi-prisoners-on-the-rock.htm. Accessed August 4, 2016.

2016   The Army and American Indian Prisoners. http://home.nps.gov/alca
        /learn/historyculture/the-army-and-american-indian-prisoners.htm.
        Accessed August 4, 2016.

Nelson, Guy
    1970   *Thunderbird: A History of the 45th Infantry Division.* 45th Infantry Divi-
            sion Association, Oklahoma City.

Newhouse, Arvid B.
    1948   SOPAC Signals. *Signals* May–June:35–39.

Newland, Samuel J., and Raymond Delaney
    1996   *Twenty Years at Haskell: American Indian Units in the Kansas National
            Guard.* United States Army War College, Carlisle Barracks, PA.

Nez, Chester, with Judith Schiess Avila
    2011   *Code Talker.* Berkeley Caliber, New York.

Nye, Wilbur S.
    1937   *Carbine and Lance: The Story of Old Fort Sill.* University of Oklahoma
            Press, Norman.

Otte, Maarten
    2018   *The American Expeditionary Forces in the Great War. Meuse-Argonne 1918:
            Breaking the Line.* Pen and Sword Books, South Yorkshire, England.

Page, Andrea M.
    2017   *Sioux Code Talkers of World War II.* Pelican, Gretna, LA.

Parker, Arthur C.
    1918   The American Indian in the World Crisis. *The American Indian*
            6(2):15–24.

Parman, Donald
    1994   *Indians and the American West in the Twentieth Century.* Indiana Univer-
            sity Press, Bloomington.

Paul, Doris A.
    1973   *The Navajo Code Talkers.* Dorrance, Pittsburgh, PA.

Perry, John
    2010   *Sergeant York.* Thomas Nelson, Nashville.

Pickering, John
    1820   *An Essay on the Uniform Orthography for the Indian Languages of North
            America.* Cambridge: University-Press-Hilliard and Metcalf.

    1830   *A Grammar of the Cherokee Language.* Mission Press, Boston.

Price, Byron
    1977   The Utopian Experiment: The Army and the Indian, 1890–1897. *By
            Valor and Arms* 3:4–11 (Spring).

Ragan, Angela
    2012   Eastern Band of Cherokee Indians Enlisted or Drafted as of December
            1917 by Branch of Service, Appendix A. Copy, courtesy of the author.

Raines, Rebecca Robbins
    1996   *Getting the Message Through: A Branch History of the U.S. Army Signal
            Corps.* Center of Military History, United States Army. US Government
            Printing Office, Washington, DC.

Rawls, James R.

  1996   *Chief Red Fox is Dead: A History of Native Americans Since 1945*. Harcourt Brace, New York.

Red Elk, Roderick

  1991   Comanche Code Talkers. *Prairie Lore* 27(1):113–114, Book 86.

  1992   Comanche Code Talkers. *Prairie Lore* 28(1):1–10, Book 88.

Richardson, Rupert N.

  1933   *The Comanche Barrier to South Plains Settlement*. Arthur H. Clark, Glendale, CA.

Riggs, Stephen R.

  1852   *Grammar and Dictionary of the Dakota Language*. Smithsonian Contributions to Knowledge 4, Washington, DC.

  1890   *A Dakota-English Dictionary*. Volume 7 of *Contributions to North American Ethnology*, edited by James Owen Dorsey. U.S. Geographical and Geological Survey of the Rocky Mountain Region, Washington, DC.

  1893   Dakota Grammar, Texts, and Ethnography. Volume 9 of *Contributions to North American Ethnology*, edited by James Owen Dorsey. U.S. Geographical and Geological Survey of the Rocky Mountain Region, Washington, DC.

Riseman, Noah Jed

  2007   "Regardless of History?": Re-assessing the Navajo Codetalkers of World War II. *Australasian Journal of American Studies* 26(2):48–73.

  2012   *Defending Whose Country*. University of Nebraska Press, Lincoln.

Robinson, Gary

  2011   *The Language of Victory. American Indian Code Talkers of World War I and World War II*. iUniverse, Bloomington, IN.

Rogers, Everett M., and Nancy R. Bartlit

  2005   *Silent Voices of World War II: When Sons of the Land of Enchantment Met Sons of the Rising Sun*. Sunstone Press, Santa Fe.

Roosevelt, Theodore.

  1990   *The Rough Riders*. Da Capo Press, New York. Originally published 1902, Scribner, New York.

Ross, Annie

  2013   "Our Mother Earth Is My Purpose": Recollections From Mr. Albert Smith, Na'ashq'iidich'izhii. *American Indian Culture and Research Journal* 37(1):105–124.

Sawyer, Sarah Elizabeth

  2018   *Anumpa Warrior: Choctaw Code Talkers of World War I, A Novel*. Rock Haven, Canton, TX.

Scott, Duncan Campbell

  1919   The Canadian Indians and the Great World War. In *Canada in the Great War: 3. Guarding the Channel Ports*, pp. 295–328. United Publishing of Canada, Toronto.

Scott, Hugh Lennox

  1928   *Some Memories of a Soldier*. Century Company, New York.

Sells, Cato

   1973 [1918]   Report of the Commissioner of Indian Affairs, September 30, 1918. In
        The American Indian and the United States: A Documentary Survey: 2, edited
        by Wilcomb E. Washburn, pp. 873–888. Random House, New York.

Singh, Simon

   1999   *The Code Book: The Evolution of Secrecy from Mary Queen of Scots to
        Quantum Cryptography.* Doubleday, New York.

   2002   *The Code Book: How to Make It, Break It, Hack it, Crack It.* Delacourte,
        New York.

Smith, Laura E.

   2016   *Horace Poolaw: Photographer of American Indian Modernity.* University
        of Nebraska Press, Lincoln.

Smith, Thomas S.

   1919   *357th Infantry. Its History From Organization Until Part of Army of Occu-
        pation 1917–1919.* J. Linzt, Trier, Germany.

Spector, Ronald H. (editor)

   1998   *Listening to the Enemy: Key Documents on the Role of Communications Intel-
        ligence in the War With Japan.* Scholarly Resources, Wilmington, DE.

Spence, Alexander White

   1919   *The History of the 36th Division, U.S.A., 1917–1919.* Typescript. 1-2, His-
        torical File, 36th Division, AEF Records, RG 120, National Archives,
        Washington, DC.

Stabler, Hollis D.

   2005   *No One Ever Asked Me. The World War II Memories of an Omaha Indian
        Soldier.* University of Nebraska Press, Lincoln.

Stanley, John W.

   1931   *Personal Experiences of a Battalion Commander and Brigade Signal Officer,
        105th Field Signal Battalion, in the Somme Offensive, September 29–October 12,
        1918.* The Infantry School, Fourth Section, Committee "H," Fort Benning,
        Georgia. Advanced Course 1930–1931. http://www.benning.army.mil/library
        /content/Virtual/Donovanpapers/wwi/. Accessed September 1, 2016.

Stallings, Laurence

   1963   *The Doughboys: The Story of the AEF, 1917–1918.* Harper & Row, New York.

Starr, Emmet

   1921   *History of the Cherokee Indians and Their Legends and Folklore.* Warden
        Company, Oklahoma City, OK. Reprinted 1993 by Oklahoma Yesterday
        Publications, Tulsa, OK.

Stein, William W.

   1986   Doing Ethnohistory with Old Newspapers: The Study of an Andean Peasant
        Movement of 1885. In *Ethnohistory: A Researcher's Guide*, edited by Dennis
        Wiedman, pp. 345–380. Studies in Third World Societies Publication Num-
        ber Thirty Five, College of William and Mary, Williamsburg, VA.

Swanton, John R., and Henry S. Halbert (editors)

   1915   *A Dictionary of the Choctaw Language.* Bureau of American Ethnology
        Bulletin 46, Washington, DC.

Swink, Lila Douglas

n.d.   Biographical Sketch of Captain Walter Veach. 5 pp. Author's copy, courtesy of Lila Swink, 2015.

Tate, Michael L.

1986   From Scout to Doughboy: The National Debate Over Integrating American Indians into the Military, 1891–1918. *Western Historical Quarterly* 17 (October):417–437.

Thompson, George Raynor, and Dixie R. Harris

1966   *The Signal Corps: The Outcome (Mid-1943 Through 1945)*. United States Army in World War II. The Technical Services. Office of the Chief of Military History, United States Army. Government Printing Office, Washington, DC.

Tohe, Laura

2012   *Code Talker Stories*. Rio Nuevo Publishers, Tucson, AZ.

Townsend, Kenneth W.

2000   *World War II and the American Indian*. University of New Mexico Press, Albuquerque.

Townsend, Una Belle

2016   *Toby and the Secret Code: A Choctaw Adventure*. Illustrated by Gwen Coleman Lester. Doodle and Peck, Cedarburg, CT.

US Army

2014   US Army Campaigns: World War I. www.history.army.mil/html /reference/army-flag/wwi.html. Accessed December 1. 2014.

Usbeck, Frank

2015   *Fellow Tribesmen: The Image of Native Americans, National Identity, and Nazi Ideology in Germany*. Berghahn Press, Brooklyn, NY.

Van de Logt, Mark

2006   Looking for Adventure: Ponca Warriors of the Forty-Fifth Infantry Division in the Korean War. *Chronicles of Oklahoma* 84(1):64–77.

2010   *War Party in Blue: Pawnee Scouts in the U.S. Army*. University of Oklahoma Press, Norman.

Van Der Rhoer, Edward

1978   *Deadly Magic*. Scribners, New York.

Viola, Herman J.

2008   *Warriors in Uniform: The Legacy of American Indian Heroism*. National Geographic, Washington, DC.

Walker, John O., William A. Graham, and Thomas Fauntleroy

1919   Official History of the 120th Infantry. "3rd North Carolina" 30th Division. From August 5, 1917, to April 17, 1919. Canal Sector -Ypres-Lys Offensive, Somme Offensive. J. P. Bell Company, Lyncburg, VA.

Walker, Willard B.

1980   Incidental Intelligence on the Cryptographic Use of Muskogee Creek in World War II Tactical Operations by the United States Army. *International Journal of American Linguistics* 46(2):144–145.

1983   More on the Cryptographic Use of Native American Languages in Tactical Operations by United States Armed Forces. *International Journal of American Linguistics* 49(1):93–97.

1996   Native Writing Systems. In *Handbook of North American Indians: 17. Languages*, edited by Ives Goddard, pp. 158–184. Smithsonian Institution, Washington, DC.

2000   The Comanche Code Talkers of World War II. *International Journal of American Linguistics* 66(4):563–564.

Welch, A. B.

1934   Richard Blue Earth, World War I Hero, Killed in Action against the Germans, Honored, Mandan ND, March 14, 1934. Directed by Col. A. B. Welch. Oral History of the Dakota Tribes 1800s–1945. http://www .welchdakotapapers.com/2011/08-richard-blue-earth-honored-mandan -nd-march-14–1934. Accessed January 9, 2013.

Welch, W. E., J .S. Aldridge, and L. V. Aldridge

1920   *The Oklahoma Spirit of '17: Biographical Volume.* Historical Publishing Co., Oklahoma City, OK.

White, W. Bruce

1976   The American Indian as Soldier, 1890–1917. *Canadian Review of American Studies* 7(Spring):15–25.

1990   "The American Army and the Indian." In *Ethnic Armies: Polyethnic Armed Forces from the Time of the Habsburgs to the Age of the Superpowers,* edited by Nandor F. Dreisziger, pp. 69–88. Wilfred Laurier University Press, Waterloo, Ontario, Canada.

White, Lonnie J.

1978   Major General Edwin St. John Greble. *Military History of Texas and the Southwest* 14(1):7–20.

1979   Indian Soldiers in the 36th Division: A Study of Native American Participation in the First World War. *Military History of Texas and the Southwest* 15:7–20.

1982   The Combat History of the 36th Division in World War I. *Military History of Texas and the Southwest* 17(4):Special Issue.

1984   *Panthers to Arrowheads: The 36th Division (Texas-Oklahoma) in World War I.* Presidial Press, Austin, TX.

1996   *The 90th Division in World War I: The Texas-Oklahoma Draft Division in the Great War.* Sunflower University Press. Manhattan, KS.

Whitlock, Flint

1998   *The Rock of Anzio. From Sicily to Dachau: A History of the U.S. 45th Infantry Division.* Westview Press. Boulder, CO.

Winegard, Timothy C.

2012   *For King and Kanata: Canadian Indians and the First World War.* University of Manitoba Press, Winnipeg, Canada.

Wise, Jennings C.

1931   *The Red Man in the New World Drama: A Politico-Legal Study with a Pageantry of American Indian History.* W. F. Roberts, Washington, DC.

Wood, David L.
  1981   American Indian Farmland and the Great War. *Agricultural History* 55(3):249–265.
Wright, Alfred, and Cyrus A. Byington
  1825   *Spelling Book, Written in the Chahta Language with an English Translation.* Morgan, Lodge, and Fisher, Cincinnati.
  1848   *The New Testament of Our Lord and Saviour Jesus Christ, Translated into the Choctaw Language.* American Bible Society, New York.
Wright, Allen
  1880   *Choctaw Leksikon: A Choctaw in English Definition.* Presbyterian Publishing Company, St. Louis.
Wright, Mike
  1986   Unsung Heroes: Indian Military "Code Talkers." *Oklahoma Observer* 18(20):19.
Wythe, Major George
  1920   *A History of the 90th Division.* The 90th Division Association, Dallas, TX. Privately Published.
Yockelson, Mitchell
  2016   *Forty Seven Days: How Pershing's Warriors Came of Age to Defeat the German Army in World War I.* NAL Caliber, New York.
Zambrano, Mike
  2015   Lost + Forgotten: The Choctaw Code Talkers of World War I. *Texas Heritage* 2:16–20.

Federal Legislation

NALA (Native American Languages Act)
  1990   Native American Languages Act of 1990, P.L. 101-477.
  1992   Native American Languages Act of 1992, P.L. 102-524.

Archival Records

AHM (Application for Headstone or Marker Form). Ancestry.com: Attchavit, Calvin (Comanche), 2806696, 1945; Billy, Albert (Choctaw), 1491485, 1959; Hampton, Benjamin Wilburn (Choctaw), 1490133, 1963; Leader, Otis W. (Choctaw), 105473, 1961; Longtail, John H. (Winnebago), 540725, 1948.
ARCIA (Annual Report of the Commissioner of Indian Affairs)
  1919   Department of the Interior 66th Congress, 2d session, House document 409. 1918–1920. Government Printing House, Washington, DC.
Billy, Schlicht
  1952   United States Army Discharge Record. Schlicht Billy, 20829665. Issued May 14, 1952. Copy courtesy of Judy Allen, Choctaw Nation.
Bloor, Colonel Alfred W., 142 Infantry Commanding Officer
  1919   "Transmitting Messages in Choctaw." Letter to the Commanding General 36th Division, Attention Captain Spence. January 23, 1919. A.P.O. No. 796. National Archives. AGO REC. World War I -File 236–32.5.

Bobb, Nora
    2001   Standard Certificate of Birth. Oklahoma State Board of Health, Bureau of Vital Statistics, State Department of Health, Oklahoma City. May 11.

Boren, Dan
    n.d.   Letter to the Congress of the United States, US House of Representatives. Copy courtesy of the Choctaw Nation of Oklahoma. Pre-2008.

Brown, CPL. Victor
    1919   United States Army Discharge Record. June 14, 1919, Camp Pike, Arkansas. Blanche B. Freeman, Notary Public, Chickasha, OK. July 26, 1920.

Callaway, John
    1992   Untitled paper. Copy in possession of the author. Choctaw Nation Archives, Durant, OK. Later published in *Bishinik* in 1996, August:4.

Camp Merritt
    1919   "142D Infantry Is in Camp Merritt, N.J." Unknown newspaper article. Release from Hoboken, NJ, June 1:1, 8. Courtesy of Kathryn Horner Widder.

CBVF (Camp Beauregard Vertical Files)
    2003   "Native American Code Talker Monument Dedication, Louisiana, Maneuvers and Military Museum Complex, Camp Beauregard, Pineville, LA. April 3. Event Brochure. Louisiana National Guard Archive, Jackson Barracks, New Orleans, LA.

CNA (Choctaw Nation Archives)
    Choctaw code talker files. Choctaw Nation Headquarters, Durant, OK.

CNOO (Choctaw Nation of Oklahoma)
    1986   "Indian-Language Communication in World War I," August 8, 1986, unpublished document courtesy of Judy Allen and the Choctaw Nation of Oklahoma.

    ca. 1990   Choctaw Code Talkers. World War I. *Bishinik*. Drawer 1210, 16th and Locust, Durant, OK.

    2013   *They Served. They Sacrificed. The Choctaw Code Talkers, United States Army, World War I, Congressional Gold Medal Recipients.* Color pamphlet published by the Choctaw Nation, November. Choctaw Nation Archives. Choctaw Nation Headquarters. Durant, OK.

    2016   *They Served. They Sacrificed: The Choctaw Code Talkers, United States Army, World War I, Congressional Gold Medal Recipients.* Color pamphlet published by the Choctaw Nation, November. Choctaw Nation Archives. Choctaw Nation Headquarters. Durant, OK. Revised from 2013.

    2018a   County Bridges, More to Honor Choctaw Code Talkers. https://www.choctawnation.com/news-events/press-media-county-bridges-more-honor-choctaw-code-talkers. Accessed April 19, 2018.

    2018b   Bridge Dedication Ceremony in Honor of Choctaw Code Talker Joseph Oklahombi. https://www.choctawnation.com/bridge-dedication-ceremony-honor-of-choctaw-code-talker-joseph-oklahombi. April 19, 2018. Accessed April 19, 2018.

    n.d.   *Choctaw Code Talkers: World War I Code Talkers Instrumental in Ending War.* Undated two-page color flier.

Co. C. 312th FSB (Field Signal Battalion)

1918   "Passenger List of Organizations and Casuals Port of Embarkation, New York, New York." August 27.

1919   "Passenger List of Organizations and Casuals Returning to the United States, Port of Embarkation, St. Nazaire, France. Co. C. 312th Field Signal Battalion." March 12.

Co. D, 143rd Infantry

1919   "Passenger List of Organizations and Casuals Returning to the United States, Port of Embarkation, Brest, France. Co. D., 143rd Infantry." May 27. Ancestry.com.

Co. E, 142nd Infantry

1918   "Passenger List of Organizations and Casuals, Port of Embarkation, Hoboken, N.J." July 18. Copy Courtesy of Kathryn Horner Widder.

1919   "Passenger List of Organizations and Casuals Returning to the United States." May 19. Ancestry.com; second copy courtesy of Kathryn Horner Widder.

Co. M, 143rd Infantry

1918   "Passenger List of Organizations and Casuals, Port of Embarkation, Newport News, VA." July 18. Ancestry.com.

Dixon, Joseph K.

1919   "Indians in WWI, Books 1–6. Book 6. Data on Indian Soldiers at Camp Dix. Camp Merritt." Camp Merritt Section, pp. 28–41. Document WW-33–01:29–42. June 7. Photos 1962–08–6440, 6445–6448, 6451–6453, June 8. Indiana University Museum of Archaeology and Anthropology, Bloomington, IN.

Eddy, First Lieutenant John R.

1919   Report on the American Indian Soldier. Records of the Historical Section of the General Staff, Records of the American Expeditionary Force, Records Group 120. National Archives and Records Administration. Washington, DC.

Edwards, James M.

1921   United States Army Discharge Record (1490047). August 13, 1921. Camp Eagle Pass, Texas. Copy courtesy of Judy Allen, Choctaw Nation.

Evacuation Hospital No. 19.

1918   "Passenger List of Organizations and Casuals, Port of Embarkation, Hoboen, NJ. Evacuation Hospital No. 19. Aug. 31." Ancestry.com.

1919   "Passenger List of Organizations and Casuals Returning to the United States. Evacuation Hospital No. 19. Aug. 3." Ancestry.com.

GDMC—George D. Meiklejohn Collection

Letters from Captain W. A. Mercer, 8th Infantry, U.S. Indian Service, Omaha and Winnebago Agency, Nebraska, to Assistant Secretary of War George D. Meiklejohn, Washington, DC. Nebraska State Historical Society. Box 18, Folder 120. April 18, 1898; April 20, 1898.

Gerrer, Father Gregory

c.1945   Unpublished Autobiography. OSB. NMAI 09–243, Box 3, Tewanna Edwards Personal Papers and Notes Collection.

HARB (Horner Application for Retirement Benefits)
:   1953   Lt. Col. Elijah W. Horner, Application for Retirement Benefits Under the Provisions of Title III, PL810–80th Congress. Adjutant General, Department of the Army. April 10. Courtesy of Kathryn Horner Widder.

Horner, Major Elijah W.
:   1942   Major E. W. Horner, F. A. Fort Warren, Wyoming, February 10, Letter to E. M. Kirby, Chief Radio Branch, Washington, DC. Copy courtesy of Kathryn Horner Widder.

IPP (Indian Pioneer Papers)
:   1937   Interview with Ben Carterby (Choctaw), June 29. Western History Collections. University of Oklahoma.

IUMAA (Indiana University Museum of Archaeology and Anthropology)
:   1919   2d Lt. Benjamin Cloud, 164th Inf., to Lt. John Eddy. Historical Division, US Army, Washington, DC. November 17. Indiana University, Bloomington, IN.

IWCD (Indian War College Data)
:   1920   Folder WW-75–09:1–6. Indiana University Museum of Archaeology and Anthropology, Bloomington, IN.

JJPC—John J. Pershing Collection
:   Letter from George D. Meiklejohn, Office of the Assistant Secretary of War to Major John J. Pershing, Assistant Adjutant-General, US Volunteers, Manila, Philippine Islands. April 16, 1900. Box 317, File 1, "Camp Vicars." Library of Congress, Manuscript Division. Washington, DC.

Kirby, E. M.
:   1942   Chief Radio Branch, Washington, DC, Telegraph to E.W. Horner, 183rd F.A., Fort Lewis, Washington, January 31. Copies courtesy of Kathryn Horner Widder and Erin Fehr, Sequoyah Research Institute, Little Rock, AR.

MCHS (McCurtain County Historical Society)
:   1982   *McCurtain County: A Pictorial History*. McCurtain County Historical Society, Idabel, OK.

NARA (National Archives and Records Administration)
:   Records Group 75, Records of the Bureau of Indian Affairs. Records Pertaining to Indians in World War I and World War II 1920–1921 and 1945. NARA Textual Reference Archives I. Washington, DC.

Box 1, World War I Folder; Responses to Circular Letter #1625. Entry Number 998 E.

Box 3, Responses to Circular Letter #1625 Entry Number 999E.

Box 24, Entry Number 998 E.

Box 25, Osage Service Records in World War I Folder. Entry Number 998 E.

Box 68. Undated 14 page list of Kiowa Agency World War I Veterans. Chief Clerk in Charge, Office of the Commission of Indian Affairs, Washington, DC.

Card File. Records of the Employees Section. Card File Relating to Indians in World War I, 1916–20. Soldiers, Decorated Surgeon, Officers, Special Medals, Nurses. Entry 977 B. NC3–75–78–7. Box 1.

John Collier, Office of Indian Affairs to the Office of the Secretary. "Mobilization of the Indian Service and Indian Resources for National Defense. June 15, 1940. Item 106196. October 1944

File, Entry Number 179, ACR 611972. See also Bernstein (1991:189n20).

Records Group 120, Records of the American Expeditionary Forces 1917–1923, General Headquarters Historical Section. NARA Textual Reference Archives II Branch, College Park, MD.

Box 2, Records of Combat Division 1917–1918, 36th Division. Hist.

History of 36th Div. Appendix 236.11.4 to Hist. Weekly Report of Shows, Ent. Officer 236.17.

Headquarters 71st Infantry Brigade, A.E.F.A.P.O. #796, 7, Nov. 1918, G-3, 71st Infantry Brigade to G-3, 36th Division, Subject: Operation Report of Engagement 27, October 1918.

Box 14, Records of Combat Division 1917–1918, 36th Division. Hist. 141st Inf. Personal Accts. 236–33.61 to Hist. 142nd Inf. Ops. Rept. Medical Troops 236–43.2. ARC ID 301641. Entry NM-91 1241.

Box 214, 216, 105th Field Signal Battalion 30'h Division.

Box 97, Records of the 30th Division, File 201 Stanley, John W., Entry NM-91, 1241.

Box 1200, File 21125. Responses to Circular Letter #1625.

Boxes 3471, 3472, 3473. General Headquarters Historical Section.

Morrissey, Lieutenant Colonel William J., 142nd Infantry, A.P.O. #796.

1919 "Terms Used by Indians over Telephone." Memo to Lieutenant John P. Eddy, Historical Section, General Headquarters, MRB. March 2.

Records Group 127, Records of the US Marine Corps. NARA Textual Reference Archives II Branch, College Park, MD.

History and Museums Division, Correspondence of Marine Divisions, 1941–46, 6th Marine Division, 2295 (G-2 Periodic Reports) through (S-3 Reports), Folder 3, Intelligence, Box 59.

NARA-PF (National Archives and Records Administration-Personnel Files, St. Louis, MO.

Cherokee: George Adair (1490079). Choctaw: Albert Billy (1491485), Mitchell Bobb (1490094), Victor Brown (1483614), Ben Carterby (1483743), Benjamin Colbert (979885), George E. Davenport (1484283); Joseph H. Davenport (1483461); Noel Johnson (1484284), James Morrison Edwards (1490047), Benjamin Hampton (1490133), Otis W, Leader (105473), Solomon B. Louis (Lewis (1480041); Pete Maytubby (1490159), Joseph Oklahombi (1483609), Robert Taylor (1490194), Walter Veach (448184106), Cabin (Calvin Wilson (1483461). Comanche: Calvin Atchavit (2806695), George Clark (2215844), Gilbert Conwoop (28064890), Edward A. Nahquaddy (2245683), Samuel Tabbytosavit (2806854). Hochunk: John H. Longtail (540725); Robert Big Thunder (540657).

OHC—Oklahoma History Center, Oklahoma City, OK.

Otis Leader Papers Record No. 81.105 Otis Leader. Federal Writer's Project, Biographies, Lacy Leflore. Box 21, FF 6.

Elmer L. Fraker to Sybil Miracle, Oklahoma Department, American Legion, June 6, 1953.

Otis W. Leader to Overton Colbert, Paris France, February 1, 1924. Undated note on painting of Otis Leader by Gregory Guerrer.

Joseph Oklahombi Papers. Record No. 97.32.01. Joseph Oklahombi to Mrs. Czarina Conlan, March 31, 1925.

Record No. 97.32.03. 28 February 1919 General Headquarters of the French Armies of the East (Decoration) Order No. 13910 "D." (Extract, Private Joseph Oklahombi 1483609 of Co. D, 141st Infantry (in French).

Record No. 97.32.04. 28 February 1919 General Headquarters of the French Armies of the East (Decoration) Order No. 13910 "D." (Extract, Private Joseph Oklahombi 1483609 of Co. D, 141st Inf. (in English).

Oklahoma Senate Resolution

1961   Enrolled Senate Resolution No. 34. Robert A. Trent, President, Oklahoma Senate. March 27.

Oklahombi, Joseph

1949   Military Discharge Record. Joseph Oklahombi, 1483609. Copy issued April 4, 1949. County Clerk's Office, McCurtain County Courthouse, Idabel, OK.

Order No. 13.910 "D." 1919. French Armies of the East, February 28, 1919. Bureau Central d'Archives Militaires, Casern Bernadotte, France. Accession No. 3076, Oklahoma History Center, Oklahoma City, OK.

Order No. 13.910 "D" Extract Copy. 2013 Extract Copy of French Order No. 13.910 "D," February 28, 1919. Issued in French by Lt-Col. Dubois, Commandant le Bureau Central d'Archives Administratives Militaires, to Mr. Dale Turner, San Antonio, TX, April 4, 1989.

Accession No. 3076, Oklahoma History Center, Oklahoma City, OK.

Reagan, Ronald

1982   Proclamation 4954—National Navajo Code Talker Day. July 28.

Scribner, John C. L., Brigadier General.

n.d.   Answering the Call: A History of the Texas National Guard, Unpublished document. Texas Military Forces Museum.

Sells, Cato

1920   Extract From the Original. Department of the Interior. United States Indian Service. Secretary of the Interior. Washington, DC. December. Copy, NMAI 09–243, Box 3, Tewanna Edwards Personal Papers and Notes Collection.

SIFCJ (*Saskatchewan Indian Federated College Journal*)

1984   Canadian Indians and World War One. 1:65–72

SRST (Standing Rock Sioux Tribe).

2013   Standing Rock Sioux Tribe Congressional Silver Medal Honoring. Event Program. December 12, 2013. Prairie Knights Casino Pavillion. Copy in possession of the author.

USADP (US Army Discharge Papers)

1919   Victor Brown, Ben Carterby, Tobias Frazier, Benjamin W. Hampton, Pete Maytubby, Joseph Oklahombi, Calvin Wilson. June 1919. Choctaw Nation Archives, Choctaw Nation Headquarters. Durant, OK.

USAFPR (United States Army Final Payment Roll)
    Mitchell Bobb, 6–16–1919; Albert Billy, 6–17–1919; Victor Brown, 6–14–1919;
        Ben Carterby, 6–6-1919; Joseph H. Davenport, 6–16–1919; Tobias W. Frazier,
        6–16–1919; Benjamin W. Hampton, 6–19–1919; Solomon B. Lewis (Louis),
        6–16–1919; Pete Maytubby, 6–16–1919; Robert Taylor, 6–16–1919. Choctaw
        Nation Archives, Choctaw Nation Headquarters. Durant, OK.
US Congress
    1920   Army Reorganization: Hearings before the Committee on Military
            Affairs, House of Representatives. Sixty-Sixth Congress, First and Sec-
            ond Sessions on H.R. 8287, H.R. 8068, H.R. 7925, H.R. 9970. Septem-
            ber 29, 1919 to February 5, 1920. Vol. II. Government Printing House.
            Washington, DC.
USASA (US Army Security Agency)
    1950   "Utilization of American Indians as Communications Linguists." Octo-
            ber 24, 1950. Central Security Service. Historic Cryptographic Collec-
            tion, Pre–World War I through World War II. Records of the National
            Security Agency Special Research History (SRH) #120, 107 pp. Records
            Group 457, Box 20, National Archives and Records Administration. Col-
            lege Park, MD.
USASS (United States Army Signal School)
    n.d.   "T.P.S. and Listening Posts." American Expeditionary Forces, France.
USDRC (United States Draft Registration Cards)
    1917   (Choctaw) Albert Billy; Mitchell Bobb, Ben Carterby, Joseph H. Davenport,
            Pete Maytubby, Joseph Oklahombi, Calvin Wilson, Jeff Wilson, Louis L.
            Gooding; (Comanche) Calvin Atchavit; Eastern Band Cherokee (Ute Crow,
            Kane George, Jesse Youngdeer, Steve Youngdeer). NARA, Choctaw Nation
            Archives, Choctaw Nation Headquarters. Durant, OK; Ancestry.com.
USMC-MYP (United States Marine Corps Military Yearbook Project)
    2009–2017   USMC MOS Codes, WW II Era. Entry "642—Code Talker." https://
            militaryyearbookproject.com/references/old-mos-codes/wwii-era/usmc
            -wwii-codes/communication/642-code talker. Accessed November 28,
            2017.
VNVPW (Virginia Nations Veterans Pow Wow)
    2002   Powwow Program. November 9–10. Copy, NMAI 09–243, Box 3,
            Tewanna Edwards Personal Papers and Notes Collection.
WVM (Wisconsin Veterans Museum). Madison, Wi. Robert Big Thunder, Nathan-
            iel H. Longtail files.

Newspapers and Periodicals

AA (*Antlers American*)
    1950   "Davenport Rites Set for Today at Old Cedar Church." ca. April 18.
    1966   "Choctaw Tongue Proved Too Tough for Germans." March 10:1,6.
    1997   "Choctaw Code-Talkers Subject of Class Study." May 29:1,8.

ABMC (*American Battle Monuments Commission*)

1944   36th Division: Summary of Operations in the World War. United States Government Printing Office, Washington, DC.

ADA (*Ardmore Daily Ardmoreite*)

1919   "American Casualties." February 4:2.

1936   "Indians Held Durant Meeting." May 31:11.

ADTT (*Ames Daily Tribune Times*)

1933   "Jobless War Hero Asks Aid." January 13:3.

AEN (*Ada Evening News*)

1921   Indian Veteran and War Figure Forgets Glory." October 5:4.

1924   "Shawnee." April 29:2.

1925   "Famous Indian Soldier Enters U. S. Hospital." September 18:3.

1933   "Otis Leader in Fight for Health. Hollis Man Chosen as Model for Indian Soldiers Conquering T-B." November 13:5.

1937   "Pension Asked for Indian Hero." April 4:5.

1953   "Joint Installation Held by Coalgate Legion, Auxiliary." August 13:7.

1958   "He's Almost Forgotten Today, But Famed Soldier Remembers. November 11:1,3.

1959   "Coalgate Legion Elects Officers." July 22:10.

AG (*Amarillo Globe*)

1940   "Choctaw Hero of AEF Ready to Fight Again." November 14:2.

AGZ (*Arkansas Gazette*)

1919   "Arkansan Led Company of Indian Braves in France. Captain Horner of Mena Lands in New York with Redskin Scouts, Who Outwitted Germans by Talking in Their Native Tongue." ca. June 1.

AIM (*American Indian Magazine*)

1917a   "Five Civilized Tribes Doing Their Bit." 5(3):143.

1917b   "The American Indians and the World War. Want U.S. Indians at Front." 5(3):198.

1919   "Played Joke on the Huns. Sioux Indians had Fun for Three Days Talking over a Tapped Telephone Wire." Summer, 7(2):101.

AL (*American Legion*)

2016   Ponce Tribal Cemetery Established 1890. https://centennial.legion.org/oklahoma/post38/gallery/ponca-tribal-cemetery-established-1890. May 13. Accessed September 23, 2019.

AR (*Arizona Republic*)

1941   "Indians Whoop Delightedly at White Man's Way of War." Sunday, January 12, Section 2, pp. 3. Phoenix, AZ.

2001   "Forgotten Heroes: Non-Navajo Code Talkers Seeking Equal Recognition." January 6:A1, A12.

ASV (*Afton Star Valley Independent*)

1932   "The Fighting Race." Nov. 3.

AT (*Ardmore Times*)

1948   "Paris Artist's Model is VA Patient." May 7:9.

AWN (*Ada Weekly News*)

  1925   "Famous Indian Soldier Enters U.S. Hospital." September 24:4.

BB (*Brownwood Bulletin*)

  1919   "Oklahoma Indian Captures Total of 171 Huns in War." July 5:1. Brownwood, TX.

BBC News (British Broadcasting Corporation Magazine)

  2014   "World War One: The Original Code Talkers." May 19. Story by Denise Winterman.   http://www.bbc.co.uk/news/magazine-26963624#page. Accessed November 8, 2015.

Bishinik / Biskinik (The Choctaw Nation Newspaper)

  1986a "D.C. Archives Acknowledge Choctaws as 1st "Code Talkers." July:2.

  1986b "Germans Confused by Choctaw Code Talkers." August:2.

  1986c "Code Talkers Suggested by Choctaw Soldier." September:2.

  1986d "Tributes to Original Choctaw Code Talkers Continue." December:3.

  1987a "Choctaw Code Talkers May Receive International Recognition." February:2, 7.

  1987b "Interest Continues in the Choctaw Code-Talkers. April:8.

  1987c "Solomon Bond Louis Underage When He Enlisted into WWI." April:8.

  1987d "Victor Brown 'Fooled the Germans' in France." April:8.

  1987e "Walter Veach Helped Organize Code-Talkers." April:8.

  1987f "Ben Hampton Remembered as WW I Code-Talker." April:8.

  1987g "Choctaw Language Also Used in WW II for Military Communications." April:9.

  1987h "Joseph Oklahombi, Oklahoma's Greatest War Hero." November:1,6. Story by Barry Plunkett.

  1989a "France to Honor Choctaw Code-Talkers." October:1, 5.

  1989b "Award Presented in Honor of Code-Talkers." November:1, 3.

  1992a "Schlicht Billy Last Living Choctaw Code-Talker Enlisted in WW II." August:4.

  1992b "History of the Choctaw Code-Talkers." August:4.

  1992c "Oklahombi Receives Father's Medals." October:3.

  1994a "Services for WW II Choctaw Code Talker, Schlicht Billy. " January:1, 4.

  1994b "Choctaw Men Were Very First Code-Talkers, Using Their Native Language for Secret Messages in WW I." June:3.

  1996   "Choctaw Code Talkers Original One to Use Native Language in War: 'From Cursing to Code Talking.'" August:4. By John Callaway.

  1997   "Rattan Class Project is Code Talker History." May:1, 4.

  2000a "Albert Billy One of First to Use Native Language to Transmit Coded Messages." March:5. By Phillip Allen.

  2000b "The Late Schlicht Billy Was Last Living Choctaw Code Talker of WWII." March:5. By Phillip Allen.

  2000c "Solomon Bond Louis Underage When He Enlisted.' March:5. By Phillip Allen.

  2000d "Victor Brown Fooled Germans with 'Code.'" March:5. By Phillip Allen.

  2000e "Ben Hampton Was Choctaw Code Talker." March:5. By Phillip Allen.

2000f   "Choctaw Code Talkers of WW I." March:4–5. By Phillip Allen.

2004b   "Ceremony to Unveil Marker at Code Talker's Gravesite." April:2

2004c   "Tombstone Unveiled at Gravesite of Original Code Talker James Edwards." June:1, 3.

2004d   "Specially Minted Medals Sought for Code Talkers." October:1, 3.

2004e   "Contributions of Code Talkers in Military History." November:3.

2005   "Display Pays Tribute to World War I Hero. Joseph Oklahombi Exhibit on Loan to Choctaw Museum Until February 18." January:1.

2006a   "Code Talker Exhibit Premieres." November:1.

2006b   "'Hidden Voices, Coded Words' Tells Story of World War I Code Talkers." December:1.

2006c   "Code Talkers Honored with Exhibits in Oklahoma City." December:3.

2007   "Special Flags Are Given to Code Talker's Families." January:1, 14.

2008a   "Native Language Turns the Tide of Battle." Part 1. By Juanita Jefferson. September:2.

2008b   "Native Language Turns the Tide of Battle." Part 2. By Juanita Jefferson. October:2.

2008c   "Native Language Turns the Tide of Battle." Part 3. By Juanita Jefferson. November:2.

2008d   "Code Talkers to Receive Awards. President Signs Law to Give Choctaw Code Talkers Congressional Medals! November:1–2.

2009   "State Honors Choctaw Code Talkers." April:1

2010a   "Wright City Honors Oklahombi." August:1.

2010b   "Choctaw Nation Honored at 2010 Drum Awards." December:1.

2011   "Quilt Show." October:9.

2013   "Highway Named in Honor of Choctaw Code Talkers." October:1.

2018a   "Code Talkers in France, Again." April:4.

2018b   "Choctaw Code Talkers from WW I and WW II Honored with Monument in Antlers." August:7.

2018c   "Conference in France to Share the Story of the Choctaw Code Talkers Begins Journey to Retrace Otis Leader's Experiences." September:14.

BN (*Blanchard News*)

2009   "Code Talkers Honored Posthumously." April 16:5. Blanchard, OK.

CLJE (Commemorating the Life of James M. Edwards, WW I Original Choctaw Code Talker)

2004   Event Program. James Folsom Cemetery. Whitesboro, Oklahoma. April 20.

Cherokee Nation

2010   "History and Legacy of Cherokee Code Talkers Sought." November 15. http://www.cherokee.org./News/Stories/32170. Accessed May 1, 2011.

CP (*Cherokee Phoenix*)

2017   "WW I Code Talkers Exhibit Opens." November 10. Story by Will Chavez. http://www.cherokeephoenix.org/Article/Index/11751. Accessed November 27, 2017.

Choctaw Days

2012   "Choctaw Days: A Celebration of Our Culture, Heritage, and Tradition. Ma e chi pisa chike! June 20–23." Event program.

Code Talkers.info

2005   Petition to the Congress of the United States on behalf of the Native American Code Talkers of World War I and World War II. http://code talkers.info/content/view/120/.

CR (*Corydon Republican*)

1921   "War Cross to an Indian." November 17.

CGL (*Chronicle of Grand Lake*)

2010   "History and Legacy of Cherokee Code Talkers Sought." November 18.

CRR (*Colgate Record-Register*)

1956   "Legion Honors Otis Leader War Record." July 26:1.

CNN (*Comanche Nation News*)

2013   Historical Day for Comanche Heroes. Special Edition, Thursday, December 12. issuu.com/comanchenation/docs/codetaker_special-edition. Accessed January 10, 2014.

Co-operator

1960   "World War I Hero Killed in Traffic Accident." Excerpt believed to be from a publication of the Wright City Mill, Wright City, Oklahoma. Provided by Jonah Oklahombi, who worked at the mill when his father died, and the Choctaw Nation.

DDD (*Durant Daily Democrat*)

1966   Untitled Photocopy. October 17–18.

1979   "Durant in the Past: Happenings of 40 Years Ago—August 16, 1939." August 16.

DH (*Denison Herald*)

1970   "Indians Save Palefaces: Choctaw Chatter Puzzled Prussians." March 15:1. Story by John Clift. Denison, TX.

DMN (*Dallas Morning News*)

1919   "Indian Awarded War Crosses for Deeds of Valor." September 30:13.

DO (*Daily Oklahoman*)

1917a   "Drafted Indians from Oklahoma Who Have Been Transferred To the 142nd Infantry: Oklahoma Indians to Form Company." November 11.

1917b   "Fifteen Tribes Represented in Indian Company." November 18:B1-2.

1918a   "Even the Indians to Learn French." February 2:4.

1918b   "Indians Squat on Floor at Capitol and Demand to Be U.S. Cavalrymen." February 8:1,10.

1918c   "Full Citizenship for Indian Urged by Gabe E. Parker." February 10:1, 4.

1918d   "Indians Carrying Share of War Load. February 10:1,6.

1918e   "Chilocco Indians in Army Service." March 3:B-3.

1918f   "Oklahoma Men Are Not Quitters. Few at Bowie Desert; Ignorant Indians Are Being Eliminated." March 4:4.

1918g   "Indians in Trenches at Bowie. Cherokees Spend Four Days and Nights at This Warfare Practice." March 24.

1918h   "Bowie Men Will March as to War." April 11.

1918i "Twenty-Seven Thousand Soldiers of Oklahoma and Texas Division March in Review, Fit for Battle." April 12.

1918j "Indian at Bowie Ready to Go." May 5:C-11,14.

1919a "Indian Tongue Used as Code to Dodge Spies. Enemy Listeners Couldn't Translate Army Orders in Choctaw." January 21:3.

1919b "Oklahoma Indian Is Model. Wounded and Gassed, French Call Him Type." February 2:Section B.

1919c "Cherokee Indian Wins War Cross and Medal." February 20.

1919d "Oklahoma Guardsmen in Action." March 9:C1, 14. Story by Captain Ben Chastaine. Part 1 of 5.

1919e "Indians Show Up Best in Open Fighting." March 15.

1919f "Oklahoma's Own Reach the Battle Line. Sooner Soldiers Called to Front to Fill Line Gap." March 16 D:1–2. Part 2 of 5. Story by Captain Ben H. Chastaine.

1919g "Choctaw Tongue Gave Surprise to the Germans." March 23, B-1.

1919h "Through Hell to the Hindenburg Line." March 23:D1,4. Story by Captain Ben H. Chastaine. Part 3 of 5.

1919i "Ranking Indian Officer in Overseas Forces, Son of Chief of the Creeks. Returns at Head of Machine Gunners." March 23, B-1.

1919j "Digging in and Holding on Death Ridge." March 30, D-1,4. Story by Captain Ben H. Chastaine. Part 4 of 5.

1919k "On the Heels of the Fleeing Foe." April 6, D-1,4. Story by Captain Ben H. Chastaine. Part 5 of 5.

1919l "Indian Yank Helped Take 171 Boches. 'People Killer' Apparently with Putnam Farmer Boy in Feat." June 29:1.

1919m "Indians Celebrate Return of Modern Warriors with Ancient War Dances. August 24:B1–2.

1919n "Seven Tribes Hold Great Scalp Dance Near Pawnee Celebrating Braves' Return." September 2:4.

1919o "Indian Use Hun Scalps in Dance." September 13:1.

1919p "Oklahoma's Greatest Indian Hero." October 19:16-B.

1937 "Our No. 1 War Hero Wants a Job." January 17:D1,8.

1941 "State Indian-Youth Put on Show for Army. Comanches Become 'Pets' at Fort Benning, Ga." January 12:A-7.

1948 "Mose Bellmard Dies, Colorful Indian Fighter in World War I." March 29.

1959 "State Doughboy Keeps His Spirit." June 7:8E.

1960 "Heroic Indian Killed." April 14:1.

1962 "Indian War Heroes Many." November 11:A23. Story by Roy P. Stewart.

DOI (Department of the Interior, Office of Indian Affairs)

1922 Office of Indian Affairs, Bulletin No. 12, American Indians and Government Administration. Washington, DC.

1927 "The American Indian in the World War." Bulletin 15. Government Printing Office. Washington, DC.

DR (Democrat Record)

1919 "Joseph Oklahombi Cited by General Petain: And Given Croix De Guerre for Conspicuous Bravery." June 26:8.

DurantDemocrat.com

2013   "Highway Named in Honor of Choctaw Code Talkers." Story by Deidre Bacon, Choctaw Nation of Oklahoma. August 17. http://durrantdemocrat .com/apps/pbcs.dll/article?AID=/2013082/news/308209989/highway -named-in-honor-of-choctaw-code-talkers.

Edwards Jr., James M.

2004   Letter read in honor of James M. Edwards Sr. during installment of new tombstone, James-Folsom Cemetery, Whiteboro, OK, April 20. Choctaw Nation Archives, Durant, OK.

FWS (*Fort Warren Sentinel*)

1941   "Capt. Horner Put Indian Sign on Germans in War. First Man to Use an Indian Language in Sending Code." June.

FWST (Fort Worth Star Telegram, Fort Worth, Texas).

1917a   Choctaw Indians Visit Relative at Camp Bowie. November 15:1

1917b   Famous Redskin Punter Who Will Play Here Sunday. November 22:8.

1917c   Commissioner Tells Indians Why This War Is Justified. December 1:8.

1918a   Indians Purchase $100,000 War Stamps. January 31:3.

1918b   Indian Chieftains in War Paint Offer 10 Cavalry Regiments. February 8:3

1918c   Guardian of Indians Goes Home Pleased. April 9:3

1918d   Making Fighting Sammies Out of Oklahoma Indians. April 14:9. Story by B. C. Utecht.

1919a   Major Robinson, Back from France, Describes Victories of the Thirty-Sixth Division. January 19:1.

1919b   Story of the 36th Division is Related in "Stars and Stripes." Official Publication of A.E.F. May 11:6.

2007   "The First Code Talkers." September 16:B1,B6.

GXM (*GX Magazine*)

2007   "Ceremony Honors WWI Choctaw Code Talkers.' 4(11):38.

HC (*Hello Choctaw*)

1976   "Choctaw War Hero, Order Given in Choctaw." Choctaw Tribal Newspaper, May 1:2.

HI (*Helena Independent*)

1942   "The Haskin Letter: Indians Volunteer Their Service. " February 18:4.

Holman, Mark

2018   "World War I Code Talker Story Revealed." Sitting Bull College Library. October 1. https://sittingbullcollege.wixsite.com/website/single-post /2018/10/01/World-War-I-Code-Talker-Story-Revealed. Accessed September 22, 2019.

HT (*Hammond Times*)

1940   "Choctaw Hero to Fight Again." October 23:25.

HINU (Haskell Indian Nations University)

2018   Haskell Cultural Center and Museum: Honoring Our Native Veterans. http://haskell.edu/cultural-center/exhibitions/tribal-military/. Accessed September 12, 2018.

HUa (Horner-Unknown-a)

c.1942 "'Lige' Horner May Again See Overseas Service." Unknown Arkansas newspaper clipping. Courtesy of Kathryn Horner Widder.

HUb (Horner-Unknown-b)

1953 "Lige Horner Completes Thirty Years of Military Service." Unknown newspaper clipping. Courtesy of Kathryn Horner Widder. Near Weiser, ID.

HUc (Horner-Unknown-c)

1953 "Horner Retires After 30 Years of Military Service." Unknown newspaper clipping Dated Thursday, June 25. Courtesy of Kathryn Horner Widder. Near Weiser, ID.

Hunhoff, Bernie

2007 The Last Lakota Code Talker. *South Dakota Magazine.* May-June. http://www.southdakotamagazine.com/clarence-wolf-guts. Accessed November 24, 2013.

IL (*Indian Leader*)

1917 Cherokee Indians of North Carolina Ready for Service in Uncle Sam's Army. XXI(9):3.

1935 Indian War Hero Rejects Hollywood. 39(13):12.

Indian Record

1970 The American Indian in the World War, Office of Indian Affairs Bulletin 15; Bureau of Indian Affairs, "Special Issue: Indians in the Military," November.

ISJ (*Indian School Journal*)

1919 Winnebago Indians Upheld Record of Ancestors in World War. 19(9):351. Carlisle Indian School. Carlisle, PA.

Indian Sign

1940 Unsourced news article. Based on four adjacent columns of printed material, this article appears to be an Oklahoma City area newspaper circa late 1940.

Kanza Newsletter

2008 "Kaw Code Talkers." 2(1):16. March.

KN (*Kaw Nation*)

2011 "A Timeline of the Kaw Nation." Developed by Kanza Museum, Crystal Douglas, museum director. http://www.kawnation.com/wp-content /uploads/2012/03/ Timeline.pdf. Accessed February 4, 2019.

KXII News

2018 "Dedication Bridges History with Future Generations." Thursday, April 19. http://www.kxii.com/content/news/Dedication-bridges-history -with-future-generations. Accessed April 20, 2018.

LC (*Lawton Constitution*)

1960 "Car Hits, Kills State War Hero." April 14:2.

1989 "Joseph Oklahombi." October 3:4B.

LJ (*Lakota Journal*)

2001 "Descendant Remembers First Lakota Code Talkers." February 4:B5.

LN (*Lima News*)

   1921   "Hero." October 20:1.

LS (*Lowell Sun*)

   1932   "Asks U.S. Aid." December 27:6. Lowell, Mass.

LSFE (La Société des Quarante Hommes et Huit Chevaux [The Society of Forty Men and Eight Horses].

   2017   History Highlights of the Forty and Eight. 40 & 8 La Société des Quarante Hommes et Huit Chevaux. http://www.fortyandeight.org/history-of-the-408/. Accessed March 18, 2017.

Masterkey

   1941   "Indians as Code Transmitters." 15(6):240, November.

MD (*McAlester Democrat*)

   1961   "Otis Leader, Former Scipio Rancher, One of War 1's Most Decorated Soldiers Dies Sat." March 30:16.

MDNR (*Miami Daily News-Record*)

   1932   "War Hero Seeks Aid." December 8:3.

MG (*McCurtain Gazette / McCurtain Daily Gazette*)

   1919   "Joseph Oklahombi Cited by General Petain." June 25:1.

   1932   "Oklahoma's Great Hero Asking Aid of Government. Joseph Oklahombi Is an Outstanding Hero of the World War." December 14:2.

   1935   "McCurtain County World War Hero Rejects Movie Offer to Keep $12.00 A Month Job." October 2:6.

   1940   Untitled photocopy, June 1.

   1960   "Joseph Oklahombi Is Killed. Truck Takes Life of World War I Hero." April 16:1.

   1989   "Wilsons, Roberts Help Honor Choctaw Code-Talkers." November 3:1.

   2004   "Some Historians Caution Against Puffery on World War I Choctaw Code Talkers." September 22:1.

   2007   "Choctaw Code Talkers Featured in Documentary." January 10:1.

MN (*McAlester News*)

   1961   "Rancher, One of War's Most Decorated Soldier Dies Sat." March. McAlester, OK. Undated news clipping, courtesy of Judy Allen, Choctaw Nation.

MNC (*McAlester News-Capital*)

   1917a   "Action of German Suspects Watched." April 6:1.

   1917b   "Spy Suspects Turn Out to Be Ranchers. Men Are Swiss: Are Stocking Up Ranch in Hughes County" April 13:8.

   1961   "Otis Leader, One of Top Heroes, Dies." March 27:2.

MSGN (*McCurtain Sunday Gazette-News*)

   1996   "Correcting Another Bit of Popular History." November 10:12. Story by Louis Coleman.

MSPTD (Muskogee Sunday Phoenix and Times Democrat)

   1955   "Typical' Doughboy Critically Ill." May 1. Section II:1.

MTD (*Muskogee Times-Democrat*)

   1919a   "Wily Yankees Outwitted Boches. Choctaw Dialect Used for Telegraphic Messages at Front: Wire-Tappers Beaten. April 26:1.

1919b "Oklahoma Indian Chosen as Model of Typical Yank." December 17:1.

MTR (*Marshalltown Times Republican*)

1941a Original Americans. February 21.

1941b Enemy Will Have Tough Time Decoding Messages of 168th. February 26.

NA (*Native American*)

1918a "Indian Soldiers." 19(11):170.

1918b "Indians Big Factor in War." 19(13):204.

1918c "The Choctaws in the War." 19(17):274–275.

NAT (*Native American Times*)

2010 "History and Legacy of Cherokee Code Talkers Sought." Nov. 11. Written by Travis Noland. http://www.nativetimes.com/life/people/4595-history-and-legacy-of-cherokee-codetakers-sought.

NCMF (National Cryptologic Museum Foundation)

(n.d.) "New Native American Code Talker Exhibit." https://cryptologic foundation.org/visit/museum/museum_exhibits/new-native-american-code-talker-exhibit.html. Accessed November 27, 2017.

NDS (*Nowata Daily Star*)

1947 "Adair School Board Member Is Killed in Auto Collision." Oct. 9.

NFG (*Niagara Falls Gazette*)

1941 "Indian Languages Become "Code" in Army Maneuvers. Classic World War Trick Again Being Employed by American Troops. August 31. By Science Service. September 2, 1941:11.

NMAI (National Museum of the American Indian)

2007 Resources, "Use of the Term Code Talker" (Native Words, Native Warriors. http://www.nmai.si.edu/education/codetalkers/html/resources.html. Accessed 2007.

NN (*Nocona News*)

1920 "The American Model. Choctaw Indian Chosen by French Sculpture for Statue of "American Fighting Man." February 13:4.

NSA/CSS (National Security Agency/Central Security Service)

2014 NSA/CSS Honors Code Talkers; Presents Plaque to National Museum of the American Indian. NSA Press Release, April 8, Fort Meade, Maryland. http://www.nsa.gov/public_info/press_room/2014/code_talkers.shtml. Accessed May 2, 2014.

NYA (*New York American*)

1921 "Amazing Code Machine That Sent Messages Safely to U.S. Army in War Baffles Experts." November 13:L-9.

NYEW (*New York Evening World*)

1919 "150 Indians Back after Fooling Foe by Choctaw Talk. Redmen Arriving To-Day on Pueblo Furnished Puzzle and Terror for Germans." May 31.

NYS (*New York Sun*)

1938 "Choctaw Stopped War Wire Tappers: Germans at St. Mihiel Finally Circumvented by Indians of the U.S. Forces." The Sun's Rays, February 2.

NYT (*New York Times*)

1917　"Indian Wants to Put $800,000 in War Bonds." Monday June 4:3.

1918　"On the Warpath." August 2, Section 1:10.

1919　"Two Soldiers Lost from Troopship." June 1:20.

1920　"Indians for the Army." February 14:10.

1940　"Comanches Again Called for Service." December 13:16.

1941a　"Indians Volunteer for Defense Army, to Speak Another Dialect." February 16:32.

1941b　"Indians' 'Code' Upsets Foe. They Speed Dial Messages by Radio in War Games." August 31:21.

OCN (*Oklahoma City News*)

1928　"Officer Who Led Indians in Rout of Germans Now Sets Type-Enemy Fooled by Wires Sent in Language of Red Men." April 5.

OCT (*Oklahoma City Times*)

1919a　"142nd Leaves City for Camp Bowie: They Traveled Kilometers, Knots and Miles to Get Here. June 12:1.

1919b　"Indian Posed for French as Typical Yank." June 30:3.

1958　"Long Memoried Friend Seeks to Aids State Hero." July 14:5.

OKN (*Oklahoma News*)

1932　"State Indian Who Captured 171 War Foes Asks U.S. Aid." December 7:1.

OMHF (Oklahoma Military Hall of Fame)

2012a　"13th Annual Banquet and Induction Ceremony Program, November 9.

2012b　Choctaw Code Talkers of World War I and World War II, Induction Certificate, November 9.

ON (*Osage News*)

2012　"Osages Included in Second Set of Code Talker Coins Reviewed by CFA." August 3. http://www.osagenews.org/en/article2012/08/03/osages-included-in-second-set-of-code-talker-coins-reviewed-by-CFA/. Accessed February 9, 2017.

2016　"Granddaughter of WWI Osage Code Talker to Receive Medal at Veteran Day Dance." Veterans Day November 11. http://www.osagenews.org/en/article2016/11/08grandaughter-of-wwI-osage-code-talker-to-receive-medal-at-veterans-day-dance. Accessed February 9, 2017.

ONO (*Osage Nation*)

2013　"Osage Code Talkers Honored with U.S. Congressional Gold Medal." December 12. http://www.osagenation.co/osage-code-talkers-honored-with-u-s-congressional-gold-medal/. Accessed December 23, 2013.

OTH (*Olean Times Herald*)

1940　"Choctaw Hero of A.E.F. Ready to Fight Again." October 29:7.

Phillips, Mary

2010　"French Artist Picked Outstanding Oklahoman as Subject of War Painting." August 17. newsok.com/french-artist-picked-outstanding.oklahoman-as-subject-of-war-painting/article/3485815. Accessed February 25, 2014.

PCN (*Ponca City News*)

1948a　"Mose Bellmard Dies after Long Illness." March 28:8.

1948b   "Bellmard Led Colorful Life." March 28:8. Story by Joel Fant.

Pyle, Gregory E.

1999   "Official State of the Nation Address by Choctaw Chief," September 6. Choctaw Nation Archives. Choctaw Nation Headquarters, Durant, OK.

2007   Letter to the Choctaw Nation. August 28. Choctaw Nation Archives, Choctaw Nation Headquarters, Durant, OK.

2012   "Medal Design for Code Talkers Ready for U.S. Mint." http://www .choctawnation.com/news-room/from-the-desk-of-brchief-gregory-epyle /medaldesign-for-code-talkers-ready-for-u-s-mint. Accessed April 28, 2014.

RES (Rattan Elementary School)

1997   Choctaw Code Talkers in World War I. Sixth Grade Boys' Reading Project, Rattan, OK.

SCP (*Sioux County Pioneer*)

1921   "Returned Soldier-Hero Buried at Cannon Ball." September 22:1.

SCT (*St. Cloud Times*)

1940   "Choctaw Hero of AEF Again Ready to Enter Battle." October 22:4.

SDA (*Somerset Daily American*)

1943   "Governor Joins Crew Lands Red Snapper." May 3:1.

Southern Workman

1918a   Hampton War Notes: Letters from France. 47(11):551–555. November.

1918b   Hampton's Honor Roll 47(12):608. December.

SP (*Seminole Producer*)

1940   "Letter Box: A Tour of Southeastern Oklahoma." By Charles Wilburn and Roy Sullivan. March 20:10.

Starr, Arigon

2014   *Tales of the Mighty Code Talkers.* Vol. 1. INC Comics, West Hollywood, CA.

Stars and Stripes

1918a   "13 Redskin Tribes in Single Company." November 8:8.

1918b   "Argonne Battle in Second Phase, Hardest Job Yet." October 11:1.

1919a   "Boche Wire Tappers Run into New Code. Sioux Observer and Receiver Make Things Easy for Gunners." Friday, January 10:5.

1919b   "Yank Indian Was Heap Big Help in Winning the War." May 30:1, 3.

TA (*Talihina American*)

2004   "WWI Original Choctaw Code Talker." April 29:1.

TAH (*Arrow Head*)

1919   "Six Choctaws among Recipients of Crosses." 1(1):2. February 27.

TDW (*Tulsa Daily World*)

1917a   "Suspected Spy Released." April 10:1.

1917b   "Hold Spy Thruout War." April 17:1.

Telephone Warriors

2007   *Telephone Warriors—Choctaw Code Talkers of WWI.* Film Premiere Program. March 1. Oklahoma History Center, Oklahoma City. OK.

Telephone Warriors Draft

2007   "Telephone Warriors: The Story of the Choctaw Code Talkers." Draft, May 31. Copy courtesy of Judy Allen and the Choctaw Nation Archives.

TMFM (Brigadier General John C. L. Scribner Texas Military Forces Museum)

2007   *The BG John C. L. Scribner Texas Military Forces Museum Honors the Choctaw Code Talkers of World War One.* Twelve-page event program. September 16.

2014   "Choctaw Indian Code Talkers of World War I." Camp Mabry. Austin, TX. http://www.texasmilitaryforcesmuseum.org/choctaw/codetalkers .htm. Accessed March 26, 2014.

TO (the *Oklahoman*)

1936   "America's Typical Soldier is at Home on Lehigh's Hilltop." Article by J. H. Biles. August 9.

1937   "Our No. 1 War Hero Wants a Job." January 17:59, 66. By R. G. Miller.

1941   "Tongue Twister Ready. Choctaw Who Foiled Germans in 1918 Wants to Go." December 21:60.

1970   "Enemy Couldn't 'Cut' Messages in Choctaw." March 22:21.

2004   "Senate to Hear Choctaw Chief: Committee Testimony Relates to World War I Code Talkers." September 21:3A.

2010   "State Doughboy Was Image of U.S. Soldier." August 17:3D.

2012   "Military Hall Honors State Heroes." August 12:6A.

2015   "Oklahombi's Honor." June 4:1A-2A.

TT (*Twin Territories*)

1991   "Otis W. Leader, America's Mr. Doughboy." 1(8):7.

TTF (*Texas Trail of Fame*)

2010   Texas Trail of Fame, 2010 Inductees Program. Fort Worth Stockyards National Historic District. Fort Worth, TX. October 23.

TW (*Tulsa World*)

1937   "How the Kaiser's Wire Tappers Were Balked by Oklahoma Indian Using Choctaw at Front." November 14, Section Four:8.

2004   "Choctaw Chief Will Tout Code Talkers." September 22:A15.

Unknown

1986   "Choctaw Code Talkers. Native Language Turns the Tide of Battle." August.

USA Veterans Magazine (The United States of America Veterans Magazine).

2006   "The WW I Unbreakable Code." Winter:8–10.

VL (*Valliant Leader*)

1987   "Oklahoma's Greatest War Hero Also Choctaw Code Talker." September 9:1. Valliant, OK. Story by Barry Plunkett.

WFTRN (*Wichita Falls Times Record News*)

2018   "Armistice Day Talks Honor Native Americans." 1B, 3B.

WP (*Washington Post*)

1919   "Y.M.C.A. Secretary Honored. W.R. Farmer, of Pittsburgh, among Those Given Service Crosses." July 22:6.

WS (*Weiser Signal*)

1938   "Eastern Papers Tell of Local Man's Experiences in World War." March 3:3.

1941   "Capt. Horner Put Indian Sign on Germans in War. First Man to Use an Indian Language in Sending Code." June 12.

YD (*Yale Democrat*)
    1921   "Joseph Oklahombi: Choctaw War Hero." October 26.

Films

Visionmaker Video
    2010   *Choctaw Code Talkers*. Valerie Red-Horse producer/director/writer, and Gale Anne Hurd producer/writer. Native American Public Telecommunications, Lincoln, NE.

Warner Brothers
    1941   *Sergeant York*. Warner Brothers Pictures Inc. Hollywood, CA.

INDEX

1st Infantry Division (WW I), 115, 163–169, 171, 172, 179, 187–189, 199, 225, 261, 270–271, 275
3rd Infantry Division (WW I), 108, 135, 190–193, 224, 225, 272
30th Infantry Division (WW I), 6, 33–42, 55, 67, 108, 176–177, 187, 189, 224–225, 275, 283n3–6
36th infantry Division (WW I), 43–117, 122–159, 170–171, 176–179, 184–185, 193–194, 199–202, 208–210, 223–225, 229, 236, 254–267, 268, 275, 286n46, 286–287n48, 287n54, 288n61, 290–291n114, 291n123, 294n152, 299n99, 306n6
90th Infantry Division (WW I), 19, 48, 100, 108, 117, 135, 177–184, 187–189, 224, 235–236, 255, 267–270, 275, 286n46, 299n99, 303n3, 304n19
7th Infantry Regiment (1st Division, WW I), 190–193, 224
119th Infantry Regiment (30th Division, WW I), 34–41, 224
120th Infantry Regiment (30th Division, WW I), 34–41, 224
141st Infantry Regiment (36th Division, WW I), 61, 63, 71, 73, 78, 83, 89–91, 107, 126, 138, 141–146, 150, 158, 287n48, 287n54
142nd Infantry Regiment (36th Division, WW I), 27–30, 45–107, 122–136, 143–146, 149–151, 176–177, 180, 185, 188–189, 193–195, 198, 202, 208, 224, 230, 254–267, 268, 273–274, 287n54, 289–290n98, 291n123, 292n127, 294n152, 295n16, 299n99, 311n2; "Millionaire Company," 50, 59; photos of, 110–117

143rd Infantry Regiment (36th Division, WW I), 47, 50, 63, 71, 91, 107, 184, 185, 224, 255
144th Infantry Regiment (36th Division, WW I), 61, 63, 71, 78

Adair, George (Cherokee; WW I), 135, 176–177, 254; photo of, 117
Adair, William (Cherokee; WW I), 303n3
Allen, Judy (Choctaw): photos of, 119–120; work with Choctaw code talkers, 83, 87, 211, 214, 254
American Expeditionary Forces (AEF), campaigns in WW I, 253; casualty rates, 29; divisional intelligence of, 66–70; field intelligence of, 63–66; Native Americans in, 14; in WW I, 1, 7, 12–14
American Indians. See Native Americans (WW I)
American Legion Post 143 (Stephen Youngdeer Post), 14, 34, 40, 284n10
American Legion posts, 21, 156–157, 162, 172–173, 237, 258–259, 262, 270, 271. See also American Legion Post 143 (Stephen Youngdeer Post)
Arn, Arnold, 161–162
Asepermy, Lanny (Comanche), 181, 212, 303n5
assimilation, US government, military and missionary motivations for, 17–20, 22–26, 31, 48, 227, 239–245, 255. See also boarding schools
Atchavit, Calvin (Comanche; WW I), 100–101, 135, 179–183, 216, 239, 267–270, 303n13; photo of, 117
Atchavit, Robert (Comanche), 183, 216
Atoka Agreement (1897), 242

Baconrind, George (Osage), 89, 104, 131, 185, 290n110, 295n114

Baker, Newton D., 16–18, 26

Barnes, Charles H. (142nd Inf., WW I), 48, 56–59, 75, 131, 202, 296n44

Bellmard, Mose (Kaw), 47, 53, 80, 194–195, 290n112

Big Thunder, Robert (Ho-Chunk), 190–192, 271–272

Billy, Albert (Choctaw), 44, 80, 86, 89, 102, 136, 203, 219, 239; biography, 254–255

Billy, Lisa (Choctaw), 211, 215

Billy, Schlicht (Choctaw; WW II), 204, 205, 219

Black, Temple (Cheyenne; 142nd Inf. Reg.), and Choctaw code talker training, 85, 94, 103–106, 128, 152, 291n123

Bloor, Alfred W. (142nd Infantry), 46, 48, 56, 68, 69–71, 77–83, 86, 89, 91–95, 100–107, 125–129, 132, 134–135, 185, 201–204, 214, 229–231, 260, 286n46, 287n48, 288n67, 291n114, 293n148, 294n152; memo (1919), 93–95; orders in Choctaw, 273–274; photo of, 111

boarding schools, 22–26, 44, 48–49, 179, 220, 223, 242, 244–245, 252, 283n25, 284n9. See also assimilation, US government, military and missionary motivations for

Bobb, Bertram (Choctaw), 206, 211, 246

Bobb, Mitchell (Choctaw), 44, 51, 80–90, 93, 98–99, 102, 106, 123, 205, 212, 219, 239, 256; biography, 255; bridge (photo), 120; photo of, 110

Boren, Dan, 121, 214–215

Brown, Nicholas E. (Choctaw), 122, 143

Brown, Victor (Choctaw), 49, 87, 89–90, 135–136, 156, 204–205, 219, 247–248; biography, 255–256

Browning Automatic Rifle (WW I), 73–75

Burke Act (1906), 20, 238

buzzer phone, 67, 69–70, 94, 100, 101, 107, 292n134; 304n19

Camp Bowie (Texas), 18, 19, 27, 43, 45–52, 80, 107, 110, 137–138, 293n151

Carr, Bob (aka Marty Beaver; Choctaw), 122

Carterby, Ben (Choctaw), 44, 45, 49, 82–83, 86–87, 89–90, 92, 136, 151–152, 205, 212, 219, 239, 247, 255, 259, 263, 289n90, 294n1; biography, 256–257

ciphers, 7–8, 10, 223, 225, 227, 234. See also codes and cryptography

CIVA. See Comanche Indian Veteran's Association (CIVA)

Chastaine, Ben H. (142nd Infantry), 42, 52–53, 56, 59, 71–81, 106, 132, 145, 149–150, 201, 214, 268, 286n38, 291n114, 293n15, 298n73

Chateau Thierry (France), 19, 27, 166–173, 190–192, 272

Cherokee, 30, 46–47, 184, 246; written language of, 243–244

Cherokee code talkers: Eastern Band (WW I), 5, 6, 33–42, 108, 176–177, 188–189, 192, 225, 230, 244, 251, 275, 283–284; Oklahoma (WW I), 117, 135, 176–177, 196, 224, 230, 251, 254

Cheyenne, 16, 24, 47, 85, 133, 193–196, 223, 237, 279, 308n1. See also Black, Temple (Cheyenne; 142nd Inf. Reg.)

Cheyenne and Arapaho, 16

Chippewa-Oneida code talkers (32nd Division, WW II), 99, 232, 234, 251, 275, 284n11, 311n1

Choctaw code talkers, WW I, 43–120; bridges named for, 218–220; code terms, 84, 96, 104–105; documentary films on, 208, 212, 221; effectiveness of, 203; idea to use in WW I, 80–83; identification of members, 83–90; individual biographies, 254–267; lists of, 88–90; Knight of the National Order of Merit (France), 205, 276; Lone Star Medal of Valor, 210, 277; memorial (photo), 116; messages by, 273–274; personal experiences of, 135–175; postwar experiences of, 121–175; postwar publicity of, 125–135; proposed future use, 130–131;

recognition of, 197–221; training at Louppy-le-Petit, 78–79, 84–85, 89, 94–96, 104–105, 135, 152, 224, 291n123; use of in WW I, 90–99; use of in WW II, 204–205, 219

Choctaw Code Talkers Association (CCTA), 207–208, 211–212, 218, 221, 247, 250, 276; committee (photo), 120; design of, 208

Choctaw Nation: language and schools, 241–243; receiving code talker Congressional Gold Medal (photo), 121; removal of, 242–243; Treaty of Dancing Rabbit Creek (1830), 242; written language, 243–244. *See also* Choctaw code talkers, WW I

Chuculate, Alexander (Cherokee), 30

Church War Cross (awarded to Choctaws), 86, 122, 267, 299n99

ciphers, 6, 8, 10, 223, 234. *See also* codes and cryptography

Civil War (communications in), 5, 9

Clark, George (Comanche), 181–183, 268–269; photo of, 117

Cloud, Benjamin (Cheyenne), 19, 223–224, 291n123, 308n1

codes and cryptography, 1–10. *See also* ciphers

code talkers. See Native Americans (WW I)

Code Talkers Recognition Act (2008), 2–3, 5, 42, 88, 185, 188, 190, 193–194, 196, 214–216, 234–235, 251, 277; author testifying for (photo), 119; US Senate testimony for (2004), 213–214

Codynah, Haddon (Comanche), 178

Coffman, Napanee Brown (Choctaw), 135, 247, 256

Colbert, Benjamin Jr. (Choctaw), 87–89, 90, 219, 299n98, 306n24, 307n39; biography, 257

Coleman, Louis, 137, 143, 153, 158–159, 307n53

Collier, John, 240

Comanche code talkers (WW I), 1–6, 1–12, 23, 46–47, 99, 100, 107, 117, 130, 135, 176–184, 193, 196, 212–216, 224, 230, 232–240, 246, 250–251,

275–280; Comanche Code Talker Trailway (2019), 221; individual biographies, 267–270; Knight of the National Order of Merit (France), 205, 276; recognition, 205, 208, 220–221; Spirit Talker Statue, 277; in WW II, 203, 220, 235

Comanche Indian Veteran's Association (CIVA), 212, 216, 250, 277, 279

Conlan, Czarina Colbert (Choctaw), 152–153, 157–158, 299n98, 301n147

Conwoop, Gilbert P. (Comanche), 181–183, 269; photo of, 117

Croix de Guerre. *See* French military medals (WW I)

Curtis Act (1898), 238, 242

Davenport, George (Choctaw), 51, 81, 86–90, 99, 134, 219, 247; biography, 257–258; photo of, 112

Davenport, Joseph (also James; Choctaw), 51, 81, 86–90, 93, 98–99, 102, 106, 123, 219, 239; biography, 258; photo of, 110

Dawes Act (1887), 20

Dixon, Joseph, 15, 16, 23, 29–31, 41, 80–81, 83–86, 98, 102–104, 123, 128–130, 223, 229, 231, 235, 239, 240, 248, 282n11–12, 293n140; and Wanamaker Expeditions, 15, 31

draft. *See* Selective Service Act (1917); Native Americans (WW I)

dugouts (German defensive structures), 30, 31, 36, 59, 61, 64–66, 69–71, 73, 76, 94, 124, 144–151, 264, 298n73

Durant, Jonas (Choctaw), 86, 88, 99, 123; biography, 267

Eddy, John, and Native American Veterans research, 16, 26, 84, 95, 100–102, 128, 132–135, 179, 223, 231, 235, 282, 292, 295, 308

Edwards, James M. (Choctaw), 45, 49, 52, 80–90, 92, 93, 98–99, 102–106, 134, 136, 197, 203, 205, 207, 212, 219, 230, 246, 263, 291, 294n1, 295n21, 309n13; biography, 258–259; photo of, 110

Edwards, James M., Jr. (Choctaw), 207
Edwards, Tewanna, 210–211, 262

First Nations Peoples (Canadian
Natives), 193
Ford, Charles M., 141–142, 145–146,
150, 297n65
Forest Ferme (France, WW I), 54, 56,
62, 70–95, 98–99, 103–104, 107, 111,
177, 198–202, 224, 251, 266, 273,
279, 286n46, 290n98, 291n114,
293n148, 294n152, 297n65,
297n68; assault on, 70–79; map of,
91; name of, 62
Fort Sill (Oklahoma), 23, 45, 157, 256,
259–266, 279, 282, 293
Frazier, Tobias (Choctaw), 45, 51,
80–81, 87–90, 99, 134–135, 152,
183, 205, 209, 212, 219, 245, 247,
289n91, 299n94; biography,
259–260; photo of, 114
Frazier, T. W. (Choctaw), 247
French military medals (WW I): Croix
de Guerre, 27, 122, 137–144, 153–154,
157–158, 167, 169–171, 174, 198, 262,
264, 299n98–99; definition, 140;
Silver Citation Star, 154

German army (WW I), 13, 38, 54–56,
106, 161; dugouts, 144–145; at Forest
Ferme, 70–84, 87, 91, 107; monitoring Allied communications, 7, 11–12,
36, 65–67, 83, 93–94, 97, 108, 129,
133–134; at St. Etienne, 57–63, 141,
145–151; views of Native Americans,
123–125, 184–185. See also Prussian
Guard Divisions
Gooding, Carrie Miller, 108–109
Gooding, Louis (Choctaw), 108–109,
294n157
Gorman, Zonnie (Diné/Navajo), 281n3
Greble, Edwin St. John, 43, 51, 291n114

Hampton, Benjamin (Choctaw), 81,
87–90, 99, 133, 204, 205, 219, 230,
247, 295n21, 296n37, 309n13; biography, 260–261; photo of, 113
Hinman, Richard (Ponca), 30–31
Hix, John, 99, 132–133

Ho-Chunk (Winnebago) code talkers (WW I), 3, 5, 6, 33, 108, 176,
190–193, 196, 225, 246, 251; article
on (photo), 118; individual biographies of, 271–272, 275
Hooker, Kathryn (Choctaw), 247
Horner, Elijah Whitt (36th Division),
29–31, 47, 52, 56, 59–62, 77, 80–85,
88–93, 96–99, 102, 103, 107, 110,
115, 123–125, 127, 129–132, 152, 185,
195, 230, 231, 233, 248–249, 260,
279, 289n86, 292n127, 295n27; letter on Choctaw code talkers (1942),
97–98; military service of, 287n51

Indian Citizenship Act (1924),
239–240
Indian Reorganization Act (1934),
240–241
Indian Scout Syndrome (Holm coinage), 17, 29, 125, 198, 227
influenza (WW I), 53, 55, 71, 165, 258,
305n28

Johnson, Noel (Choctaw; WW I), 51,
81, 86–88, 93, 99, 106, 112, 123, 136,
219; biography, 261; death of, 261;
photo of, 112
Johnston, Philip, 311n1

Kahn, Julius (California), and Indian
Cavalry Bill (HR 3970), 15–17, 240
Kirk, C. (Klamath), 130

Lavine, Abraham Lincoln (142nd
Infantry), 80, 84, 86, 89, 91, 185,
290n.114, 295n27; article by,
130–131
Lawless, Beth (Choctaw): photo of, 216;
school class project of, 206
Leader, Otis W. (Choctaw), 44, 87–90,
134, 160–175, 183, 197–198, 210–212,
219, 276, 302, 308; biography,
261–262; capture of Germans,
167–168; as code talker, 170–171;
military awards of, 167, 171; painting
of, 164–165; photo of, 115; suspected
as spy, 160–164, 173
Lee, Crockett, 161–162, 301n38

Lewis, Solomon. *See* Louis (Lewis), Solomon
Locke, Benjamin Davis (Choctaw), 46–47, 251, 311n2
Longtail, John (Ho-Chunk), 190–192, 272
Loudner, Don (Hunkpapa Dakota), 213
Louis (Lewis), Solomon, 45, 49, 51, 81–83, 86–90, 93, 98–99, 102, 106, 110, 122–123, 131, 136, 199, 204–205, 219, 221, 249, 284, 289n91, 290n110, 297n54, 299n96; biography of, 262–263; photo of, 116
Louisiana maneuvers/war games (1941), 207, 232, 274, 311n1

Mahseet, Harold (Comanche/Ottawa), 48, 50–51, 285n18
Marty, Karl, 161–162
May, Karl, 123
Maytubby, Pete (Chickasaw/Choctaw), 45, 51, 52, 81–82, 86–90, 99, 102, 205, 219, 239, 289, 310n45; biography of, 263
McKenzie, Parker P. (Kiowa), 239
McMillian, Ruth Frazier (Choctaw), 209, 212–215, 245, 247, 259–260
Meadows, William C.: Native American code talker research, 3–6, 208, 214, 277; US Senate testimony of (photo), 119
Meiklejohn, George D., 15
Meriam Report (*The Problem of Indian Administration*, 1928), 240
Meskwaki code talkers (34th Division, WW II), 2, 3, 99, 196, 213, 232, 234, 251, 275
Meuse-Argonne campaign (WW I), 54–78. *See also* Forest Ferme (France, WW I); St. Etienne (WW I)
Mexican border, Indian service on, 15, 34–35, 43, 46, 163, 185, 223, 266, 311n2
Morgan, Thomas J., 242
Morrissey, William J. (36th Division, WW I), 56, 80–84, 100–105, 127–128, 195, 226, 235, 255; Choctaw code terms, 95–96

Nahquaddy, Albert, Jr. (Comanche), 178, 183, 303n9
Nahquaddy, Albert, Sr. (Comanche), 178, 181, 183–184; biography of, 269; photo of, 117
Nashoba, Nuchi (Choctaw), 211, 216, 247; photo of, 120
National Guard, Native American service in, 19–22, 26, 28, 49; Louisiana, 207, 277; North Carolina, 34, 40–41; North Dakota, 187, 223, 270, 271; Oklahoma and Texas, 43–49, 101, 129, 157, 179, 204, 208–210, 259, 265
National Personnel Records (1973 fire), 4
Native American code talking (NACT): alleged secrecy of, 5, 125–35, 229–230; basis of success, 225; "code talker," as term, 1, 230–235; Congressional Gold Medal ceremony, 216; Cryptologic Hall of Honor award, 220; definitions, 1, 226, 230–235; effectiveness of, 203; factors of success, 225; groups used in WW I, 224; influences on culture, 235–238; influences on US armed forces, 222–225, 227–229; literature on, 3–6, 11–12; origins of, 7, 32, 225; proposed future use of, 129–131, 225, 291n123; recognition of, 17, 197–221, 235–238, 275–280; research and oral history of, 1–6, 246–249; statues of, 165, 207, 250, 261, 277, 301; timeline, 275–280; types of, 226, 230, 234, 305n43. *See also* Code Talkers Recognition Act (2008); *names of individual tribes*
Native American language orthographies, 243–244
Native American Languages Act of 1990 (Public Law 101-477), 241
Native American Languages Act of 1992 (Public Law 102-524), 241
Native Americans (WW I): acculturation and economic motivations for military service, 25–26; as scouts, 16, 29, 23–24, 27, 29, 30, 64, 100–102, 125, 128, 191, 198, 228,

Native Americans (WW I) (*continued*)
230, 235–236, 293n136–137, 295n24;
civilian contributions, 31–32; community send-offs, 21; community
homecomings, 25, 221, 225, 237;
congressional hearings on (1920),
103, 129–130; dependency theory, 22;
draft of, 13–14, 19, 20–22, 26, 34, 40,
44–49, 137, 152, 162, 164, 179–183,
235, 238–239, 255–256, 260–264,
267–269, 297n54; English fluency,
48–50, 151, 305n32; enlistment of, 14,
20–22, 26, 45, 47, 51, 151, 178, 235,
284n9; German views of, 123–125,
184–185; images and stereotypes of, 3,
17–19, 25–29, 101, 123, 125, 128, 227;
Indian Scout Program, 17, 23–24; language use and US policy, 240–243;
Lt. John Eddy study of, 100–102; military service of, 24–25; motivations for
service, 21–26; population in 1917, 14;
postwar celebrations and revivals, 22,
25, 237; postwar publicity of, 27–30,
125; praise of, 50, 122–23, 203, 235–
238; proposed all-Indian units, 14–18,
101–102, 128–130, 226–227, 240; service in WW I, 12–32; as snipers, 29,
56, 60, 73, 124, 191, 260; syncretism
of military service, 24–25; traditional
cultural motivations for military
service, 23–25; units with concentrations of, 19, 179; US citizenship of,
13–16, 19–23, 27, 31, 222, 235–240,
266, 282n11–12, 283n25, 308n66;
written languages of, 243–246. *See
also* assimilation, US government,
military and missionary motivations
for; boarding schools; Indian scout
syndrome (Holm coinage); National
Guard, Native American service in
Native Words, Native Warriors (exhibit),
2–3, 208, 277
Navajo code talkers (US Marine Corps,
WW II), 1–4, 107–109, 188–189,
203, 230, 233–235, 251, 275–279,
311n1; and "code talker" term, 233;
declassification, 229; distribution of,
189; MOS number 642, 4, 234–235;

Navajo Code Talker Day, 204;
recognition of, 213, 219; secrecy,
126; sources on, 11–12. *See also* US
Marine Corps
Nelson, David R. (142nd Infantry),
97–98, 195, 291n115, 292n127
Nelson, Jeff (also Jeff Nilson/Wilson;
Choctaw), 45, 82, 86–90, 99, 205,
219; biography of, 263–264; photo
of, 116

Oklahoma Military Hall of Fame, 212,
278–279
Oklahombi, Jonah (Choctaw), 156–158,
247, 264–265
Oklahombi, Joseph (Choctaw), 5,
43–44, 49, 57, 68, 69, 82, 86–87,
89–92, 122, 134, 136–159, 170–171,
175, 197–198, 205, 217–219, 239,
247, 279, 291, 294n1, 297–298n54–
56, 299n96, 299n98, 300n104,
307n53; biography of, 264–265;
military awards, 153–154, 157–158;
monument for, 159; movie offer, 155;
photo of, 114
Oneida code talkers (32nd Division,
WW II). See Chippewa-Oneida code
talkers (32nd Division, WW II)
Onondaga declaration of war on Germany, 23
Osage code talkers (WW I), 3–6,
46–47, 104, 176, 184–186, 196, 224,
230, 244, 246, 284n11, 292n127,
304n20, 21, 26

Page, Andrea (Hunkpapa Lakota), 12
Parker, Gabe (Choctaw), 18, 27, 51, 255,
283n25
Pershing, John J., 15, 24, 27, 54, 56, 75,
85, 123, 165, 171, 200, 226, 261, 264,
282n12
Picotte, Paul (Yankton), 187, 190,
305n28
Pollard, Liz, 1–2
Prussian Guard divisions, 60, 62, 73,
75, 81–82, 86, 92, 124, 168, 186,
286n46, 290–291n114
Pushmataha (Choctaw), 54

Pyle, Gregory (Choctaw), 87, 207, 209, 213–215, 246; photos of, 119, 121

radio (WW I), 7, 9, 12, 64–70, 94, 107, 227–228, 232–234
Ragan, Angela, 34, 40–41, 284n10
Robinson, George A. (111th Field Signal Battalion), 70, 107, 126–127, 134–135, 229
rolling artillery barrage, 71–72, 77, 167
Roosevelt, Theodore, 24
Rough Riders (Spanish-American War), 24,
runners (pedestrian messengers), losses of in WW I, 68–70

Sawyer, Sarah Elizabeth (Choctaw), 221, 279
Scott, Hugh L., 16–17, 282n15–16
Sedan (France), strategic importance of, 55, 200
Selective Service Act (1917), 13, 20, 33
Sells, Cato, 14–18, 22, 26, 51, 169–170, 237, 282n7
Silver Citation Star. See US armed forces medals (WW I)
Silver Star (US military award). See US armed forces medals (WW I)
Smith, William R., 29, 52, 63, 70–71, 93, 107, 123–129, 135, 181, 295n27
Society of American Indians (SAI), 16–18
Spence, Alexander W. (36th Division), 93, 129, 291n120, 295n16
Stanley, John W. (30th Division, WW I), 33, 35–39, 42, 188, 251, 283n4, 283n6, 284n7
St. Etienne (WW I), 28, 30, 52–63, 68–72, 76, 79–84, 87, 92–95, 103, 124, 135–138, 141–152, 155–159, 200–202, 264, 286n46, 290n114, 297n68; salient during (October 8, 1918), 61, 141, 145. See also Meuse-Argonne campaign (WW I)
St. Mihiel (WW I), 54, 66, 68, 92, 124, 155, 166, 169, 171–174, 179–183, 191, 239, 267–270, 286n46, 289–290n98, 290–291n114

Tabbytosavit (Tabbytosevit), Samuel (Comanche), 181–184, 269–270; biography of, 267–268; photo of, 117
Taylor, Robert (Choctaw), 45, 49, 51, 81–82, 86–90, 99, 102, 205, 219, 263; biography of, 265; photo of, 113
telegraph, 9; in WW I, 64, 67–69, 223, 291
Texas Military Forces Museum (Austin), 159, 209–210, 295n25
TPS (telegraphie par sol), use in WW I, 65, 67
Troop L, 7th Cavalry (Fort Sill, OK), 23

US armed forces (WW I): changes in signals intelligence, 227–229; divisional organization, 13; in France, 54; reorganization, 52–53; signals intelligence, 9
US armed forces medals: description of, 154; origin, 154; Silver Star (1932–), 137–144, 153–159; WW I Silver Citation Star, 137, 140–142, 153–154, 157–158, 171; WW I Victory Button, 153; WW I Victory Medal, 137, 140–141, 153–154, 297n64. See also French military medals (WW I)
US Congress, House Committee on Military Affairs (1920), 129–130, 240
US Marine Corps: in WW I, 13, 30, 60, 123, 168; MOS 642, 234–235. See also Navajo code talkers (US Marine Corps, WW II)

Veach, Charles Walter (Choctaw), 43–49, 51–53, 87–90, 99, 204–205, 211–212, 219, 285n15, 286n38, 290n112, 291n121, 292n127; biography of, 265–267
Veach, Columbus E. (Choctaw), 47, 53, 80, 211, 266–267

Whirlwind Horse, John (Lakota), 187–188, 239
Widder, John, 248

Widder, Kathryn Horner, 96, 115, 248–249, 279

Wilson, Calvin (also Cabin; Choctaw), 45, 51, 81–82, 86–90, 93, 98–99, 102, 106, 219, 239, 263; biography of, 267; photos of, 110, 116

Wilson, Evangeline (Choctaw), 120, 207, 289n86

Wilson, Woodrow, 13, 135, 256

Wilson (Nilson), Jeff. *See* Nelson, Jeff (also Jeff Nilson/Wilson; Choctaw)

Winnebago. *See* Ho-Chunk (Winnebago) code talkers (WW I)

York, Alvin, 137–139, 153, 159, 201, 297n56, 300n104

Youngdeer, Stephen (Cherokee), 40; American Legion Post 143, 34, 40